MW00592600

Tax and Securities Sources for Equity Compensation

Certified Equity Professional Institute

2005 Edition

Tax and Securities Sources for Equity Compensation

Certified Equity Professional Institute

2005 Edition

The National Center for Employee Ownership
Oakland, California

This publication is designed to provide accurate and authoritative information regarding the subject matter covered. It is sold with the understanding that the publisher is not engaged in rendering legal, accounting, or other professional services. If legal advice or other expert assistance is required, the services of a competent professional should be sought.

Tax and Securities Sources for Equity Compensation, 2005 Edition
Editor and book designer: Scott S. Rodrick

Copyright © 2005 by The National Center for Employee Ownership (NCEO). All rights reserved. No claim is made to original government works; however, the gathering, compilation, and arrangement of such materials are subject to the NCEO's copyright. No part of this book may be reproduced or transmitted in any form or by any means, electronic or mechanical, including photocopying, recording, or by any information storage and retrieval system, without prior written permission from the publisher.

The National Center for Employee Ownership
1736 Franklin Street, 8th Floor
Oakland, CA 94612
(510) 208-1300
(510) 272-9510 (fax)
E-mail: *nceo@nceo.org*
Web site: *http://www.nceo.org/*

2004 (first) edition: February 2004, reprinted May 2004
2005 (second) edition: February 2005

ISBN: 1-932924-06-X

Contents

Part 2—Taxation

Regulations

IRS Releases

Preface

This book, prepared for the Certified Equity Professional Institute (CEPI) at Santa Clara University, is a collection of tax and securities source materials relevant to the study of equity compensation. The CEPI offers a course of study leading to certification as a Certified Equity Professional. The CEPI curriculum committee selected the materials included here as being essential for those involved with equity compensation. For more information about the CEPI program, please see *http://cepi.scu.edu/*.

This book is intended for education and general reference and is neither an official publication nor a comprehensive legal reference. Notes on legislative and regulatory history are not included. Practitioners and corporate personnel should consult the latest versions of these sources (as available from government and other sites) when conducting business.

The materials included here were collected from various government sources and other reliable sources available online. (The New York Stock Exchange Listed Company Manual was taken directly from the NYSE's site at *www.nyse.com*.) One may encounter these materials formatted in various ways in various publications and online sources. We formatted them in a basic, consistent manner similar to that used, for example, for the Code of Federal Regulations (parts of which are included in this book); see *http://www.gpoaccess.gov/cfr/*. Where a complex form is involved (e.g., SEC Form 3), the actual form has been reproduced.

The book has two basic divisions: Part I, consisting of securities-related materials, and Part II, consisting of tax-related materials. Within each of those two main divisions, the materials are organized by type (statute, regulations of a certain type, etc.). An index is provided at the end.

Part I

Securities

Securities Act of 1933

Section 4—Exempted Transactions

The provisions of Section 5 shall not apply to:

(1) Transactions by any person other than an issuer, underwriter, or dealer.

(2) Transactions by an issuer not involving any public offering.

(3) Transactions by a dealer (including an underwriter no longer acting as an underwriter in respect of the security involved in such transaction), except:

(A) Transactions taking place prior to the expiration of 40 days after the first date upon which the security was *bona fide* offered to the public by the issuer or by or through an underwriter,

(B) Transactions in a security as to which a registration statement has been filed taking place prior to the expiration of 40 days after the effective date of such registration statement or prior to the expiration of 40 days after the first date upon which the security was *bona fide* offered to the public by the issuer or by or through an underwriter after such effective date, whichever is later (excluding in the computation of such 40 days any time during which a stop order issued under Section 8 is in effect as to the security), or such shorter period as the Commission may specify by rules and regulations or order, and

(C) Transactions as to securities constituting the whole or a part of an unsold allotment to or subscription by such dealer as a participant in the distribution of such securities by the issuer or by or through an underwriter.

With respect to transactions referred to in clause (B), if securities of the issuer have not previously been sold pursuant to an earlier effective registration statement, the applicable period, instead of 40 days, shall be 90 days, or such shorter period as the Commission may specify by rules and regulations or order.

(4) Brokers' transactions executed upon customers' orders on any exchange or in the over-the-counter market but not the solicitation of such orders.

(5)(A) Transactions involving offers or sales of one or more promissory notes directly secured by a first lien on a single parcel of real estate upon which is located a dwelling or other residential or commercial structure, and participation interests in such notes:

(i) Where such securities are originated by a savings and loan association, savings bank, commercial bank, or similar banking institution which is supervised and examined by a federal or state authority, and are offered and sold subject to the following conditions:

(a) The minimum aggregate sales price per purchaser shall not be less than $250,000;

(b) The purchaser shall pay cash either at the time of the sale or within 60 days thereof; and

(c) Each purchaser shall buy for his own account only; or

(ii) Where such securities are originated by a mortgagee approved by the Secretary of Housing and Urban Development pursuant to Sections 203 and 211 of the National Housing Act and are offered or sold subject to the three conditions specified in subparagraph (A)(i) to any institution described in such subparagraph or to any insurance company subject to the supervision of the insurance commissioner, or any agency or officer performing like function, of any state or territory of the United States or the District of Columbia, or the Federal Home Loan Mortgage Corporation, the Federal National Mortgage Association, or the Government National Mortgage Association.

(B) Transactions between any of the entities described in subparagraph (A)(i) or (A)(ii) hereof involving non-assignable contracts to buy or sell the foregoing securities which are to be completed within two years, where the seller of the foregoing securities pursuant to any such contract is one of the parties described in subparagraph (A)(i) or (A)(ii) who may originate such securities and the purchaser of such securities pursuant to any such contract is any institution described in subparagraph (A)(i) or any insurance company described in subparagraph (A)(ii), the Federal Home Loan Mortgage Corporation, Federal National Mortgage Association, or the Government National Mortgage Association and where the foregoing securities are subject to the three conditions for sale set forth in subparagraphs (A)(i)(a) through (c).

(C) The exemption provided by subparagraphs (A) and (B) hereof shall not apply to resales of the securities acquired pursuant thereto, unless each of the conditions for sale contained in subparagraphs (A)(i)(a) through (c) are satisfied.

(6) Transactions involving offers or sales by an issuer solely to one or more accredited investors, if the aggregate offering price of an issue of securities offered in reliance on this paragraph does not exceed the amount allowed under Section 3(b) of this title, if there is no advertising or public solicitation in connection with the transaction by the issuer or anyone acting on the issuer's behalf, and if the issuer files such notice with the Commission as the Commission shall prescribe.

Section 5—Prohibitions Relating to Interstate Commerce and the Mails

(a) Unless a registration statement is in effect as to a security, it shall be unlawful for any person, directly or indirectly:

(1) To make use of any means or instruments of transportation or communication in interstate commerce or of the mails to sell such security through the use or medium of any prospectus or otherwise; or

(2) To carry or cause to be carried through the mails or in interstate commerce, by any means or instruments of transportation, any such security for the purpose of sale or for delivery after sale.

(b) It shall be unlawful for any person, directly or indirectly:

(1) To make use of any means or instruments of transportation or communication in interstate commerce or of the mails to carry or transmit any prospectus relating to any security with respect to which a registration statement has been filed under this title, unless such prospectus meets the requirements of Section 10; or

(2) To carry or to cause to be carried through the mails or in interstate commerce any such security for the purpose of sale or for delivery after sale, unless accompanied or preceded by a prospectus that meets the requirements of subsection (a) of Section 10.

(c) It shall be unlawful for any person, directly or indirectly, to make use of any means or instruments of transportation or communication in interstate commerce or of the mails to offer to sell or offer to buy through the use or medium of any prospectus or otherwise any security, unless a registration statement has been filed as to such security, or while the registration statement is the subject of a refusal order or stop order or (prior to the effective date of the registration statement) any public proceeding or examination under Section 8.

Securities Exchange Act of 1934

Section 10—Regulation of the Use of Manipulative and Deceptive Devices

It shall be unlawful for any person, directly or indirectly, by the use of any means or instrumentality of interstate commerce or of the mails, or of any facility of any national securities exchange:

(a)(1) To effect a short sale, or to use or employ any stop-loss order in connection with the purchase or sale, of any security registered on a national securities exchange, in contravention of such rules and regulations as the Commission may prescribe as necessary or appropriate in the public interest or for the protection of investors.

(2) Paragraph (1) of this subsection shall not apply to security futures products.

(b) To use or employ, in connection with the purchase or sale of any security registered on a national securities exchange or any security not so registered, or any securities-based swap agreement (as defined in Section 206B of the Gramm-Leach-Bliley Act), any manipulative or deceptive device or contrivance in contravention of such rules and regulations as the Commission may prescribe as necessary or appropriate in the public interest or for the protection of investors.

Rules promulgated under subsection (b) that prohibit fraud, manipulation, or insider trading (but not rules imposing or specifying reporting or recordkeeping requirements, procedures, or standards as prophylactic measures against fraud, manipulation, or insider trading), and judicial precedents decided under subsection (b) and rules promulgated thereunder that prohibit fraud, manipulation, or insider trading, shall apply to security-based swap agreements (as defined in Section 206B of the Gramm-Leach-Bliley Act) to the same extent as they apply to securities. Judicial precedents decided under Section 17(a) of the Securities Act of 1933 and Sections 9, 15, 16, 20, and 21A of this title, and judicial precedents decided under applicable rules promulgated under such sections, shall apply to security-based swap agreements (as defined in Section 206B of the Gramm-Leach-Bliley Act) to the same extent as they apply to securities.

Section 16(a)—Directors, Officers, and Principal Stockholders

(1) *Directors, Officers, and Principal Stockholders Required to File.* Every person who is directly or indirectly the beneficial owner of more than 10 percent of any class of any equity security (other than an exempted security) which is registered pursuant to Section 12, or who is a director

or an officer of the issuer of such security, shall file the statements required by this subsection with the Commission (and, if such security is registered on a national securities exchange, also with the exchange).

(2) *Time of Filing.* The statements required by this subsection shall be filed—

(A) At the time of the registration of such security on a national securities exchange or by the effective date of a registration statement filed pursuant to Section 12(g);

(B) Within 10 days after he or she becomes such beneficial owner, director, or officer;

(C) If there has been a change in such ownership, or if such person shall have purchased or sold a security-based swap agreement (as defined in Section 206(b) of the Gramm-Leach-Bliley Act (15 U.S.C. 78c note)) involving such equity security, before the end of the second business day following the day on which the subject transaction has been executed, or at such other time as the Commission shall establish, by rule, in any case in which the Commission determines that such 2-day period is not feasible.

(3) *Contents of Statements.* A statement filed—

(A) Under subparagraph (A) or (B) of paragraph (2) shall contain a statement of the amount of all equity securities of such issuer of which the filing person is the beneficial owner; and

(B) Under subparagraph (C) of such paragraph shall indicate ownership by the filing person at the date of filing, any such changes in such ownership, and such purchases and sales of the security-based swap agreements as have occurred since the most recent such filing under such subparagraph.

(4) *Electronic Filing and Availability.* Beginning not later than 1 year after the date of enactment of the Sarbanes-Oxley Act of 2002

(A) A statement filed under subparagraph (C) of paragraph (2) shall be filed electronically;

(B) The Commission shall provide each such statement on a publicly accessible Internet site not later than the end of the business day following that filing; and (C) The issuer (if the issuer maintains a corporate website) shall provide that statement on that corporate website, not later than the end of the business day following that filing.

Section 16(b)—Profits from Purchase and Sale of Security Within Six Months

(b) *Profits from Purchase and Sale of Security Within Six Months.* For the purpose of preventing the unfair use of information which may have been obtained by such beneficial owner, director, or officer by reason of his relationship to the issuer, any profit realized by him from any purchase and sale, or any sale and purchase, of any equity security of such issuer (other than an exempted security) or a security-based swap agreement (as defined in Section 206B of the Gramm-Leach-Bliley Act) involving any such equity security within any period of less than six months, unless such security or security-based swap agreement was acquired in good faith in connection with a debt previously contracted, shall inure to and be recoverable by the issuer, irrespective of any intention on the part of such beneficial owner, director, or officer in entering into such transaction of holding the security or security-based swap agreement purchased or of not repurchasing the security or security-based swap agreement sold for a period exceeding six months. Suit to recover such profit may be instituted at law or in equity in any court of competent jurisdiction by the issuer, or by the owner of any security of the issuer in the name and in behalf of the issuer if the issuer shall fail or refuse to bring such suit within sixty days after request or shall fail diligently to prosecute the same thereafter; but no such suit shall be brought more than two years after the date such profit was realized. This subsection shall not be construed to cover any transaction where such beneficial owner was not such both at the time of the purchase and sale, or the sale and purchase, of the security or security-based swap agreement (as defined in Section 206B of the Gramm-Leach-Bliley Act) involved, or any transaction or transactions which the Commission by rules and regulations may exempt as not comprehended within the purpose of this subsection.

Regulation D

Rules Governing the Limited Offer and Sale of Securities Without Registration Under the Securities Act of 1933

Preliminary Notes

1. The following rules relate to transactions exempted from the registration requirements of Section 5 of the Securities Act of 1933 (the "Act"). Such transactions are not exempt from the antifraud, civil liability, or other provisions of the federal securities laws. Issuers are reminded of their obligation to provide such further material information, if any, as may be necessary to make the information required under this regulation, in light of the circumstances under which it is furnished, not misleading.

2. Nothing in these rules obviates the need to comply with any applicable state law relating to the offer and sale of securities. Regulation D is intended to be a basic element in a uniform system of federal-state limited offering exemptions consistent with the provisions of Sections 18 and 19(c) of the Act. In those states that have adopted Regulation D, or any version of Regulation D, special attention should be directed to the applicable state laws and regulations, including those relating to registration of persons who receive remuneration in connection with the offer and sale of securities, to disqualification of issuers and other persons associated with offerings based on state administrative orders or judgments, and to requirements for filings of notices of sales.

3. Attempted compliance with any rule in Regulation D does not act as an exclusive election; the issuer can also claim the availability of any other applicable exemption. For instance, an issuer's failure to satisfy all the terms and conditions of Rule 506 shall not raise any presumption that the exemption provided by Section 4(2) of the Act is not available.

4. These rules are available only to the issuer of the securities and not to any affiliate of that issuer or to any other person for resales of the issuer's securities. The rules provide an exemption only for the transactions in which the securities are offered or sold by the issuer, not for the securities themselves.

5. These rules may be used for business combinations that involve sales by virtue of Rule 145(a) or otherwise.

6. In view of the objectives of these rules and the policies underlying the Act, Regulation D is not available to any issuer for any transaction or chain of transactions that, although in technical compliance with these rules, is part of a plan or scheme to evade the registration provisions of the Act. In such cases, registration under the Act is required.

7. Securities offered and sold outside the United States in accordance with Regulation S need not be registered under the Act. *See* Release No. 33-6863. Regulation S may be relied upon for such offers and sales even if coincident offers and sales are made in accordance with Regulation D inside the United States. Thus, for example, persons who are offered and sold securities in accordance with Regulation S would not be counted in the calculation of the number of purchasers under Regulation D. Similarly, proceeds from such sales would not be included in the aggregate offering price. The provisions of this note, however, do not apply if the issuer elects to rely solely on Regulation D for offers or sales to persons made outside the United States.

Rule 501—Definitions and Terms Used in Regulation D

As used in Regulation D, the following terms shall have the meaning indicated:

(a) *Accredited Investor.* "Accredited investor" shall mean any person who comes within any of the following categories, or who the issuer reasonably believes comes within any of the following categories, at the time of the sale of the securities to that person:

(1) Any bank as defined in Section 3(a)(2) of the Act, or any savings and loan association or other institution as defined in Section 3(a)(5)(A) of the Act whether acting in its individual or fiduciary capacity; any broker or dealer registered pursuant to Section 15 of the Securities Exchange Act of 1934; any insurance company as defined in Section 2(13) of the Act; any investment company registered under the Investment Company Act of 1940 or a business development company as defined in Section 2(a)(48) of that Act; any Small Business Investment Company licensed by the U.S. Small Business Administration under Section 301(c) or (d) of the Small Business Investment Act of 1958; any plan established and maintained by a state, its political subdivisions, or any agency or instrumentality of a state or its political subdivisions, for the benefit of its employees, if such plan has total assets in excess of $5,000,000; any employee benefit plan within the meaning of the Employee Retirement Income Security Act of 1974 if the investment decision is made by a plan fiduciary, as defined in Section 3(21) of such Act, which is either a bank, savings and loan association, insurance company, or registered investment adviser, or if the employee benefit plan has total assets in excess of $5,000,000 or, if a self-directed plan, with investment decisions made solely by persons that are accredited investors;

(2) Any private business development company as defined in Section 202(a)(22) of the Investment Advisers Act of 1940;

(3) Any organization described in Section 501(c)(3) of the Internal Revenue Code, corporation, Massachusetts or similar business trust, or

partnership, not formed for the specific purpose of acquiring the securities offered, with total assets in excess of $5,000,000;

(4) Any director, executive officer, or general partner of the issuer of the securities being offered or sold, or any director, executive officer, or general partner of a general partner of that issuer;

(5) Any natural person whose individual net worth, or joint net worth with that person's spouse, at the time of his purchase exceeds $1,000,000;

(6) Any natural person who had an individual income in excess of $200,000 in each of the two most recent years or joint income with that person's spouse in excess of $300,000 in each of those years and has a reasonable expectation of reaching the same income level in the current year;

(7) Any trust, with total assets in excess of $5,000,000, not formed for the specific purpose of acquiring the securities offered, whose purchase is directed by a sophisticated person as described in Rule 506(b)(2)(ii); and

(8) Any entity in which all of the equity owners are accredited investors.

(b) *Affiliate.* An "affiliate" of, or person "affiliated" with, a specified person shall mean a person that directly, or indirectly through one or more intermediaries, controls or is controlled by, or is under common control with, the person specified.

(c) *Aggregate Offering Price.* "Aggregate offering price" shall mean the sum of all cash, services, property, notes, cancellation of debt, or other consideration to be received by an issuer for issuance of its securities. Where securities are being offered for both cash and non-cash consideration, the aggregate offering price shall be based on the price at which the securities are offered for cash. Any portion of the aggregate offering price attributable to cash received in a foreign currency shall be translated into United States currency at the currency exchange rate in effect at a reasonable time prior to or on the date of the sale of the securities. If securities are not offered for cash, the aggregate offering price shall be based on the value of the consideration as established by *bona fide* sales of that consideration made within a reasonable time, or, in the absence of sales, on the fair value as determined by an accepted standard. Such valuations of non-cash consideration must be reasonable at the time made.

(d) *Business Combination.* "Business combination" shall mean any transaction of the type specified in paragraph (a) of Rule 145 under the Act and any transaction involving the acquisition by one issuer, in exchange for all or a part of its own or its parent's stock, of stock of another issuer if, immediately after the acquisition, the acquiring issuer has control of the other issuer (whether or not it had control before the acquisition).

(e) *Calculation of Number of Purchasers.* For purposes of calculating the number of purchasers under Rules 505(b) and 506(b) only, the following shall apply:

(1) The following purchasers shall be excluded:

(i) Any relative, spouse or relative of the spouse of a purchaser who has the same principal residence as the purchaser;

(ii) Any trust or estate in which a purchaser and any of the persons related to him as specified in paragraph (e)(1)(i) or (e)(1)(iii) of this Rule 501 collectively have more than 50 percent of the beneficial interest (excluding contingent interests);

(iii) Any corporation or other organization of which a purchaser and any of the persons related to him as specified in paragraph (e)(1)(i) or (e)(1)(ii) of this Rule 501 collectively are beneficial owners of more than 50 percent of the equity securities (excluding directors' qualifying shares) or equity interests; and

(iv) Any accredited investor.

(2) A corporation, partnership or other entity shall be counted as one purchaser. If, however, that entity is organized for the specific purpose of acquiring the securities offered and is not an accredited investor under paragraph (a)(8) of this Rule 501, then each beneficial owner of equity securities or equity interests in the entity shall count as a separate purchaser for all provisions of Regulation D, except to the extent provided in paragraph (e)(1) of this Rule 501.

(3) A non-contributory employee benefit plan within the meaning of Title I of the Employee Retirement Income Security Act of 1974 shall be counted as one purchaser where the trustee makes all investment decisions for the plan.

Note. The issuer must satisfy all the other provisions of Regulation D for all purchasers whether or not they are included in calculating the number of purchasers. Clients of an investment adviser or customers of a broker or dealer shall be considered the "purchasers" under Regulation D regardless of the amount of discretion given to the investment adviser or broker or dealer to act on behalf of the client or customer.

(f) *Executive Officer.* "Executive officer" shall mean the president, any vice-president in charge of a principal business unit, division or function (such as sales, administration or finance), any other officer who performs a policy-making function, or any other person who performs similar policy-making functions for the issuer. Executive officers of subsidiaries may be deemed executive officers of the issuer if they perform such policy-making functions for the issuer.

(g) *Issuer.* The definition of the term "issuer" in Section 2(4) of the Act shall apply, except that in the case of a proceeding under the Federal

Bankruptcy Code, the trustee or debtor in possession shall be considered the issuer in an offering under a plan of reorganization, if the securities are to be issued under the plan.

(h) *Purchaser Representative.* "Purchaser representative" shall mean any person who satisfies all of the following conditions or who the issuer reasonably believes satisfies all of the following conditions:

(1) Is not an affiliate, director, officer or other employee of the issuer, or beneficial owner of 10 percent or more of any class of the equity securities or 10 percent or more of the equity interest in the issuer, except where the purchaser is:

(i) A relative of the purchaser representative by blood, marriage or adoption and not more remote than a first cousin;

(ii) A trust or estate in which the purchaser representative and any persons related to him as specified in paragraph (h)(1)(i) or (h)(1)(iii) of this Rule 501 collectively have more than 50 percent of the beneficial interest (excluding contingent interest) or of which the purchaser representative serves as trustee, executor, or in any similar capacity; or

(iii) A corporation or other organization of which the purchaser representative and any persons related to him as specified in paragraph (h)(1)(i) or (h)(1)(ii) of this Rule 501 collectively are the beneficial owners of more than 50 percent of the equity securities (excluding directors' qualifying shares) or equity interests;

(2) Has such knowledge and experience in financial and business matters that he is capable of evaluating, alone, or together with other purchaser representatives of the purchaser, or together with the purchaser, the merits and risks of the prospective investment;

(3) Is acknowledged by the purchaser in writing, during the course of the transaction, to be his purchaser representative in connection with evaluating the merits and risks of the prospective investment; and

(4) Discloses to the purchaser in writing a reasonable time prior to the sale of securities to that purchaser any material relationship between himself or his affiliates and the issuer or its affiliates that then exists, that is mutually understood to be contemplated, or that has existed at any time during the previous two years, and any compensation received or to be received as a result of such relationship.

Notes.

1. A person acting as a purchaser representative should consider the applicability of the registration and antifraud provisions relating to brokers and dealers under the Securities Exchange Act of 1934 ("Exchange Act") and relating to investment advisers under the Investment Advisers Act of 1940.

2. The acknowledgment required by paragraph (h)(3) and the disclosure required by paragraph (h)(4) of this Rule 501 must be made with specific reference to each prospective investment. Advance blanket acknowledgment, such as for "all securities transactions" or "all private placements," is not sufficient.

3. Disclosure of any material relationships between the purchaser representative or his affiliates and the issuer or its affiliates does not relieve the purchaser representative of his obligation to act in the interest of the purchaser.

Rule 502—General Conditions to Be Met

The following conditions shall be applicable to offers and sales made under Regulation D:

(a) *Integration.* All sales that are part of the same Regulation D offering must meet all of the terms and conditions of Regulation D. Offers and sales that are made more than six months before the start of a Regulation D offering or are made more than six months after completion of a Regulation D offering will not be considered part of that Regulation D offering, so long as during those six-month periods there are no offers or sales of securities by or for the issuer that are of the same or a similar class as those offered or sold under Regulation D, other than those offers or sales of securities under an employee benefit plan as defined in Rule 405 under the Act.

Note. The term "offering" is not defined in the Act or in Regulation D. If the issuer offers or sells securities for which the safe harbor rule in paragraph (a) of this Rule 502 is unavailable, the determination as to whether separate sales of securities are part of the same offering (*i.e.* are considered "integrated") depends on the particular facts and circumstances. Generally, transactions otherwise meeting the requirements of an exemption will not be integrated with simultaneous offerings being made outside the United States in compliance with Regulation S. *See* Release No. 33-6863.

The following factors should be considered in determining whether offers and sales should be integrated for purposes of the exemptions under Regulation D:

(a) Whether the sales are part of a single plan of financing;

(b) Whether the sales involve issuance of the same class of securities;

(c) Whether the sales have been made at or about the same time;

(d) Whether the same type of consideration is being received; and

(e) Whether the sales are made for the same general purpose.

See Release No. 33-4552 (November 6, 1962).

(b) *Information Requirements.*

(1) *When Information Must be Furnished.* If the issuer sells securities under Rule 505 or Rule 506 to any purchaser that is not an accredited investor, the issuer shall furnish the information specified in paragraph (b)(2) of this Rule 502 to such purchaser a reasonable time prior to sale. The issuer is not required to furnish the specified information to purchasers when it sells securities under Rule 504, or to any accredited investor.

Note. When an issuer provides information to investors pursuant to paragraph (b)(1), it should consider providing such information to accredited investors as well, in view of the anti-fraud provisions of the federal securities laws.

(2) *Type of Information to be Furnished.* (i) If the issuer is not subject to the reporting requirements of Section 13 or 15(d) of the Exchange Act, at a reasonable time prior to the sale of securities the issuer shall furnish to the purchaser, to the extent material to an understanding of the issuer, its business, and the securities being offered:

(A) *Non-Financial Statement Information.* As if the issuer is eligible to use Regulation A (Rules 251–263), the same kind of information as would be required in Part II of Form 1-A. If the issuer is not eligible to use Regulation A, the same kind of information as required in Part I of a registration statement filed under the Securities Act on the form that the issuer would be entitled to use.

(B) *Financial Statement Information.*

(1) *Offerings up to $2,000,000.* The information required in Item 310 of Regulation S-B, except that only the issuer's balance sheet, which shall be dated within 120 days of the start of the offering, must be audited.

(2) *Offerings up to $7,500,000.* The financial statements information required in Form SB-2. If an issuer, other than a limited partnership, cannot obtain audited financial statements without unreasonable effort or expense, then only the issuer's balance sheet, which shall be dated within 120 days of the start of the offering, must be audited. If the issuer is a limited partnership and cannot obtain the required financial statements without unreasonable effort or expense, it may furnish financial statements that have been prepared on the basis of federal income tax requirements and examined and reported on in accordance with generally accepted auditing standards by an independent public or certified accountant.

(3) *Offerings Over $7,500,000.* The financial statement as would be required in a registration statement filed under the Act on the form that the issuer would be entitled to use. If an issuer, other than a limited partnership, cannot obtain audited financial statements without unreasonable effort or expense, then only the issuer's balance sheet, which shall be

dated within 120 days of the start of the offering, must be audited. If the issuer is a limited partnership and cannot obtain the required financial statements without unreasonable effort or expense, it may furnish financial statements that have been prepared on the basis of federal income tax requirements and examined and reported on in accordance with generally accepted auditing standards by an independent public or certified accountant.

(C) If the issuer is a foreign private issuer eligible to use Form 20-F, the issuer shall disclose the same kind of information required to be included in a registration statement filed under the Act on the form that the issuer would be entitled to use. The financial statements need be certified only to the extent required by paragraph (b)(2)(i)(B)*(1)*, *(2)* or *(3)* of the section, as appropriate. (ii) If the issuer is subject to the reporting requirements of Section 13 or 15(d) of the Exchange Act, at a reasonable time prior to the sale of securities the issuer shall furnish to the purchaser the information specified in paragraph (b)(2)(ii)(A) or (B) of this Rule 502, and in either event the information specified in paragraph (b)(2)(ii)(C) of this Rule 502:

(A) The issuer's annual report to shareholders for the most recent fiscal year, if such annual report meets the requirements of Rule 14a-3 or 14c-3 under the Exchange Act, the definitive proxy statement filed in connection with that annual report, and, if requested by the purchaser in writing, a copy of the issuer's most recent Form 10-K or Form 10-KSB under the Exchange Act.

(B) The information contained in an annual report on Form 10-K or 10-KSB under the Exchange Act or in a registration statement on Form S-1, SB-1, SB-2 or S-11 under the Act or on Form 10 or 10-SB under the Exchange Act, whichever filing is the most recent required to be filed.

(C) The information contained in any reports or documents required to be filed by the issuer under Sections 13(a), 14(a), 14(c) and 15(d) of the Exchange Act since the distribution or filing of the report or registration statement specified in paragraph (A) or (B), and a brief description of the securities being offered, the use of the proceeds from the offering, and any material changes in the issuer's affairs that are not disclosed in the documents furnished.

(D) If the issuer is a foreign private issuer, the issuer may provide in lieu of the information specified in paragraph (b)(2)(ii)(A) or (B) of this section, the information contained in its most recent filing on Form 20-F or Form F-1.

(iii) Exhibits required to be filed with the Commission as part of a registration statement or report, other than an annual report to shareholders or parts of that report incorporated by reference in a Form 10-K or Form 10-KSB report, need not be furnished to each purchaser that is not an accredited investor if the contents of material exhibits are identified and such exhibits are made available to a purchaser, upon his written request, a reasonable time prior to his purchase.

(iv) At a reasonable time prior to the sale of securities to any purchaser that is not an accredited investor in a transaction under Rule 505 or 506, the issuer shall furnish to the purchaser a brief description in writing of any material written information concerning the offering that has been provided by the issuer to any accredited investor but not previously delivered to such unaccredited purchaser. The issuer shall furnish any portion or all of this information to the purchaser, upon his written request a reasonable time prior to his purchase.

(v) The issuer shall also make available to each purchaser at a reasonable time prior to his purchase of securities in a transaction under Rule 505 or 506, the opportunity to ask questions and receive answers concerning the terms and conditions of the offering and to obtain any additional information which the issuer possesses or can acquire without unreasonable effort or expense that is necessary to verify the accuracy of information furnished under paragraph (b)(2)(i) or (ii) of this Rule 502.

(vi) For business combinations or exchange offers, in addition to information required by Form S-4, the issuer shall provide to each purchaser at the time the plan is submitted to security holders, or, with an exchange, during the course of the transaction and prior to sale, written information about any terms or arrangements of the proposed transactions that are materially different from those for all other security holders. For purposes of this subsection, an issuer which is not subject to the reporting requirements of Section 13 or 15(d) of the Exchange Act may satisfy the requirements of Part I.B. or C. of Form S-4 by compliance with paragraph (b)(2)(i) of this Rule 502.

(vii) At a reasonable time prior to the sale of securities to any purchaser that is not an accredited investor in a transaction under Rule 505 or Rule 506, the issuer shall advise the purchaser of the limitations on resale in the manner contained in paragraph (d)(2) of this Rule 502. Such disclosure may be contained in other materials required to be provided by this paragraph.

(c) *Limitation on Manner of Offering.* Except as provided in Rule 504(b)(1), neither the issuer nor any person acting on its behalf shall offer or sell the securities by any form of general solicitation or general advertising, including, but not limited to, the following:

(1) Any advertisement, article, notice or other communication published in any newspaper, magazine, or similar media or broadcast over television or radio; and

(2) Any seminar or meeting whose attendees have been invited by any general solicitation or general advertising;

Provided, however, that publication by an issuer of a notice in accordance with Rule 135c shall not be deemed to constitute general solicitation or general advertising for purposes of this section; *provided further,* that, if the requirements of Rule 135e are satisfied, providing any journalist with access to press conferences held outside of the United States, to meetings with issuer or selling security holder representatives conducted outside of the United States, or to written press-related materials released outside the United States, at or in which a present or proposed offering of securities is discussed, will not be deemed to constitute general solicitation or general advertising for purposes of this Rule 502.

(d) *Limitations on Resale.* Except as provided in Rule 504(b)(1), securities acquired in a transaction under Regulation D shall have the status of securities acquired in a transaction under Section 4(2) of the Act and cannot be resold without registration under the Act or an exemption therefrom. The issuer shall exercise reasonable care to assure that the purchasers of the securities are not underwriters within the meaning of Section 2(11) of the Act, which reasonable care may be demonstrated by the following:

(1) Reasonable inquiry to determine if the purchaser is acquiring the securities for himself or for other persons;

(2) Written disclosure to each purchaser prior to sale that the securities have not been registered under the Act and, therefore, cannot be resold unless they are registered under the Act or unless an exemption from registration is available; and (3) Placement of a legend on the certificate or other document that evidences the securities stating that the securities have not been registered under the Act and setting forth or referring to the restrictions on transferability and sale of the securities.

While taking these actions will establish the requisite reasonable care, it is not the exclusive method to demonstrate such care. Other actions by the issuer may satisfy this provision. In addition, Rule 502(b)(2)(vii) requires the delivery of written disclosure of the limitations on resale to investors in certain instances.

Rule 503—Filing of Notice of Sales

(a) An issuer offering or selling securities in reliance on Rule 504, 505 or 506 shall file with the Commission five copies of a notice on Form D no later than 15 days after the first sale of securities.

(b) One copy of every notice on Form D shall be manually signed by a person duly authorized by the issuer.

(c) If sales are made under Rule 505, the notice shall contain an undertaking by the issuer to furnish to the Commission, upon the written request of its staff, the information furnished by the issuer under Rule 502(b)(2) to any purchaser that is not an accredited investor.

(d) Amendments to notices filed under paragraph (a) of this Rule 503 need only report the issuer's name and the information required by Part C and any material change in the facts from those set forth in Parts A and B.

(e) A notice on Form D shall be considered filed with the Commission under paragraph (a) of this Rule 503:

(1) As of the date on which it is received at the Commission's principal office in Washington, DC; or

(2) As of the date on which the notice is mailed by means of United States registered or certified mail to the Commission's principal office in Washington, DC, if the notice is delivered to such office after the date on which it is required to be filed.

Rule 504—Exemption for Limited Offerings and Sales of Securities Not Exceeding $1,000,000

(a) *Exemption.* Offers and sales of securities that satisfy the conditions in paragraph (b) of this Rule 504 by an issuer that is not:

(1) Subject to the reporting requirements of Section 13 or 15(d) of the Exchange Act;

(2) An investment company; or

(3) A development stage company that either has no specific business plan or purpose or has indicated that its business plan is to engage in a merger or acquisition with an unidentified company or companies, or other entity or person, shall be exempt from the provision of Section 5 of the Act under Section 3(b) of the Act.

(b) *Conditions to be Met.*

(1) *General Conditions.* To qualify for exemption under this Rule 504, offers and sales must satisfy the terms and conditions of Rule 501 and Rule 502(a), (c) and (d), except that the provisions of Rule 502(c) and (d) will not apply to offers and sales of securities under this Rule 504 that are made:

(i) Exclusively in one or more states that provide for the registration of the securities, and require the public filing and delivery to investors of a substantive disclosure document before sale, and are made in accordance with those state provisions;

(ii) In one or more states that have no provision for the registration of the securities or the public filing or delivery of a disclosure document before sale, if the securities have been registered in at least one state that provides for such registration, public filing and delivery before sale, offers and sales are made in that state in accordance with such provisions, and the disclosure document is delivered before sale to all purchasers (including those in the states that have no such procedure); or

(iii) Exclusively according to state law exemptions from registration that permit general solicitation and general advertising so long as sales are made only to "accredited investors" as defined in Rule 501(a).

(2) The aggregate offering price for an offering of securities under this Rule 504, as defined in Rule 501(c), shall not exceed $1,000,000, less the aggregate offering price for all securities sold within the 12 months before the start of and during the offering of securities under this Rule 504, in reliance on any exemption under Section 3(b), or in violation of Section 5(a) of the Securities Act.

Example 1. The calculation of the aggregate offering price is illustrated as follows:

If an issuer sold $900,000 on June 1, 1987 under this Rule 504 and an additional $4,100,000 on December 1, 1987 under Rule 505, the issuer could not sell any of its securities under this Rule 504 until December 1, 1988. Until then the issuer must count the December 1, 1987 sale towards the $1,000,000 limit within the preceding 12 months.

Example 2. If a transaction under Rule 504 fails to meet the limitation on the aggregate offering price, it does not affect the availability of this Rule 504 for the other transactions considered in applying such limitation. For example, if an issuer sold $1,000,000 worth of its securities on January 1, 1988 under this Rule 504 and an additional $500,000 worth on July 1, 1988, this Rule 504 would not be available for the later sale, but would still be applicable to the January 1, 1988 sale.

Rule 505—Exemption for Limited Offers and Sales of Securities Not Exceeding $5,000,000

(a) *Exemption.* Offers and sales of securities that satisfy the conditions in paragraph (b) of this Rule 505 by an issuer that is not an investment company shall be exempt from the provisions of Section 5 of the Act under Section 3(b) of the Act.

(b) *Conditions to be Met.*

(1) *General Conditions.* To qualify for exemption under this Rule 505, offers and sales must satisfy the terms and conditions of Rules 501 and 502.

(2) *Specific Conditions.*

(i) *Limitation on Aggregate Offering Price.* The aggregate offering price for an offering of securities under this Rule 505, as defined in Rule 501(c), shall not exceed $5,000,000, less the aggregate offering price for all securities sold within the 12 months before the start of and during the offering of securities under this Rule 505 in reliance on any exemption under Section 3(b) of the Act or in violation of Section 5(a) of the Act.

Note. The calculation of the aggregate offering price is illustrated as follows:

Example 1. If an issuer sold $2,000,000 of its securities on June 1, 1982 under this Rule 505 and an additional $1,000,000 on September 1, 1982, the issuer would be permitted to sell only $2,000,000 more under this Rule 505 until June 1, 1983. Until that date the issuer must count both prior sales towards the $5,000,000 limit. However, if the issuer made its third sale on June 1, 1983, the issuer could then sell $4,000,000 of its securities because the June 1, 1982 sale would not be within the preceding 12 months.

Example 2. If an issuer sold $500,000 of its securities on June 1, 1982 under Rule 504 and an additional $4,500,000 on December 1, 1982 under this Rule 505, then the issuer could not sell any of its securities under this Rule 505 until June 1, 1983. At that time it could sell an additional $500,000 of its securities.

(ii) *Limitation on Number of Purchasers.* There are no more than or the issuer reasonable believes that there are no more than 35 purchasers of securities from the issuer in any offering under this Rule 505.

Note. See Rule 501(e) for the calculation of the number of purchasers and Rule 502(a) for what may or may not constitute an offering under this section.

(iii) *Disqualifications.* No exemption under this section shall be available for the securities of any issuer described in Rule 262 of Regulation A, except that for purposes of this section only:

(A) The term "filing of the offering statement required by Rule 252" as used in Rule 262(a), (b) and (c) shall mean the first sale of securities under this section;

(B) The term "underwriter" as used in Rule 262(b) and (c) shall mean a person that has been or will be paid directly or indirectly remuneration for solicitation of purchasers in connection with sales of securities under this section; and

(C) Paragraph (b)(2)(iii) of this Rule 505 shall not apply to any issuer if the Commission determines, upon a showing of good cause, that it is not necessary under the circumstances that the exemption be denied. Any such determination shall be without prejudice to any other action by the Commission in any other proceeding or matter with respect to the issuer or any other person.

Rule 506—Exemption for Limited Offers and Sales without Regard to Dollar Amount of Offering

(a) *Exemption.* Offers and sales of securities by an issuer that satisfy the conditions in paragraph (b) of this Rule 506 shall be deemed to be transactions not involving any public offering within the meaning of Section 4(2) of the Act.

(b) *Conditions to be Met.*

(1) *General Conditions.* To qualify for an exemption under this Rule 506, offers and sales must satisfy all the terms and conditions of Rules 501 and 502.

(2) *Specific Conditions.*

(i) *Limitation on Number of Purchasers.* There are no more than or the issuer reasonably believes that there are no more than 35 purchasers of securities from the issuer in any offering under this Rule 506.

Note. See Rule 501(e) for the calculation of the number of purchasers and Rule 502(a) for what may or may not constitute an offering under this Rule 506.

(ii) *Nature of Purchasers.* Each purchaser who is not an accredited investor either alone or with his purchaser representative(s) has such knowledge and experience in financial and business matters that he is capable of evaluating the merits and risks of the prospective investment, or the issuer reasonably believes immediately prior to making any sale that such purchaser comes within this description.

Rule 507—Disqualifying Provision Relating to Exemptions Under Rule 504, Rule 505 and Rule 506

(a) No exemption under Rule 504, Rule 505 or Rule 506 shall be available for an issuer if such issuer, any of its predecessors or affiliates have been subject to any order, judgment, or decree of any court of competent jurisdiction temporarily, preliminarily or permanently enjoining such person for failure to comply with Rule 503.

(b) Paragraph (a) of this Rule 507 shall not apply if the Commission determines, upon a showing of good cause, that it is not necessary under the circumstances that the exemption be denied.

Rule 508—Insignificant Deviations from a Term, Condition or Requirement of Regulation D

(a) A failure to comply with a term, condition or requirement of Rule 504, Rule 505 or Rule 506 will not result in the loss of the exemption from the requirements of Section 5 of the Act for any offer or sale to a particular individual or entity, if the person relying on the exemption shows:

(1) The failure to comply did not pertain to a term, condition or requirement directly intended to protect that particular individual or entity;

(2) The failure to comply was insignificant with respect to the offering as a whole, provided that any failure to comply with paragraph (c) of Rule 502, paragraph (b)(2) of Rule 504, paragraphs (b)(2)(i) and (ii) of Rule 505 and paragraph (b)(2)(i) of Rule 506 shall be deemed to be significant to the offering as a whole; and

(3) A good faith and reasonable attempt was made to comply with all applicable terms, conditions and requirements of Rule 504, Rule 505 or Rule 506.

(b) A transaction made in reliance on Rule 504, Rule 505 or Rule 506 shall comply with all applicable terms, conditions and requirements of Regulation D. Where an exemption is established only through reliance upon paragraph (a) of this Rule 508, the failure to comply shall nonetheless be actionable by the Commission under Section 20 of the Act.

Rule 144

Persons Deemed Not to Be Engaged in a Distribution and Therefore Not Underwriters

Preliminary Note to Rule 144

Rule 144 is designed to implement the fundamental purposes of the Act, as expressed in its preamble, "To provide full and fair disclosure of the character of the securities sold in interstate commerce and through the mails, and to prevent fraud in the sale thereof . . ." The rule is designed to prohibit the creation of public markets in securities of issuers concerning which adequate current information is not available to the public. At the same time, where adequate current information concerning the issuer is available to the public, the rule permits the public sale in ordinary trading transactions of limited amounts of securities owned by persons controlling, controlled by or under common control with the issuer and by persons who have acquired restricted securities of the issuer.

Certain basic principles are essential to an understanding of the requirement of registration in the Act:

1. If any person utilizes the jurisdictional means to sell any non-exempt security to any other person, the security must be registered unless a statutory exemption can be found for the transaction.

2. In addition to the exemptions found in Section 3, four exemptions applicable to transactions in securities are contained in Section 4. Three of these Section 4 exemptions are clearly not available to anyone acting as an "underwriter" of securities. (The fourth, found in Section 4(4), is available only to those who act as brokers under certain limited circumstances.) An understanding of the term "underwriter" is therefore important to anyone who wishes to determine whether or not an exemption from registration is available for his sale of securities.

The term "underwriter" is broadly defined in Section 2(11) of the Act to mean any person who has purchased from an issuer with a view to, or offers or sells for an issuer in connection with, the distribution of any security, or participates or has a direct or indirect participation in any such undertaking, or participates or has a participation in the direct or indirect underwriting of any such undertaking. The interpretation of this definition has traditionally focused on the words "with a view to" in the phrase "purchased from an issuer with a view to . . . distribution." Thus, an investment banking firm which arranges with an issuer for the public sale of its securities is clearly an "underwriter" under that section. Individual investors who are not professionals in the securities business may also be "underwriters" within the meaning of that term as used in the Act if they act as links in a chain of transactions through which securities move from an issuer to the public. Since it is difficult to ascertain the mental state of the purchaser at the time of his acquisition, subsequent acts and circumstances have been considered to determine whether such person took with a view to distribution at the time of his acquisition. Emphasis has been placed on factors such as the length of time the person has held the securities and whether there has been an unforeseeable change in circumstances of the holder. Experience has shown, however, that reliance upon such factors as the above has not assured adequate protection of investors through the maintenance of informed trading markets and has led to uncertainty in the application of the registration provisions of the Act.

It should be noted that the statutory language of Section 2(11) is in the disjunctive. Thus, it is insufficient to conclude that a person is not an underwriter solely because he did not purchase securities from an issuer with a view to their distribution. It must also be established that the person is not offering or selling for an issuer in connection with the distribution of the securities, does not participate or have a direct or indirect participation in any such undertaking, and does not participate or have a participation in the direct or indirect underwriting of such an undertaking.

In determining when a person is deemed not to be engaged in a distribution, several factors must be considered.

First, the purpose and underlying policy of the Act to protect investors requires that there be adequate current information concerning the issuer, whether the resales of securities by persons result in a distribution or are effected in trading transactions. Accordingly, the availability of the rule is conditioned on the existence of adequate current public information.

Secondly, a holding period prior to resale is essential, among other reasons, to assure that those persons who buy under a claim of a Section 4(2) exemption have assumed the economic risks of investment, and therefore are not acting as conduits for sale to the public of unregistered securities, directly or indirectly, on behalf of an issuer. It should be noted that there is nothing in Section 2(11) which places a time limit on a person's status as an underwriter. The public has the same need for protection afforded by registration whether the securities are distributed shortly after their purchase or after a considerable length of time.

A third factor, which must be considered in determining what is deemed not to constitute a "distribution," is the impact of the particular transaction or transactions on the trading markets. Section 4(1) was intended to exempt only routine trading transactions between individual investors with respect to securities already issued and not to exempt distributions by issuers or acts of other individuals who engage in steps necessary to such distributions. Therefore, a person reselling securities under Section 4(1) of the Act must sell the securities in such limited quantities and in such a manner as not to disrupt the trading markets. The larger the amount of securities involved, the more likely it is that such resales may involve methods of offering and amounts of compensation usually associated with a distribution rather than routine trading transactions. Thus, solicitation of buy orders or the payment of extra compensation are not permitted by the rule.

In summary, if the sale in question is made in accordance with *all* of the provisions of the rule, as set forth below, any person who sells restricted securities shall be deemed not to be engaged in a distribution of such securities and therefore not an underwriter thereof. The rule also provides that any person who sells restricted or other securities on behalf of a person in a control relationship with the issuer shall be deemed not to be engaged in a distribution of such securities and therefore not to be an underwriter thereof, if the sale is made in accordance with *all the conditions of the rule.*

Rule 144

(a) *Definitions.* The following definitions shall apply for the purposes of this rule:

(1) An "affiliate" of an issuer is a person that directly, or indirectly through one or more intermediaries, controls, or is controlled by, or is under common control with, such issuer.

(2) The term "person" when used with reference to a person for whose account securities are to be sold in reliance upon this rule includes, in addition to such person, all of the following persons:

(i) Any relative or spouse of such person, or any relative of such spouse, any one of whom has the same home as such person;

(ii) Any trust or estate in which such person or any of the persons specified in paragraph (a)(2)(i) of this section collectively own 10 percent or more of the total beneficial interest or of which any of such persons serve as trustee, executor or in any similar capacity; and

(iii) Any corporation or other organization (other than the issuer) in which such person or any of the persons specified in paragraph (a)(2)(i) of this section are the beneficial owners collectively of 10 percent or more of any class of equity securities or 10 percent or more of the equity interest.

(3) The term "restricted securities" means:

(i) Securities acquired directly or indirectly from the issuer, or from an affiliate of the issuer, in a transaction or chain of transactions not involving any public offering;

(ii) Securities acquired from the issuer that are subject to the resale limitations of Rule 502(d) under Regulation D or Rule 701(c);

(iii) Securities acquired in a transaction or chain of transactions meeting the requirementsof Rule 144A;

(iv) Securities acquired from the issuer in a transaction subject to the conditions of Regulation CE;

(v) Equity securities of domestic issuers acquired in a transaction or chain of transactions subject to the conditions of Rule 901 or Rule 903 under Regulation S;

(vi) Securities acquired in a transaction made under Securities Act Rule 801 to the same extent and proportion that the securities held by the security holder of the class with respect to which the rights offering was made were as of the record date for the rights offering "restricted securities" within the meaning of this paragraph (a)(3); and

(vii) Securities acquired in a transaction made under Securities Act Rule 802 to the same extent and proportion that the securities that were tendered or exchanged in the exchange offer or business combination were "restricted securities" within the meaning of this paragraph (a)(3).

(b) *Conditions to be Met.* Any affiliate or other person who sells restricted securities of an issuer for his own account, or any person who sells restricted or any other securities for the account of an affiliate of the issuer of such securities, shall be deemed not to be engaged in a distribution of such securities and therefore not to be an underwriter thereof within the meaning of Section 2(11) of the Act if all of the conditions of this rule are met.

(c) *Current Public Information.* There shall be available adequate current public information with respect to the issuer of the securities. Such information shall be deemed to be available only if either of the following conditions is met:

(1) *Filing of Reports.* The issuer has securities registered pursuant to Section 12 of the Securities Exchange Act of 1934, has been subject to the reporting requirements of Section 13 of that Act for a period of at least 90 days immediately preceding the sale of the securities and has filed all the reports required to be filed thereunder during the 12 months preceding such sale (or for such shorter period that the issuer was required to file such reports), other than Form 8-K reports (§ 249.308 of this chapter); or has securities registered pursuant to the Securities Act of 1933, has been subject to the reporting requirements of Section 15(d) of the Securities Exchange Act of 1934 for a period of at least 90 days immediately preceding the sale of the securities and has filed all the reports required to be filed thereunder during the 12 months preceding such sale (or for such shorter period that the issuer was required to file such reports), other

than Form 8-K reports (§ 249.308 of this chapter). The person for whose account the securities are to be sold shall be entitled to rely upon a statement in whichever is the most recent report, quarterly or annual, required to be filed and filed by the issuer that such issuer has filed all reports required to be filed by Section 13 or 15(d) of the Securities Exchange Act of 1934 during the preceding 12 months (or for such shorter period that the issuer was required to file such reports), other than Form 8-K reports (§ 249.308 of this chapter), and has been subject to such filing requirements for the past 90 days, unless he knows or has reason to believe that the issuer has not complied with such requirements. Such person shall also be entitled to rely upon a written statement from the issuer that it has complied with such reporting requirements unless he knows or has reasons to believe that the issuer has not complied with such requirements.

(2) *Other Public Information.* If the issuer is not subject to Section 13 or 15(d) of the Securities Exchange Act of 1934, there is publicly available the information concerning the issuer specified in paragraphs (a)(5)(i) to (xiv), inclusive, and paragraph (a)(5)(xvi) of Rule 15c2-11 under that Act or, if the issuer is an insurance company, the information specified in Section 12(g)(2)(G)(i) of that Act.

(d) *Holding Period For Restricted Securities.* If the securities sold are restricted securities, the following provisions apply:

(1) *General Rule.* A minimum of one year must elapse between the later of the date of the acquisition of the securities from the issuer or from an affiliate of the issuer, and any resale of such securities in reliance on this section for the account of either the acquiror or any subsequent holder of those securities. If the acquiror takes the securities by purchase, the one-year period shall not begin until the full purchase price or other consideration is paid or given by the person acquiring the securities from the issuer or from an affiliate of the issuer.

(2) *Promissory Notes, Other Obligations or Installment Contracts.* Giving the issuer or affiliate of the issuer from whom the securities were purchased a promissory note or other obligation to pay the purchase price, or entering into an installment purchase contract with such seller, shall not be deemed full payment of the purchase price unless the promissory note, obligation or contract:

(i) Provides for full recourse against the purchaser of the securities;

(ii) Is secured by collateral, other than the securities purchased, having a fair market value at least equal to the purchase price of the securities purchased; and

(iii) Shall have been discharged by payment in full prior to the sale of the securities.

(3) *Determination of Holding Period.* The following provisions shall apply for the purpose of determining the period securities have been held:

(i) *Stock Dividends, Splits and Recapitalizations.* Securities acquired from the issuer as a dividend or pursuant to a stock split, reverse split or recapitalization shall be deemed to have been acquired at the same time as the securities on which the dividend or, if more than one, the initial dividend was paid, the securities involved in the split or reverse split, or the securities surrendered in connection with the recapitalization;

(ii) *Conversions.* If the securities sold were acquired from the issuer for a consideration consisting solely of other securities of the same issuer surrendered for conversion, the securities so acquired shall be deemed to have been acquired at the same time as the securities surrendered for conversion;

(iii) *Contingent Issuance of Securities.* Securities acquired as a contingent payment of the purchase price of an equity interest in a business, or the assets of a business, sold to the issuer or an affiliate of the issuer shall be deemed to have been acquired at the time of such sale if the issuer or affiliate was then committed to issue the securities subject only to conditions other than the payment of further consideration for such securities. An agreement entered into in connection with any such purchase to remain in the employment of, or not to compete with, the issuer or affiliate or the rendering of services pursuant to such agreement shall not be deemed to be the payment of further consideration for such securities;

(iv) *Pledged Securities.* Securities which are *bona fide* pledged by an affiliate of the issuer when sold by the pledgee, or by a purchaser, after a default in the obligation secured by the pledge, shall be deemed to have been acquired when they were acquired by the pledgor, except that if the securities were pledged without recourse they shall be deemed to have been acquired by the pledgee at the time of the pledge or by the purchaser at the time of purchase;

(v) *Gifts of Securities.* Securities acquired from an affiliate of the issuer by gift shall be deemed to have been acquired by the donee when they were acquired by the donor;

(vi) *Trusts.* Where a trust settlor is an affiliate of the issuer, securities acquired from the settlor by the trust, or acquired from the trust by the beneficiaries thereof, shall be deemed to have been acquired when such securities were acquired by the settlor;

(vii) *Estates.* Where a deceased person was an affiliate of the issuer, securities held by the estate of such person or acquired from such estate by the beneficiaries thereof shall be deemed to have been acquired when they were acquired by the deceased person, except that no holding period is required if the estate is not an affiliate of the issuer or if the securities are sold by a beneficiary of the estate who is not such an affiliate.

Note. While there is no holding period or amount limitation for estates and beneficiaries thereof which are not affiliates of the issuer, paragraphs (c), (h) and (i) of the rule apply to securities sold by such persons in reliance upon the rule.

(viii) *Rule 145(a) Transactions.* The holding period for securities acquired in a transaction specified in Rule 145(a) shall be deemed to commence on the date the securities were acquired by the purchaser in such transaction. This provision shall not apply, however, to a transaction effected solely for the purpose of forming a holding company.

(e) *Limitation on Amount of Securities Sold.* Except as hereinafter provided, the amount of securities which may be sold in reliance upon this rule shall be determined as follows:

(1) *Sales by Affiliates.* If restricted or other securities are sold for the account of an affiliate of the issuer, the amount of securities sold, together with all sales of restricted and other securities of the same class for the account of such person within the preceding three months, shall not exceed the greater of: (i) one percent of the shares or other units of the class outstanding as shown by the most recent report or statement published by the issuer; or (ii) the average weekly reported volume of trading in such securities on all national securities exchanges and/or reported through the automated quotation system of a registered securities association during the four calendar weeks preceding the filing of notice required by paragraph (h), or if no such notice is required the date of receipt of the order to execute the transaction by the broker or the date of execution of the transaction directly with a market maker; or (iii) the average weekly volume of trading in such securities reported through the consolidated transaction reporting system contemplated by Rule 11Aa3-1 under the Securities Exchange Act of 1934 during the four-week period specified in subdivision (ii) of this paragraph.

(2) *Sales by Persons Other Than Affiliates.* The amount of restricted securities sold for the account of any person other than an affiliate of the issuer, together with all other sales of restricted securities of the same class for the account of such person within the preceding three months, shall not exceed the amount specified in paragraph (e)(1)(i), (1)(ii) or (1)(iii) of this section, whichever is applicable, unless the conditions in paragraph (k) of this rule are satisfied.

(3) *Determination of Amount.* For the purpose of determining the amount of securities specified in paragraphs (e)(1) and (2) of this rule, the following provisions shall apply:

(i) Where both convertible securities and securities of the class into which they are convertible are sold, the amount of convertible securities sold shall be deemed to be the amount of securities of the class into which they are convertible for the purpose of determining the aggregate amount of securities of both classes sold;

(ii) The amount of securities sold for the account of a pledgee thereof, or for the account of a purchaser of the pledged securities, during any period of three months within one year after a default in the obligation secured by the pledge, and the amount of securities sold during the same three-month period for the account of the pledgor shall not exceed, in the aggregate, the amount specified in paragraph (e)(1) or (2) of this section, whichever is applicable;

(iii) The amount of securities sold for the account of a donee thereof during any period of three months within one year after the donation, and the amount of securities sold during the same three-month period for the account of the donor, shall not exceed, in the aggregate, the amount specified in paragraph (e)(1) or (2) of this section, whichever is applicable;

(iv) Where securities were acquired by a trust from the settlor of the trust, the amount of such securities sold for the account of the trust during any period of three months within one year after the acquisition of the securities by the trust, and the amount of securities sold during the same three-month period for the account of the settlor, shall not exceed, in the aggregate, the amount specified in paragraph (e)(1) or

(2) of this section, whichever is applicable;

(v) The amount of securities sold for the account of the estate of a deceased person, or for the account of a beneficiary of such estate, during any period of three months and the amount of securities sold during the same period for the account of the deceased person prior to his death shall not exceed, in the aggregate, the amount specified in subparagraph (1) or (2) of this paragraph, whichever is applicable; *provided*, that no limitation on amount shall apply if the estate or beneficiary thereof is not an affiliate of the issuer;

(vi) When two or more affiliates or other persons agree to act in concert for the purpose of selling securities of an issuer, all securities of the same class sold for the account of all such persons during any period of three months shall be aggregated for the purpose of determining the limitation on the amount of securities sold;

(vii) The following sales of securities need not be included in determining the amount of securities sold in reliance upon this section: securities sold pursuant to an effective registration statement under the Act; securities sold pursuant to an exemption provided by Regulation A under the Act; securities sold in a transaction exempt pursuant to Section 4 of the Act and not involving any public offering; and securities sold offshore pursuant to Regulation S under the Act.

(f) *Manner of Sale.* The securities shall be sold in "brokers' transactions" within the meaning of Section 4(4) of the Act or in transactions directly with a "market maker," as that term is defined in Section 3(a)(38) of the Securities Exchange Act of 1934, and the person selling the securities shall not: (1) solicit or arrange for the solicitation of orders to buy the securities in anticipation of or in connection with such transaction, or (2) make any payment in connection with the offer or sale of the securities to any person other than the broker who executes the order to sell the securities. The requirements of this paragraph, however, shall not apply to securities sold for the account of the estate of a deceased person or for the account of a beneficiary of such estate provided the estate or beneficiary thereof is not an affiliate of the issuer; nor shall they apply to securities sold for the account of any person other than an affiliate of the issuer, *provided* the conditions of paragraph (k) of this rule are satisfied.

(g) *Brokers' Transactions.* The term "brokers' transactions" in Section 4(4) of the Act shall for the purposes of this rule be deemed to include transactions by a broker in which such broker:

(1) Does no more than execute the order or orders to sell the securities as agent for the person for whose account the securities are sold; and receives no more than the usual and customary broker's commission;

(2) Neither solicits nor arranges for the solicitation of customers' orders to buy the securities in anticipation of or in connection with the transaction; *provided,* that the foregoing shall not preclude: *(i)* inquiries by the broker of other brokers or dealers

who have indicated an interest in the securities within the preceding 60 days, *(ii)* inquiries by the broker of his customers who have indicated an unsolicited *bona fide* interest in the securities within the preceding 10 business days, or *(iii)* the publication by the broker of bid and ask quotations for the security in an inter-dealer quotation system provided that such quotations are incident to the maintenance of a *bona fide* inter-dealer market for the security for the broker's own account and that the broker has published *bona fide* bid and ask quotations for the security in an inter-dealer quotation system on each of at least 12 days within the preceding 30 calendar days with no more than four business days in succession without such two-way quotations;

Note to Subparagraph (g)(2)(ii). The broker should obtain and retain in his files written evidence of indications of *bona fide* unsolicited interest by his customers in the securities at the time such indications are received.

(3) After reasonable inquiry is not aware of circumstances indicating that the person for whose account the securities are sold is an underwriter with respect to the securities or that the transaction is a part of a distribution of securities of the issuer. Without limiting the foregoing, the broker shall be deemed to be aware of any facts or statements contained in the notice required by paragraph (h) below.

Notes. (i) The broker, for his own protection, should obtain and retain in his files a copy of the notice required by paragraph (h).

(ii) The reasonable inquiry required by paragraph (g)(3) of this section should include, but not necessarily be limited to, inquiry as to the following matters:

a. The length of time the securities have been held by the person for whose account they are to be sold. If practicable, the inquiry should include physical inspection of the securities;

b. The nature of the transaction in which the securities were acquired by such person; c. The amount of securities of the same class sold during the past three months by all persons whose sales are required to be taken into consideration pursuant to paragraph (e) of this section;

d. Whether such person intends to sell additional securities of the same class through any other means;

e. Whether such person has solicited or made any arrangement for the solicitation of buy orders in connection with the proposed sale of securities;

f. Whether such person has made any payment to any other person in connection with the proposed sale of the securities; and

g. The number of shares or other units of the class outstanding, or the relevant trading volume.

(h) *Notice of Proposed Sale.* If the amount of securities to be sold in reliance upon the rule during any period of three months exceeds 500 shares or other units or has an aggregate sale price in excess of $10,000, three copies of a notice on Form 144 shall be filed with the Commission at its principal office in Washington, DC; and if such securities are admitted to trading on any national securities exchange, one copy of such notice shall also be transmitted to the principal exchange on which such securities are so admitted. The Form 144 shall be signed by the person for whose account the securities are to be sold and shall be transmitted for filing concurrently with either the placing with a broker of an order to execute a sale of securities in reliance upon this rule or the execution directly with a market maker of such a sale. Neither the filing of such notice nor the failure of the Commission to comment thereon shall be deemed to preclude the Commission from taking any action it deems necessary or appropriate with respect to the sale of the securities referred to in such notice. The requirements of this paragraph, however, shall not apply to securities sold for the account of any person other than an affiliate of the issuer, provided the conditions of paragraph (k) of this rule are satisfied.

(i) *Bona Fide Intention to Sell.* The person filing the notice required by paragraph (h) shall have a *bona fide* intention to sell the securities referred to therein within a reasonable time after the filing of such notice.

(j) *Non-Exclusive Rule.* Although this rule provides a means for reselling restricted securities and securities held by affiliates without registration, it is not the exclusive means for reselling such securities in that manner. Therefore, it does not eliminate or otherwise affect the availability of any exemption for resales under the Securities Act that a person or entity may be able to rely upon.

(k) *Termination of Certain Restrictions on Sales of Restricted Securities by Persons Other Than Affiliates.* The requirements of paragraphs (c), (e), (f) and (h) of this section shall not apply to restricted securities sold for the account of a person who is not an affiliate of the issuer at the time of the sale and has not been an affiliate during the preceding three months, *provided* a period of at least two years has elapsed since the later of the date the securities were acquired from the issuer or from an affiliate of the issuer. The two-year period shall be calculated as described in paragraph (d) of this section.

Rule 428

Documents Constituting a Section 10(a) Prospectus for Form S-8 Registration Statement; Requirements Relating to Offerings of Securities Registered on Form S-8

(a)(1) Where securities are to be offered pursuant to a registration statement on Form S-8, the following, taken together, shall constitute a prospectus that meets the requirements of Section 10(a) of the Act:

(i) The document(s), or portions thereof as permitted by paragraph (b)(1)(ii) of this section, containing the employee benefit plan information required by Item 1 of the form;

(ii) The statement of availability of registrant information, employee benefit plan annual reports and other information required by Item 2; and

(iii) The documents containing registrant information and employee benefit plan annual reports that are incorporated by reference in the registration statement pursuant to Item 3.

(2) The registrant shall maintain a file of the documents that, pursuant to paragraph (a) of this section, at any time are part of the Section 10(a) prospectus, except for documents required to be incorporated by reference in the registration statement pursuant to Item 3 of Form S-8. Each such document shall be included in the file until five years after it is last used as part of the Section 10(a) prospectus to offer or sell securities pursuant to the plan. With respect to documents containing specifically designated portions that constitute part of the Section 10(a) prospectus pursuant to paragraph (b)(1)(ii) of this section, the entire document shall be maintained in the file. Upon request, the registrant shall furnish to the Commission or its staff a copy of any or all of the documents included in the file.

(b) Where securities are offered pursuant to a registration statement on Form S-8:

(1)(i) The registrant shall deliver or cause to be delivered, to each employee who is eligible to participate (or selected by the registrant to participate, in the case of a stock option or other plan with selective participation) in an employee benefit plan to which the registration statement relates, the information required by Part I of Form S-8. The information shall be in written form and shall be updated in writing in a timely manner to reflect any material changes during any period in which offers or sales are being made. When updated information is furnished, documents previously furnished need not be redelivered, but the registrant shall furnish promptly without charge to each employee, upon written or oral request, a copy of all documents containing the plan information required by Part I that then constitute part of the Section 10(a) prospectus.

(ii) The registrant may designate an entire document or only portions of a document as constituting part of the Section 10(a) prospectus. If the registrant designates only portions of a document as constituting part of the prospectus, rather than the entire document, a statement clearly identifying such portions, for example, by reference to section headings, section numbers, paragraphs or page numbers within the document must be included in a conspicuous place in the forepart of the document, or such portions must be specifically designated throughout the text of the document. Registrants shall not designate only words or sentences within a paragraph as part of a prospectus. Unless the portions of a document constituting part of the Section 10(a) prospectus are clearly identified, the entire document shall constitute part of the prospectus.

(iii) The registrant shall date any document constituting part of the Section 10(a) prospectus or containing portions constituting part of the prospectus and shall include the following printed, stamped or typed legend in a conspicuous place in the forepart of the document, substituting the bracketed language as appropriate: "This document [Specifically designated portions of this document] constitutes [constitute] part of a prospectus covering securities that have been registered under the Securities Act of 1933."

(iv) The registrant shall revise the document(s) containing the plan information sent or given to newly eligible participants pursuant to paragraph (b)(1)(i) of this section, if documents containing updating information would obscure the readability of the plan information.

(2) The registrant shall deliver or cause to be delivered with the document(s) containing the information required by Part I of Form S-8, to each employee to whom such information is sent or given, a copy of any one of the following:

(i) The registrant's annual report to security holders containing the information required by Rule 14a-3(b) under the Securities Exchange Act of 1934 ("Exchange Act") for its latest fiscal year;

(ii) The registrant's annual report on Form 10-K or Form 10-KSB, U5S, or 20-F for its latest fiscal year;

(iii) The latest prospectus filed pursuant to Rule 424(b) under the Act that contains audited financial statements for the registrant's latest fiscal year, *provided* that the financial statements are not incorporated by reference from another filing, and provided further that such prospectus contains substantially the information required by Rule 14a-3(b), or the registration statement was on Form SB-2 or F-1; or

(iv) The registrant's effective Exchange Act registration statement on Form 10 or Form 10-SB or 20-F containing audited financial statements for the registrant's latest fiscal year.

Instructions.

1. If a registrant has previously sent or given an employee a copy of any document specified in clauses (i)-(iv) of paragraph (b)(2) for the latest fiscal year, it need not be re-delivered, but the registrant shall furnish promptly, without charge, a copy of such document upon written or oral request of the employee.

2. If the latest fiscal year of the registrant has ended within 120 days (or 190 days with respect to foreign private issuers eligible to file on Form 20-F) prior to the delivery of the documents containing the information specified by Part I of Form S-8, the registrant may deliver a document containing financial statements for the fiscal year preceding the latest fiscal year, provided that within the 120- or 190-day period a document containing financial statements for the latest fiscal year is furnished to each employee.

2T. With regard to issuers that are eligible to rely on and are electing to comply with Release No. 34-45589 (March 18, 2002) (which may be viewed on the Commission's website at www.sec.gov) or a temporary rule adopted in Release 33-8070 (March 18, 2002) published on March 22, 2002 in the Federal Register, until September 13, 2002 (or December 16, 2002 with respect to foreign private issuers), if the latest fiscal year has ended within 180 days (or 250 days with respect to foreign private issuers) prior to the delivery of documents containing the information specified by Part I of Form S-8, the issuer may deliver a document containing financial statements for the fiscal year preceding the latest fiscal year, provided that within the 180 or 250 day period a document containing financial statements for the latest fiscal year is furnished to each employee. This temporary instruction will expire on December 31, 2002.

(3) The registrant shall deliver or cause to be delivered promptly, without charge, to each employee to whom information is required to be delivered, upon written or oral request, a copy of the information that has been incorporated by reference pursuant to Item 3 of Form S-8 (not including exhibits to the information that is incorporated by reference unless such exhibits are specifically incorporated by reference into the information that the registration statement incorporates).

(4) Where interests in a plan are registered, the registrant shall deliver or cause to be delivered promptly, without charge, to each employee to whom information is required to be delivered, upon written or oral request, a copy of the then latest annual report of the plan filed pursuant to Section 15(d) of the Exchange Act, whether on Form 11-K or included as part of the registrant's annual report on Form 10-K or Form 10-KSB.

(5) The registrant shall deliver or cause to be delivered to all employees participating in a stock option plan or plan fund that invests in registrant securities (and other plan participants who request such information orally or in writing) who do not otherwise receive such material, copies of all reports, proxy statements and other communications distributed to its security holders generally, provided that such material is sent or delivered no later than the time it is sent to security holders.

(c) As used in this rule, the term "employee benefit plan" is defined in Rule 405 of Regulation C and the term "employee" is defined in General Instruction A.1 of Form S-8.

Rule 701

Exemption for Offers and Sales of Securities Pursuant to Certain Compensatory Benefit Plans and Contracts Relating to Compensation

Preliminary Notes.

1. This Rule 701 relates to transactions exempted from the registration requirements of Section 5 of the Securities Act. These transactions are not exempt from the antifraud, civil liability, or other provisions of the federal securities laws. Issuers and persons acting on their behalf have an obligation to provide investors with disclosure adequate to satisfy the antifraud provisions of the federal securities laws.

2. In addition to complying with this Rule 701, the issuer also must comply with any applicable state law relating to the offer and sale of securities.

3. An issuer that attempts to comply with this Rule 701, but fails to do so, may claim any other exemption that is available.

4. This Rule 701 is available only to the issuer of the securities. Affiliates of the issuer may not use this Rule 701 to offer or sell securities. This Rule 701 also does not cover resales of securities by any person. This Rule 701 provides an exemption only for the transactions in which the securities are offered or sold by the issuer, not for the securities themselves.

5. The purpose of this Rule 701 is to provide an exemption from the registration requirements of the Securities Act for securities issued in compensatory circumstances. This Rule 701 is not available for plans or schemes to circumvent this purpose, such as to raise capital. This Rule 701 also is not available to exempt any transaction that is in technical compliance with this Rule 701 but is part of a plan or scheme to evade the registration provisions of the Securities Act. In any of these cases, registration under the Securities Act is required unless another exemption is available.

(a) *Exemption.* Offers and sales made in compliance with all of the conditions of this Rule 701 are exempt from Section 5 of the Securities Act.

(b) *Issuers Eligible to Use this Rule 701.*

(1) *General.* This Rule 701 is available to any issuer that is not subject to the reporting requirements of Section 13 or 15(d) of the Securities Exchange Act of 1934 (the "Exchange Act") and is not an investment company registered or required to be registered under the Investment Company Act of 1940 (15 U.S.C. 80a-1 *et seq.*).

(2) *Issuers That Become Subject to Reporting.* If an issuer becomes subject to the reporting requirements of Section 13 or 15(d) of the Exchange Act after it has made offers complying with this Rule 701, the issuer may nevertheless rely on this section to sell the securities previously offered to the persons to whom those offers were made.

(3) *Guarantees by Reporting Companies.* An issuer subject to the reporting requirements of Section 13 or 15(d) of the Exchange Act may rely on this Rule 701 if it is merely guaranteeing the payment of a subsidiary's securities that are sold under this Rule 701.

(c) *Transactions Exempted by This Rule 701.* This Rule 701 exempts offers and sales of securities (including plan interests and guarantees pursuant to paragraph (d)(2)(ii) of this Rule 701) under a written compensatory benefit plan (or written compensation contract) established by the issuer, its parents, its majority-owned subsidiaries or majority-owned subsidiaries of the issuer's parent, for the participation of their employees, directors, general partners, trustees (where the issuer is a business trust), officers, or consultants and advisors, and their family members who acquire such securities from such persons through gifts or domestic relations orders. This Rule 701 exempts offers and sales to former employees, directors, general partners, trustees, officers, consultants and advisors only if such persons were employed by or providing services to the issuer at the time the securities were offered. In addition, the term "employee" includes insurance agents who are exclusive agents of the issuer, its subsidiaries or parents, or derive more than 50% of their annual income from those entities.

(1) *Special Requirements for Consultants and Advisors.* This Rule 701 is available to consultants and advisors only if:

(i) They are natural persons;

(ii) They provide *bona fide* services to the issuer, its parents, its majority-owned subsidiaries or majority-owned subsidiaries of the issuer's parent; and

(iii) The services are not in connection with the offer or sale of securities in a capital- raising transaction, and do not directly or indirectly promote or maintain a market for the issuer's securities.

(2) *Definition of "Compensatory Benefit Plan."* For purposes of this Rule 701, a compensatory benefit plan is any purchase, savings, option, bonus, stock appreciation, profit sharing, thrift, incentive, deferred compensation, pension or similar plan.

(3) Definition of "Family Member." For purposes of this Rule 701, family member includes any child, stepchild, grandchild, parent, stepparent, grandparent, spouse, former spouse, sibling, niece, nephew, mother-in-law, father-in-law, son-in-law, daughterin-law, brother-in-law, or sister-

in-law, including adoptive relationships, any person sharing the employee's household (other than a tenant or employee), a trust in which these persons have more than fifty percent of the beneficial interest, a foundation in which these persons (or the employee) control the management of assets, and any other entity in which these persons (or the employee) own more than fifty percent of the voting interests.

(d) *Amounts That May Be Sold.*

(1) *Offers.* Any amount of securities may be offered in reliance on this Rule 701. However, for purposes of this Rule 701, sales of securities underlying options must be counted as sales on the date of the option grant.

(2) *Sales.* The aggregate sales price or amount of securities sold in reliance on this Rule 701 during any consecutive 12-month period must not exceed the greatest of the following:

(i) $1,000,000;

(ii) 15% of the total assets of the issuer (or of the issuer's parent if the issuer is a wholly-owned subsidiary and the securities represent obligations that the parent fully and unconditionally guarantees), measured at the issuer's most recent balance sheet date (if no older than its last fiscal year end); or

(iii) 15% of the outstanding amount of the class of securities being offered and sold in reliance on this Rule 701, measured at the issuer's most recent balance sheet date (if no older than its last fiscal year end).

(3) *Rules for Calculating Prices and Amounts.*

(i) *Aggregate Sales Price.* The term *aggregate sales price* means the sum of all cash, property, notes, cancellation of debt or other consideration received or to be received by the issuer for the sale of the securities. Non-cash consideration must be valued by reference to *bona fide* sales of that consideration made within a reasonable time or, in the absence of such sales, on the fair value as determined by an accepted standard. The value of services exchanged for securities issued must be measured by reference to the value of the securities issued. Options must be valued based on the exercise price of the option.

(ii) *Time of the Calculation.* With respect to options to purchase securities, the aggregate sales price is determined when an option grant is made (without regard to when the option becomes exercisable). With respect to other securities, the calculation is made on the date of sale. With respect to deferred compensation or similar plans, the calculation is made when the irrevocable election to defer is made.

(iii) *Derivative Securities.* In calculating outstanding securities for purposes of paragraph (d)(2)(iii) of this Rule 701, treat the securities underlying all currently exercisable or convertible options, warrants, rights or other securities, other than those issued under this exemption, as outstanding. In calculating the amount of securities sold for other purposes of paragraph (d)(2) of this Rule 701, count the amount of securities that would be acquired upon exercise or conversion in connection with sales of options, warrants, rights or other exercisable or convertible securities, including those to be issued under this exemption.

(iv) *Other Exemptions.* Amounts of securities sold in reliance on this Rule 701 do not affect "aggregate offering prices" in other exemptions, and amounts of securities sold in reliance on other exemptions do not affect the amount that may be sold in reliance on this Rule 701.

(e) *Disclosure That Must Be Provided.* The issuer must deliver to investors a copy of the compensatory benefit plan or the contract, as applicable. In addition, if the aggregate sales price or amount of securities sold during any consecutive 12-month period exceeds $5 million, the issuer must deliver the following disclosure to investors a reasonable period of time before the date of sale:

(1) If the plan is subject to the Employee Retirement Income Security Act of 1974 ("ERISA") (29 U.S.C. 1104 - 1107), a copy of the summary plan description required by ERISA;

(2) If the plan is not subject to ERISA, a summary of the material terms of the plan;

(3) Information about the risks associated with investment in the securities sold pursuant to the compensatory benefit plan or compensation contract; and

(4) Financial statements required to be furnished by Part F/S of Form 1-A (Regulation A Offering Statement) under Regulation A. Foreign private issuers as defined in Securities Act Rule 405 must provide a reconciliation to generally accepted accounting principles in the United States (U.S. GAAP) if their financial statements are not prepared in accordance with U.S. GAAP (Item 17 of Form 20-F). The financial statements required by this Rule 701 must be as of a date no more than 180 days before the sale of securities in reliance on this exemption.

(5) If the issuer is relying on paragraph (d)(2)(ii) of this Rule 701 to use its parent's total assets to determine the amount of securities that may be sold, the parent's financial statements must be delivered. If the parent is subject to the reporting requirements of Section 13 or 15(d) of the Exchange Act, the financial statements of the parent required by Rule 10-01 of Regulation S-X and Item 310 of Regulation S-B, as applicable, must be delivered.

(6) If the sale involves a stock option or other derivative security, the issuer must deliver disclosure a reasonable period of time before the date of exercise or conversion. For deferred compensation or similar plans, the

issuer must deliver disclosure to investors a reasonable period of time before the date the irrevocable election to defer is made.

(f) *No Integration With Other Offerings.* Offers and sales exempt under this Rule 701 are deemed to be a part of a single, discrete offering and are not subject to integration with any other offers or sales, whether registered under the Securities Act or otherwise exempt from the registration requirements of the Securities Act.

(g) *Resale Limitations.*

(1) Securities issued under this section are deemed to be "restricted securities" as defined in Securities Act Rule 144.

(2) Resales of securities issued pursuant to this Rule 701 must be in compliance with the registration requirements of the Securities Act or an exemption from those requirements.

(3) Ninety days after the issuer becomes subject to the reporting requirements of Section 13 or 15(d) of the Exchange Act, securities issued under this Rule 701 may be resold by persons who are not affiliates (as defined in Securities Act Rule 144) in reliance on Securities Act Rule 144 without compliance with paragraphs (c), (d), (e) and (h) of Securities Act Rule 144, and by affiliates without compliance with paragraph (d) of Securities Act Rule 144.

Rule 10b-5

Employment of Manipulative and Deceptive Devices

It shall be unlawful for any person, directly or indirectly, by the use of any means or instrumentality of interstate commerce, or of the mails, or of any facility of any national securities exchange:

(a) To employ any device, scheme, or artifice to defraud,

(b) To make any untrue statement of a material fact or to omit to state a material fact necessary in order to make the statements made, in the light of the circumstances under which they were made, not misleading, or

(c) To engage in any act, practice, or course of business which operates or would operate as a fraud or deceit upon any person, in connection with the purchase or sale of any security.

Rule 10b5-1

Trading "on the Basis of" Material Nonpublic Information in Insider Trading Cases

Preliminary Note to Rule 10b5-1: This provision defines when a purchase or sale constitutes trading "on the basis of" material nonpublic information in insider trading cases brought under Section 10(b) of the Exchange Act and Rule 10b-5 thereunder. The law of insider trading is otherwise defined by judicial opinions construing Rule 10b-5, and Rule 10b5-1 does not modify the scope of insider trading law in any other respect.

(a) *General.* The "manipulative and deceptive devices" prohibited by Section 10(b) of the Exchange Act and Rule 10b-5 thereunder include, among other things, the purchase or sale of a security of any issuer, on the basis of material nonpublic information about that security or issuer, in breach of a duty of trust or confidence that is owed directly, indirectly, or derivatively, to the issuer of that security or the shareholders of that issuer, or to any other person who is the source of the material nonpublic information.

(b) *Definition of "On the Basis Of."* Subject to the affirmative defenses in paragraph (c) of this Rule 10b5-1, a purchase or sale of a security of an issuer is "on the basis of" material nonpublic information about that security or issuer if the person making the purchase or sale was aware of the material nonpublic information when the person made the purchase or sale.

(c) *Affirmative Defenses.*

(1)(i) Subject to paragraph (c)(1)(ii) of this Rule 10b5-1, a person's purchase or sale is not "on the basis of" material nonpublic information if the person making the purchase or sale demonstrates that:

(A) Before becoming aware of the information, the person had:

(*1*) Entered into a binding contract to purchase or sell the security,

(*2*) Instructed another person to purchase or sell the security for the instructing person's account, or

(*3*) Adopted a written plan for trading securities;

(B) The contract, instruction, or plan described in paragraph (c)(1)(i)(A):

(*1*) Specified the amount of securities to be purchased or sold and the price at which and the date on which the securities were to be purchased or sold;

(2) Included a written formula or algorithm, or computer program, for determining the amount of securities to be purchased or sold and the price at which and the date on which the securities were to be purchased or sold; or

(3) Did not permit the person to exercise any subsequent influence over how, when, or whether to effect purchases or sales; provided, in addition, that any other person who, pursuant to the contract, instruction, or plan, did exercise such influence must not have been aware of the material nonpublic information when doing so; and

(C) The purchase or sale that occurred was pursuant to the contract, instruction, or plan. A purchase or sale is not "pursuant to a contract, instruction, or plan" if, among other things, the person who entered into the contract, instruction, or plan altered or deviated from the contract, instruction, or plan to purchase or sell securities (whether by changing the amount, price, or timing of the purchase or sale), or entered into or altered a corresponding or hedging transaction or position with respect to those securities.

(ii) Paragraph (c)(1)(i) of this Rule 10b5-1 is applicable only when the contract, instruction, or plan to purchase or sell securities was given or entered into in good faith and not as part of a plan or scheme to evade the prohibitions of this Rule 10b5-1.

(iii) This subparagraph defines certain terms as used in paragraph (c).

(A) *Amount.* "Amount" means either a specified number of shares or other securities or a specified dollar value of securities.

(B) *Price.* "Price" means the market price on a particular date or a limit price, or a particular dollar price.

(C) *Date.* "Date" means, in the case of a market order, the specific day of the year on which the order is to be executed (or as soon thereafter as is practicable under ordinary principles of best execution). "Date" means, in the case of a limit order, a day of the year on which the limit order is in force.

(2) A person other than a natural person also may demonstrate that a purchase or sale of securities is not "on the basis of" material nonpublic information if the person demonstrates that:

(i) The individual making the investment decision on behalf of the person to purchase or sell the securities was not aware of the information; and

(ii) The person had implemented reasonable policies and procedures, taking into consideration the nature of the person's business, to ensure that individuals making investment decisions would not violate the laws prohibiting trading on the basis of material nonpublic information. These policies and procedures may include those that restrict any purchase, sale, and causing any purchase or sale of any security as to which the person has material nonpublic information, or those that prevent such individuals from becoming aware of such information.

Regulation 13D–G

Rule 13d-1. Filing of Schedules 13D and 13G.

(a) Any person who, after acquiring directly or indirectly the beneficial ownership of any equity security of a class which is specified in paragraph (i) of this Rule 13d-1, is directly or indirectly the beneficial owner of more than five percent of the class shall, within 10 days after the acquisition, file with the Commission, a statement containing the information required by Schedule 13D.

(b)(1) A person who would otherwise be obligated under paragraph (a) of this Rule 13d-1 to file a statement on Schedule 13D may, in lieu thereof, file with the Commission, a short-form statement on Schedule 13G, *provided*, that:

(i) Such person has acquired such securities in the ordinary course of his business and not with the purpose nor with the effect of changing or influencing the control of the issuer, nor in connection with or as a participant in any transaction having such purpose or effect, including any transaction subject to Rule 13d-3(b); and

(ii) Such person is:

(A) A broker or dealer registered under Section 15 of the Exchange Act;

(B) A bank as defined in Section 3(a)(6) of the Exchange Act;

(C) An insurance company as defined in Section 3(a)(19) of the Exchange Act;

(D) An investment company registered under Section 8 of the Investment Company Act;

(E) Any person registered as an investment adviser under Section 203 of the Investment Advisers Act or under the laws of any state;

(F) An employee benefit plan as defined in Section 3(3) of the Employee Retirement Income Security Act of 1974, as amended, ("ERISA") that is subject to the provisions of ERISA, or any such plan that is not subject to ERISA that is maintained primarily for the benefit of the employees of a state or local government or instrumentality, or an endowment fund;

(G) A parent holding company or control person, provided the aggregate amount held directly by the parent or control person, and directly and indirectly by their subsidiaries or affiliates that are not persons specified in Rule 13d-1(b)(1)(ii)(A) through

(I), does not exceed one percent of the securities of the subject class;

(H) A savings association as defined in Section 3(b) of the Federal Deposit Insurance Act;

(I) A church plan that is excluded from the definition of an investment company under Section 3(c)(14) of the Investment Company Act; and

(J) A group, provided that all the members are persons specified in Rule 13d-1(b)(1)(ii)(A) through (I); and

(iii) Such person has promptly notified any other person (or group within the meaning of Section 13(d)(3) of the Act) on whose behalf it holds, on a discretionary basis, securities exceeding five percent of the class, of any acquisition or transaction on behalf of such other person which might be reportable by that person under Section 13(d) of the Act. This paragraph only requires notice to the account owner of information which the filing person reasonably should be expected to know and which would advise the account owner of an obligation he may have to file a statement pursuant to Section 13(d) of the Act or an amendment thereto.

(2) The Schedule 13G filed pursuant to paragraph (b)(1) of this Rule 13d-1 shall be filed within 45 days after the end of the calendar year in which the person became obligated under paragraph (b)(1) of this section to report the person's beneficial ownership as of the last day of the calendar year, *provided*, that it shall not be necessary to file a Schedule 13G unless the percentage of the class of equity security specified in paragraph (i) of this Rule 13d-1 beneficially owned as of the end of the calendar year is more than five percent; however, if the person's direct or indirect beneficial ownership exceeds 10 percent of the class of equity securities prior to the end of the calendar year, the initial Schedule 13G shall be filed within 10 days after the end of the first month in which the person's direct or indirect beneficial ownership exceeds 10 percent of the class of equity securities, computed as of the last day of the month.

(c) A person who would otherwise be obligated under paragraph (a) of this Rule 13d-1 to file a statement on Schedule 13D may, in lieu thereof, file with the Commission, within 10 days after an acquisition described in paragraph (a) of this Rule 13d-1, a short-form statement on Schedule 13G, *provided*, that the person:

(1) Has not acquired the securities with any purpose, or with the effect of, changing or influencing the control of the issuer, or in connection with or as a participant in any transaction having that purpose or effect, including any transaction subject to Rule 13d-3(b);

(2) Is not a person reporting pursuant to paragraph (b)(1) of this Rule 13d-1; and

(3) Is not directly or indirectly the beneficial owner of 20 percent or more of the class.

(d) Any person who, as of the end of any calendar year, is or becomes directly or indirectly the beneficial owner of more than five percent of any equity security of a class specified in paragraph (i) of this Rule 13d-1 and who is not required to file a statement under paragraph (a) of this Rule 13d-1 by virtue of the exemption provided by Section 13(d)(6)(A) or (B) of the Exchange Act, or because the beneficial ownership was acquired prior to December 22, 1970, or because the person otherwise (except for the exemption provided by Section 13(d)(6)(C) of the Exchange Act) is not required to file a statement, shall file with the Commission, within 45 days after the end of the calendar year in which the person became obligated to report under this paragraph(d), a statement containing the information required by Schedule 13G.

(e)(1) Notwithstanding paragraphs (b) and (c) of this Rule 13d-1 and Rule 13d-2(b), a person that has reported that it is the beneficial owner of more than five percent of a class of equity securities in a statement on Schedule 13G pursuant to paragraph (b) or (c) of this Rule 13d-1, or is required to report the acquisition but has not yet filed the schedule, shall immediately become subject to Rule 13d-1(a) and Rule 13d-2(a) and shall file a statement on Schedule 13D within 10 days if, and shall remain subject to those requirements for so long as, the person:

(i) Has acquired or holds the securities with a purpose or effect of changing or influencing control of the issuer, or in connection with or as a participant in any transaction having that purpose or effect, including any transaction subject to Rule 13d-3(b); and

(ii) Is at that time the beneficial owner of more than five percent of a class of equity securities described in Rule 13d-1(i).

(2) From the time the person has acquired or holds the securities with a purpose or effect of changing or influencing control of the issuer, or in connection with or as a participant in any transaction having that purpose or effect until the expiration of the tenth day from the date of the filing of the Schedule 13D pursuant to this Rule 13d-1, that person shall not:

(i) Vote or direct the voting of the securities described therein; or

(ii) Acquire an additional beneficial ownership interest in any equity securities of the issuer of the securities, nor of any person controlling the issuer.

(f)(1) Notwithstanding paragraph (c) of this Rule 13d-1 and Rule 13d-2(b), persons reporting on Schedule 13G pursuant to paragraph (c) of this Rule 13d-1 shall immediately become subject to Rule 13d-1(a) and Rule 13d-2(a) and shall remain subject to those requirements for so long as, and shall file a statement on Schedule 13D within 10 days of the date on which, the person's beneficial ownership equals or exceeds 20 percent of the class of equity securities.

(2) From the time of the acquisition of 20 percent or more of the class of equity securities until the expiration of the tenth day from the date of the filing of the Schedule 13D pursuant to this Rule 13d-1, the person shall not:

(i) Vote or direct the voting of the securities described therein, or

(ii) Acquire an additional beneficial ownership interest in any equity securities of the issuer of the securities, nor of any person controlling the issuer.

(g) Any person who has reported an acquisition of securities in a statement on Schedule 13G pursuant to paragraph (b) of this Rule 13d-1, or has become obligated to report on the Schedule 13G but has not yet filed the Schedule, and thereafter ceases to be a person specified in paragraph (b)(1)(ii) of this Rule 13d-1 or determines that it no longer has acquired or holds the securities in the ordinary course of business shall immediately become subject to Rule 13d-1(a) or Rule 13d-1(c) (if the person satisfies the requirements specified in Rule 13d-1(c)), and Rule 13d-2(a), (b) or (d), and shall file, within 10 days thereafter, a statement on Schedule 13D or amendment to Schedule 13G, as applicable, if the person is a beneficial owner at that time of more than five percent of the class of equity securities.

(h) Any person who has filed a Schedule 13D pursuant to paragraph (e), (f) or (g) of this Rule 13d-1 may again report its beneficial ownership on Schedule 13G pursuant to paragraphs (b) or (c) of this Rule 13d-1 provided the person qualifies thereunder, as applicable, by filing a Schedule 13G once the person determines that the provisions of paragraph (e), (f) or (g) of this Rule 13d-1 no longer apply.

(i) For the purpose of this regulation, the term "equity security" means any equity security of a class which is registered pursuant to Section 12 of the Exchange Act, or any equity security of any insurance company which would have been required to be so registered except for the exemption contained in Section 12(g)(2)(G) of the Exchange Act, or any equity security issued by a closed-end investment company registered under the Investment Company Act; *provided*, such term shall not include securites of a class of non-voting securites.

(j) For the purposes of Sections 13(d) and 13(g), any person, in determining the amount of outstanding securities of a class of equity securities, may rely upon information set forth in the issuer's most recent quarterly or annual report, and any current report subsequent thereto, filed with the Commission pursuant to this Act, unless he knows or has reason to believe that the information contained therein is inaccurate.

(k)(1) Whenever two or more persons are required to file a statement containing the information required by Schedule 13D or Schedule 13G with respect to the same securities, only one statement need be filed; *provided* that:

(i) Each person on whose behalf the statement is filed is individually eligible to use the schedule on which the information is filed;

(ii) Each person on whose behalf the statement is filed is responsible for the timely filing of such statement and any amendments thereto, and for the completeness and accuracy of the information concerning such person contained therein; such person is not responsible for the completeness or accuracy of the information concerning the other persons making the filing, unless such person knows or has reason to believe that such information is inaccurate; and

(iii) Such statement identifies all such persons, contains the required information with regard to each such person, indicates that such statement is filed on behalf of all such persons, and includes, as an exhibit, their agreement in writing that such a statement is filed on behalf of each of them.

(2) A group's filing obligation may be satisfied either by a single joint filing or by each of the group's members making an individual filing. If the group's members elect to make their own filings, each such filing should identify all members of the group, but the information provided concerning the other persons making the filing need only reflect information which the filing person knows or has reason to know.

Rule 13d-2. Filing of Amendments to Schedule 13D or 13G.

(a) If any material change occurs in the facts set forth in the Schedule 13D required by Rule 13d-1(a), including, but not limited to, any material increase or decrease in the percentage of the class beneficially owned, the person or persons who were required to file the statement shall promptly file or cause to be filed with the Commission an amendment disclosing that change. An acquisition or disposition of beneficial ownership of securities in an amount equal to one percent or more of the class of securities shall be deemed "material" for purposes of this Rule 13d-1; acquisitions or dispositions of less than those amounts may bematerial, depending upon the facts and circumstances.

(b) Notwithstanding paragraph (a) of this Rule 13d-2, and provided that the person filing a Schedule 13G pursuant to Rule 13d-1(b) or Rule 13d-1(c) continues to meet the requirements set forth therein, any person who has filed a Schedule 13G pursuant to Rule 13d-1(b), Rule 13d-1(c) or Rule 13d-1(d) shall amend the statement within forty-five days after the end of each calendar year if, as of the end of the calendar year, there are any changes in the information reported in the previous filing on that Schedule; *provided, however,* that an amendment need not be filed with respect to a change in the percent of class outstanding previously reported if the change results solely from a change in the aggregate number of securities outstanding. Once an amendment has been filed reflecting beneficial ownership of five percent or less of the class of securities, no additional filings are required unless the person thereafter becomes the beneficial owner of more than five percent of the class and is required to file pursuant to Rule 13d-1.

(c) Any person relying on Rule 13d-1(b) that has filed its initial Schedule 13G pursuant to that paragraph shall, in addition to filing any amendments pursuant to Rule 13d-2(b), file an amendment on Schedule 13G within 10 days after the end of the first month in which the person's direct or indirect beneficial ownership, computed as of the last day of the month, exceeds 10 percent of the class of equity securities. Thereafter, that person shall, in addition to filing any amendments pursuant to Rule 13d-2(b), file an amendment on Schedule 13G within 10 days after the end of the first month in which the person's direct or indirect beneficial ownership, computed as of the last day of the month, increases or decreases by more than five percent of the class of equity securities. Once an amendment has been filed reflecting beneficial ownership of five percent or less of the class of securities, no additional filings are required by this paragraph (c).

(d) Any person relying on Rule 13d-1(c) and has filed its initial Schedule 13G pursuant to that paragraph shall, in addition to filing any amendments pursuant to Rule 13d-2(b), file an amendment on Schedule 13G promptly upon acquiring, directly or indirectly, greater than 10 percent of a class of equity securities specified in Rule 13d-1(d), and thereafter promptly upon increasing or decreasing its beneficial ownership by more than five percent of the class of equity securities. Once an amendment has been filed reflecting beneficial ownership of five percent or less of the class of securities, no additional filings are required by this paragraph (d).

(e) The first electronic amendment to a paper format Schedule 13D or Schedule 13G shall restate the entire text of the Schedule 13D or Schedule 13G, but previously filed paper exhibits to such schedules are not required to be restated electronically. *See* Rule 102 of Regulation S-T regarding amendments to exhibits previously filed in paper format. Notwithstanding the foregoing, if the sole purpose of filing the first electronic Schedule 13D or 13G amendment is to report a change in beneficial ownership that would terminate the filer's obligation to report, the amendment need not include a restatement of the entire text of the Schedule being amended.

Note to Rule 13d-2: For persons filing a short-form statement pursuant to Rule 13d-1(b) or (c), *see also* Rules 13d-1(e), (f), and (g).

Rule 13d-3. Determination of Beneficial Owner.

(a) For the purposes of Sections 13(d) and 13(g) of the Act, a beneficial owner of a security includes any person who, directly or indirectly, through any contract, arrangement, understanding, relationship, or otherwise has or shares:

(1) Voting power which includes the power to vote, or to direct the voting of, such security, and/or

(2) Investment power which includes the power to dispose, or to direct the disposition of, such security.

(b) Any person who, directly or indirectly, creates or uses a trust, proxy, power of attorney, pooling arrangement or any other contract, arrangement, or device with the purpose or effect of divesting such person of beneficial ownership of a security or preventing the vesting of such beneficial ownership as part of a plan or scheme to evade the reporting requirements of Section 13(d) or 13(g) of the Act, shall be deemed for purposes of such sections to be the beneficial owner of such security.

(c) All securities of the same class beneficially owned by a person, regardless of the form which such beneficial ownership takes, shall be aggregated in calculating the number of shares beneficially owned by such person.

(d) Notwithstanding the provisions of paragraphs (a) and (c) of this rule:

(1)(i) A person shall be deemed to be the beneficial owner of a security, subject to the provisions of paragraph (b) of this rule, if that person has the right to acquire beneficial ownership of such security, as defined in Rule 13d-4(a) within 60 days, including but not limited to any right to acquire: (A) through the exercise of any option, warrant or right; (B) through the conversion of a security; (C) pursuant to the power to revoke a trust, discretionary account, or similar arrangement; or (D) pursuant to the automatic termination of a trust, discretionary account or similar arrangement; *provided, however*, any person who acquires a security or power specified in paragraph (A), (B) or (C) above, with the purpose or effect of changing or influencing the control of the issuer, or in connection with or as a participant in any transaction having such purpose or effect, immediately upon such acquisition shall be deemed to be the beneficial owner of the securities which may be acquired through the exercise or conversion of such security or power. Any securities not outstanding which are subject to such options, warrants, rights or conversion privileges shall be deemed to be outstanding for the purpose of computing the percentage of outstanding securities of the class owned by such person, but shall not be deemed to be outstanding for the purpose of computing the percentage of the class by any other person.

(ii) Paragraph (d)(1)(i) of this section remains applicable for the purpose of determining the obligation to file with respect to the underlying security even though the option, warrant, right or convertible security is of a class of equity security, as defined in Rule 13d-1(i), and may therefore give rise to a separate obligation to file.

(2) A member of a national securities exchange shall not be deemed to be a beneficial owner of securities held directly or indirectly by it on behalf of another person solely because such member is the record holder of such securities and, pursuant to the rules of such exchange, may direct the vote of such securities, without instruction, on other than contested matters or matters that may affect substantially the rights or privileges of the holders of the securities to be voted, but is otherwise precluded by the rules of such exchange from voting without instruction.

(3) A person who in the ordinary course of business is a pledgee of securities under a written pledge agreement shall not be deemed to be the beneficial owner of such pledged securities until the pledgee has taken all formal steps necessary which are required to declare a default, and determines that the power to vote or to direct the vote or to dispose or to direct the disposition of such pledged securities will be exercised, *provided* that:

(i) The pledgee agreement is *bona fide* and was not entered into with the purpose nor with the effect of changing or influencing the control of the issuer, nor in connection with any transaction having such purpose or effect, including any transaction subject to Rule 13d-3(b);

(ii) The pledgee is a person specified in Rule 13d-1(b)(ii), including persons meeting the conditions set forth in paragraph (G) thereof; and

(iii) The pledgee agreement, prior to default, does not grant to the pledgee:

(A) The power to vote or to direct the vote of the pledged securities; or

(B) The power to dispose or direct the disposition of the pledged securities, other than the grant of such power(s) pursuant to a pledge agreement under which credit is extended subject to Regulation T and in which the pledgee is a broker or dealer registered under Section 15 of the Act.

(4) A person engaged in business as an underwriter of securities who acquires securities through his participation in good faith in a firm commitment underwriting registered under the Securities Act of 1933 shall not be deemed to be the beneficial owner of such securities until the expiration of 40 days after the date of such acquisition.

Rule 13d-4. Disclaimer of Beneficial Ownership.

Any person may expressly declare in any statement filed that the filing of such statement shall not be construed as an admission that such person is, for the purposes of Section 13(d) or 13(g) of the Act, the beneficial owner of any securities covered by the statement.

Rule 13d-5. Acquisition of Securities.

(a) A person who becomes a beneficial owner of securities shall be deemed to have acquired such securities for purposes of Section 13(d)(1) of the Act, whether such acquisition was through purchase or otherwise. However, executors or administrators of a decedent's estate generally will be presumed not to have acquired beneficial ownership of the securities in the decedent's estate until such time as such executors or administrators are qualified under local law to perform their duties.

(b)(1) When two or more persons agree to act together for the purpose of acquiring, holding, voting or disposing of equity securities of an issuer, the group formed thereby shall be deemed to have acquired beneficial ownership, for purposes of Sections 13(d) and 13(g) of the Act, as of the date of such agreement, of all equity securities of that issuer beneficially owned by any such persons.

(2) Notwithstanding the previous paragraph, a group shall be deemed not to have acquired any equity securities beneficially owned by the other members of the group solely by virtue of their concerted actions relating to the purchase of equity securities directly from an issuer in a transaction not involving a public offering; *provided* that:

(i) All the members of the group are persons specified in Rule 13d-1(b)(1)(ii);

(ii) The purchase is in the ordinary course of each member's business and not with the purpose nor with the effect of changing or influencing control of the issuer, nor in connection with or as a participant in any transaction having such purpose or effect, including any transaction subject to Rule 13d-3(b);

(iii) There is no agreement among, or between any members of the group to act together with respect to the issuer or its securities except for the purpose of facilitating the specific purchase involved; and

(iv) The only actions among or between any members of the group with respect to the issuer or its securities subsequent to the closing date of the non-public offering are those which are necessary to conclude ministerial matters directly related to the completion of the offer or sale of the securities.

Rule 13d-6. Exemption of Certain Acquisitions.

The acquisition of securities of an issuer by a person who, prior to such acquisition, was a beneficial owner of more than five percent of the outstanding securities of the same class as those acquired shall be exempt from Section 13(d) of the Act, provided that:

(a) The acquisition is made pursuant to preemptive subscription rights in an offering made to all holders of securities of the class to which the preemptive subscription rights pertain;

(b) Such person does not acquire additional securities except through the exercise of his *pro rata* share of the preemptive subscription rights; and

(c) The acquisition is duly reported, if required, pursuant to Section 16(a) of the Act and the rules and regulations thereunder.

Rule 13d-7. Dissemination.

One copy of the Schedule filed pursuant to Rule 13d-1 and Rule 13d-2 shall be sent to the issuer of the security at its principal executive office, by registered or certified mail. A copy of Schedules filed pursuant to Rule 13d-1(a) and Rule 13d-2(a) shall also be sent to each national securities exchange where the security is traded.

Schedule 13D

OMB APPROVAL	
OMB Number:	3235-0145
Expires:	December 31, 2005
Estimated average burden hours per response	15

UNITED STATES
SECURITIES AND EXCHANGE COMMISSION
Washington, D.C. 20549

SCHEDULE 13D

Under the Securities Exchange Act of 1934
(Amendment No. _____)*

_____

(Name of Issuer)

_____

(Title of Class of Securities)

_____

(CUSIP Number)

_____

(Name, Address and Telephone Number of Person Authorized to
Receive Notices and Communications)

_____

(Date of Event which Requires Filing of this Statement)

If the filing person has previously filed a statement on Schedule 13G to report the acquisition that is the subject of this Schedule 13D, and is filing this schedule because of §§240.13d-1(e), 240.13d-1(f) or 240.13d-1(g), check the following box. ☐

Note: Schedules filed in paper format shall include a signed original and five copies of the schedule, including all exhibits. See §240.13d-7 for other parties to whom copies are to be sent.

* The remainder of this cover page shall be filled out for a reporting person's initial filing on this form with respect to the subject class of securities, and for any subsequent amendment containing information which would alter disclosures provided in a prior cover page.

The information required on the remainder of this cover page shall not be deemed to be "filed" for the purpose of Section 18 of the Securities Exchange Act of 1934 ("Act") or otherwise subject to the liabilities of that section of the Act but shall be subject to all other provisions of the Act (however, see the Notes).

Persons who respond to the collection of information contained in this form are not required to respond unless the form displays a currently valid OMB control number.

SEC 1746 (11–03)

CUSIP No. ....

1.	Names of Reporting Persons.	
	I.R.S. Identification Nos. of above persons (entities only).	

....

2.	Check the Appropriate Box if a Member of a Group (See Instructions)
	(a) ....
	(b) ....
3.	SEC Use Only ....
4.	Source of Funds (See Instructions) ....
5.	Check if Disclosure of Legal Proceedings Is Required Pursuant to Items 2(d) or 2(e) ....
6.	Citizenship or Place of Organization ....

Number of	7.	Sole Voting Power ....
Shares Bene-		
ficially by	8.	Shared Voting Power ....
Owned by Each		
Reporting	9.	Sole Dispositive Power ....
Person With		
	10.	Shared Dispositive Power ....

11.	Aggregate Amount Beneficially Owned by Each Reporting Person ....
12.	Check if the Aggregate Amount in Row (11) Excludes Certain Shares (See Instructions) ....
13.	Percent of Class Represented by Amount in Row (11) ....
14.	Type of Reporting Person (See Instructions)

....
....
....
....

Instructions for Cover Page

(1)   *Names and I.R.S. Identification Numbers of Reporting Persons* — Furnish the full legal name of each person for whom the report is filed - i.e., each person required to sign the schedule itself - including each member of a group. Do not include the name of a person required to be identified in the report but who is not a reporting person. Reporting persons that are entities are also requested to furnish their I.R.S. identification numbers, although disclosure of such numbers is voluntary, not mandatory (see "SPECIAL INSTRUCTIONS FOR COMPLYING WITH SCHEDULE 13D" below).

(2)   If any of the shares beneficially owned by a reporting person are held as a member of a group and the membership is expressly affirmed, please check row 2(a). If the reporting person disclaims membership in a group or describes a relationship with other persons but does not affirm the existence of a group, please check row 2(b) [unless it is a joint filing pursuant to Rule 13d-1(k)(1) in which case it may not be necessary to check row 2(b)].

(3)   The 3rd row is for SEC internal use; please leave blank.

(4)   Classify the source of funds or other consideration used or to be used in making purchases as required to be disclosed pursuant to Item 3 of Schedule 13D and insert the appropriate symbol (or symbols if more than one is necessary) in row (4):

Category of Source	Symbol
Subject Company (Company whose securities are being acquired)	SC
Bank	BK
Affiliate (of reporting person)	AF
Working Capital (of reporting person)	WC
Personal Funds (of reporting person)	PF
Other	OO

(5)   If disclosure of legal proceedings or actions is required pursuant to either Items 2(d) or 2(e) of Schedule 13D, row 5 should be checked.

(6)   *Citizenship or Place of Organization* - Furnish citizenship if the named reporting person is a natural person. Otherwise, furnish place of organization. (See Item 2 of Schedule 13D.)

(7)-(11), (13)   *Aggregate Amount Beneficially Owned by Each Reporting Person, etc.* — Rows (7) through (11) inclusive, and (13) are to be completed in accordance with the provisions of Item 5 of Schedule 13D. All percentages are to be rounded off to nearest tenth (one place after decimal point).

(12)   Check if the aggregate amount reported as beneficially owned in row (11) does not include shares which the reporting person discloses in the report but as to which beneficial ownership is disclaimed pursuant to Rule 13d-4 [17 CFR 240.13d-4] under the Securities Exchange Act of 1934.

(14)   *Type of Reporting Person* — Please classify each "reporting person" according to the following breakdown and place the appropriate symbol (or symbols, i.e., if more than one is applicable, insert all applicable symbols) on the form:

Category	Symbol
Broker-Dealer	BD
Bank	BK
Insurance Company	IC
Investment Company	IV
Investment Adviser	IA
Employee Benefit Plan or Endowment Fund	EP
Parent Holding Company/Control Person	HC
Savings Association	SA
Church Plan	CP
Corporation	CO
Partnership	PN
Individual	IN
Other	OO

Notes:

Attach as many copies of the second part of the cover page as are needed, one reporting person per page.

Filing persons may, in order to avoid unnecessary duplication, answer items on the schedules (Schedule 13D, 13G or 14D-1) by appropriate cross references to an item or items on the cover page(s). This approach may only be used where the cover page item or items provide all the disclosure required by the schedule item. Moreover, such a use of a cover page item will result in the item becoming a part of the schedule and accordingly being considered as "filed" for purposes of Section 18 of the Securities Exchange Act or otherwise subject to the liabilities of that section of the Act.

Reporting persons may comply with their cover page filing requirements by filing either completed copies of the blank forms available from the Commission, printed or typed facsimiles, or computer printed facsimiles, provided

.

the documents filed have identical formats to the forms prescribed in the Commission's regulations and meet existing Securities Exchange Act rules as to such matters as clarity and size (Securities Exchange Act Rule 12b-12).

SPECIAL INSTRUCTIONS FOR COMPLYING WITH SCHEDULE 13D

Under Sections 13(d) and 23 of the Securities Exchange Act of 1934 and the rules and regulations thereunder, the Commission is authorized to solicit the information required to be supplied by this schedule by certain security holders of certain issuers.

Disclosure of the information specified in this schedule is mandatory, except for I.R.S. identification numbers, disclosure of which is voluntary. The information will be used for the primary purpose of determining and disclosing the holdings of certain beneficial owners of certain equity securities. This statement will be made a matter of public record. Therefore, any information given will be available for inspection by any member of the public.

Because of the public nature of the information, the Commission can utilize it for a variety of purposes, including referral to other governmental authorities or securities self-regulatory organizations for investigatory purposes or in connection with litigation involving the Federal securities laws or other civil, criminal or regulatory statutes or provisions. I.R.S. identification numbers, if furnished, will assist the Commission in identifying security holders and, therefore, in promptly processing statements of beneficial ownership of securities.

Failure to disclose the information requested by this schedule, except for I.R.S. identification numbers, may result in civil or criminal action against the persons involved for violation of the Federal securities laws and rules promulgated thereunder.

General Instructions

A.   The item numbers and captions of the items shall be included but the text of the items is to be omitted. The answers to the items shall be so prepared as to indicate clearly the coverage of the items without referring to the text of the items. Answer every item. If an item is inapplicable or the answer is in the negative, so state.

B.   Information contained in exhibits to the statements may be incorporated by reference in answer or partial answer to any item or sub-item of the statement unless it would render such answer misleading, incomplete, unclear or confusing. Material incorporated by reference shall be clearly identified in the reference by page, paragraph, caption or otherwise. An express statement that the specified matter is incorporated by reference shall be made at the particular place in the statement where the information is required. A copy of any information or a copy of the pertinent pages of a document containing such information which is incorporated by reference shall be submitted with this statement as an exhibit and shall be deemed to be filed with the Commission for all purposes of the Act.

C.   If the statement is filed by a general or limited partnership, syndicate, or other group, the information called for by Items 2-6, inclusive, shall be given with respect to (i) each partner of such general partnership; (ii) each partner who is denominated as a general partner or who functions as a general partner of such limited partnership; (iii) each member of such syndicate or group; and (iv) each person controlling such partner or member. If the statement is filed by a corporation or if a person referred to in (i), (ii), (iii) or (iv) of this Instruction is a corporation, the information called for by the above mentioned items shall be given with respect to (a) each executive officer and director of such corporation; (b) each person controlling such corporation; and (c) each executive officer and director of any corporation or other person ultimately in control of such corporation.

Item 1. Security and Issuer

State the title of the class of equity securities to which this statement relates and the name and address of the principal executive offices of the issuer of such securities.

Item 2. Identity and Background

If the person filing this statement or any person enumerated in Instruction C of this statement is a corporation, general partnership, limited partnership, syndicate or other group of persons, state its name, the state or other place of its

4

organization, its principal business, the address of its principal office and the information required by (d) and (e) of this Item. If the person filing this statement or any person enumerated in Instruction C is a natural person, provide the information specified in (a) through (f) of this Item with respect to such person(s).

(a)   Name;

(b)   Residence or business address;

(c)   Present principal occupation or employment and the name, principal business and address of any corporation or other organization in which such employment is conducted;

(d)   Whether or not, during the last five years, such person has been convicted in a criminal proceeding (excluding traffic violations or similar misdemeanors) and, if so, give the dates, nature of conviction, name and location of court, and penalty imposed, or other disposition of the case;

(e)   Whether or not, during the last five years, such person was a party to a civil proceeding of a judicial or administrative body of competent jurisdiction and as a result of such proceeding was or is subject to a judgment, decree or final order enjoining future violations of, or prohibiting or mandating activities subject to, federal or state securities laws or finding any violation with respect to such laws; and, if so, identify and describe such proceedings and summarize the terms of such judgment, decree or final order; and

(f)   Citizenship.

Item 3. Source and Amount of Funds or Other Consideration

State the source and the amount of funds or other consideration used or to be used in making the purchases, and if any part of the purchase price is or will be represented by funds or other consideration borrowed or otherwise obtained for the purpose of acquiring, holding, trading or voting the securities, a description of the transaction and the names of the parties thereto. Where material, such information should also be provided with respect to prior acquisitions not previously reported pursuant to this regulation. If the source of all or any part of the funds is a loan made in the ordinary course of business by a bank, as defined in Section 3(a)(6) of the Act, the name of the bank shall not be made available to the public if the person at the time of filing the statement so requests in writing and files such request, naming such bank, with the Secretary of the Commission. If the securities were acquired other than by purchase, describe the method of acquisition.

Item 4. Purpose of Transaction

State the purpose or purposes of the acquisition of securities of the issuer. Describe any plans or proposals which the reporting persons may have which relate to or would result in:

(a)   The acquisition by any person of additional securities of the issuer, or the disposition of securities of the issuer;

(b)   An extraordinary corporate transaction, such as a merger, reorganization or liquidation, involving the issuer or any of its subsidiaries;

(c)   A sale or transfer of a material amount of assets of the issuer or any of its subsidiaries;

(d)   Any change in the present board of directors or management of the issuer, including any plans or proposals to change the number or term of directors or to fill any existing vacancies on the board;

(e)   Any material change in the present capitalization or dividend policy of the issuer;

(f)   Any other material change in the issuer's business or corporate structure including but not limited to, if the issuer is a registered closed-end investment company, any plans or proposals to make any changes in its investment policy for which a vote is required by section 13 of the Investment Company Act of 1940;

(g)   Changes in the issuer's charter, bylaws or instruments corresponding thereto or other actions which may impede the acquisition of control of the issuer by any person;

(h)   Causing a class of securities of the issuer to be delisted from a national securities exchange or to cease to be authorized to be quoted in an inter-dealer quotation system of a registered national securities association;

(i)   A class of equity securities of the issuer becoming eligible for termination of registration pursuant to Section 12(g)(4) of the Act; or

(j)   Any action similar to any of those enumerated above.

Item 5. Interest in Securities of the Issuer

(a)   State the aggregate number and percentage of the class of securities identified pursuant to Item 1 (which may be based on the number of securities outstanding as contained in the most recently available filing with the Commission by the issuer unless the filing person has reason to believe such information is not current) beneficially owned (identifying those shares which there is a right to acquire) by each person named in Item 2. The above mentioned information should also be furnished with respect to persons who, together with any of the persons named in Item 2, comprise a group within the meaning of Section 13(d)(3) of the Act;

(b)   For each person named in response to paragraph (a), indicate the number of shares as to which there is sole power to vote or to direct the vote, shared power to vote or to direct the vote, sole power to dispose or to direct the disposition, or shared power to dispose or to direct the disposition. Provide the applicable information required by Item 2 with respect to each person with whom the power to vote or to direct the vote or to dispose or direct the disposition is shared;

(c)   Describe any transactions in the class of securities reported on that were effected during the past sixty days or since the most recent filing of Schedule 13D (§240.13d-191), whichever is less, by the persons named in response to paragraph (a).

   Instruction.   The description of a transaction required by Item 5(c) shall include, but not necessarily be limited to: (1) the identity of the person covered by Item 5(c) who effected the transaction; (2) the date of the transaction; (3) the amount of securities involved; (4) the price per share or unit; and (5) where and how the transaction was effected.

(d)   If any other person is known to have the right to receive or the power to direct the receipt of dividends from, or the proceeds from the sale of, such securities, a statement to that effect should be included in response to this item and, if such interest relates to more than five percent of the class, such person should be identified. A listing of the shareholders of an investment company registered under the Investment Company Act of 1940 or the beneficiaries of an employee benefit plan, pension fund or endowment fund is not required.

(e)   If applicable, state the date on which the reporting person ceased to be the beneficial owner of more than five percent of the class of securities.

   Instruction.   For computations regarding securities which represent a right to acquire an underlying security, see Rule 13d-3(d)(1) and the note thereto.

Item 6. Contracts, Arrangements, Understandings or Relationships with Respect to Securities of the Issuer

   Describe any contracts, arrangements, understandings or relationships (legal or otherwise) among the persons named in Item 2 and between such persons and any person with respect to any securities of the issuer, including but not limited to transfer or voting of any of the securities, finder's fees, joint ventures, loan or option arrangements, puts or calls, guarantees of profits, division of profits or loss, or the giving or withholding of proxies, naming the persons with whom such contracts, arrangements, understandings or relationships have been entered into. Include such information for any of the securities that are pledged or otherwise subject to a contingency the occurrence of which would give another person voting power or investment power over such securities except that disclosure of standard default and similar provisions contained in loan agreements need not be included.

Item 7. Material to Be Filed as Exhibits

The following shall be filed as exhibits: copies of written agreements relating to the filing of joint acquisition statements as required by §240.13d-1(k) and copies of all written agreements, contracts, arrangements, understandings, plans or proposals relating to: (1) the borrowing of funds to finance the acquisition as disclosed in Item 3; (2) the acquisition of issuer control, liquidation, sale of assets, merger, or change in business or corporate structure or any other matter as disclosed in Item 4; and (3) the transfer or voting of the securities, finder's fees, joint ventures, options, puts, calls, guarantees of loans, guarantees against loss or of profit, or the giving or withholding of any proxy as disclosed in Item 6.

Signature

After reasonable inquiry and to the best of my knowledge and belief, I certify that the information set forth in this statement is true, complete and correct.

_____

Date

_____

Signature

_____

Name/Title

The original statement shall be signed by each person on whose behalf the statement is filed or his authorized representative. If the statement is signed on behalf of a person by his authorized representative (other than an executive officer or general partner of the filing person), evidence of the representative's authority to sign on behalf of such person shall be filed with the statement: provided, however, that a power of attorney for this purpose which is already on file with the Commission may be incorporated by reference. The name and any title of each person who signs the statement shall be typed or printed beneath his signature.

Attention: Intentional misstatements or omissions of fact constitute Federal criminal violations (See 18 U.S.C. 1001)

Schedule 13G

OMB APPROVAL	
OMB Number:	3235-0145
Expires:	December 31, 2005
Estimated average burden	
hours per response........11	

UNITED STATES
SECURITIES AND EXCHANGE COMMISSION
Washington, D.C. 20549

SCHEDULE 13G

Under the Securities Exchange Act of 1934

(Amendment No. _____)*

_____
(Name of Issuer)

_____
(Title of Class of Securities)

_____
(CUSIP Number)

_____
(Date of Event Which Requires Filing of this Statement)

Check the appropriate box to designate the rule pursuant to which this Schedule is filed:

☐ Rule 13d-1(b)

☐ Rule 13d-1(c)

☐ Rule 13d-1(d)

*The remainder of this cover page shall be filled out for a reporting person's initial filing on this form with respect to the subject class of securities, and for any subsequent amendment containing information which would alter the disclosures provided in a prior cover page.

The information required in the remainder of this cover page shall not be deemed to be "filed" for the purpose of Section 18 of the Securities Exchange Act of 1934 ("Act") or otherwise subject to the liabilities of that section of the Act but shall be subject to all other provisions of the Act (however, see the Notes).

Persons who respond to the collection of information contained in this form are not required to respond unless the form displays a currently valid OMB control number.

CUSIP No. ....

---

1. Names of Reporting Persons.
    I.R.S. Identification Nos. of above persons (entities only).
....

2. Check the Appropriate Box if a Member of a Group (See Instructions)

    (a) ....

    (b) ....

3. SEC Use Only ....

4. Citizenship or Place of Organization ....

| Number of Shares Bene-ficially by Owned by Each Reporting Person With: | 5. Sole Voting Power .... |
| 6. Shared Voting Power .... |
| 7. Sole Dispositive Power.. |
| 8. Shared Dispositive Power .... |

9. Aggregate Amount Beneficially Owned by Each Reporting Person..

10. Check if the Aggregate Amount in Row (9) Excludes Certain Shares (See Instructions)............................

11. Percent of Class Represented by Amount in Row (9) ....

12. Type of Reporting Person (See Instructions)

....

....

....

....

....

....

INSTRUCTIONS FOR SCHEDULE 13G

Instructions for Cover Page

(1) *Names and I.R.S. Identification Numbers of Reporting Persons*—Furnish the full legal name of each person for whom the report is filed—i.e., each person required to sign the schedule itself—including each member of a group. Do not include the name of a person required to be identified in the report but who is not a reporting person. Reporting persons that are entities are also requested to furnish their I.R.S. identification numbers, although disclosure of such numbers is voluntary, not mandatory (see "SPECIAL INSTRUCTIONS FOR COMPLYING WITH SCHEDULE 13G" below).

(2) If any of the shares beneficially owned by a reporting person are held as a member of a group and that membership is expressly affirmed, please check row 2(a). If the reporting person disclaims membership in a group or describes a relationship with other persons but does not affirm the existence of a group, please check row 2(b) [unless it is a joint filing pursuant to Rule 13d-1(k)(1) in which case it may not be necessary to check row 2(b)].

(3) The third row is for SEC internal use; please leave blank.

(4) *Citizenship or Place of Organization*—Furnish citizenship if the named reporting person is a natural person. Otherwise, furnish place of organization.

(5)-(9), (11) *Aggregate Amount Beneficially Owned By Each Reporting Person, Etc.*—Rows (5) through (9) inclusive, and (11) are to be completed in accordance with the provisions of Item 4 of Schedule 13G. All percentages are to be rounded off to the nearest tenth (one place after decimal point).

(10) Check if the aggregate amount reported as beneficially owned in row (9) does not include shares as to which beneficial ownership is disclaimed pursuant to Rule 13d-4 (17 CFR 240.13d-4] under the Securities Exchange Act of 1934.

(12) *Type of Reporting Person*—Please classify each "reporting person" according to the following breakdown (see Item 3 of Schedule 13G) and place the appropriate symbol on the form:

Category	*Symbol*
Broker Dealer	BD
Bank	BK
Insurance Company	IC
Investment Company	IV
Investment Adviser	IA
Employee Benefit Plan, Pension Fund, or Endowment Fund	EP
Parent Holding Company/Control Person	HC
Savings Association	SA
Church Plan	CP
Corporation	CO
Partnership	PN
Individual	IN
Other	OO

Notes:

Attach as many copies of the second part of the cover page as are needed, one reporting person per page.

Filing persons may, in order to avoid unnecessary duplication, answer items on the schedules (Schedule 13D, 13G or 14D-1) by appropriate cross references to an item or items on the cover page(s). This approach may only be used where the cover page item or items provide all the disclosure required by the schedule item. Moreover, such a use of a cover page item will result in the item becoming a part of the schedule and accordingly being considered as "filed" for purposes of Section 18 of the Securities Exchange Act or otherwise subject to the liabilities of that section of the Act.

Reporting persons may comply with their cover page filing requirements by filing either completed copies of the blank forms available from the Commission, printed or typed facsimiles, or computer printed facsimiles, provided the documents filed have identical formats to the forms prescribed in the Commission's regulations and meet existing Securities Exchange Act rules as to such matters as clarity and size (Securities Exchange Act Rule 12b-12).

SPECIAL INSTRUCTIONS FOR COMPLYING WITH SCHEDULE 13G

Under Sections 13(d), 13(g), and 23 of the Securities Exchange Act of 1934 and the rules and regulations thereunder, the Commission is authorized to solicit the information required to be supplied by this schedule by certain security holders of certain issuers.

Disclosure of the information specified in this schedule is mandatory, except for I.R.S. identification numbers, disclosure of which is voluntary. The information will be used for the primary purpose of determining and disclosing the holdings of certain beneficial owners of certain equity securities. This statement will be made a matter of public record. Therefore, any information given will be available for inspection by any member of the public.

Because of the public nature of the information, the Commission can use it for a variety of purposes, including referral to other governmental authorities or securities self-regulatory organizations for investigatory purposes or in connection with litigation involving the Federal securities laws or other civil, criminal or regulatory statutes or provisions. I.R.S. identification numbers, if furnished, will assist the Commission in identifying security holders and, therefore, in promptly processing statements of beneficial ownership of securities.

Failure to disclose the information requested by this schedule, except for I.R.S. identification numbers, may result in civil or criminal action against the persons involved for violation of the Federal securities laws and rules promulgated thereunder.

GENERAL INSTRUCTIONS

A. Statements filed pursuant to Rule 13d-1(b) containing the information required by this schedule shall be filed not later than February 14 following the calendar year covered by the statement or within the time specified in Rules 13d-1(b)(2) and 13d-2(c). Statements filed pursuant to Rule 13d-1(c) shall be filed within the time specified in Rules 13d-1(c), 13d-2(b) and 13d-2(d). Statements filed pursuant to Rule 13d-1(d) shall be filed not later than February 14 following the calendar year covered by the statement pursuant to Rules 13d-1(d) and 13d-2(b).

B. Information contained in a form which is required to be filed by rules under section 13(f) (15 U.S.C. 78m(f)) for the same calendar year as that covered by a statement on this schedule may be incorporated by reference in response to any of the items of this schedule. If such information is incorporated by reference in this schedule, copies of the relevant pages of such form shall be filed as an exhibit to this schedule.

C. The item numbers and captions of the items shall be included but the text of the items is to be omitted. The answers to the items shall be so prepared as to indicate clearly the coverage of the items without referring to the text of the items. Answer every item. If an item is inapplicable or the answer is in the negative, so state.

Item 1.

(a) Name of Issuer

(b) Address of Issuer's Principal Executive Offices

Item 2.

(a) Name of Person Filing

(b) Address of Principal Business Office or, if none, Residence

(c) Citizenship

(d) Title of Class of Securities

(e) CUSIP Number

Item 3. If this statement is filed pursuant to §§240.13d-1(b) or 240.13d-2(b) or (c), check whether the person filing is a:

(a) ☐ Broker or dealer registered under section 15 of the Act (15 U.S.C. 78o).

(b) ☐ Bank as defined in section 3(a)(6) of the Act (15 U.S.C. 78c).

(c) ☐ Insurance company as defined in section 3(a)(19) of the Act (15 U.S.C. 78c).

(d) ☐ Investment company registered under section 8 of the Investment Company Act of 1940 (15 U.S.C 80a-8).

(e) ☐ An investment adviser in accordance with §240.13d-1(b)(1)(ii)(E);

(f) ☐ An employee benefit plan or endowment fund in accordance with §240.13d-1(b)(1)(ii)(F);

(g) ☐ A parent holding company or control person in accordance with § 240.13d-1(b)(1)(ii)(G);

(h) ☐ A savings associations as defined in Section 3(b) of the Federal Deposit Insurance Act (12 U.S.C. 1813);

(i) ☐ A church plan that is excluded from the definition of an investment company under section 3(c)(14) of the Investment Company Act of 1940 (15 U.S.C. 80a-3);

(j) ☐   Group, in accordance with §240.13d-1(b)(1)(ii)(J).

Item 4. Ownership.

Provide the following information regarding the aggregate number and percentage of the class of securities of the issuer identified in Item 1.

(a) Amount beneficially owned: _____.

(b) Percent of class: _____.

(c) Number of shares as to which the person has:

     (i)   Sole power to vote or to direct the vote _____.

     (ii)   Shared power to vote or to direct the vote _____.

     (iii)   Sole power to dispose or to direct the disposition of _____.

     (iv)   Shared power to dispose or to direct the disposition of _____.

Instruction. For computations regarding securities which represent a right to acquire an underlying security *see* §240.13d-3(d)(1).

Item 5. Ownership of Five Percent or Less of a Class

If this statement is being filed to report the fact that as of the date hereof the reporting person has ceased to be the beneficial owner of more than five percent of the class of securities, check the following ☐.

Instruction: Dissolution of a group requires a response to this item.

Item 6. Ownership of More than Five Percent on Behalf of Another Person.

If any other person is known to have the right to receive or the power to direct the receipt of dividends from, or the proceeds from the sale of, such securities, a statement to that effect should be included in response to this item and, if such interest relates to more than five percent of the class, such person should be identified. A listing of the shareholders of an investment company registered under the Investment Company Act of 1940 or the beneficiaries of employee benefit plan, pension fund or endowment fund is not required.

Item 7. Identification and Classification of the Subsidiary Which Acquired the Security Being Reported on By the Parent Holding Company

If a parent holding company has filed this schedule, pursuant to Rule 13d-1(b)(ii)(G), so indicate under Item 3(g) and attach an exhibit stating the identity and the Item 3 classification of the relevant subsidiary. If a parent holding company has filed this schedule pursuant to Rule 13d-1(c) or Rule 13d-1(d), attach an exhibit stating the identification of the relevant subsidiary.

Item 8. Identification and Classification of Members of the Group

If a group has filed this schedule pursuant to §240.13d-1(b)(1)(ii)(J), so indicate under Item 3(j) and attach an exhibit stating the identity and Item 3 classification of each member of the group. If a group has filed this schedule pursuant to §240.13d-1(c) or §240.13d-1(d), attach an exhibit stating the identity of each member of the group.

Item 9. Notice of Dissolution of Group

Notice of dissolution of a group may be furnished as an exhibit stating the date of the dissolution and that all further filings with respect to transactions in the security reported on will be filed, if required, by members of the group, in their individual capacity. See Item 5.

Item 10. Certification

(a)   The following certification shall be included if the statement is filed pursuant to §240.13d-1(b):

> By signing below I certify that, to the best of my knowledge and belief, the securities referred to above were acquired and are held in the ordinary course of business and were not acquired and are not held for the purpose of or with the effect of changing or influencing the control of the issuer of the securities and were not acquired and are not held in connection with or as a participant in any transaction having that purpose or effect.

(b)   The following certification shall be included if the statement is filed pursuant to §240.13d-1(c):

> By signing below I certify that, to the best of my knowledge and belief, the securities referred to above were not acquired and are not held for the purpose of or with the effect of changing or influencing the control of the issuer of the securities and were not acquired and are not held in connection with or as a participant in any transaction having that purpose or effect.

SIGNATURE

After reasonable inquiry and to the best of my knowledge and belief, I certify that the information set forth in this statement is true, complete and correct.

_____

Date

_____

Signature

_____

Name/Title

The original statement shall be signed by each person on whose behalf the statement is filed or his authorized representative. If the statement is signed on behalf of a person by his authorized representative other than an executive officer or general partner of the filing person, evidence of the representative's authority to sign on behalf of such person shall be filed with the statement, provided, however, that a power of attorney for this purpose which is already on file with the Commission may be incorporated by reference. The name and any title of each person who signs the statement shall be typed or printed beneath his signature.

NOTE: Schedules filed in paper format shall include a signed original and five copies of the schedule, including all exhibits. *See* §240.13d-7 for other parties for whom copies are to be sent.

Attention: Intentional misstatements or omissions of fact constitute Federal criminal violations (See 18 U.S.C. 1001)

Regulation 14A

Solicitation of Proxies

ATTENTION ELECTRONIC FILERS

THIS REGULATION SHOULD BE READ IN CONJUNCTION WITH REGULATION S-T (PART 232 OF THIS CHAPTER), WHICH GOVERNS THE PREPARATION AND SUBMISSION OF DOCUMENTS IN ELECTRONIC FORMAT. MANY PROVISIONS RELATING TO THE PREPARATION AND SUBMISSION OF DOCUMENTS IN PAPER FORMAT CONTAINED IN THIS REGULATION ARE SUPERSEDED BY THE PROVISIONS OF REGULATION S-T FOR DOCUMENTS REQUIRED TO BE FILED IN ELECTRONIC FORMAT.

Rule 14a-1 (Reg. §240.14a-1). Definitions

Reg. §240.14a-1. Unless the context otherwise requires, all terms used in this regulation have the same meanings as in the Act or elsewhere in the general rules and regulations thereunder. In addition, the following definitions apply unless the context otherwise requires:

(a) *Associate.* The term "associate," used to indicate a relationship with any person, means (1) any corporation or organization (other than the registrant or a majority owned subsidiary of the registrant) of which such person is an officer or partner or is, directly or indirectly, the beneficial owner of 10 percent or more of any class of equity securities; (2) any trust or other estate in which such person has a substantial beneficial interest or as to which such person serves as trustee or in a similar fiduciary capacity; and (3) any relative or spouse of such person, or any relative of such spouse, who has the same home as such person or who is a director or officer of the registrant or any of its parents or subsidiaries.

(b) *Employee benefit plan.* For purposes of §§240.14a-13, 240.14b-1 and 240.14b-2, the term "employee benefit plan" means any purchase, savings, option, bonus, appreciation, profit sharing, thrift, incentive, pension or similar plan solely for employees, directors, trustees or officers.

(c) *Entity that exercises fiduciairy powers.* The term "entity that exercises fiduciary powers" means any entity that holds securities in nominee name or otherwise on behalf of a beneficial owner but does not include a clearing agency registered pursuant to section 17A of the Act or a broker or a dealer.

(d) *Exempt employee benefit plan securities.* For purposes of §§240.14a-13, 240.14b-l and 240.14b-2, the term "exempt employee benefit plan securities" means: (1) securities of the registrant held by an employee benefit plan, as defined in paragraph (b) of this section, where such plan is established by the registrant; or (2) if notice regarding the current solicitation has been given pursuant to §240.14a-13(a)(1)(ii)(C) or if notice regarding the current request for a list of names, addresses and securities positions of beneficial owners has been given pursuant to §240.14a-13(b)(3), securities of the registrant held by an employee benefit plan, as defined in paragraph (b) of this section, where such plan is established by an affiliate of the registrant.

(e) *Last fiscal year.* The term "last fiscal year" of the registrant means the last fiscal year of the registrant ending prior to the date of the meeting for which proxies are to be solicited or if the solicitation involves written authorizations or consents in lieu of a meeting, the earliest date they may be used to effect corporate action.

(f) *Proxy.* The term "proxy" includes every proxy, consent or authorization within the meaning of section 14(a) of the Act. The consent or authorization may take the form of failure to object or to dissent.

(g) *Proxy statement.* The term "proxy statement" means the statement required by §240.14a-3(a) whether or not contained in a single document.

(h) *Record date.* The term "record date" means the date as of which the record holders of securities entitled to vote at a meeting or by written consent or authorization shall be determined.

(i) *Record holder.* For purposes of §§240.14a-13, 240.14b-1 and 240.14b-2, the term "record holder" means any broker, dealer, voting trustee, bank, association or other entity that exercises fiduciary powers which holds securities of record in nominee name or otherwise or as a participant in a clearing agency registered pursuant to section 17A of the Act.

(j) *Registrant.* The term "registrant" means the issuer of the securities in respect of which proxies are to be solicited.

(k) *Respondent bank.* For purposes of §§240.14a-13, 240.14b-l and 240.14b-2, the term "respondent bank" means any bank, association or other entity that exercises fiduciary powers which holds securities on behalf of beneficial owners and deposits such securities for safekeeping with another bank, association or other entity that exercises fiduciary powers.

(l) *Solicitation.*

(1) The terms "solicit" and "solicitation" include:

(i) Any request for a proxy whether or not accompanied by or included in a form of proxy;

(ii) Any request to execute or not to execute, or to revoke, a proxy; or

(iii) The furnishing of a form of proxy or other communication to security holders under circumstances reasonably calculated to result in the procurement, withholding or revocation of a proxy.

(2) The terms do not apply, however, to:

(i) The furnishing of a form of proxy to a security holder upon the unsolicited request of such security holder;

(ii) The performance by the registrant of acts required by §240.14a-7;

(iii) The performance by any person of ministerial acts on behalf of a person soliciting a proxy; or

(iv) A communication by a security holder who does not otherwise engage in a proxy solicitation (other than a solicitation exempt under §240.14a-2) stating how the security holder intends to vote and the reasons therefor, provided that the communication:

(A) is made by means of speeches in public forums, press releases, published or broadcast opinions, statements or advertisements appearing in a broadcast media, or newspaper, magazine or other bona fide publication disseminated on a regular basis,

(B) is directed to persons to whom the security holder owes a fiduciary duty in connection with the voting of securities of a registrant held by the security holder, or

(C) is made in response to unsolicited requests for additional information with respect to a prior communication by the security holder made pursuant to this paragraph (l)(2)(iv).

Rule 14a-2 (Reg. §240.14a-2). Solicitations to Which §240.14a-3 to §240.14a-15 Apply

Reg. §240.14a-2. Sections 240.14a-3 to 240.14a-15, except as specified below, apply to every solicitation of a proxy with respect to securities registered pursuant to Section 12 of the Act (15 U.S.C. 78l), whether or not trading in such securities has been suspended. To the extent specified below, certain of these sections also apply to roll-up transactions that do not involve an entity with securities registered pursuant to Section 12 of the Act.

(a) Sections 240.14a-3 to 240.14a-15 do not apply to the following:

(1) Any solicitation by a person in respect to securities carried in his name or in the name of his nominee (otherwise than as voting trustee) or held in his custody, if such person —

(i) Receives no commission or remuneration for such solicitation, directly or indirectly, other than reimbursement of reasonable expenses,

(ii) Furnishes promptly to the person solicited (or such person's household in accordance with 240.14a-3(e)(1)) a copy of all soliciting material with respect to the same subject matter or meeting received from all persons who shall furnish copies thereof for such purpose and who shall, if requested, defray the reasonable expenses to be incurred in forwarding such material, and

(iii) In addition, does no more than impartially instruct the person solicited to forward a proxy to the person, if any, to whom the person solicited desires to give a proxy, or impartially request from the person solicited instructions as to the authority to be conferred by the proxy and state that a proxy will be given if no instructions are received by a certain date.

(2) Any solicitation by a person in respect of securities of which he is the beneficial owner;

(3) Any solicitation involved in the offer and sale of securities registered under the Securities Act of 1933: Provided, That this paragraph shall not apply to securities to be issued in any transaction of the character specified in paragraph (a) of Rule 145 under that Act;

(4) Any solicitation with respect to a plan of reorganization under Chapter 11 of the Bankruptcy Reform Act of 1978, as amended, if made after the entry of an order approving the written disclosure statement concerning a plan of reorganization pursuant to section 1125 of said Act and after, or concurrently with, the transmittal of such disclosure statement as required by section 1125 of said Act;

(5) Any solicitation which is subject to Rule 62 under the Public Utility Holding Company Act of 1935; and

(6) Any solicitation through the medium of a newspaper advertisement which informs security holders of a source from which they may obtain copies of a proxy statement, form of proxy and any other soliciting material and does no more than (i) name the registrant, (ii) state the reason for the advertisement, and (iii) identify the proposal or proposals to be acted upon by security holders.

(b) Sections 240.14a-3 to 240.14a-6 (other than 14a-6(g)), 240.14a-8, and 240.14a-10 to 14a-15 do not apply to the following:

(1) Any solicitation by or on behalf of any person who does not, at any time during such solicitation, seek directly or indirectly, either on its own or another's behalf, the power to act as proxy for a security holder and does not furnish or otherwise request, or act on behalf of a person who furnishes or requests, a form of revocation, abstention, consent or authorization. Provided, however, that the exemptions set forth in this paragraph shall not apply to:

(i) the registrant or an affiliate or associate of the registrant (other than an officer or director or any person serving in a similar capacity);

(ii) an officer or director of the registrant or any person serving in a similar capacity engaging in a solicitation financed directly or indirectly by the registrant;

(iii) an officer, director, affiliate or associate of a person that is ineligible to rely on the exemption set forth in this paragraph (other than persons specified in paragraph (b)(1)(i) of this section), or any person serving in a similar capacity;

(iv) any nominee for whose election as a director proxies are solicited;

(v) any person soliciting in opposition to a merger, recapitalization, reorganization, sale of assets or other extraordinary transaction recommended or approved by the board of directors of the registrant who is proposing or intends to propose an alternative transaction to which such person or one of its affiliates is a party;

(vi) any person who is required to report beneficial ownership of the registrant's equity securities on a Schedule 13D [§240.13d-101], unless such person has filed a Schedule 13D and has not disclosed pursuant to Item 4 thereto an intent, or reserved the right, to engage in a control transaction, or any contested solicitation for the election of directors;

(vii) any person who receives compensation from an ineligible persons directly related to the solicitation of proxies, other than pursuant to §240.14a-13;

(viii) where the registrant is an investment company registered under the Investment Company Act of 1940 [15 U.S.C. 80a-1 et seq.], an "interested person" of that investment company, as that term is defined in Section 2(a)(19) of the Investment Company Act [15 U.S.C. 80a-2];

(ix) any person who, because of a substantial interest in the subject matter of the solicitation, is likely to receive a benefit from a successful solicitation that would not be shared pro rata by all other holders of the same class of securities, other than a benefit arising from the person's employment with the registrant; and

(x) any person acting on behalf of any of the foregoing.

(2) Any solicitation made otherwise than on behalf of the registrant where the total number of persons solicited is not more than ten; and

(3) The furnishing of proxy voting advice by any person (the "advisor") to any other person with whom the advisor has a business relationship, if:

(i) The advisor renders financial advice in the ordinary course of his business;

(ii) The advisor discloses to the recipient of the advice any significant relationship with the registrant or any of its affiliates, or a security holder proponent of the matter on which advice is given, as well as any material interests of the advisor in such matter.

(iii) The advisor receives no special commission or remuneration for furnishing the proxy voting advice from any person other than a recipient of the advice and other persons who receive similar advice under this subsection; and

(iv) The proxy voting advice is not furnished on behalf of any person soliciting proxies or on behalf of a participant in an election subject to the provisions of Rule 14a-11.

(4) Any solicitation in connection with a roll-up transaction as defined in Item 901(c) of Regulation S-K (§229.901 of this chapter) in which the holder of a security that is the subject of a proposed roll-up transaction engages in preliminary communications with other holders of securities that are the subject of the same limited partnership roll-up transaction for the purpose of determining whether to solicit proxies, consents, or authorizations in opposition to the proposed limited partnership roll-up transaction; provided, however, that:

(i) This exemption shall not apply to a security holder who is an affiliate of the registrant or general partner or sponsor; and

(ii) This exemption shall not apply to a holder of five percent (5%) or more of the outstanding securities of a class that is the subject of the proposed roll-up transaction who engages in the business of buying and selling limited partnership interests in the secondary market unless that holder discloses to the persons to whom the communications are made such ownership interest and any relations of the holder to the parties of the transaction or to the transaction itself, as required by §240.14a-6(n)(1) and specified in the Notice of Exempt Preliminary Roll-up Communication (§240.14a-104). If the communication is oral, this disclosure may be provided to the security holder orally. Whether the communication is written or oral, the notice required by §240.14a-6(n) and §240.14a-104 shall be furnished to the Commission.

Rule 14a-3 (Reg. §240.14a-3). Information to be Furnished to Security Holders

Reg. §240.14a-3. (a) No solicitation subject to this regulation shall be made unless each person solicited is concurrently furnished or has previously been furnished with a publicly-filed preliminary or definitive written proxy statement containing the information specified in Schedule 14A (§240.14a-101) or with a publicly-filed preliminary or definitive written proxy statement included in a registration statement filed under the Securities Act of 1933 on Form S-4 or F-4 (§239.25 or §239.34 of this chapter) or Form N-14 (§239.23) and containing the information specified in such Form.

(b) If the solicitation is made on behalf of the registrant other than an investment company registered under the Investment Company Act of 1940, and relates to an annual (or special meeting in lieu of the annual) meeting of security holders, or written consent in lieu of such meeting, at which directors are to be elected, each proxy statement furnished pursuant to paragraph (a) of this section shall be accompanied or preceded by an annual report to security holders as follows:

Note to Small Business Issuers. A "small business issuer," defined under Rule 12b-2 of the Exchange Act (§240.12b-2), shall refer to the disclosure items in Regulation S-B (§228.10-702 of this chapter) rather than Regulation S-K (§229.10-702 of this chapter). If there is no comparable disclosure item in Regulation S-B, a small business issuer need not provide the information requested. A small business issuer shall provide the information in Item 310(a) of Regulation S-B in lieu of the financial information required by Rule 14a-3(b)(1) (§240.14a-3(b)(1)). Small business issuers using the transitional small business issuers disclosure format in the filing of their most recent annual report on Form 10-KSB (§249.310b of this chapter) need not provide the information specified below. Rather, those small business issuers shall provide only the financial statements required to be filed in their most recent Form 10-KSB. The inclusion of additional information, including information required of non-transitional small business issuers, in the annual report to security holders will not cause the issuer to be ineligible for the transitional disclosure forms.

(1) The report shall include, for the registrant and its subsidiaries consolidated, audited balance sheets as of the end of each of the two most recent fiscal years and audited statements of income and cash flows for each of the three most recent fiscal years prepared in accordance with Regulation S-X (Part 210 of this chapter), except that the provisions of Article 3 (other than §210.3-03(e), 210.3-04 and 210.3-20) and Article 11 shall not apply. Any financial statement schedules or exhibits or separate financial statements which may otherwise be required in filings with the Commission may be omitted. If the financial statements of the registrant and its subsidiaries consolidated in the annual report filed or to be filed with the Commission are not required to be audited, the financial statements required by this paragraph may be unaudited.

Note 1: If the financial statements for a period prior to the most recently completed fiscal year have been examined by a predecessor accountant, the separate report of the predecessor accountant may be omitted in the report to security holders provided the registrant has obtained from the predecessor accountant a reissued report covering the prior period presented and the successor accountant clearly indicates in the scope paragraph of his report (a) that the financial statements of the prior period were examined by other accountants, (b) the date of their report, (c) the type of opinion expressed by the predecessor accountant, and (d) the substantive reasons therefor, if it was other than unqualified. It should be noted, however, that the separate report of any predecessor accountant is required in filings with the Commission. If, for instance, the financial statements in the annual report to security holders are incorporated by reference in a Form 10-K and Form 10-KSB, the separate report of a predecessor accountant shall be filed in Part II or in Part IV as a financial statement schedule.

Note 2: For purposes of complying with §240.14a-3, if the registrant has changed its fiscal closing date, financial statements covering two years and one period of nine to 12 months shall be deemed to satisfy the requirements for statements of income and cash flows for the three most recent fiscal years.

(2) (i) Financial statements and notes thereto shall be presented in roman type at least as large and as legible as 10-point modern type. If necessary for convenient presentation, the financial statements may be in roman type as large and as legible as 8-point modern type. All type shall be leaded at least 2 points.

(ii) Where the annual report to security holders is delivered through an electronic medium, issuers may satisfy legibility requirements applicable to printed documents, such as type size and font, by presenting all required information in a format readily communicated to investors.

(3) The report shall contain the supplementary financial information required by Item 302 of Regulation S-K (§229.302 of this chapter).

(4) The report shall contain information concerning changes in and disagreements with accountants on accounting and financial disclosure required by Item 304 of Regulation S-K (§229.304 of this chapter).

(5) (i) The report shall contain the selected financial data required by Item 301 of Regulation S-K (§229.301 of this chapter).

(ii) The report shall contain management's discussion and analysis of financial condition and results of operations required by Item 303 of Regulation S-K (§229.303 of this chapter) or, if applicable, a plan of operation required by Item 303(a) of Regulation S-B (§228.303(a) of this chapter).

(iii) The report shall contain the quantitative and qualitative disclosures about market risk required by Item 305 of Regulation S-K (§229.305 of this chapter).

(6) The report shall contain a brief description of the business done by the registrant and its subsidiaries during the most recent fiscal year which will, in the opinion of management, indicate the general nature and scope of the business of the registrant and its subsidiaries.

(7) The report shall contain information relating to the registrant's industry segments, classes of similar products or services, foreign and domestic operations and exports sales required by paragraphs (b), (c)(1)(i) and (d) of Item 101 of Regulation S-K (§229.101 of this chapter).

(8) The report shall identify each of the registrant's directors and executive officers, and shall indicate the principal occupation or employment of each such person and the name and principal business of any organization by which such person is employed.

(9) The report shall contain the market price of and dividends on the registrant's common equity and related security holder matters required by Item 201(a), (b) and (c) of Regulation S-K (§229.201 of this chapter).

(10) The registrant's proxy statement, or the report, shall contain an undertaking in bold face or otherwise reasonably prominent type to provide without charge to each person solicited upon the written request of any such person, a copy of the registrant's annual report on Form 10-K and Form 10-KSB, including the financial statements and the financial statement schedules, required to be filed with the Commission pursuant to Rule 13a-1 under the Act for the registrant's most recent fiscal year, and shall indicate the name and address (including title or department) of the person to whom such a written request is to be directed. In the discretion of management, a registrant need not undertake to furnish without charge copies of all exhibits to its Form 10-K and Form 10-KSB provided the copy of the annual report on Form 10-K and Form 10-KSB furnished without charge to requesting security holders is accompanied by a list briefly describing all the exhibits not contained therein and indicating that the registrant will furnish any exhibit upon the payment of a specified reasonable fee which fee shall be limited to the registrant's reasonable expenses in furnishing such exhibit. If the registrant's annual report to security holders complies with all of the disclosure requirements of Form 10-K and Form 10-KSB and is filed with the Commission in satisfaction of its Form 10-K and Form 10-KSB filing requirements, such registrant need not furnish a separate Form 10-K and Form 10-KSB to security holders who receive a copy of such annual report.

Note: Pursuant to the undertaking required by paragraph (b)(10) of this section, a registrant shall furnish a copy of its annual report on Form 10-K (§249.310 of this chapter) and Form 10-KSB (§249.310b of this chapter) to a beneficial owner of its securities upon receipt of a written request from such person. Each request must set forth a good faith representation that, as of the record date for the solicitation requiring the furnishing of the annual report to security holders pursuant to paragraph (b) of this section, the person making the request was a beneficial owner of securities entitled to vote.

(11) Subject to the foregoing requirements, the report may be in any form deemed suitable by management and the information required by

paragraphs (b)(5) to (b)(10) of this section may be presented in an appendix or other separate section of the report, provided that the attention of security holders is called to such presentation.

Note: Registrants are encouraged to utilize tables, schedules, charts and graphic illustrations of present financial information in an understandable manner. Any presentation of financial information must be consistent with the data in the financial statements contained in the report and, if appropriate, should refer to relevant portions of the financial statements and notes thereto.

(12) [Reserved]

(13) Paragraph (b) of this section shall not apply, however, to solicitations made on behalf of the registrant before the financial statements are available if a solicitation is being made at the same time in opposition to the registrant and if the registrant's proxy statement includes an undertaking in bold-face type to furnish such annual report to all persons being solicited at least 20 calendar days before the date of the meeting or, if the solicitation refers to a written consent or authorization in lieu of a meeting, at least 20 calendar days prior to the earliest date on which it may be used to effect corporate action.

(c) Seven copies of the report sent to security holders pursuant to this rule shall be mailed to the Commission, solely for its information, not later than the date on which such report is first sent or given to security holders or the date on which preliminary copies, or definitive copies, if preliminary filing was not required, of solicitation material are filed with the Commission pursuant to Rule 14a-6(a), whichever date is later. The report is not deemed to be "soliciting material" or to be "filed" with the Commission or subject to this regulation otherwise than as provided in this Rule, or to the liabilities of section 18 of the Act, except to the extent that the registrant specifically requests that it be treated as a part of the proxy soliciting material or incorporates it in the proxy statement or other filed report by reference.

(d) An annual report to security holders prepared on an integrated basis pursuant to General Instruction H to Form 10-K (§249.310) and Form 10-KSB (§249.310b) may also be submitted in satisfaction of this rule. When filed as the annual report on Form 10-K and Form 10-KSB, responses to the Items of that form are subject to section 18 of the Act notwithstanding paragraph (c).

(e) (1) (i) A registrant will be considered to have delivered an annual report to security holders of record who share an address if:

(A) The registrant delivers one annual reportor proxy statement, as applicable, to the shared address;

(B) The registrant addresses the annual report or proxy statement, as applicable, to the security holders a group (for example, "ABC Fund [or Corporation] Shareholders," "Jane Doe and Household," "The Smith Family") or to each of the security holders individually (for example, "John Doe and Richard Jones"), or to the security holders in a form to which each of the security holders has consented in writing;

Note to paragraph (e)(1)(i)(B):

Unless the company addresses the annual report or proxy statement to the security holders as a group or to each of the security holders individually, it must obtain, from each security holder to be included in the householded group, a separate affirmative written consent to the specific form of address the company will use.

(C) The security holders consent, in accordance with paragraph (e)(1)(ii) of this section, to delivery of one annual report or proxy statement, as applicable;

(D) With respect to delivery of the proxy statement, the registrant delivers, together with or subsequent to delivery of the proxy statement, a separate proxy card for each security holder at the shared address; and

(E) The registrant includes an undertaking in the proxy statement to deliver promptly upon written or oral request a separate copy of the annual report or proxy statement, as applicable, to a security holder at a shared address to which a single copy of the document was delivered.

(ii) Consent.

(A) Affirmative written consent. Each security holder must affirmatively consent, in writing, to delivery of one annual report or proxy statement, as applicable. A security holder's affirmative written consent will only be considered valid if the security holder has been informed of:

(1) The duration of the consent;

(2) The specific types of documents to which the consent will apply;

(3) The procedures the security holder must follow to revoke consent; and

(4) The registrant's obligation to begin sending individual copies to a security holder within thirty days after the security holder revokes consent.

(B) Implied consent. The registrant need not obtain written consent from a security holder under paragraph (e)(1)(i)(C) of this section if all of the following conditions are met:

(1) The security holder has the same last name as the other security holders at the shared address or the registrant reasonably believes that the security holders are members of the same family;

(2) The registrant has sent the security holder a notice at least 60 days before the registrant begins to rely on this section concerning delivery of annual reports and proxy statements to that security holder. The notice must:

(i) Be a separate written document;

(ii) State that only one annual report or proxy statement, as applicable, will be delivered to the shared address unless the registrant receives contrary instructions;

(iii) Include a toll-free telephone number, or be accompanied by a reply form that is pre-addressed with postage provided, that the security holder can use to notify the registrant that he or she wishes to receive a separate annual report or proxy statement;

(iv) State the duration of the consent;

(v) Explain how a security holder can revoke consent;

(vi) State that the registrant will begin sending individual copies to a security holder within thirty days after the security holder revokes consent; and

(vii) Contain the following prominent statement, or similar clear and understandable statement, in bold-face type: "Important Notice Regarding Delivery of Security Holder Documents." This statement also must appear on the envelope in which the notice is delivered. Alternatively, if the notice is delivered separately from other communications to security holders, this statement may appear either on the notice or on the envelope in which the notice is delivered.

Note to §240.14a-3(e)(1)(ii)(B)(2): The notice should be written in plain English. See §230.421(d)(2) of this chapter for a discussion of plain English principles.

(3) The registrant has not received the reply form or other notification indicating that the security holder wishes to continue to receive an individual copy of the annual report or proxy statement, as applicable, within 60 days after the registrant sent the notice; and

(4) The registrant delivers the document to a post office box or to a residential street address.

Note to §240.14a-3(e)(1)(ii)(B)(4): The registrant can assume a street address is residential unless registrant has information that indicates the street address is a business.

(iii) Revocation of consent. If a security holder, orally or in writing, revokes consent to delivery of one annual report or proxy statement to a shared address, the registrant must begin sending individual copies to that security holder within 30 days after the registrant receives revocation of the security holder's consent.

(iv) Definition of address. Unless otherwise indicated, for purposes of this section, address means a street address, a post office box number, an electronic mail address, a facsimile telephone number, or other similar destination to which paper or electronic documents are delivered, unless otherwise provided in this section. If the registrant has reason to believe that the address is a street address of a multi-unit building, the address must include the unit number.

Note to paragraph (e)(1).

A person other than the registrant making a proxy solicitation may deliver a single proxy statement to security holders of record or beneficial owners who have separate accounts and share an address if: (a) the registrant or intermediary has followed the procedures in this section; and (b) the registrant or intermediary makes available the shared address information to the person in accordance with §240.14a-7(a)(2)(i) and (ii).

(2) Notwithstanding paragraphs (a) and (b) of this section, unless state law requires otherwise, a registrant is not required to send an annual report or proxy statement to a security holder if:

(i) an annual report and a proxy statement for two consecutive annual meetings; or

(ii) all, and at least two, payments (if sent by first class mail) of dividends or interest on securities, or dividend reinvestment confirmations, during a twelve month period, have been mailed to such security holder's address and have been returned undeliverable. If any such security holder delivers or causes to be delivered to the registrant written notice setting forth his then current address for security holder communications purposes, the registrant's obligation to deliver an annual report or a proxy statement under this section is reinstated.

(f) The provisions of paragraph (a) of this section shall not apply to a communication made by means of speeches in public forums, press releases, published or broadcast opinions, statements, or advertisements appearing in a broadcast media, newspaper, magazine or other bona fide publication disseminated on a regular basis, provided that:

(1) no form of proxy, consent or authorization or means to execute the same is provided to a security holder in connection with the communication; and

(2) at the time the communication is made, a definitive proxy statement is on file with the Commission pursuant to § 240.14a-6(b).

Rule 14a-4 (Reg. §240.14a-4). Requirements as to Proxy

(a) The form of proxy (1) shall indicate in bold-face type whether or not the proxy is solicited on behalf of the registrant's board of directors or, if provided other than by a majority of the board of directors, shall indicate in bold-face type on whose behalf the solicitation is made; (2) shall provide a specifically designated blank space for dating the proxy card; and (3) shall identify clearly and impartially each separate matter intended to be acted upon, whether or not related to or conditioned on the approval of other matters, and whether proposed by the registrant or by security holders. No reference need be made, however, to proposals as to which discretionary authority is conferred pursuant to paragraph (c) of this section.

Note to paragraph (a)(3) (electronic filers): Electronic filers shall satisfy the filing requirements of Rule 14a-6(a) or (b) (§240.14a-6(a) or (b)) with respect to the form of proxy by filing the form of proxy as an appendix at the end of the proxy statement. Forms of proxy shall not be filed as exhibits or separate documents within an electronic submission.

(b) (1) Means shall be provided in the form of proxy whereby the person solicited is afforded an opportunity to specify by boxes a choice between approval or disapproval of, or abstention with respect to, each separate matter referred to therein as intended to be acted upon, other than elections to office. A proxy may confer discretionary authority with respect to matters as to which a choice is not specified by the security holder provided that the form of proxy states in bold-face type how it is intended to vote the shares represented by the proxy in each such case.

(2) A form of proxy which provides for the election of directors shall set forth the names of persons nominated for election as directors. Such form of proxy shall clearly provide any of the following means for security holders to withhold authority to vote for each nominee:

(i) a box opposite the name of each nominee which may be marked to indicate that authority to vote for such nominee is withheld; or

(ii) an instruction in bold-face type which indicates that the security holder may withhold authority to vote for any nominee by lining through or otherwise striking out the name of any nominee; or

(iii) designated blank spaces in which the security holder may enter the names of nominees with respect to whom the shareholder chooses to withhold authority to vote; or

(iv) any other similar means, provided that clear instructions are furnished indicating how the security holder may withhold authority to vote for any nominee.

Such form of proxy also may provide a means for the security holder to grant authority to vote for the nominees set forth, as a group, provided that there is a similar means for the security holder to withhold authority to vote for such group of nominees. Any such form of proxy which is executed by the security holder in such manner as not to withhold authority to vote for the election of any nominee shall be deemed to grant such authority, provided that the form of proxy so states in bold-face type.

Instructions:

Paragraph (2) does not apply in the case of a merger, consolidation or other plan if the election of directors is an integral part of the plan.

If applicable state law gives legal effect to votes cast against a nominee, then in lieu of, or in addition to, providing a means for security holders to withhold authority to vote, the issuer should provide a similar means for security holders to vote against each nominee.

(c) A proxy may confer discretionary authority to vote on any of the following matters:

(1) For an annual meeting of shareholders, if the registrant did not have notice of the matter at least 45 days before the date on which the registrant first mailed its proxy materials for the prior year's annual meeting of shareholders (or date specified by an advance notice provision), and a specific statement to that effect is made in the proxy statement or form of proxy. If during the prior year the registrant did not hold an annual meeting, or if the date of the meeting has changed more than 30 days from the prior year, then notice must not have been received a reasonable time before the registrant mails its proxy materials for the current year.

(2) In the case in which the registrant has received timely notice in connection with an annual meeting of shareholders (as determined under paragraph (c)(1) of this section), if the registrant includes, in the proxy statement, advice on the nature of the matter and how the registrant intends to exercise its discretion to vote on each matter. However, even if the registrant includes this information in its proxy statement, it may not exercise discretionary voting authority on a particular proposal if the proponent:

(i) Provides the registrant with a written statement, within the timeframe determined under paragraph (c)(1) of this section, that the proponent intends to deliver a proxy statement and form of proxy to holders of at least the percentage of the company's voting shares required under applicable law to carry the proposal;

(ii) Includes the same statement in its proxy materials filed under §240.14a-6; and

(iii) Immediately after soliciting the percentage of shareholders required to carry the proposal, provides the registrant with a statement from any solicitor or other person with knowledge that the necessary steps have been taken to deliver a proxy statement and form of proxy to holders of at least the percentage of the company's voting shares required under applicable law to carry the proposal.

(3) For solicitations other than for annual meetings or for solicitations by persons other than the registrant, matters which the persons making the solicitation do not know, a reasonable time before the solicitation, are to be presented at the meeting, if a specific statement to that effect is made in the proxy statement or form of proxy.

(4) Approval of the minutes of the prior meeting if such approval does not amount to ratification of the action taken at that meeting;

(5) The election of any person to any office for which a bona fide nominee is named in the proxy statement and such nominee is unable to serve or for good cause will not serve.

(6) Any proposal omitted from the proxy statement and form of proxy pursuant to §240.14a-8 or §240.14a-9 of this chapter.

(7) Matters incident to the conduct of the meeting.

(d) No proxy shall confer authority (1) to vote for the election of any person to any office for which a bona fide nominee is not named in the proxy statement, (2) to vote at any annual meeting other than the next annual meeting (or any adjournment thereof) to be held after the date on which the proxy statement and form of proxy are first sent or given to security holders, (3) to vote with respect to more than one meeting (and any adjournment thereof) or more than one consent solicitation or (4) to consent to or authorize any action other than the action proposed to be taken in the proxy statement, or matters referred to in paragraph (c) of this rule. A person shall not be deemed to be a bona fide nominee and he shall not be named as such unless he has consented to being named in the proxy statement and to serve if elected. Provided, however, that nothing in this section 240.14a-4 shall prevent any person soliciting in support of nominees who, if elected, would constitute a minority of the board of directors, from seeking authority to vote for nominees named in the registrant's proxy statement, so long as the soliciting party:

(i) seeks authority to vote in the aggregate for the number of director positions then subject to election;

(ii) represents that it will vote for all the registrant nominees, other than those registrant nominees specified by the soliciting party;

(iii) provides the security holder an opportunity to withhold authority with respect to any other registrant nominee by writing the name of that nominee on the form of proxy; and

(iv) states on the form of proxy and in the proxy statement that there is no assurance that the registrant's nominees will serve if elected with any of the soliciting party's nominees.

(e) The proxy statement or form of proxy shall provide, subject to reasonable specified conditions, that the shares represented by the proxy will be voted and that where the person solicited specifies by means of a ballot provided pursuant to paragraph (b) a choice with respect to any matter to be acted upon, the shares will be voted in accordance with the specifications so made.

(f) No person conducting a solicitation subject to this regulation shall deliver a form of proxy, consent or authorization to any security holder unless the security holder concurrently receives, or has previously received, a definitive proxy statement that has been filed with the Commission pursuant to §240.14a-6(b).

Rule 14a-5 (Reg. §240.14a-5). Presentation of Information in Proxy Statement

(a) The information included in the proxy statement shall be clearly presented and the statements made shall be divided into groups according to subject matter and the various groups of statements shall be preceded by appropriate headings. The order of items and sub-items in the schedule need not be followed. Where practicable and appropriate, the information shall be presented in tabular form. All amounts shall be stated in figures. Information required by more than one applicable item need not be repeated. No statement need be made in response to any item or sub-item which is inapplicable.

(b) Any information required to be included in the proxy statement as to terms of securities or other subject matter which from a standpoint of practical necessity must be determined in the future may be stated in terms of present knowledge and intention. To the extent practicable, the authority to be conferred concerning each such matter shall be confined within limits reasonably related to the need for discretionary authority. Subject to the foregoing, information which is not known to the persons on whose behalf the solicitation is to be made and which it is not reasonably within the power of such persons to ascertain or procure may be omitted, if a brief statement of the circumstances rendering such information unavailable is made.

(c) Any information contained in any other proxy soliciting material which has been furnished to each person solicited in connection with the same meeting or subject matter may be omitted from the proxy statement, if a clear reference is made to the particular document containing such information.

(d) (1) All printed proxy statements shall be in roman type at least as large and as legible as 10-point modern type, except that to the extent necessary for convenient presentation financial statements and other tabular data, but not the notes thereto, may be in roman type at least as large and as legible as 8-point modern type. All such type shall be leaded at least 2 points.

(2) Where a proxy statement is delivered through an electronic medium, issuers may satisfy legibility requirements applicable to printed documents, such as type size and font, by presenting all required information in a format readily communicated to investors.

(e) All proxy statements shall disclose, under an appropriate caption, the following dates:

(1) The deadline for submitting shareholder proposals for inclusion in the registrant's proxy statement and form of proxy for the registrant's next annual meeting, calculated in the manner provided in §240.14a-8(d)(Question 4); and

(2) The date after which notice of a shareholder proposal submitted outside the processes of §240.14a-8 is considered untimely, either calculated in the manner provided by §240.14a-4(c)(1) or as established by the registrant's advance notice provision, if any, authorized by applicable state law.

(f) If the date of the next annual meeting is subsequently advanced or delayed by more than 30 calendar days from the date of the annual meeting to which the proxy statement relates, the registrant shall, in a timely manner, inform shareholders of such change, and the new dates referred to in paragraphs (e)(1) and (e)(2) of this section, by including a notice, under Item 5, in its earliest possible quarterly report on Form 10-Q (§249.308a of this chapter) or Form 10-QSB (§249.308b of this chapter), or, in the case of investment companies, in a shareholder report under §270.30d-1 of this chapter under the Investment Company Act of 1940, or, if impracticable, any means reasonably calculated to inform shareholders.

Rule 14a-6 (Reg. §240.14a-6). Filing Requirements

(a) Preliminary proxy statement. Five preliminary copies of the proxy statement and form of proxy shall be filed with the Commission at least 10 calendar days prior to the date definitive copies of such material are first sent or given to security holders, or such shorter period prior to that date as the Commission may authorize upon a showing of good cause thereunder. A registrant, however, shall not file with the Commission a preliminary proxy statement, form of proxy or other soliciting material to be furnished to security holders concurrently therewith if the solicitation relates to an annual (or special meeting in lieu of the annual) meeting, or for an investment company registered under the Investment Company Act of 1940 (15 U.S.C. 80a-1 et seq.) or a business development company, if the solicitation relates to any meeting of security holders at which the only matters to be acted upon are:

(1) the election of directors;

(2) the election, approval or ratification of accountant(s);

(3) a security holder proposal included pursuant to Rule 14a-8 (§240.14a-8 of this chapter);

(4) the approval or ratification of a plan as defined in paragraph (a)(7)(ii) of Item 402 of Regulation S-K (§229.402(a)(7)(ii) of this chapter) or amendments to such a plan;

(5) with respect to an investment company registered under the Investment Company Act of 1940 or a business development company, a proposal to continue, without change, any advisory or other contract or agreement that previously has been the subject of a proxy solicitation for which proxy material was filed with the Commission pursuant to this rule; and/or

(6) with respect to an open-end investment company registered under the Investment Company Act of 1940, a proposal to increase the number of shares authorized to be issued.

This exclusion from filing preliminary proxy material does not apply if the registrant comments upon or refers to a solicitation in opposition in connection with the meeting in its proxy material.

Note 1: The filing of revised material does not recommence the ten day time period unless the revised material contains material revisions or material new proposal(s) that constitute a fundamental change in the proxy material.

Note 2: The official responsible for the preparation of the preliminary material should make every effort to verify the accuracy and completeness of the information required by the applicable rules. The preliminary material should be filed with the Commission at the earliest practicable date.

Note 3: Solicitation in Opposition. For purposes of the exclusion from filing preliminary proxy material, a "solicitation in opposition" includes: (a) any solicitation opposing a proposal supported by the registrant; and (b) any solicitation supporting a proposal that the registrant does not expressly support, other than a security holder proposal included in the registrant's proxy material pursuant to Rule 14a-8 (§240.14a-8 of this chapter). The inclusion of a security holder proposal in the registrant's proxy material pursuant to Rule 14a-8 does not constitute a "solicitation in opposition," even if the registrant opposes the proposal and/or includes a statement in opposition to the proposal.

Note 4: A registrant that is filing proxy material in preliminary form only because the registrant has commented on or referred to a solicitation in opposition should indicate that fact in a transmittal letter when filing the preliminary material with the Commission.

(b) Definitive proxy statement and other soliciting material. Eight definitive copies of the proxy statement, form of proxy and all other soliciting materials, in the same form as the materials sent to security holders, must be filed with the Commission no later than the date they are first sent or given to security holders. Three copies of these materials also must be filed with, or mailed for filing to, each national securities exchange on which the registrant has a class of securities listed and registered.

(c) Personal solicitation materials. If part or all of the solicitation involves personal solicitation, then eight copies of all written instructions or other materials that discuss, review or comment on the merits of any matter to be acted on, that are furnished to persons making the actual solicitation for their use directly or indirectly in connection with the solicitation, must be filed with the Commission no later than the date the materials are first sent or given to these persons.

(d) Release dates. All preliminary proxy statements and forms of proxy filed pursuant to paragraph (a) of this section shall be accompanied by a statement of the date on which definitive copies thereof filed pursuant to paragraph (b) of this section are intended to be released to security holders. All definitive material filed pursuant to paragraph (b) of this section shall be accompanied by a statement of the date on which copies of such material were related to security holders, or, if not released, the date on which copies thereof are intended to be released. All material filed pursuant to paragraph (c) of this section shall be accompanied by a statement of the date on which copies thereof were released to the individual who will make the actual solicitation or it not released, the date on which copies thereof are intended to be released.

(e) (1) Public availability of information. All copies of preliminary proxy statements and forms of proxy filed pursuant to paragraph (a) of this section shall be clearly marked "Preliminary Copies," and shall be deemed available for public inspection unless confidential treatment is obtained pursuant to paragraph (e)(2) of this section.

(2) Confidential treatment. If action will be taken on any matter specified in Item 14 of Schedule 14A (§240.14a-101), all copies of the preliminary proxy statement and form of proxy filed under paragraph (a) of this section will be for the information of the Commission only and will not be deemed available for public inspection until filed with the Commission in definitive form so long as:

(i) The proxy statement does not relate to a matter or proposal subject to §240.13e-3 or a roll-up transaction as defined in Item 901(c) of Regulation S-K (§229.901(c) of this chapter);

(ii) Neither the parties to the transaction nor any persons authorized to act on their behalf have made any public communications relating to the transaction except for statements where the content is limited to the information specified in §230.135 of this chapter; and

(iii) The materials are filed in paper and marked "Confidential, For Use of the Commission Only." In all cases, the materials may be disclosed to any department or agency of the United States Government and to the Congress, and the Commission may make any inquiries or investigation into the materials as may be necessary to conduct an adequate review by the Commission.

Instruction to paragraph (e)(2): If communications are made publicly that go beyond the information specified in §230.135 of this chapter, the preliminary proxy materials must be re-filed promptly with the Commission as public materials.

(f) Communications not required to be filed. Copies of replies to inquiries from security holders requesting further information and copies of communications which do no more than request that forms of proxy theretofore solicited be signed and returned need not be filed pursuant to this rule.

(g) Solicitations subject to §240.14a-2(b)(1).

(1) Any person who:

(i) engages in a solicitation pursuant to §240.14a-2(b)(1), and

(ii) at the commencement of that solicitation owns beneficially securities of the class which is the subject of the solicitation with a market value of over $5 million, shall furnish or mail to the Commission, not later than three days after the date the written solicitation is first sent or given to any security holder, five copies of a statement containing the information specified in the Notice of Exempt Solicitation [§240.14a-103] which statement shall attach as an exhibit all written soliciting materials. Five copies of an amendment to such statement shall be furnished or mailed to the Commission, in connection with dissemination of any additional communications, not later than three days after the date the additional material is first sent or given to any security holder. Three copies of the Notice of Exempt Solicitation and amendments thereto shall, at the same time the materials are furnished or mailed to the Commission, be furnished or mailed to each national securities exchange upon which any class of securities of the registrant is listed and registered.

(2) Notwithstanding paragraph (g)(1) of this section, no such submission need be made with respect to oral solicitations (other than with respect to scripts used in connection with such oral solicitations), speeches delivered in a public forum, press releases, published or broadcast opinions, statements, and advertisements appearing in a broadcast media, or a newspaper, magazine or other bona fide publication dissemination on a regular basis.

(h) Revised material. Where any proxy statement, form of proxy or other material filed pursuant to this rule is amended or revised, two of the copies of such amended or revised material filed pursuant to this rule (or in the case of investment companies registered under the Investment Company Act of 1940, three of such copies) shall be marked to indicate clearly and precisely the changes effected therein. If the amendment or revision alters the text of the material the changes in such text shall be indicated by means of underscoring or in some other appropriate manner.

(i) Fees. At the time of filing the proxy solicitation material, the persons upon whose behalf the solicitation is made, other than investment companies registered under the Investment Company Act of 1940, shall pay to the Commission the following applicable fee:

(1) For preliminary proxy material involving acquisitions, mergers, spinoffs, consolidations or proposed sales or other dispositions of substantially all the assets of the company, a fee established in accordance with Rule 0-11 (240.0-11 of this chapter) shall be paid. No refund shall be given.

(2) For all other proxy submissions and submissions made pursuant to §240.14a-6(g), no fee shall be required.

(j) Merger proxy materials.

(1) Any proxy statement, form of proxy or other soliciting material required to be filed by this section that also is either

(i) included in a registration statement filed under the Securities Act of 1933 on Forms S-4 (§239.25 of this chapter), F-4 (§239.34 of this chapter) or N-14 (§239.23 of this chapter); or

(ii) filed under §230.424, §230.425 or §230.497 of this chapter is required to be filed only under the Securities Act, and is deemed filed under this section.

(2) Under paragraph (j)(1) of this section, the fee required by paragraph (i) of this section need not be paid.

(k) Computing time periods. In computing time periods beginning with the filing date specified in Regulation 14A (§§240.14a-1 to §§240.14b-1 of this chapter), the filing date shall be counted as the first day of the time period and midnight of the last day shall constitute the end of the specified time period.

(l) Roll-up transactions. If a transaction is a roll-up transaction as defined in Item 901(c) of Regulation S-K [17 CFR 229.901(c)] and is registered (or authorized to be registered) on Form S-4 (17 CFR 229.25) or Form F-4 (17 CFR 229.34), the proxy statement of the sponsor or the general partner as defined in Item 901(d) and Item 901(a), respectively, of Regulation S-K (17 CFR 229.901) must be distributed to security holders no later than the lesser of 60 calendar days prior to the date on which the meeting of security holders is held or action is taken, or the maximum number of days permitted for giving notice under applicable state law.

(m) Cover Page. Proxy materials filed with the Commission shall include a cover page in the form set in Schedule 14A (§ 240.14a101 of this chapter). The cover page required by this paragraph need not be distributed to security holders.

(n) Solicitations subject to §240.14a-2(b)(4). Any person who:

(1) Engages in a solicitation pursuant to §240.14a-2(b)(4), and

(2) At the commencement of that solicitation both owns five percent (5%) or more of the outstanding securities of a class that is the subject of the proposed roll-up transaction, and engages in the business of buying and selling limited partnership interests in the secondary market, shall furnish or mail to the Commission, not later than three days after the date an oral or written solicitation by that person is first made, sent or provided to any security holder, five copies of a statement containing the information specified in the Notice of Exempt Preliminary Roll-up Communication (§ 240.14a-104). Five copies of any amendment to such statement shall be furnished or mailed to the Commission not later than three days after a communication containing revised material is first made, sent or provided to any security holder.

(o) Solicitations before furnishing a definitive proxy statement. Solicitations that are published, sent or given to security holders before they have been furnished a definitive proxy statement must be made in accordance with §240.14a-12 unless there is an exemption available under §240.14a-2.

Rule 14a-7 (Reg. §240.14a-7). Obligations of Registrants to Provide a List of, or Mail Soliciting Material to, Security Holders

(a) If the registrant has made or intends to make a proxy solicitation in connection with a security holder meeting or action by consent or authorization, upon the written request by any record or beneficial holder of securities of the class entitled to vote at the meeting or to execute a consent or authorization to provide a list of security holders or to mail the requesting security holder's materials, regardless of whether the request references this section, the registrant shall:

(1) deliver to the requesting security holder within five business days after receipt of the request:

(i) notification as to whether the registrant has elected to mail the security holder's soliciting materials or provide a security holder list if the election under paragraph (b) is to be made by the registrant;

(ii) a statement of the approximate number of record holders and beneficial holders, separated by type of holder and class, owning securities in the same class or classes as holders which have been or are to be solicited on management's behalf, or any more limited group of such holders designated by the security holder if available or retrievable under the registrant's or its transfer agent's security holder data systems; and

(iii) the estimated cost of mailing a proxy statement, form of proxy or other communication to such holders, including to the extent known or reasonably available, the estimated costs of any bank, broker, and similar person through whom the registrant has solicited or intends to solicit beneficial owners in connection with the security holder meeting or action.

(2) perform the acts set forth in either paragraphs (a)(2)(i) or (a)(2)(ii) of this section, at the registrant's or requesting security holder's option, as specified in paragraph (b) of this section:

(i) Mail copies of any proxy statement, form of proxy or other soliciting material furnished by the security holder to the record holders, including banks, brokers, and similar entities, designated by the security holder. A sufficient number of copies must be mailed to the banks, brokers, and similar entities for distribution to all beneficial owners designated by the security holder. If the registrant has received affirmative written or implied consent to deliver a single proxy statement to security holders at a shared address in accordance with the procedures in §240.14a-3(e)(1), a single copy of the proxy statement furnished by the security holder shall be mailed to that address. The registrant shall mail the security holder material with reasonable promptness after tender of the material to be mailed, envelopes or other containers therefor, postage or payment for postage and other reasonable expenses of effecting such mailing. The registrant shall not be responsible for the content of the material; or

(ii) Deliver the following information to the requesting security holder within five business days of receipt of the request: a reasonably current list of the names, addresses and security positions of the record holders, including banks, brokers and similar entities holding securities in the same class or classes as holders which have been or are to be solicited on management's behalf, or any more limited group of such holders designated by the security holder if available or retrievable under the registrant's or its transfer agent's security holder data systems; the most recent list of names, addresses and security positions of beneficial owners as specified in §240.14a-13(b), in the possession, or which subsequently comes into the possession, of the registrant; and the names of security holders at a shared address that have consented to delivery of a single copy of proxy materials to a shared address, if the registrant has received written or implied consent in accordance with §240.14a-3(e)(1). All security holder list information shall be in the form requested by the security holder to the extent that such form is available to the registrant without undue burden or expense. The registrant shall furnish the security holder with updated record holder information on a daily basis or, if not available on a daily basis, at the shortest reasonable intervals, provided, however, the registrant need not provide beneficial or record holder information more current than the record date for the meeting or action.

(b) If the registrant is soliciting or intends to solicit with respect to a proposal that is subject to §240.13e-3 or a roll-up transaction as defined in Item 901(c) of Regulation S-K [§229.901(c) of this chapter], the requesting security holder shall have the option set forth in paragraph (a)(2) of this section. With respect to all other requests pursuant to this section, the registrant shall have the option to either mail the security holder's material or furnish the security holder list as set forth in paragraph (a)(2) of this section.

(c) At the time of a list request, the security holder making the request shall:

(1) if holding the registrant's securities through a nominee, provide the registrant with a statement by the nominee or other independent third party, or a copy of a current filing made with the Commission and furnished to the registrant, confirming such holder's beneficial ownership; and

(2) provide the registrant with an affidavit, declaration, affirmation or other similar document provided for under applicable state law identifying the proposal or other corporate action that will be the subject of the security holder's solicitation or communication and attesting that:

(i) the security holder will not use the list information for any purpose other than to solicit security holders with respect to the same meeting or action by consent or authorization for which the registrant is soliciting or intends to solicit or to communicate with security holders with respect to a solicitation commenced by the registrant; and

(ii) the security holder will not disclose such information to any person other than a beneficial owner for whom the request was made and an employee or agent to the extent necessary to effectuate the communication or solicitation.

(d) The security holder shall not use the information furnished by the registrant pursuant to paragraph (a)(2)(ii) of this section for any purpose other than to solicit security holders with respect to the same meeting or action by consent or authorization for which the registrant is soliciting or intends to solicit or to communicate with security holders with respect to a solicitation commenced by the registrant; or disclose such information to any person other than an employee, agent, or beneficial owner for whom a request was made to the extent necessary to effectuate the communication or solicitation. The security holder shall return the information provided pursuant to paragraph (a)(2)(ii) of this section and shall not retain any copies thereof or of any information derived from such information after the termination of the solicitation.

(e) The security holder shall reimburse the reasonable expenses incurred by the registrant in performing the acts requested pursuant to paragraph (a) of this section.

Note to §240.14a-7.

(1) Reasonably prompt methods of distribution to security holders may be used instead of mailing. If an alternative distribution method is chosen, the costs of that method should be considered where necessary rather than the costs of mailing.

(2)When providing the information required by §240.14a-7(a)(1)(ii), if the registrant has received affirmative written or implied consent to delivery of a single copy of proxy materials to a shared address in accordance with §240.14a-3(e)(1), it shall exclude from the number of record holders those to whom it does not have to deliver a separate proxy statement.

Rule 14a-8 (Reg. §240.14a-8). Shareholder Proposals

This section addresses when a company must include a shareholder's proposal in its proxy statement and identify the proposal in its form of proxy when the company holds an annual or special meeting of shareholders. In summary, in order to have your shareholder proposal included on a company's proxy card, and included along with any supporting statement in its proxy statement, you must be eligible and follow certain procedures. Under a few specific circumstances, the company is permitted to exclude your proposal, but only after submitting its reasons to the Commission. We structured this section in a question-and-answer format so that it is easier to understand. The references to "you" are to a shareholder seeking to submit the proposal.

(a) Question 1: What is a proposal?

A shareholder proposal is your recommendation or requirement that the company and/or its board of directors take action, which you intend to present at a meeting of the company's shareholders. Your proposal should state as clearly as possible the course of action that you believe the company should follow. If your proposal is placed on the company's proxy card, the company must also provide in the form of proxy means for shareholders to specify by boxes a choice between approval or disapproval, or abstention. Unless otherwise indicated, the word "proposal" as used in this section refers both to your proposal, and to your corresponding statement in support of your proposal (if any).

(b) Question 2: Who is eligible to submit a proposal, and how do I demonstrate to the company that I am eligible?

(1) In order to be eligible to submit a proposal, you must have continuously held at least $2,000 in market value, or 1%, of the company's securities entitled to be voted on the proposal at the meeting for at least one year by the date you submit the proposal. You must continue to hold those securities through the date of the meeting.

(2) If you are the registered holder of your securities, which means that your name appears in the company's records as a shareholder, the company can verify your eligibility on its own, although you will still have to provide the company with a written statement that you intend to continue to hold the securities through the date of the meeting of shareholders. However, if like many shareholders you are not a registered holder, the company likely does not know that you are a shareholder, or how many shares you own. In this case, at the time you submit your proposal, you must prove your eligibility to the company in one of two ways:

(i) The first way is to submit to the company a written statement from the "record" holder of your securities (usually a broker or bank) verifying that, at the time you submitted your proposal, you continuously held the securities for at least one year. You must also include your own written statement that you intend to continue to hold the securities through the date of the meeting of shareholders; or

(ii) The second way to prove ownership applies only if you have filed a Schedule 13D (§240.13d-101), Schedule 13G (§240.13d-102), Form 3 (§249.103 of this chapter), Form 4 (§249.104 of this chapter) and/or Form 5 (§249.105 of this chapter), or amendments to those documents or updated forms, reflecting your ownership of the shares as of or before the date on which the one-year eligibility period begins. If you have filed one of these documents with the SEC, you may demonstrate your eligibility by submitting to the company:

(A) A copy of the schedule and/or form, and any subsequent amendments reporting a change in your ownership level;

(B) Your written statement that you continuously held the required number of shares for the one-year period as of the date of the statement; and

(C) Your written statement that you intend to continue ownership of the shares through the date of the company's annual or special meeting.

(c) Question 3: How many proposals may I submit?

Each shareholder may submit no more than one proposal to a company for a particular shareholders' meeting.

(d) Question 4: How long can my proposal be?

The proposal, including any accompanying supporting statement, may not exceed 500 words.

(e) Question 5: What is the deadline for submitting a proposal?

(1) If you are submitting your proposal for the company's annual meeting, you can in most cases find the deadline in last year's proxy statement. However, if the company did not hold an annual meeting last year, or has changed the date of its meeting for this year more than 30 days from last year's meeting, you can usually find the deadline in one of the company's quarterly reports on Form 10-Q (§249.308a of this chapter) or 10-QSB (§249.308b of this chapter), or in shareholder reports of investment companies under §270.30d-1 of this chapter of the Investment Company Act of 1940. In order to avoid controversy, shareholders should submit their proposals by means, including electronic means, that permit them to prove the date of delivery.

(2) The deadline is calculated in the following manner if the proposal is submitted for a regularly scheduled annual meeting. The proposal must be received at the company's principal executive offices not less than 120 calendar days before the date of the company's proxy statement released to shareholders in connection with the previous year's annual meeting. However, if the company did not hold an annual meeting the previous year, or if the date of this year's annual meeting has been changed by more than 30 days from the date of the previous year's meeting, then the deadline is a reasonable time before the company begins to print and mail its proxy materials.

(3) If you are submitting your proposal for a meeting of shareholders other than a regularly scheduled annual meeting, the deadline is a reasonable time before the company begins to print and mail its proxy materials.

(f) Question 6: What if I fail to follow one of the eligibility or procedural requirements explained in answers to Questions 1 through 4 of this section?

(1) The company may exclude your proposal, but only after it has notified you of the problem, and you have failed adequately to correct it. Within 14 calendar days of receiving your proposal, the company must notify you in writing of any procedural or eligibility deficiencies, as well as of the time frame for your response. Your response must be postmarked , or transmitted electronically, no later than 14 days from the date you received the company's notification. A company need not provide you such notice of a deficiency if the deficiency cannot be remedied, such as if you fail to submit a proposal by the company's properly determined deadline. If the company intends to exclude the proposal, it will later have to

make a submission under §240.14a-8 and provide you with a copy under Question 10 below, §240.14a-8(j).

(2) If you fail in your promise to hold the required number of securities through the date of the meeting of shareholders, then the company will be permitted to exclude all of your proposals from its proxy materials for any meeting held in the following two calendar years.

(g) Question 7: Who has the burden of persuading the Commission or its staff that my proposal can be excluded?

Except as otherwise noted, the burden is on the company to demonstrate that it is entitled to exclude a proposal.

(h) Question 8: Must I appear personally at the shareholders' meeting to present the proposal?

(1) Either you, or your representative who is qualified under state law to present the proposal on your behalf, must attend the meeting to present the proposal. Whether you attend the meeting yourself or send a qualified representative to the meeting in your place, you should make sure that you, or your representative, follow the proper state law procedures for attending the meeting and/or presenting your proposal.

(2) If the company holds its shareholder meeting in whole or in part via electronic media, and the company permits you or your representative to present your proposal via such media, then you may appear through electronic media rather than traveling to the meeting to appear in person.

(3) If you or your qualified representative fail to appear and present the proposal, without good cause, the company will be permitted to exclude all of your proposals from its proxy materials for any meetings held in the following two calendar years.

(i) Question 9: If I have complied with the procedural requirements, on what other bases may a company rely to exclude my proposal?

(1) Improper under state law: If the proposal is not a proper subject for action by shareholders under the laws of the jurisdiction of the company's organization;

Note to paragraph (i)(1): Depending on the subject matter, some proposals are not considered proper under state law if they would be binding on the company if approved by shareholders. In our experience, most proposals that are cast as recommendations or requests that the board of directors take specified action are proper under state law. Accordingly, we will assume that a proposal drafted as a recommendation or suggestion is proper unless the company demonstrates otherwise.

(2) Violation of law: If the proposal would, if implemented, cause the company to violate any state, federal, or foreign law to which it is subject;

Note to paragraph (i)(2): We will not apply this basis for exclusion to permit exclusion of a proposal on grounds that it would violate foreign law if compliance with the foreign law would result in a violation of any state or federal law.

(3) Violation of proxy rules: If the proposal or supporting statement is contrary to any of the Commission's proxy rules, including §240.14a-9, which prohibits materially false or misleading statements in proxy soliciting materials;

(4) Personal grievance; special interest: If the proposal relates to the redress of a personal claim or grievance against the company or any other person, or if it is designed to result in a benefit to you, or to further a personal interest, which is not shared by the other shareholders at large;

(5) Relevance: If the proposal relates to operations which account for less than 5 percent of the company's total assets at the end of its most recent fiscal year, and for less than 5 percent of its net earnings and gross sales for its most recent fiscal year, and is not otherwise significantly related to the company's business;

(6) Absence of power/authority: If the company would lack the power or authority to implement the proposal;

(7) Management functions: If the proposal deals with a matter relating to the company's ordinary business operations;

(8) Relates to election: If the proposal relates to an election for membership on the company's board of directors or analogous governing body;

(9) Conflicts with company's proposal: If the proposal directly conflicts with one of the company's own proposals to be submitted to shareholders at the same meeting;

Note to paragraph (i)(9): A company's submission to the Commission under this section should specify the points of conflict with the company's proposal.

(10) Substantially implemented: If the company has already substantially implemented the proposal;

(11) Duplication: If the proposal substantially duplicates another proposal previously submitted to the company by another proponent that will be included in the company's proxy materials for the same meeting;

(12) Resubmissions: If the proposal deals with substantially the same subject matter as another proposal or proposals that has or have been previously included in the company's proxy materials within the preceding 5 calendar years, a company may exclude it from its proxy materials for any meeting held within 3 calendar years of the last time it was included if the proposal received:

(i) Less than 3% of the vote if proposed once within the preceding 5 calendar years;

(ii) Less than 6% of the vote on its last submission to shareholders if proposed twice previously within the preceding 5 calendar years; or

(iii) Less than 10% of the vote on its last submission to shareholders if proposed three times or more previously within the preceding 5 calendar years; and

(13) Specific amount of dividends: If the proposal relates to specific amounts of cash or stock dividends.

(j) Question 10: What procedures must the company follow if it intends to exclude my proposal?

(1) If the company intends to exclude a proposal from its proxy materials, it must file its reasons with the Commission no later than 80 calendar days before it files its definitive proxy statement and form of proxy with the Commission. The company must simultaneously provide you with a copy of its submission. The Commission staff may permit the company to make its submission later than 80 days before the company files its definitive proxy statement and form of proxy, if the company demonstrates good cause for missing the deadline.

(2) The company must file six paper copies of the following:

(i) The proposal;

(ii) An explanation of why the company believes that it may exclude the proposal, which should, if possible, refer to the most recent applicable authority, such as prior Division letters issued under the rule; and

(iii) A supporting opinion of counsel when such reasons are based on matters of state or foreign law.

(k) Question 11: May I submit my own statement to the Commission responding to the company's arguments?

Yes, you may submit a response, but it is not required. You should try to submit any response to us, with a copy to the company, as soon as possible after the company makes its submission. This way, the Commission staff will have time to consider fully your submission before it issues its response. You should submit six paper copies of your response.

(l) Question 12: If the company includes my shareholder proposal in its proxy materials, what information about me must it include along with the proposal itself?

(1) The company's proxy statement must include your name and address, as well as the number of the company's voting securities that you hold. However, instead of providing that information, the company may

instead include a statement that it will provide the information to shareholders promptly upon receiving an oral or written request.

(2) The company is not responsible for the contents of your proposal or supporting statement.

(m) Question 13: What can I do if the company includes in its proxy statement reasons why it believes shareholders should not vote in favor of my proposal, and I disagree with some of its statements?

(1) The company may elect to include in its proxy statement reasons why it believes shareholders should vote against your proposal. The company is allowed to make arguments reflecting its own point of view, just as you may express your own point of view in your proposal's supporting statement.

(2) However, if you believe that the company's opposition to your proposal contains materially false or misleading statements that may violate our anti-fraud rule, §240.14a-9, you should promptly send to the Commission staff and the company a letter explaining the reasons for your view, along with a copy of the company's statements opposing your proposal. To the extent possible, your letter should include specific factual information demonstrating the inaccuracy of the company's claims. Time permitting, you may wish to try to work out your differences with the company by yourself before contacting the Commission staff.

(3) We require the company to send you a copy of its statements opposing your proposal before it mails its proxy materials, so that you may bring to our attention any materially false or misleading statements, under the following timeframes:

(i) If our no-action response requires that you make revisions to your proposal or supporting statement as a condition to requiring the company to include it in its proxy materials, then the company must provide you with a copy of its opposition statements no later than 5 calendar days after the company receives a copy of your revised proposal; or

(ii) In all other cases, the company must provide you with a copy of its opposition statements no later than 30 calendar days before its files definitive copies of its proxy statement and form of proxy under §240.14a-6.

Rule 14a-9 (Reg. §240.14a-9). False or Misleading Statements

(a) No solicitation subject to this regulation shall be made by means of any proxy statement, form of proxy, notice of meeting or other communication, written or oral, containing any statement which, at the time and in the light of the circumstances under which it is made, is false or misleading with respect to any material fact, or which omits to state any material fact necessary in order to make the statements therein not false or misleading or necessary to correct any statement in any earlier communication with respect to the solicitation of a proxy for the same meeting or subject matter which has become false or misleading.

(b) The fact that a proxy statement, form of proxy or other soliciting material has been filed with or examined by the Commission shall not be deemed a finding by the Commission that such material is accurate or complete or not false or misleading, or that the Commission has passed upon the merits of or approved any statement contained therein or any matter to be acted upon by security holders. No representation contrary to the foregoing shall be made.

Note: The following are some examples of what, depending upon particular facts and circumstances, may be misleading within the meaning of this section.

(a) Predictions as to specific future market values.

(b) Material which directly or indirectly impugns character, integrity or personal reputation, or directly or indirectly makes charges concerning improper, illegal or immoral conduct or associations, without factual foundation.

(c) Failure to so identify a proxy statement, form of proxy and other soliciting material as to clearly distinguish it from the soliciting material of any other person or persons soliciting for the same meeting or subject matter.

(d) Claims made prior to a meeting regarding the results of a solicitation.

Rule 14a-10 (Reg. §240.14a-10). Prohibition of Certain Solicitations

No person making a solicitation which is subject to §§240.14a-1 to 240.14a-10 shall solicit:

(a) any undated or post-dated proxy, or

(b) any proxy which provides that it shall be deemed to be dated as of any date subsequent to the date on which it is signed by the security holder.

Rule 14a-11 (Reg. §240.14a-11). [Removed and Reserved.]

Rule 14a-12 (Reg. §240.14a-12). Solicitation Before Furnishing a Proxy Statement.

(a) Notwithstanding the provisions of §240.14a-3(a), a solicitation may be made before furnishing security holders with a proxy statement meeting the requirements of §240.14a-3(a) if:

(1) Each written communication includes:

(i) The identity of the participants in the solicitation (as defined in Instruction 3 to Item 4 of Schedule 14A (§240.14a-101)) and a description of their direct or indirect interests, by security holdings or otherwise, or a prominent legend in clear, plain language advising security holders where they can obtain that information; and

(ii) A prominent legend in clear, plain language advising security holders to read the proxy statement when it is available because it contains important information. The legend also must explain to investors that they can get the proxy statement, and any other relevant documents, for free at the Commission's web site and describe which documents are available free from the participants; and

(2) A definitive proxy statement meeting the requirements of §240.14a-3(a) is sent or given to security holders solicited in reliance on this section before or at the same time as the forms of proxy, consent or authorization are furnished to or requested from security holders.

(b) Any soliciting material published, sent or given to security holders in accordance with paragraph (a) of this section must be filed with the Commission no later than the date the material is first published, sent or given to security holders. Three copies of the material must at the same time be filed with, or mailed for filing to, each national securities exchange upon which any class of securities of the registrant is listed and registered. The soliciting material must include a cover page in the form set forth in Schedule 14A (§240.14a-101) and the appropriate box on the cover page must be marked. Soliciting material in connection with a registered offering is required to be filed only under §230.424 or §230.425 of this chapter, and will be deemed filed under this section.

(c) Solicitations by any person or group of persons for the purpose of opposing a solicitation subject to this regulation by any other person or group of persons with respect to the election or removal of directors at any annual or special meeting of security holders also are subject to the following provisions:

(1) Application of this rule to annual report. Notwithstanding the provisions of §240.14a-3(b) and (c), any portion of the annual report referred to in §240.14a-3(b) that comments upon or refers to any solicitation subject to this rule, or to any participant in the solicitation, other

than the solicitation by the management, must be filed with the Commission as proxy material subject to this regulation. This must be filed in electronic format unless an exemption is available under Rules 201 or 202 of Regulation S-T (§232.201 or §232.202 of this chapter).

(2) Use of reprints or reproductions. In any solicitation subject to this §240.14a-12(c), soliciting material that includes, in whole or part, any reprints or reproductions of any previously published material must:

(i) State the name of the author and publication, the date of prior publication, and identify any person who is quoted without being named in the previously published material.

(ii) Except in the case of a public or official document or statement, state whether or not the consent of the author and publication has been obtained to the use of the previously published material as proxy soliciting material.

(iii) If any participant using the previously published material, or anyone on his or her behalf, paid, directly or indirectly, for the preparation or prior publication of the previously published material, or has made or proposes to make any payments or give any other consideration in connection with the publication or republication of the material, state the circumstances.

Instructions to §240.14a-12:

If paper filing is permitted, file eight copies of the soliciting material with the Commission, except that only three copies of the material specified by §240.14a-12(c)(1) need be filed.

Any communications made under this section after the definitive proxy statement is on file but before it is disseminated also must specify that the proxy statement is publicly available and the anticipated date of dissemination.

Rule 14a-13 (Reg. §240.14a-13). Obligation of Registrants in Communicating With Beneficial Owners

(a) If the registrant knows that securities of any class entitled to vote at a meeting (or by written consents or authorizations if no meeting is held) with respect to which the registrant intends to solicit proxies, consents or authorizations are held of record by a broker, dealer, voting trustee, bank, association, or other entity that exercises fiduciary powers in nominee name or otherwise, the registrant shall:

(1) By first class mail or other equally prompt means:

(i) inquire of each such record holder:

(A) whether other persons are the beneficial owners of such securities and if so, the number of copies of the proxy and other soliciting material necessary to supply such material to such beneficial owners;

(B) in the case of an annual (or special meeting in lieu of the annual) meeting, or written consents in lieu of such meeting, at which directors are to be elected, the number of copies of the annual report to security holders necessary to supply such report to beneficial owners to whom such reports are to be distributed by such record holder or its nominee not by the registrant; and

(C) if the record holder has an obligation under §240.14b-1(b)(3) or §240.14b-2(b)(4)(ii) and (iii), whether an agent has been designated to act on its behalf in fulfilling such obligation and, if so, the name and address of such agent; and

(D) whether it holds the registrant's securities on behalf of any respondent bank and, if so, the name and address of each such respondent bank; and

(ii) indicate to each such record holder:

(A) whether the registrant, pursuant to paragraph (c) of this section, intends to distribute the annual report to security holders to beneficial owners of its securities whose names, addresses and securities positions are disclosed pursuant to §240.14b-1(c) and §240.14b-2(e)(2) and (3);

(B) the record date; and

(C) at the option of the registrant, any employee benefit plan established by an affiliate of the registrant that holds securities of the registrant that the registrant elects to treat as exempt employee benefit plan securities;

(2) Upon receipt of a record holder's or respondent bank's response indicating, pursuant to §240.14b-2(b)(1)(i), the names and addresses of its respondent banks, within one business day after the date such response is received, make an inquiry of and give notification to each such respondent bank in the same manner required by paragraph (a)(1) of this section; Provided, however, the inquiry required by paragraphs (a)(1) and (a)(2) of this section shall not cover beneficial owners of exempt employee benefit plan securities;

(3) Make the inquiry required by paragraph (a)(1) of this section at least 20 business days prior to the record date of the meeting of security holders, or (i) if such inquiry is impracticable 20 business days prior to the record date of a special meeting, as many days before the record date of such meeting as is practicable or, (ii) if consents or authorizations are solicited, and such inquiry is impracticable 20 business days before the earliest date on which they may be used to effect corporate action, as many days before that date as is practicable, or (iii) at such later time as

the rules of a national securities exchange on which the class of securities in question is listed may permit for good cause shown; Provided, however, that if a record holder or respondent bank has informed the registrant that a designated office(s) or department(s) is to receive such inquiries, the inquiry shall be made to such designated office(s) or department(s); and

(4) Supply, in a timely manner, each record holder and respondent bank of whom the inquiries required by paragraphs (a)(1) and (a)(2) of this section are made with copies of the proxy, other proxy soliciting material, and/or the annual report to security holders, in such quantities, assembled in such form and at such place(s), as the record holder or respondent banks may reasonably request in order to send such material to each beneficial owner of securities who is to be furnished with such material by the record holder or respondent bank; and

(5) Upon the request of any record holder or respondent bank that is supplied with proxy soliciting material and/or annual reports to security holders pursuant to paragraph (a)(4) of this section, pay its reasonable expenses for completing the mailing of such material to beneficial owners.

Note 1: If the registrant's list of security holders indicates that some of its securities are registered in the name of a clearing agency registered pursuant to section 17A of the Act (e.g., "Cede & Co.," nominee for the Depository Trust Company), the registrant shall make appropriate inquiry of the clearing agency and thereafter of the participants in such clearing agency who may hold on behalf of a beneficial owner or respondent bank, and shall comply with the above paragraph with respect to any such participant [see §240.14a-1(i)].

Note 2: The attention of registrants is called to the fact that each broker, dealer, bank, association and other entity that exercises fiduciary powers has an obligation pursuant to §240.14b-1, §240.14b-2 (except as provided therein with respect to exempt employee benefit plan securities held in nominee name) and, with respect to brokers and dealers, applicable self-regulatory organization requirements to obtain and forward, within the time periods prescribed therein, (a) proxies (or in lieu thereof requests for voting instructions) and proxy soliciting materials to all beneficial owners on whose behalf it holds securities, and (b) annual reports to security holders to beneficial owners on whose behalf it holds securities, unless the registrant has notified the record holder or respondent bank that it has assumed responsibility to mail such material to beneficial owners whose names, addresses and securities positions are disclosed pursuant to §240.14b-1(b)(3) and §240.14b-2(b)(4)(ii) and (iii).

Note 3. The attention of registrants is called to the fact that registrants have an obligation, pursuant to paragraph (d) of this section, to cause proxies (or in lieu thereof requests for voting instructions), proxy soliciting material and annual reports to security holders to be furnished, in a timely manner, to beneficial owners of exempt employee benefit plan securities.

(b) Any registrant requesting pursuant to §240.14b-1(c)(3) or §240.14b-2(e)(2) and (3) a list of names, addresses and securities positions of beneficial owners of its securities who either have consented or have not objected to disclosure of such information shall:

(1) By first class mail or other equally prompt means, inquire of each record holder and each respondent bank identified to the registrant pursuant to §240.14b-2(b)(4)(i) whether such record holder or respondent bank holds the registrant's securities on behalf of any respondent banks and, if so, the name and address of each such respondent bank;

(2) Request such list to be compiled as of a date no earlier than five business days after the date the registrant's request is received by the record holder or respondent bank; Provided, however, that if the record holder or respondent bank has informed the registrant that a designated office(s) or department(s) is to receive such requests, the request shall be made to such designated office(s) or department(s);

(3) Make such request to the following persons that hold the registrant's securities on behalf of beneficial owners: all brokers, dealers, banks, associations and other entities that exercise fiduciary powers; Provided, however, such request shall not cover beneficial owners of exempt employee benefit plan securities as defined in §240.14a-1(d)(1); and, at the option of the registrant, such request may give notice of any employee benefit plan established by an affiliate of the registrant that holds securities of the registrant that the registrant elects to treat as exempt employee benefit plan securities.

(4) Use the information furnished in response to such request exclusively for purposes of corporate communications; and

(5) Upon the request of any record holder or respondent bank to whom such request is made, pay the reasonable expenses, both direct and indirect, of providing beneficial owner information.

Note: A registrant will be deemed to have satisfied its obligations under paragraph (b) of this section by requesting consenting and non-objecting beneficial owner lists from a designated agent acting on behalf of the record holder or respondent bank and paying to that designated agent the reasonable expenses of providing the beneficial owner information.

(c) A registrant, at its option, may mail its annual report to security holders to the beneficial owners whose identifying information is provided by record holders and respondent banks, pursuant to §240.14b-1(c) or §240.14b-2(e)(2) and (3), provided that such registrant notifies the record holders and respondent banks, at the time it makes the inquiry required by paragraph (a) of this section, that the registrant will mail the annual report to security holders to the beneficial owners so identified.

(d) If a registrant solicits proxies, consents or authorizations from record holders and respondent banks who hold securities on behalf of beneficial owners, the registrant shall cause proxies (or in lieu thereof requests for voting instructions), proxy soliciting material and annual reports to security holders to be furnished, in a timely manner, to beneficial owners of exempt employee benefit plan securities.

Rule 14a-14 (Reg. §240.14a-14). Modified or Superseded Documents

(a) Any statement contained in a document incorporated or deemed to be incorporated by reference shall be deemed to be modified or superseded, for purposes of the proxy statement, to the extent that a statement contained in the proxy statement or in any other subsequently filed document that also is or is deemed to be incorporated by reference modifies or replaces such statement.

(b) The modifying or superseding statement may, but need not, state it has modified or superseded a prior statement or include any other information set forth in the document that is not so modified or superseded. The making of a modifying or superseding statement shall not be deemed an admission that the modified or superseded statement, when made, constituted an untrue statement of a material fact, an omission to state a material fact necessary to make a statement not misleading, or the employment of a manipulative, deceptive, or fraudulent device, contrivance, scheme, transaction, act, practice, course of business or artifice to defraud, as those terms are used in the Securities Act of 1933, the Securities Exchange Act of 1934 ("the Act"), the Public Utility Holding Company Act of 1935, the Investment Company Act of 1940, or the rules and regulations thereunder.

(c) Any statement so modified shall not be deemed in its unmodified form to constitute part of the proxy statement for purposes of the Act. Any statement so superseded shall not be deemed to constitute a part of the proxy statement for purposes of the Act.

Rule 14a-15 (Reg. §240.14a-15). Differential and Contingent Compensation in Connection With Roll-up Transactions

(a) It shall be unlawful for any person to receive compensation for soliciting proxies, consents, or authorizations directly from security holders in connection with a roll-up transaction as provided in paragraph (b) of this section, if the compensation is:

(1) Based on whether the solicited proxy, consent, or authorization either approves or disapproves the proposed roll-up transaction; or

(2) Contingent on the approval, disapproval, or completion of the roll-up transaction.

(b) This section is applicable to a roll-up transaction as defined in Item 901(c) of Regulation S-K (§229.901(c) of this chapter), except for a transaction involving only:

(1) Finite-life entities that are not limited partnerships;

(2) Partnerships whose investors will receive new securities or securities in another entity that are not reported under a transaction reporting plan declared effective before December 17, 1993 by the Commission under Section 11A of the Act (15 U.S.C. 78k-1); or

(3) Partnerships whose investors' securities are reported under a transaction reporting plan declared effective before December 17, 1993 by the Commission under Section 11A of the Act (15 U.S.C. 78k-1).

Schedule 14A

Proxy Statement Pursuant to Section 14(a) of the Securities Exchange Act of 1934 (Amendment No.)

Filed by the Registrant [ ]

Filed by a Party other than the Registrant [ ]

Check the appropriate box:

[ ] Preliminary Proxy Statement

[ ] Confidential, for Use of the Commission Only (as permitted by Rule 14a-6(e)(2))

[ ] Definitive Proxy Statement

[ ] Definitive Additional Materials

[ ] Soliciting Material Pursuant to §240.14a-12

(Name of Registrant as Specified In Its Charter)

(Name of Person(s) Filing Proxy Statement, if other than the Registrant)

Payment of Filing Fee (Check the appropriate box):

[ ] No fee required.

[ ] Fee computed on table below per Exchange Act Rules 14a-6(i)(4) and 0-11.

1) Title of each class of securities to which transaction applies:

---

2) Aggregate number of securities to which transaction applies:

3) Per unit price or other underlying value of transaction computed pursuant to Exchange Act Rule 0-11 (set forth the amount on which the filing fee is calculated and state how it was determined):

---

4) Proposed maximum aggregate value of transaction:

---

5) Total fee paid:

_____

[ ] Fee paid previously with preliminary materials.

[ ] Check box if any part of the fee is offset as provided by Exchange Act Rule 0-11(a)(2) and identify the filing for which the offsetting fee was paid previously. Identify the previous filing by registration statement number, or the Form or

Schedule and the date of its filing.

1) Amount Previously Paid:

_____

2) Form, Schedule or Registration Statement No.:

_____

3) Filing Party:

_____

4) Date Filed:

_____

Reg. § 240.14a-101. Notes:

A. Where any item calls for information with respect to any matter to be acted upon and such matter involves other matters with respect to which information is called for by other items of this Schedule, the information called for by such other items shall also be given. For example, where a solicitation of security holders is for the purpose of approving the authorization of additional securities which are to be used to acquire another specified company, and the registrants' security holders will not have a separate opportunity to vote upon the transaction, the solicitation to authorize the securities is also a solicitation with respect to the acquisition. Under those facts, information required by Items 11, 13 and 14 shall be furnished.

B. Where any item calls for information with respect to any matter to be acted upon at the meeting, such item need be answered in the registrant's soliciting material only with respect to proposals to be made by or on behalf of the registrant.

C. Except as otherwise specifically provided, where any item calls for information for a specified period with regard to directors, executive officers, officers or other persons holding specified positions or relationships, the information shall be given with regard to any person who held any of the specified positions or relationships at any time during the period. Information need not be included for any portion of the period during which such person did not hold any such position or relationship, provided a statement to that effect is made.

D. Information may be incorporated by reference only in the manner and to the extent specifically permitted in the items of this schedule. Where incorporation by reference is used, the following shall apply:

1. Any incorporation by reference of information pursuant to the provisions of this Schedule shall be subject to the provisions of §228.10(f) and §229.10(d) restricting incorporation by reference of documents which incorporate by reference other information. A registrant incorporating any documents, or portions of documents, shall include a statement on the last page(s) of the proxy statement as to which documents, or portions of documents, are incorporated by reference. Information shall not be incorporated by reference in any case where such incorporation would render the statement incomplete, unclear or confusing.

2. If a document is incorporated by reference but not delivered to security holders, include an undertaking to provide, without charge, to each person to whom a proxy statement is delivered, upon written or oral request of such person and by first class mail or other equally prompt means within one business day of receipt of such request, a copy of any and all of the information that has been Incorporated by reference in the proxy statement (not including exhibits to the information that is incorporated by reference unless such exhibits are specifically incorporated by reference into the information that the proxy statement incorporates), and the address (including title or department) and telephone numbers to which such a request is to be directed. This includes information contained in documents filed subsequent to the date on which definitive copies of the proxy statement are sent or given to security holders, up to the date of responding to the request.

3. If a document or portion of a document other than an annual report sent to security holders pursuant to the requirements of Rule 14a-3 (§240.14a-3 of this chapter) with respect to the same meeting or solicitation of consents or authorizations as that to which the proxy statement relates is incorporated by reference in the manner permitted by Item 13(b) or 14(b) of this schedule, the proxy statement must be sent to security holders no later than 20 business days prior to the date on which the meeting of such security holders is held or, if no meeting is held, at least 20 business days prior to the date the votes, consents or authorizations may be used to effect the corporate action.

4. *Electronic filings.* If any of the information required by Items 13 or 14 of this Schedule is incorporated by reference from an annual or quarterly report to security holders, such report, or any portion thereof incorporated

by reference, shall be filed in electronic format with the proxy statement. This provision shall not apply to registered investment companies.

E. In Items 13 and 14 of this Schedule, the reference to "meets the requirements of Form S-2" shall refer to a registrant or to an "other person" specified in Item 14(a) of this Schedule which meets the requirements for use of Form S-2 (§239.12 of this chapter) and the reference to "meets the requirement of Form S-3" shall refer to a registrant or to an "other person" specified in Item 14(a) of this Schedule which meets the following requirements.

1. the registrant or other person meets the requirements of General Instruction I.A. of Form S-3 (§239.13 of this chapter);

and

2. one of the following is met:

(i) the registrant or other person meets the aggregate market value requirement of General Instruction I.B.1 of Form S-3;

or

(ii) action is to be taken as described in Items 11, 12 and 14 of this Schedule which concerns non-convertible debt or preferred securities which are "investment grade securities" as defined in General Instruction I.B.2 of Form S-3, except that the time by which the rating must be assigned shall be the date on which definitive copies of the proxy statement are first sent or given to security holders; or

(iii) the registrant or other person is a majority-owned subsidiary and one of the conditions of General Instruction I.C. of Form S-3 is met.

F. Note to Small Business Issuers—Registrants and acquirees that meet the definition of "small business issuer" under Rule 12b-2 of the Exchange Act (§240.12b-2) shall refer to the disclosure items in Regulation S-B (§228.10 et seq. of this chapter) and not Regulation S-K (§229.10 et seq. of this chapter). If there is no comparable disclosure item in Regulation S-B, small business issuers need not provide the information requested. Small business issuers shall provide the financial information in Item 310 of Regulation S-B in lieu of the financial statements required in Schedule 14A.

G. Special Note for Small Business Issuers.

(1) Registrants and acquirees which meet the definition of "small business issuer" in Rule 12b-2 of the Exchange Act and filed their latest annual report in accordance with "Information Required in Annual Report of Transitional Small Business Issuers" in form 10-KSB shall refer to this "Special Note for Small Business Issuers" with respect to the specified items in this Schedule. If paragraph G(2) or G(3), below, does not contain

an alternative disclosure instruction, small business issuers should comply with the disclosure item in this schedule, as modified by Instruction F.

(2) Registrants and acquirees which relied upon Alternative 1 in their most recent Form 10-KSB may provide the following information (Question numbers are in reference to Model A of Form 1-A): (a) Questions 37 and 38 instead of Item 6(d); (b) Question 43 instead of Item 7(a); (c) Questions 29-36 and 39 instead of Item 7(b); (d) Questions 40-42 instead of Item 8; (e) Questions 40-42 instead of Item 10; (e) the information required in Part F/S of Form 10-SB instead of the financial statement requirements of Items 13 or 14; (f) Questions 4, 11 and 47-50 instead of Item 13(a)(1)(3); (g) Question 3 instead of Item 14(b)(3)(i)(A) and (B); and (h) Questions 4, 11 and 47-50 instead of Item 14(b)(3)(i)(H).

(3) Registrants and acquirees which relied upon Alternative 2 in their most recent Form 10-KSB may provide the following information ("Model B" refers to Model B of Form 1-A): (a) Item 10 of Model B instead of Item 6(d) of Schedule 14A; (b) Item 8(d) of Model B instead of Item 7(a) of Schedule 14A: (c) Items 8(a)-8(c) and Item II of Model B instead of Item 7(b) of Schedule 14A; (d) Item 9 of Model B instead of Item 8 of Schedule 14A; (e) Item 9 of Model B instead of Item 10 of Schedule 14A; (f) the information required in Part F/S of Form 10-SB instead of the financial statement requirements of Items 13 or 14 of Schedule 14A; (g) Item 6(a)(3)(i) of Model B instead of Item 13(a)(1)(3) of Schedule 14A; (h) Items 6 and 7 of Model B instead of Item 14(b)(3)(i)(A) and (B) of Schedule 14A; and (i) Item 6(a)(3)(i) of Model B instead of Item 14(b)(3)(i)(H) of Schedule 14A.

Item 1. Date, Time and Place Information

(a) State the date, time and place of the meeting of security holders, and the complete mailing address, including Zip Code, of the principal executive officers of the registrant, unless such information is otherwise disclosed in material furnished to security holders with or preceding the proxy statement. If action is to be taken by written consent, state the date by which consents are to be submitted if state law requires that such a date be specified or if the person soliciting intends to set a date.

(b) On the first page of the proxy statement, as delivered to security holders, state the approximate date on which the proxy statement and form of proxy are first sent or given to security holders.

(c) Furnish the information required to be in the proxy statement by Rule 14a-5(e) (§240.14a-5(e) of this chapter).

Item 2. Revocability of Proxy

State whether or not the person giving the proxy has the power to revoke it. If the right of revocation before the proxy is exercised is limited or is subject to compliance with any formal procedure, briefly describe such limitation or procedure.

Item 3. Dissenters' Right of Appraisal

Outline briefly the rights of appraisal or similar rights of dissenters with respect to any matter to be acted upon and indicate any statutory procedure required to be followed by dissenting security holders in order to perfect such rights. Where such rights may be exercised only within a limited time after the date of adoption of a proposal, the filing of a charter amendment or other similar act, state whether the persons solicited will be notified of such date.

Instructions.

1. Indicate whether a security holder's failure to vote against a proposal will constitute a waiver of his appraisal or similar rights and whether a vote against a proposal will be deemed to satisfy any notice requirements under State law with respect to appraisal rights. If the State law is unclear, state what position will be taken in regard to these matters.

2. Open-end investment companies registered under the Investment Company Act of 1940 are not required to respond to this item.

Item 4. Persons Making the Solicitation

(a) *Solicitations not subject to Rule 14a-12(c) (§240.14a-12(c) of this chapter).*

(1) If the solicitation is made by the registrant, so state. Give the name of any director of the registrant who has informed the registrant in writing that he intends to oppose any action intended to be taken by the registrant and indicate the action which he intends to oppose.

(2) If the solicitation is made otherwise than by the registrant, so state and give the names of the participants in the solicitation, as defined in paragraphs (a)(iii), (iv), (v) and (vi) of Instruction 3 to this Item.

(3) If the solicitation is to be made otherwise than by the use of the malls, describe the methods to be employed. If the solicitation is to be made by specially engaged employees or paid solicitors, state (i) the material features of any contract or arrangement for such solicitation and identify the parties, and (ii) the cost or anticipated cost thereof.

(4) State the names of the persons by whom the cost of solicitation has been or will be borne, directly or indirectly.

(b) *Solicitations subject to Rule 14a-12(c) (§240.14a-12(c) of this chapter).*

(1) State by whom the solicitation is made and describe the methods employed and to be employed to solicit security holders.

(2) If regular employees of the registrant or any other participant in a solicitation have been or are to be employed to solicit security holders, describe the class or classes of employees to be so employed, and the manner and nature of their employment for such purpose.

(3) If specially engaged employees, representatives or other persons have been or are to be employed to solicit security holders, state (i) the material features of any contract or arrangement for such solicitation and the identity of the parties, (ii) the cost or anticipated cost thereof, and (iii) the approximate number of such employees or employees of any other person (naming such other person) who will solicit security holders).

(4) State the total amount estimated to be spent and the total expenditures to date for, in furtherance of, or in connection with the solicitation of security holders.

(5) State by whom the cost of the solicitation will be borne. If such cost is to be borne initially by any person other than the registrant, state whether reimbursement will be sought from the registrant, and, if so, whether the question of such reimbursement will be submitted to a vote of security holders.

(6) If any such solicitation is terminated pursuant to a settlement between the registrant and any other participant in such solicitation, describe the terms of such settlement, including the cost or anticipated cost thereof to the registrant.

Instructions.

1. With respect to solicitations subject to Rule 14a-12(c) (§240.14a-12(c) of this chapter), costs and expenditures within the meaning of this Item 4 shall include fees for attorneys, accountants, public relations or financial advisers, solicitors, advertising, printing, transportation, litigation and other costs incidental to the solicitation, except that the registrant may exclude the amount of such costs represented by the amount normally expended for a solicitation for an election of directors in the absence of a contest, and costs represented by salaries and wages of regular employees and officers, provided a statement to that effect is included in the proxy statement.

2. The information required pursuant to paragraph (b)(6) of this Item should be included in any amended or revised proxy statement or other soliciting materials relating to the same meeting or subject matter furnished to security holders by the registrant subsequent to the date of settlement.

3. For purposes of this Item 4 and Item 5 of this Schedule 14A:

(a) The terms "participant" and "participant in a solicitation" include the following:

(i) the registrant;

(ii) any director of the registrant, and any nominee for whose election as a director proxies are solicited;

(iii) any committee or group which solicits proxies, any member of such committee or group, and any person whether or not named as a member who, acting alone or with one or more other persons, directly or indirectly takes the initiative, or engages, in organizing, directing, or arranging for the financing of any such committee or group;

(iv) any person who finances or joins with another to finance the solicitation of proxies, except persons who contribute not more than $500 and who are not otherwise participants;

(v) any person who lends money or furnishes credit or enters into any other arrangements, pursuant to any contract or understanding with a participant, for the purpose of financing or otherwise inducing the purchase, sale, holding or voting of securities of the registrant by any participant or other persons, in support of or in opposition to a participant; except that such terms do not include a bank, broker or dealer who, in the ordinary course of business, lends money or executes orders for the purchase or sale of securities and who is not otherwise a participant; and

(vi) any person who solicits proxies.

(b) The terms "participant" and "participant in a solicitation" do not include:

(i) any person or organization retained or employed by a participant to solicit security holders and whose activities are limited to the duties required to be performed in the course of such employment;

(ii) any person who merely transmits proxy soliciting material or performs other ministerial or clerical duties;

(iii) any person employed by a participant in the capacity of attorney, accountant, or advertising, public relations or financial adviser, and whose activities are limited to the duties required to be performed in the course of such employment;

(iv) any person regularly employed as an officer or employee of the registrant or any of its subsidiaries who is not otherwise a participant; or

(v) any officer or director of, or any person regularly employed by, any other participant, if such officer, director or employee is not otherwise a participant.

Item 5. Interest of Certain Persons in Matters to Be Acted Upon

(a) *Solicitations not subject to Rule 14a-12(c) (§240.14a-12(c) of this chapter).* Describe briefly any substantial interest, direct or indirect, by security holdings or otherwise, of each of the following persons in any matter to be acted upon, other than elections to office:

(1) If the solicitation is made on behalf of the registrant, each person who has been a director or executive officer of the registrant at any time since the beginning of the last fiscal year.

(2) If the solicitation is made otherwise than on behalf of the registrant, each participant in the solicitation, as defined in paragraphs (a)(iii), (iv), (v), and (vi) of Instruction 3 to Item 4 of this Schedule 14A.

(3) Each nominee for election as a director of the registrant.

(4) Each associate of any of the foregoing persons.

Instruction. Except in the case of a solicitation subject to this regulation made in opposition to another solicitation subject to this regulation, the sub-item (a) shall not apply to any interest arising from the ownership of securities of the registrant where the security holder receives no extra or special benefit not shared on a pro rata basis by all other holders of the same class.

(b) *Solicitation subject to Rule 14a-12(c) (§240.14a-12(c) of this chapter).* With respect to any solicitation subject to Rule 14a-12(c).

(1) Describe briefly any substantial interest, direct or indirect, by security holdings or otherwise, of each participant as defined in paragraphs (a)(ii), (iii), (iv), (v) and (vi) of Instruction 3 to Item 4 of this Schedule 14A, in any matter to be acted upon at the meeting, and include with respect to each participant the following information, or a fair and adequate summary thereof:

(i) Name and business address of the participant.

(ii) The participant's present principal occupation or employment and the name, principal business and address of any corporation or other organization in which such employment is carried on.

(iii) State whether or not, during the past ten years, the participant has been convicted in a criminal proceeding (excluding traffic violations or similar misdemeanors) and, if so, give dates, nature of conviction, name and location of court, and penalty imposed or other disposition of the case. A negative answer need not be included in the proxy statement or other soliciting material.

(iv) State the amount of each class of securities of the registrant which the participant owns beneficially, directly or indirectly.

(v) State the amount of each class of securities of the registrant which the participant owns of record but not beneficially.

(vi) State with respect to all securities of the registrant purchased or sold within the past two years, the dates on which they were purchased or sold and the amount purchased or sold on each such date.

(vii) If any part of the purchase price or market value of any of the shares specified in paragraph (b)(1)(vi) of this Item is represented by funds borrowed or otherwise obtained for the purpose of acquiring or holding such securities, so state and indicate the amount of the indebtedness as of the latest practicable date. If such funds were borrowed or obtained otherwise than pursuant to a margin account or bank loan in the regular course of business of a bank, broker or dealer, briefly describe the transaction, and state the names of the parties.

(viii) State whether or not the participant is, or was within the past year, a party to any contract, arrangements or understandings with any person with respect to any securities of the registrant, including, but not limited to, joint ventures, loan or option arrangements, puts or calls, guarantees against loss or guarantees of profit, division of losses or profits, or the giving or withholding of proxies. If so, name the parties to such contracts, arrangements or understandings and give the details thereof.

(ix) State the amount of securities of the registrant owned beneficially, directly or indirectly, by each of the participant's associates and the name and address of each such associate.

(x) State the amount of each class of securities of any parent or subsidiary of the registrant which the participant owns beneficially, directly or indirectly.

(xi) Furnish for the participant and associates of the participant the information required by Item 404(a) of Regulation S-K (§229.404(a) of this chapter).

(xii) State whether or not the participant or any associates of the participant have any arrangement or understanding with any person—

(A) with respect to any future employment by the registrant or its affiliates; or

(B) with respect to any future transactions to which the registrant or any of its affiliates will or may be a party.

If so, describe such arrangement or understanding and state the names of the parties thereto.

(2) With respect to any person, other than a director or executive officer of the registrant acting solely in that capacity, who is a party to an arrangement or understanding pursuant to which a nominee for election as director is proposed to be elected, describe any substantial interest, direct or indirect, by security holdings or otherwise, that such person has in any matter to be acted upon at the meeting, and furnish the information called for by paragraphs (b)(1)(xi) and (xii) of this Item.

Instruction: For purposes of this Item 5, beneficial ownership shall be determined in accordance with Rule 13d-3 under the Act (Section 240.13d-3 of this chapter).

Item 6. Voting Securities and Principal Holders Thereof

(a) As to each class of voting securities of the registrant entitled to be voted at the meeting (or by written consents or authorizations if no meeting is held), state the number of shares outstanding and the number of votes to which each class is entitled.

(b) State the record date, if any, with respect to this solicitation. If the right to vote or give consent is not to be determined, in whole or in part, by reference to a record date, indicate the criteria for the determination of security holders entitled to vote or give consent.

(c) If action is to be taken with respect to the election of directors and if the persons solicited have cumulative voting rights:

(1) Make a statement that they have such rights, (2) briefly describe such rights, (3) state briefly the conditions precedent to the exercise thereof, and (4) if discretionary authority to cumulate votes is solicited, so indicate.

(d) Furnish the information required by Item 403 of Regulation S-K (§229.403 of this chapter) to the extent known by the persons on whose behalf the solicitation is made.

(e) If, to the knowledge of the persons on whose behalf the solicitation is made, a change in control of the registrant has occurred since the beginning of its last fiscal year, state the name of the person(s) who acquired such control, the amount and the source of the consideration used by such person or persons; the basis of the control, the date and a description of the transaction(s) which resulted in the change of control and the percentage of voting securities of the registrant now beneficially owned directly or indirectly by the person(s) who acquired control; and the identity of the person(s) from whom control was assumed. If the source of all or any part of the consideration used is a loan made in the ordinary course of business by a bank as defined by section 3(a)(6) of the Act, the identity of such bank shall be omitted provided a request for confidentiality has been made pursuant to section 13(d)(1)(B) of the Act by the person(s) who acquired control. In lieu thereof, the material shall indicate that the identity of the bank has been so omitted and filed separately with the Commission.

Instructions.

1. State the terms of any loans or pledges obtained by the new control group for the purposes of acquiring control, and the names of the lenders or pledgees.

2. Any arrangements or understandings among members of both the former and new control groups and their associates with respect to election of directors or other matters should be described.

Item 7. Directors and Executive Officers

If action is to be taken with respect to the election of directors, furnish the following information in tabular form to the extent practicable. If, however, the solicitation is made on behalf of persons other than the registrant, the information required need be furnished only as to nominees of the persons making the solicitation.

(a) The information required by Instruction 4 to Item 103 of Regulation S-K (§229.103 of this chapter) with respect to directors and executive officers.

(b) The information required by Items 401, 404(a) and (c), and 405 of Regulation S-K (§229.401, §229.404 and §229.405 of this chapter).

(c) The information required by Item 404(b) of Regulation S-K (§229.404 of this chapter).

(d) (1) State whether or not the registrant has standing audit, nominating and compensation committees of the Board of Directors, or committees performing similar functions. If the registrant has such committees, however designated, identify each committee member, state the number of committee meetings held by each such committee during the last fiscal year and describe briefly the functions performed by such committees. Such disclosure need not be provided to the extent it is duplicative of disclosure provided in accordance with Item 401(i) of Regulation S-K (§229.401(i) of this chapter).

(2) If the registrant has a nominating or similar committee, state whether the committee will consider nominees recommended by security holders and, if so, describe the procedures to be followed by security holders in submitting such recommendations.

(3) If the registrant has an audit committee:

(i) Provide the information required by Item 306 of Regulation S-K (17 CFR 229.306).

(ii) State whether the registrant's Board of Directors has adopted a written charter for the audit committee.

(iii) Include a copy of the written charter, if any, as an appendix to the registrant's proxy statement, unless a copy has been included as an appendix to the registrant's proxy statement within the registrant's past three fiscal years.

(iv) (A) If the registrant is a listed issuer, as defined in § 240.10A-3:

(1) Disclose whether the members of the audit committee are independent, as independence for audit committee members is defined in the listing standards applicable to the listed issuer. If the registrant does not have a separately designated audit committee, or committee performing

similar functions, the registrant must provide the disclosure with respect to all members of its board of directors.

(2) If the listed issuer's board of directors determines, in accordance with the listing standards applicable to the listed issuer, to appoint a director to the audit committee who is not independent (apart from the requirements in § 240.10A-3) because of exceptional or limited or similar circumstances, disclose the nature of the relationship that makes that individual not independent and the reasons for the board of directors' determination.

(B) If the registrant, including a small business issuer, is not a listed issuer, disclose whether the registrant has an audit committee established in accordance with section 3(a)(58)(A) of the Act (15 U.S.C. 78c(a)(58)(A)) and, if so, whether the members of the committee are independent. In determining whether a member is independent, the registrant must use a definition for audit committee member independence of a national securities exchange registered pursuant to section 6(a) of the Act (15 U.S.C. 78f(a)) or a national securities association registered pursuant to section 15A(a) of the Act (15 U.S.C. 78o-3(a)) that has been approved by the Commission (as such definition may be modified or supplemented), and state which definition was used. Whichever definition is chosen must be applied consistently to all members of the audit committee.

(v) The information required by paragraph (d)(3) of this Item shall not be deemed to be "soliciting material," or to be "filed" with the Commission or subject to Regulation 14A or 14C (17 CFR 240.14a-1 *et seq.* or 240.14c-1 *et seq.*), other than as provided in this Item, or to the liabilities of section 18 of the Exchange Act (15 U.S.C. § 78r), except to the extent that the registrant specifically requests that the information be treated as soliciting material or specifically incorporates it by reference into a document filed under the Securities Act or the Exchange Act. Such information will not be deemed to be incorporated by reference into any filing under the Securities Act or the Exchange Act, except to the extent that the registrant specifically incorporates it by reference.

(vi) The disclosure required by this paragraph (d)(3) need only be provided one time during any fiscal year.*

(vii) Investment companies registered under the Investment Company Act of 1940 (15 U.S.C. § 80a-1 *et seq.*), other than closed-end investment companies, need not provide the information required by this paragraph (d)(3).

(e) In lieu of paragraphs (a) through (d)(2) of this Item, investment companies registered under the Investment Company Act of 1940 (15 U.S.C. 80a) must furnish the information required by Item 22(b) of this Schedule 14A.

(f) State the total number of meetings of the board of directors (including regularly scheduled and special meetings) which were held during the last full fiscal year. Name each incumbent director who during the last full fiscal year attended fewer then 75 percent of the aggregate of (1) the total number of meetings of the board of directors (held during the period for which he has been a director) and (2) the total number of meetings held by all committees of the board on which he served (during the periods that he served).

(g) If a director has resigned or declined to stand for re-election to the board of directors since the date of the last annual meeting of security holders because of a disagreement with the registrant on any matter relating to the registrant's operations, policies or practices, and if the director has furnished the registrant with a letter describing such disagreement and requesting that the matter be disclosed, the registrant shall state the date of resignation or declination to stand for reelection and summarize the director's description of the disagreement. If the registrant believes that the description provided by the director is incorrect or incomplete, it may include a brief statement presenting its views of the disagreement.

Item 8. Compensation of Directors and Executive Officers

Furnish the information required by Item 402 (§ 229.402 of this chapter) of Regulation S-K if action is to be taken with regard to:

(a) the election of directors;

(b) any bonus, profit sharing or other compensation plan, contract or arrangement in which any director, nominee for election as a director, or executive officer of the registrant will participate;

(c) any pension or retirement plan in which any such person will participate; or

(d) the granting or extension to any such person of any options, warrants or rights to purchase any securities, other than warrants or rights issued to security holders as such, on a pro rata basis. However, if the solicitation is made on behalf of persons other than the registrant, the information required need be furnished only as to nominees of the persons making the solicitation and associates of such nominees. In the case of investment companies registered under the Investment Company Act of 1940 and registrants that have elected to be regulated as business development companies, furnish the information required by Item 22(b)(13) of this Schedule.

Instruction. If an otherwise reportable compensation plan became subject to such requirements because of an acquisition or merger and, within one year of the acquisition or merger, such plan was terminated for purposes of prospective eligibility, the registrant may furnish a description of its obligation to the designated individuals pursuant to the compensation plan. Such description may be furnished in lieu of a description of the compensation plan in the proxy statement.

Item 9. Independent Public Accountants

If the solicitation is made on behalf of the registrant and relates to (1) the annual (or special meeting in lieu of annual) meeting of security holders at which directors are to be elected, or a solicitation of consents or authorizations in lieu of such meeting or (2) the election, approval or ratification of the registrant's accountant, furnish the following information describing the registrant's relationship with its independent public accountant:

(a) The name of the principal accountant selected or being recommended to security holders for election, approval or ratification for the current year. If no accountant has been selected or recommended, so state and briefly describe the reasons therefor.

(b) The name of the principal accountant for the fiscal year most recently completed if different from the accountant selected or recommended for the current year or if no accountant has yet been selected or recommended for the current year.

(c) The proxy statement shall indicate (1) whether or not representatives of the principal accountant for the current year and for the most recently completed fiscal year are expected to be present at the security holders' meeting, (2) whether or not they will have the opportunity to make a statement if they desire to do so and (3) whether or not such representatives are expected to be available to respond to appropriate questions.

(d) If during the registrant's two most recent fiscal years or any subsequent interim period, (1) an independent accountant who was previously engaged as the principal accountant to audit the registrant's financial statements, or an independent accountant on whom the principal accountant expressed reliance in its report regarding a significant subsidiary, has resigned (or indicated it has declined to stand for reelection after the completion of the current audit) or was dismissed, or (2) a new independent accountant has been engaged as either the principal accountant to audit the registrant's financial statements or as an independent accountant on whom the principal accountant has expressed or is expected to express reliance in its report regarding a significant subsidiary, then, notwithstanding any previous disclosure, provide the information required by Item 304(a) of Regulation S-K (§229.304 of this chapter).

(e) (1) Disclose, under the caption Audit Fees, the aggregate fees billed for each of the last two fiscal years for professional services rendered by the principal accountant for the audit of the registrant's annual financial statements and review of financial statements included in the registrant's Form 10-Q (17 CFR 249.308a) or 10-QSB (17 CFR 249.308b) or services that are normally provided by the accountant in connection with statutory and regulatory filings or engagements for those fiscal years.

(2) Disclose, under the caption Audit-Related Fees, the aggregate fees billed in each of the last two fiscal years for assurance and related services by the principal accountant that are reasonably related to the performance of the audit or review of the registrant's financial statements and are not reported under paragraph (e)(1) of this section. Registrants shall describe the nature of the services comprising the fees disclosed under this category.

(3) Disclose, under the caption Tax Fees, the aggregate fees billed in each of the last two fiscal years for professional services rendered by the principal accountant for tax compliance, tax advice, and tax planning. Registrants shall describe the nature of the services comprising the fees disclosed under this category.

(4) Disclose, under the caption All Other Fees, the aggregate fees billed in each of the last two fiscal years for products and services provided by the principal accountant, other than the services reported in paragraphs (e)(1) through (e)(3) of this section. Registrants shall describe the nature of the services comprising the fees disclosed under this category.

(5)(i) Disclose the audit committee's pre-approval policies and procedures described in 17 CFR 210.2-01(c)(7)(i).

(ii) Disclose the percentage of services described in each of paragraphs (e)(2) through (e)(4) of this section that were approved by the audit committee pursuant to 17 CFR 210.2-01(c)(7)(i)(C).

(6) If greater than 50 percent, disclose the percentage of hours expended on the principal accountant's engagement to audit the registrant's financial statements for the most recent fiscal year that were attributed to work performed by persons other than the principal accountant's full-time, permanent employees.

(7) If the registrant is an investment company, disclose the aggregate non-audit fees billed by the registrant's accountant for services rendered to the registrant, and to the registrant's investment adviser (not including any subadviser whose role is primarily portfolio management and is subcontracted with or overseen by another investment adviser), and any entity controlling, controlled by, or under common control with the adviser that provides ongoing services to the registrant for each of the last two fiscal years of the registrant.

(8) If the registrant is an investment company, disclose whether the audit committee of the board of directors has considered whether the

provision of non-audit services that were rendered to the registrant's investment adviser (not including any subadviser whose role is primarily portfolio management and is subcontracted with or overseen by another investment adviser), and any entity controlling, controlled by, or under common control with the investment adviser that provides ongoing services to the registrant that were not pre-approved pursuant to 17 CFR 210.2-01(c)(7)(ii) is compatible with maintaining the principal accountant's independence.

Instruction to Item 9(e).

For purposes of Item 9(e)(2), (3), and (4), registrants that are investment companies must disclose fees billed for services rendered to the registrant and separately, disclose fees required to be approved by the investment company registrant's audit committee pursuant to 17 CFR 210.2-01(c)(7)(ii). Registered investment companies must also disclose the fee percentages as required by item 9(e)(5)(ii) for the registrant and separately, disclose the fee percentages as required by item 9(e)(5)(ii) for the fees required to be approved by the investment company registrant's audit committee pursuant to 17 CFR 210.2-01(c)(7)(ii).

Item 10. Compensation Plans

If action is to be taken with respect to any plan pursuant to which cash or noncash compensation may be paid or distributed, furnish the following information:

(a) *Plans Subject to Securityholder Action.*

(1) Describe briefly the material features of the plan being acted upon, identify each class of persons who will be eligible to participate therein, indicate the approximate number of persons in each such class and state the basis of such participation.

(2) (i) In the tabular format specified below, disclose the benefits or amounts that will be received by or allocated to each of the following under the plan being acted upon, if such benefits or amounts are determinable:

NEW PLAN BENEFITS

Plan Name

Name and Position	Dollar Value ($)	Number of Units
CEO		
A		
B		
C		
D		
Executive Group		
Non-Executive Director Group		
Non-Executive Officer Employee Group		

(ii) The table required by paragraph (a)(2)(i) of this Item shall provide information as to the following persons:

(A) Each person (stating name and position) specified in paragraph (a)(3) of Item 402 of Regulation S-K (§ 229.402(a)(3) of this chapter);

Instruction. In the case of investment companies registered under the Investment Company Act of 1940, furnish the information for Compensated Persons as defined in Item 22(b)(13) of this Schedule in lieu of the persons specified in paragraph (a)(3) of Item 402 of Regulation S-K (§229.402(a)(3) of this chapter).

(B) All current executive officers as a group;

(C) All current directors who are not executive officers as a group; and

(D) All employees, including all current officers who are not executive officers, as a group.

Instruction to New Plan Benefits Table. Additional columns should be added for each plan with respect to which security holder action is to be taken.

(iii) If the benefits or amounts specified in paragraph (a)(2)(i) of this Item are not determinable, state the benefits or amounts which would have been received by or allocated to each of the following for the last completed fiscal year if the plan had been in effect, if such benefits or amounts may be determined in the table specified in paragraph (a)(2)(i) of this Item:

(A) Each person (stating name and position) specified in paragraph (a) (3) of Item 402 of Regulation S-K (§ 229.402(a)(3) of this chapter);

(B) All current executive officers as a group;

(C) All current directors who are not executive officers as a group; and

(D) All employees, including all current officers who are not executive officers, as a group.

(3) If the plan to be acted upon can be amended, otherwise than by a vote of security holders, to increase the cost thereof to the registrant or to alter the allocation of the benefits as between the persons and groups specified in paragraph (a)(2) of this item, state the nature of the amendments which can be so made.

(b) *Additional Information Regarding Specific Plans Subject to Security Holder Action.*

(1) With respect to any pension or retirement plan submitted for security holder action, state:

(i) The approximate total amount necessary to fund the plan with respect to past services, the period over which such amount is to be paid and the estimated annual payments necessary to pay the total amount over such period; and

(ii) The estimated annual payment to be made with respect to current services. In the case of a pension or retirement plan, information called for by paragraph (a)(2) of this Item may be furnished in the format specified by paragraph (f)(1) of Item 402 of Regulation S-K (§ 229.402(f)(1) of this chapter).

Instruction. In the case of investment companies registered under the Investment Company Act of 1940, refer to instruction 4 if Item 22(b)(13)(i) of this Schedule in lieu of paragraph (f)(1) of Item 402 of Regulation S-K (§229.402(f)(1) of this chapter).

(2) (i) With respect to any specific grant of or any plan containing options, warrants or rights submitted for security holder action, state:

(A) The title and amount of securities underlying such options, warrants or rights;

(B) The prices, expiration dates and other material conditions upon which the options, warrants or rights may be exercised;

(C) The consideration received or to be received by the registrant or subsidiary for the granting or extension of the options, warrants or rights;

(D) The market value of the securities underlying the options, warrants, or rights as of the latest practicable date; and

(E) In the case of options, the federal income tax consequences of the issuance and exercise of such options to the recipient and the registrant; and

(ii) State separately the amount of such options received or to be received by the following persons if such benefits or amounts are determinable:

(A) Each person (stating name and position) specified in paragraph (a)(3) of Item 402 of Regulation S-K (§ 229.402(a)(3) of this chapter);

(B) All current executive officers as a group;

(C) All current directors who are not executive officers as a group;

(D) Each nominee for election as a director;

(E) Each associate of any of such directors, executive officers or nominees;

(F) Each other person who received or is to receive 5 percent of such options, warrants or rights; and

(G) All employees, including all current officers who are not executive officers, as a group.

Instructions.

1. The term "plan" as used in this Item means any plan as defined in paragraph (a)(7)(ii) of Item 402 of Regulation S-K (§229.402(a)(7)(ii) of this chapter).

2. If action is to be taken with respect to a material amendment or modification of an existing plan, the item shall be answered with respect to the plan as proposed to be amended or modified and shall indicate any material differences from the existing plan.

3. If the plan to be acted upon is set forth in a written document, three copies thereof shall be filed with the Commission at the time copies of the proxy statement and form of proxy are first filed pursuant to paragraph (a) or (b) of §240.14a-6. Electronic filers shall file with the Commission a copy of such written plan document in electronic format as an appendix to the proxy statement. It need not be provided to security holders unless it is a part of the proxy statement.

4. Paragraph (b)(2)(ii) does not apply to warrants or rights to be issued to security holders as such on a pro rata basis.

5. The Commission should be informed, as supplemental information, when the proxy statement is first filed, as to when the options, warrants or rights and the shares called for thereby will be registered under the Securities Act or, if such registration is not contemplated, the section of the Securities Act or rule of the Commission under which exemption

from such registration is claimed and the facts relied upon to make the exemption available.

Item 11. Authorization or Issuance of Securities Otherwise than for Exchange

If action is to be taken with respect to the authorization or issuance of any securities otherwise than for exchange for outstanding securities of the registrant, furnish the following information:

(a) State the title and amount of securities to be authorized or issued.

(b) Furnish the information required by Item 202 of Regulation S-K (§229.202 of this chapter). If the terms of the securities cannot be stated or estimated with respect to any or all of the securities to be authorized, because no offering thereof is contemplated in the proximate future, and if no further authorization by security holders for the issuance thereof is to be obtained, it should be stated that the terms of the securities to be authorized, including dividend or interest rates, conversion prices, voting rights, redemption prices, maturity dates, and similar matters will be determined by the board of directors. If the securities are additional shares of common stock of a class outstanding, the description may be omitted except for a statement of the preemptive rights, if any. Where the statutory provisions with respect to preemptive rights are so indefinite or complex that they cannot be stated in summarized form, it will suffice to make a statement in the form of an opinion of counsel as to the existence and extent of such rights.

(c) Describe briefly the transaction in which the securities are to be issued including a statement as to (1) the nature and approximate amount of consideration received or to be received by the registrant and (2) the approximate amount devoted to each purpose so far as determinable for which the net proceeds have been or are to be used. If it is impracticable to describe the transaction in which the securities are to be issued, state the reason, indicate the purpose of the authorization of the securities, and state whether further authorization for the issuance of the securities by a vote of security holders will be solicited prior to such issuance.

(d) If the securities are to be issued otherwise than in a public offering for cash, state the reasons for the proposed authorization or issuance and the general effect thereof upon the rights of existing security holders.

(e) Furnish the information required by Item 13(a) of this Schedule.

Item 12. Modification or Exchange of Securities

If action is to be taken with respect to the modification of any class of securities of the registrant, or the issuance or authorization for issuance of securities of the registrant in exchange for outstanding securities of the registrant, furnish the following information:

(a) If outstanding securities are to be modified, state the title and amount thereof. If securities are to be issued in exchange for outstanding securities, state the title and amount of securities to be so issued, the title and amount of outstanding securities to be exchanged therefor and the basis of the exchange.

(b) Describe any material differences between the outstanding securities and the modified or new securities in respect of any of the matters concerning which information would be required in the description of the securities in Item 202 of Regulation S-K (§229.202 of this chapter).

(c) State the reasons for the proposed modification or exchange and the general effect thereof upon the rights of existing security holders.

(d) Furnish a brief statement as to arrears in dividends or as to defaults in principal or interest in respect to the outstanding securities which are to be modified or exchanged and such other information as may be appropriate in the particular case to disclose adequately the nature and effect of the proposed action.

(e) Outline briefly any other material features of the proposed modification or exchange. If the plan of proposed action is set forth in a written document, file copies thereof with the Commission in accordance with §240.14a-8.

(f) Furnish the information required by Item 13(a) of this Schedule.

Instruction. If the existing security is presently listed and registered on a national securities exchange, state whether the registrant intends to apply for listing and registration of the new or reclassified security on such exchange or any other exchange. If the registrant does not intend to make such application, state the effect of the termination of such listing and registration.

Item 13. Financial and Other Information

(*See* Notes D and E at the beginning of this Schedule.)

(a) *Information required.* If action is to be taken with respect to any matter specified in Items 11 or 12, furnish the following information:

(1) Financial statements meeting the requirements of Regulation S-X, including financial information required by rule 3-05 and Article 11 of Regulation S-X with respect to transactions other than that pursuant to which action is to be taken as described in this proxy statement;

(2) Item 302 of Regulation S-K, supplementary financial information;

(3) Item 303 of Regulation S-K, management's discussion and analysis of financial condition and results of operations;

(4) Item 304 of Regulation S-K, changes in and disagreements with accountants on accounting and financial disclosure;

(5) Item 305 of Regulation S-K, quantitative and qualitative disclosures about market risk; and

(6) A statement as to whether or not representatives of the principal accountants for the current year and for the most recently completed fiscal year:

(i) are expected to be present at the security holders' meeting;

(ii) will have the opportunity to make a statement if they desire to do so; and

(iii) are expected to be available to respond to appropriate questions.

(b) *Incorporation by reference.* The information required pursuant to paragraph (a) of this Item may be incorporated by reference into the proxy statement as follows:

(1) *S-3 registrants.* If the registrant meets the requirements of Form S-3 (see Note E to this Schedule), it may incorporate by reference to previously-filed documents any of the information required by paragraph (a) of this Item, provided that the requirements of paragraph (c) are met. Where the registrant meets the requirements of Form S-3 and has elected to furnish the required information by incorporation by reference, the registrant may elect to update the information so incorporated by reference to information in subsequently filed documents.

(2) *All registrants.* The registrant may incorporate by reference any of the information required by paragraph (a) of this Item, provided that the information is contained in an annual report to security holders or a previously-filed statement or report, such report or statement is delivered to security holders with the proxy statement and the requirements of paragraph (c) are met.

(c) *Certain conditions applicable to incorporation by reference.* Registrants eligible to incorporate by reference into the proxy statement the information required by paragraph (a) of this Item in the manner specified by paragraphs (b)(1) and (b)(2) may do so only if:

(1) the information is not required to be included in the proxy statement pursuant to the requirement of another Item;

(2) the proxy statement identifies on the last page(s) the information incorporated by reference; and

(3) the material incorporated by reference substantially meets the requirements of this Item or the appropriate portions of this Item.

Instructions to Item 13.

1. Notwithstanding the provisions of this Item, any or all of the information required by paragraph (a) of this Item, not material for the exercise of prudent judgment in regard to the matter to be acted upon may be

omitted. In the usual case the information is deemed material to the exercise of prudent judgment where the matter to be acted upon is the authorization or issuance of a material amount of senior securities, but the information is not deemed material where the matter to be acted upon is the authorization or issuance of common stock, otherwise than in an exchange, merger, consolidation, acquisition or similar transaction, the authorization of preferred stock without present intent to issue or the authorization of preferred stock for issuance for cash in an amount constituting fair value.

2. In order to facilitate compliance with Rule 2-02(a) of Regulation S-X, one copy of the definitive proxy statement filed with the Commission shall include a manually signed copy of the accountant's report. If the financial statements are incorporated by reference, a manually signed copy of the accountant's report shall be filed with the definitive proxy statement.

3. Notwithstanding the provisions of Regulation S-X, no schedules other than those prepared in accordance with Rules 12-15, 12-28 and 12-29 (or, for management investment companies, Rules 12-12 through 12-14) of that regulation need be furnished in the proxy statement.

4. Unless registered on a national securities exchange or otherwise required to furnish such information, registered investment companies need not furnish the information required by paragraphs (a)(2) or (3) of this Item.

5. If the registrant submits preliminary proxy material incorporating by reference financial statements required by this Item, the registrant should furnish a draft of the financial statements if the document from which they are incorporated has not been filed with or furnished to the Commission.

6. A registered investment company need not comply with Items (a)(2), (a)(3), and (a)(5) of this Item 13.

Item 14. Mergers, Consolidations, Acquisitions and Similar Matters

(See Notes A, D and E at the beginning of this Schedule.)

Instructions to Item 14.

1. In transactions in which the consideration offered to security holders consists wholly or in part of securities registered under the Securities Act of 1933, furnish the information required by Form S-4 (§239.25 of this chapter), Form F-4 (§239.34 of this chapter), or Form N-14 (§239.23 of this chapter), as applicable, instead of this Item. Only a Form S-4, Form F-4, or Form N-14 must be filed in accordance with §240.14a-6(j).

2. (a) In transactions in which the consideration offered to security holders consists wholly of cash, the information required by paragraph

(c)(1) of this Item for the acquiring company need not be provided unless the information is material to an informed voting decision (e.g., the security holders of the target company are voting and financing is not assured).

(b). Additionally, if only the security holders of the target company are voting:

i. The financial information in paragraphs (b)(8) - (11) of this Item for the acquiring company and the target need not be provided; and

ii. The information in paragraph (c)(2) of this Item for the target company need not be provided.

If, however, the transaction is a going-private transaction (as defined by §240.13e-3), then the information required by paragraph (c)(2) of this Item must be provided and to the extent that the going-private rules require the information specified in paragraph (b)(8) - (b)(11) of this Item, that information must be provided as well.

(3). In transactions in which the consideration offered to security holders consists wholly of securities exempt from registration under the Securities Act of 1933 or a combination of exempt securities and cash, information about the acquiring company required by paragraph (c)(1) of this Item need not be provided if only the security holders of the acquiring company are voting, unless the information is material to an informed voting decision. If only the security holders of the target company are voting, information about the target company in paragraph (c)(2) of this Item need not be provided. However, the information required by paragraph (c)(2) of this Item must be provided if the transaction is a going-private (as defined by § 240.13e-3) or roll-up (as described by Item 901 of Regulation S-K (§ 229.901 of this chapter)) transaction.

(4). The information required by paragraphs (b)(8) - (11) and (c) need not be provided if the plan being voted on involves only the acquiring company and one or more of its totally held subsidiaries and does not involve a liquidation or a spin-off.

(5). To facilitate compliance with Rule 2-02(a) of Regulation S-X (§210.2-02(a) of this chapter) (technical requirements relating to accountants' reports), one copy of the definitive proxy statement filed with the Commission must include a signed copy of the accountant's report. If the financial statements are incorporated by reference, a signed copy of the accountant's report must be filed with the definitive proxy statement. Signatures may be typed if the document is filed electronically on EDGAR. See Rule 302 of Regulation S-T (§232.302 of this chapter).

(6). Notwithstanding the provisions of Regulation S-X, no schedules other than those prepared in accordance with §210.12-15, §210.12-28 and §210.12-29 of this chapter (or, for management investment companies, §§210.12-12 through 210.12-14 of this chapter) of that regulation need be furnished in the proxy statement.

(7). If the preliminary proxy material incorporates by reference financial statements required by this Item, a draft of the financial statements must be furnished to the Commission staff upon request if the document from which they are incorporated has not been filed with or furnished to the Commission.

(a). Applicability. If action is to be taken with respect to any of the following transactions, provide the information required by this Item:

(1). A merger or consolidation;

(2). An acquisition of securities of another person;

(3). An acquisition of any other going business or the assets of a going business;

(4). A sale or other transfer of all or any substantial part of assets; or

(5). A liquidation or dissolution.

(b). Transaction information. Provide the following information for each of the parties to the transaction unless otherwise specified:

(1). Summary term sheet. The information required by Item 1001 of Regulation M-A (§229.1001 of this chapter).

(2). Contact information. The name, complete mailing address and telephone number of the principal executive offices.

(3). Business conducted. A brief description of the general nature of the business conducted.

(4). Terms of the transaction. The information required by Item 1004(a)(2) of Regulation M-A (§229.1004 of this chapter).

(5). Regulatory approvals. A statement as to whether any federal or state regulatory requirements must be complied with or approval must be obtained in connection with the transaction and, if so, the status of the compliance or approval.

(6). Reports, opinions, appraisals. If a report, opinion or appraisal materially relating to the transaction has been received from an outside party, and is referred to in the proxy statement, furnish the information required by Item 1015(b) of Regulation M-A (§229.1015 of this chapter).

(7). Past contacts, transactions or negotiations. The information required by Items 1005(b) and 1011(a)(1) of Regulation M-A (§229.1005 of this chapter and §229.1011 of this chapter), for the parties to the transaction and their affiliates during the periods for which financial statements are presented or incorporated by reference under this Item.

(8). Selected financial data. The selected financial data required by Item 301 of Regulation S-K (§229.301 of this chapter).

(9). Pro forma selected financial data. If material, the information required by Item 301 of Regulation S-K (§229.301 of this chapter) for the acquiring company, showing the pro forma effect of the transaction.

(10). Pro forma information. In a table designed to facilitate comparison, historical and pro forma per share data of the acquiring company and historical and equivalent pro forma per share data of the target company for the following Items:

(i) Book value per share as of the date financial data is presented pursuant to Item 301 of Regulation S-K (§229.301 of this chapter);

(ii) Cash dividends declared per share for the periods for which financial data is presented pursuant to Item 301 of Regulation S-K (§229.301 of this chapter); and

(iii) Income (loss) per share from continuing operations for the periods for which financial data is presented pursuant to Item 301 of Regulation S-K (§229.301 of this chapter).

Instructions to paragraphs (b)(8), (b)(9) and (b)(10):

1. For a business combination accounted for as a purchase, present the financial information required by paragraphs (b)(9) and (b)(10) only for the most recent fiscal year and interim period. For a business combination accounted for as a pooling, present the financial information required by paragraphs (b)(9) and (b)(10) (except for information with regard to book value) for the most recent three fiscal years and interim period. For purposes of these paragraphs, book value information need only be provided for the most recent balance sheet date.

2. Calculate the equivalent pro forma per share amounts for one share of the company being acquired by multiplying the exchange ratio times each of:

(i) The pro forma income (loss) per share before non-recurring charges or credits directly attributable to the transaction;

(ii) The pro forma book value per share; and

(iii) The pro forma dividends per share of the acquiring company.

3. Unless registered on a national securities exchange or otherwise required to furnish such information, registered investment companies need not furnish the information required by paragraphs (b)(8) and (b)(9) of this Item.

(11) Financial information. If material, financial information required by Article 11 of Regulation S-X (§§210.10-01 through 229.11-03 of this chapter) with respect to this transaction.

Instructions to paragraph (b)(11):

1. Present any Article 11 information required with respect to transactions other than those being voted upon (where not incorporated by reference) together with the pro forma information relating to the transaction being voted upon. In presenting this information, you must clearly distinguish between the transaction being voted upon and any other transaction.

2. If current pro forma financial information with respect to all other transactions is incorporated by reference, you need only present the pro forma effect of this transaction.

(c). Information about the parties to the transaction.

(1) Acquiring company. Furnish the information required by Part B (Registrant Information) of Form S-4 (§239.25 of this chapter) or Form F-4 (§239.34 of this chapter), as applicable, for the acquiring company. However, financial statements need only be presented for the latest two fiscal years and interim periods.

(2) Acquired company. Furnish the information required by Part C (Information with Respect to the Company Being Acquired) of Form S-4 (§239.25 of this chapter) or Form F-4 (§239.34 of this chapter), as applicable.

(d) Information about parties to the transaction: registered investment companies and business development companies.

If the acquiring company or the acquired company is an investment company registered under the Investment Company Act of 1940 or a business development company as defined by Section 2(a)(48) of the Investment Company Act of 1940, provide the following information for that company instead of the information specified by paragraph (c) of this Item:

(1) Information required by Item 101 of Regulation S-K (§229.101 of this chapter), description of business;

(2) Information required by Item 102 of Regulation S-K (§229.102 of this chapter), description of property;

(3) Information required by Item 103 of Regulation S-K (§229.103 of this chapter), legal proceedings;

(4) Information required by Item 201 of Regulation S-K (§229.201 of this chapter), market price of and dividends on the registrant's common equity and related stockholder matters;

(5) Financial statements meeting the requirements of Regulation S-X, including financial information required by Rule 3-05 and Article 11 of Regulation S-X (§210.3-05 and §210.11-01 through §210.11-03 of this

chapter) with respect to transactions other than that as to which action is to be taken as described in this proxy statement;

(6) Information required by Item 301 of Regulation S-K (§229.301 of this chapter), selected financial data;

(7) Information required by Item 302 of Regulation S-K (§229.302 of this chapter), supplementary financial information;

(8) Information required by Item 303 of Regulation S-K (§229.303 of this chapter), management's discussion and analysis of financial condition and results of operations; and

(9) Information required by Item 304 of Regulation S-K (§229.304 of this chapter), changes in and disagreements with accountants on accounting and financial disclosure.

Instruction to paragraph (d) of Item 14:

Unless registered on a national securities exchange or otherwise required to furnish such information, registered investment companies need not furnish the information required by paragraphs (d)(6), (d)(7) and (d)(8) of this Item.

(e) Incorporation by reference.

(1) The information required by paragraph (c) of this section may be incorporated by reference into the proxy statement to the same extent as would be permitted by Form S-4 (§239.25 of this chapter) or Form F-4 (§239.34 of this chapter), as applicable.

(2) Alternatively, the registrant may incorporate by reference into the proxy statement the information required by paragraph (c) of this Item if it is contained in an annual report sent to security holders in accordance with §240.14a-3 of this chapter with respect to the same meeting or solicitation of consents or authorizations that the proxy statement relates to and the information substantially meets the disclosure requirements of Item 14 or Item 17 of Form S-4 (§239.25 of this chapter) or Form F-4 (§239.34 of this chapter), as applicable.

Item 15. Acquisition or Disposition of Property

If action is to be taken with respect to the acquisition or disposition of any property, furnish the following information:

(a) Describe briefly the general character and location of the property.

(b) State the nature and amount of consideration to be paid or received by the registrant or any subsidiary. To the extent practicable, outline briefly the facts bearing upon the question of the fairness of the consideration.

(c) State the name and address of the transferer or transferee, as the case may be and the nature of any material relationship of such person to the registrant or any affiliate of the registrant.

(d) Outline briefly any other material features of the contract or transaction.

Item 16. Restatement of Accounts

If action is to be taken with respect to the restatement of any asset, capital, or surplus account of the registrant, furnish the following information:

(a) State the nature of the restatement and the date as of which it is to be effective.

(b) Outline briefly the reasons for the restatement and for the selection of the particular effective date.

(c) State the name and amount of each account (including any reserve accounts) affected by the restatement and the effect of the restatement thereon. Tabular presentation of the amounts shall be made when appropriate, particularly in the case of recapitalizations.

(d) To the extent practicable, state whether and the extent, if any, to which the restatement will, as of the date thereof, alter the amount available for distribution to the holders of equity securities.

Item 17. Action with Respect to Reports

If action is to be taken with respect to any report of the registrant or of its directors, officers or committees or any minutes of a meeting of its security holders furnish the following information:

(a) State whether or not such action is to constitute approval or disapproval of any of the matters referred to in such reports or minutes.

(b) Identify each of such matters which it is intended will be approved or disapproved, and furnish the information required by the appropriate item or items of this schedule with respect to each such matter.

Item 18. Matters Not Required to Be Submitted

If action is to be taken with respect to any matter which is not required to be submitted to a vote of security holders, state the nature of such matter, the reasons for submitting it to a vote of security holders and what action is intended to be taken by the registrant in the event of a negative vote on the matter by the security holders.

Item 19. Amendment of Charter, Bylaws or Other Documents

If action is to be taken with respect to any amendment of the registrant's charter, bylaws or other documents as to which information is not required above, state briefly the reasons for and the general effect of such amendment.

Instructions.

1. Where the matter to be acted upon is the classification of directors, state whether vacancies which occur during the year may

be filled by the board of directors to serve only until the next annual meeting or may be so filled for the remainder of the full term.

2. Attention is directed to the discussion of disclosure regarding anti-takeover and similar proposals in Release No. 34-15230 (October 13, 1978).

Item 20. Other Proposed Action

If action is to be taken on any matter not specifically referred to in this Schedule 14A, describe briefly the substance of each such matter in substantially the same degree of detail as is required by Items 5 to 19, inclusive, of this Schedule, and, with respect to investment companies registered under the Investment Company Act of 1940, Item 22 of this Schedule.

Item 21. Voting procedures

As to each matter which is to be submitted to a vote of security holders, furnish the following information:

(a) State the vote required for approval or election, other than for the approval of auditors.

(b) Disclose the method by which votes will be counted, including the treatment and effect of abstentions and broker nonvotes under applicable state law as well as registrant charter and by-law provisions.

Item 22.Information required in investment company proxy statement.

(a) *General*

(1) *Definitions.* Unless the context otherwise requires, terms used in this Item that are defined in § 240.14a-1 (with respect to proxy soliciting material), in § 240.14c-1 (with respect to information statements), and in the Investment Company Act of 1940 shall have the same meanings provided therein and the following terms shall also apply:

(i) *Administrator.* The term "Administrator" shall mean any person who provides significant administrative or business affairs management services to a Fund.

(ii) *Affiliated Broker.* The term "Affiliated Broker" shall mean any broker:

(A) That is an affiliated person of the Fund;

(B) That is an affiliated person of such person; or

(C) An affiliated person of which is an affiliated person of the Fund, its investment adviser, principal underwriter, or Administrator.

(iii) *Distribution Plan.* The term "Distribution Plan" shall mean a plan adopted pursuant to Rule 12b-1 under the Investment Company Act of 1940 (§ 270.12b-1 of this chapter).

(iv) *Family of Investment Companies.* The term "Family of Investment Companies" shall mean any two or more registered investment companies that:

(A) Share the same investment adviser or principal underwriter; and

(B) Hold themselves out to investors as related companies for purposes of investment and investor services.

(v) *Fund.* The term "Fund" shall mean a Registrant or, where the Registrant is a series company, a separate portfolio of the Registrant.

(vi) *Fund Complex.* The term "Fund Complex" shall mean two or more Funds that:

(A) Hold themselves out to investors as related companies for purposes of investment and investor services; or

(B) Have a common investment adviser or have an investment adviser that is an affiliated person of the investment adviser of any of the other Funds.

(vii) *Immediate Family Member.* The term "Immediate Family Member" shall mean a person's spouse; child residing in the person's household (including step and adoptive children); and any dependent of the person, as defined in section 152 of the Internal Revenue Code (26 U.S.C. 152).

(viii) *Officer.* The term "Officer" shall mean the president, vice-president, secretary, treasurer, controller, or any other officer who performs policy-making functions.

(ix) *Parent.* The term "Parent" shall mean the affiliated person of a specified person who controls the specified person directly or indirectly through one or more intermediaries.

(x) *Registrant.* The term "Registrant" shall mean an investment company registered under the Investment Company Act of 1940 (15 U.S.C. 80a) or a business development company as defined by section 2(a)(48) of the Investment Company Act of 1940 (15 U.S.C. 80a-2(a)(48)).

(xi) *Sponsoring Insurance Company.* The term "Sponsoring Insurance Company" of a Fund that is a separate account shall mean the insurance company that establishes and maintains the separate account and that owns the assets of the separate account.

(x) *Subsidiary*. The term "Subsidiary" shall mean an affiliated person of a specified person who is controlled by the specified person directly, or indirectly through one or more intermediaries.

(2) [Removed and Reserved]

(3) *General Disclosure*. Furnish the following information in the proxy statement of a Fund or Funds:

(i) State the name and address of the Fund's investment adviser, principal underwriter, and Administrator.

(ii) When a Fund proxy statement solicits a vote on proposals affecting more than one Fund or class of securities of a Fund (unless the proposal or proposals are the same and affect all Fund or class shareholders), present a summary of all of the proposals in tabular form on one of the first three pages of the proxy statement and indicate which Fund or class shareholders are solicited with respect to each proposal.

(iii) Unless the proxy statement is accompanied by a copy of the Fund's most recent annual report, state prominently in the proxy statement that the Fund will furnish, without charge, a copy of the annual report and the most recent semi-annual report succeeding the annual report, if any, to a shareholder upon request, providing the name, address, and toll-free telephone number of the person to whom such request shall be directed (or, if no toll-free telephone number is provided, a self-addressed postage paid card for requesting the annual report). The Fund should provide a copy of the annual report and the most recent semi-annual report succeeding the annual report, if any, to the requesting shareholder by first class mail, or other means designed to assure prompt delivery, within three business days of the request.

(iv) If the action to be taken would, directly or indirectly, establish a new fee or expense or increase any existing fee or expense to be paid by the Fund or its shareholders, provide a table showing the current and pro forma fees (with the required examples) using the format prescribed in the appropriate registration statement form under the Investment Company Act of 1940 (for open-end management investment companies, Item 2 of Form N-1A (§ 239.15A); for closed-end management investment companies, Item 3 of Form N-2 (§ 239.14); and for separate accounts that offer variable annuity contracts, Item 3 of Form N-3 (§ 239.17a)).

Instructions.

1. Where approval is sought only for a change in asset breakpoints for a pre-existing fee that would not have increased the fee for the previous year (or have the effect of increasing fees or expenses, but for any other

reason would not be reflected in a pro forma fee table), describe the likely effect of the change in lieu of providing pro forma fee information.

2. An action would indirectly establish or increase a fee or expense where, for example, the approval of a new investment advisory contract would result in higher custodial or transfer agency fees.

3. The tables should be prepared in a manner designed to facilitate understanding of the impact of any change in fees or expenses.

4. A Fund that offers its shares exclusively to one or more separate accounts and thus is not required to include a fee table in its prospectus (*see* Item 2(a)(ii) of Form N-1A (§ 239.15A)) should nonetheless prepare a table showing current and pro forma expenses and disclose that the table does not reflect separate account expenses, including sales load.

(v) If action is to be taken with respect to the election of directors or the approval of an advisory contract, describe any purchases or sales of securities of the investment adviser or its Parents, or Subsidiaries of either, since the beginning of the most recently completed fiscal year by any director or any nominee for election as a director of the Fund.

Instructions.

1. Identify the parties, state the consideration, the terms of payment and describe any arrangement or understanding with respect to the composition of the board of directors of the Fund or of the investment adviser, or with respect to the selection of appointment of any person to any office with either such company.

2. Transactions involving securities in an amount not exceeding one percent of the outstanding securities of any class of the investment adviser or any of its Parents or Subsidiaries may be omitted.

(b) *Election of Directors.* If action is to be taken with respect to the election of directors of a Fund, furnish the following information in the proxy statement in addition to the information (and in the format) required by paragraphs (d)(3), (f) and (g) of Item 7 of Schedule 14A.

Instructions to introductory text of paragraph (b).

1 Furnish information with respect to a prospective investment adviser to the extent applicable.

2. If the solicitation is made by or on behalf of a person other than the Fund or an investment adviser of the Fund, provide information only as to nominees of the person making the solicitation.

3. When providing information about directors and nominees for election as directors in response to this Item 22(b), furnish information for directors or nominees who are or would be "interested persons" of the Fund within the meaning of section 2(a)(19) of the Investment Company

Act of 1940 (15 U.S.C. 80a-2(a)(19)) separately from the information for directors or nominees who are not or would not be interested persons of the Fund. For example, when furnishing information in a table, you should provide separate tables (or separate sections of a single table) for directors and nominees who are or would be interested persons and for directors or nominees who are not or would not be interested persons. When furnishing information in narrative form, indicate by heading or otherwise the directors or nominees who are or would be interested persons and the directors or nominees who are not or would not be interested persons.

4. No information need be given about any director whose term of office as a director will not continue after the meeting to which the proxy statement relates.

(1) Provide the information required by the following table for each director, nominee for election as director, Officer of the Fund, person chosen to become an Officer of the Fund, and, if the Fund has an advisory board, member of the board. Explain in a footnote to the table any family relationship between the persons listed.

(1)	(2)	(3)	(4)	(5)	(6)
Name, Address, and Age	Position(s) Held with Fund	Term of Office and Length of Time Served	Principal Occupation(s) During Past 5 Years	Number of Portfolios in Fund Complex Overseen by Director or Nominee for Director	Other Directorships Held by Director or Nominee for Director

Instructions to paragraph (b)(1).

1. For purposes of this paragraph, the term "family relationship" means any relationship by blood, marriage, or adoption, not more remote than first cousin.

2. No nominee or person chosen to become a director or Officer who has not consented to act as such may be named in response to this Item. In this regard, see Rule 14a-4(d) under the Exchange Act (§ 240.14a-4(d)).

3. If fewer nominees are named than the number fixed by or pursuant to the governing instruments, state the reasons for this procedure and that the proxies cannot be voted for a greater number of persons than the number of nominees named.

4. For each director or nominee for election as director who is or would be an "interested person" of the Fund within the meaning of sec-

tion 2(a)(19) of the Investment Company Act of 1940 (15 U.S.C. 80a-2(a)(19)), describe, in a footnote or otherwise, the relationship, events, or transactions by reason of which the director or nominee is or would be an interested person.

5. State the principal business of any company listed under column (4) unless the principal business is implicit in its name.

6. Include in column (5) the total number of separate portfolios that a nominee for election as director would oversee if he were elected.

7. Indicate in column (6) directorships not included in column (5) that are held by a director or nominee for election as director in any company with a class of securities registered pursuant to section 12 of the Exchange Act (15 U.S.C. 78*l*), or subject to the requirements of section 15(d) of the Exchange Act (15 U.S.C. 78o(d)), or any company registered as an investment company under the Investment Company Act of 1940 (15 U.S.C. 80a), as amended, and name the companies in which the directorships are held. Where the other directorships include directorships overseeing two or more portfolios in the same Fund Complex, identify the Fund Complex and provide the number of portfolios overseen as a director in the Fund Complex rather than listing each portfolio separately.

(2) For each individual listed in column (1) of the table required by paragraph (b)(1) of this Item, except for any director or nominee for election as director who is not or would not be an "interested person" of the Fund within the meaning of section 2(a)(19) of the Investment Company Act of 1940 (15 U.S.C. 80a-2(a)(19)), describe any positions, including as an officer, employee, director, or general partner, held with affiliated persons or principal underwriters of the Fund.

Instruction to paragraph (b)(2). When an individual holds the same position(s) with two or more registered investment companies that are part of the same Fund Complex, identify the Fund Complex and provide the number of registered investment companies for which the position(s) are held rather than listing each registered investment company separately.

(3) Describe briefly any arrangement or understanding between any director, nominee for election as director, Officer, or person chosen to become an Officer, and any other person(s) (naming the person(s)) pursuant to which he was or is to be selected as a director, nominee, or Officer.

Instruction to paragraph (b)(3). Do not include arrangements or understandings with directors or Officers acting solely in their capacities as such.

(4) Unless disclosed in the table required by paragraph (b)(1) of this Item, describe any positions, including as an officer, employee, director,

or general partner, held by any director or nominee for election as director, who is not or would not be an "interested person" of the Fund within the meaning of section 2(a)(19) of the Investment Company Act of 1940 (15 U.S.C. 80a-2(a)(19)), or Immediate Family Member of the director or nominee, during the past five years, with:

(i) The Fund;

(ii) An investment company, or a person that would be an investment company but for the exclusions provided by sections 3(c)(1) and 3(c)(7) of the Investment Company Act of 1940 (15 U.S.C. 80a-3(c)(1) and (c)(7)), having the same investment adviser, principal underwriter, or Sponsoring Insurance Company as the Fund or having an investment adviser, principal underwriter, or Sponsoring Insurance Company that directly or indirectly controls, is controlled by, or is under common control with an investment adviser, principal underwriter, or Sponsoring Insurance Company of the Fund;

(iii) An investment adviser, principal underwriter, Sponsoring Insurance Company, or affiliated person of the Fund; or

(iv) Any person directly or indirectly controlling, controlled by, or under common control with an investment adviser, principal underwriter, or Sponsoring Insurance Company of the Fund.

Instruction to paragraph (b)(4). When an individual holds the same position(s) with two or more portfolios that are part of the same Fund Complex, identify the Fund Complex and provide the number of portfolios for which the position(s) are held rather than listing each portfolio separately.

(5) For each director or nominee for election as director, state the dollar range of equity securities beneficially owned by the director or nominee as required by the following table:

(i) In the Fund; and

(ii) On an aggregate basis, in any registered investment companies overseen or to be overseen by the director or nominee within the same Family of Investment Companies as the Fund.

(1)	(2)	(3)
Name of Director or Nominee	Dollar Range of Equity Securities in the Fund	Aggregate Dollar Range of Equity Securities in All Funds Overseen or to be Overseen by Director or Nominee in Family of Investment Companies

Instructions to paragraph (b)(5).

1. Information should be provided as of the most recent practicable date. Specify the valuation date by footnote or otherwise.

2. Determine "beneficial ownership" in accordance with rule 16a-1(a)(2) under the Exchange Act (§ 240.16a-1(a)(2)).

3. If action is to be taken with respect to more than one Fund, disclose in column (2) the dollar range of equity securities beneficially owned by a director or nominee in each such Fund overseen or to be overseen by the director or nominee.

4. In disclosing the dollar range of equity securities beneficially owned by a director or nominee in columns (2) and (3), use the following ranges: none, $1-$10,000, $10,001-$50,000, $50,001-$100,000, or over $100,000.

(6) For each director or nominee for election as director who is not or would not be an "interested person" of the Fund within the meaning of section 2(a)(19) of the Investment Company Act of 1940 (15 U.S.C. 80a-2(a)(19), and his Immediate Family Members, furnish the information required by the following table as to each class of securities owned beneficially or of record in:

(i) An investment adviser, principal underwriter, or Sponsoring Insurance Company of the Fund; or

(ii) A person (other than a registered investment company) directly or indirectly controlling, controlled by, or under common control with an investment adviser, principal underwriter, or Sponsoring Insurance Company of the Fund:

(1)	(2)	(3)	(4)	(5)	(6)
Name of Director or Nominee	Name of Owners and Relationships to Director or Nominee	Company	Title of Class	Value of Securities	Percent of Class

Instructions to paragraph (b)(6).

1. Information should be provided as of the most recent practicable date. Specify the valuation date by footnote or otherwise.

2. An individual is a "beneficial owner" of a security if he is a "beneficial owner" under either rule 13d-3 or rule 16a-1(a)(2) under the Exchange Act (§§ 240.13d-3 or 240.16a-1(a)(2)).

3. Identify the company in which the director, nominee, or Immediate Family Member of the director or nominee owns securities in column (3). When the company is a person directly or indirectly controlling, controlled

by, or under common control with an investment adviser, principal underwriter, or Sponsoring Insurance Company, describe the company's relationship with the investment adviser, principal underwriter, or Sponsoring Insurance Company.

4. Provide the information required by columns (5) and (6) on an aggregate basis for each director (or nominee) and his Immediate Family Members.

(7) Unless disclosed in response to paragraph (b)(6) of this Item, describe any direct or indirect interest, the value of which exceeds $60,000, of each director or nominee for election as director who is not or would not be an "interested person" of the Fund within the meaning of section 2(a)(19) of the Investment Company Act of 1940 (15 U.S.C. 80a-2(a)(19)), or Immediate Family Member of the director or nominee, during the past five years, in:

(i) An investment adviser, principal underwriter, or Sponsoring Insurance Company of the Fund; or

(ii) A person (other than a registered investment company) directly or indirectly controlling, controlled by, or under common control with an investment adviser, principal underwriter, or Sponsoring Insurance Company of the Fund.

Instructions to paragraph (b)(7)

1. A director, nominee, or Immediate Family Member has an interest in a company if he is a party to a contract, arrangement, or understanding with respect to any securities of, or interest in, the company.

2. The interest of the director (or nominee) and the interests of his Immediate Family Members should be aggregated in determining whether the value exceeds $60,000.

(8) Describe briefly any material interest, direct or indirect, of any director or nominee for election as director who is not or would not be an "interested person" of the Fund within the meaning of section 2(a)(19) of the Investment Company Act of 1940 (15 U.S.C. 80a-2(a)(19)), or Immediate Family Member of the director or nominee, in any transaction, or series of similar transactions, since the beginning of the last two completed fiscal years of the Fund, or in any currently proposed transaction, or series of similar transactions, in which the amount involved exceeds $60,000 and to which any of the following persons was or is to be a party:

(i) The Fund;

(ii) An Officer of the Fund;

(iii) An investment company, or a person that would be an investment company but for the exclusions provided by sections 3(c)(1) and 3(c)(7) of the Investment Company Act of 1940 (15 U.S.C. 80a-3(c)(1) and (c)(7)), having the same investment adviser, principal underwriter, or Sponsoring Insurance Company as the Fund or having an investment adviser, principal underwriter, or Sponsoring Insurance Company that directly or indirectly controls, is controlled by, or is under common control with an investment adviser, principal underwriter, or Sponsoring Insurance Company of the Fund;

(iv) An Officer of an investment company, or a person that would be an investment company but for the exclusions provided by sections 3(c)(1) and 3(c)(7) of the Investment Company Act of 1940 (15 U.S.C. 80a-3(c)(1) and (c)(7)), having the same investment adviser, principal underwriter, or Sponsoring Insurance Company as the Fund or having an investment adviser, principal underwriter, or Sponsoring Insurance Company that directly or indirectly controls, is controlled by, or is under common control with an investment adviser, principal underwriter, or Sponsoring Insurance Company of the Fund;

(v) An investment adviser, principal underwriter, or Sponsoring Insurance Company of the Fund;

(vi) An Officer of an investment adviser, principal underwriter, or Sponsoring Insurance Company of the Fund;

(vii) A person directly or indirectly controlling, controlled by, or under common control with an investment adviser, principal underwriter, or Sponsoring Insurance Company of the Fund; or

(viii) An Officer of a person directly or indirectly controlling, controlled by, or under common control with an investment adviser, principal underwriter, or Sponsoring Insurance Company of the Fund.

Instructions to paragraph (b)(8).

1. Include the name of each director, nominee, or Immediate Family Member whose interest in any transaction or series of similar transactions is described and the nature of the circumstances by reason of which the interest is required to be described.

2. State the nature of the interest, the approximate dollar amount involved in the transaction, and, where practicable, the approximate dollar amount of the interest.

3. In computing the amount involved in the transaction or series of similar transactions, include all periodic payments in the case of any lease or other agreement providing for periodic payments.

4. Compute the amount of the interest of any director, nominee, or Immediate Family Member of the director or nominee without regard to the amount of profit or loss involved in the transaction(s).

5. As to any transaction involving the purchase or sale of assets, state the cost of the assets to the purchaser and, if acquired by the seller within

two years prior to the transaction, the cost to the seller. Describe the method used in determining the purchase or sale price and the name of the person making the determination.

6. If the proxy statement relates to multiple portfolios of a series Fund with different fiscal years, then, in determining the date that is the beginning of the last two completed fiscal years of the Fund, use the earliest date of any series covered by the proxy statement.

7. Disclose indirect, as well as direct, material interests in transactions. A person who has a position or relationship with, or interest in, a company that engages in a transaction with one of the persons listed in paragraphs (b)(8)(i) through (b)(8)(viii) of this Item may have an indirect interest in the transaction by reason of the position, relationship, or interest. The interest in the transaction, however, will not be deemed "material" within the meaning of paragraph (b)(8) of this Item where the interest of the director, nominee, or Immediate Family Member arises solely from the holding of an equity interest (including a limited partnership interest, but excluding a general partnership interest) or a creditor interest in a company that is a party to the transaction with one of the persons specified in paragraphs (b)(8)(i) through (b)(8)(viii) of this Item, and the transaction is not material to the company.

8. The materiality of any interest is to be determined on the basis of the significance of the information to investors in light of all the circumstances of the particular case. The importance of the interest to the person having the interest, the relationship of the parties to the transaction with each other, and the amount involved in the transaction are among the factors to be considered in determining the significance of the information to investors.

9. No information need be given as to any transaction where the interest of the director, nominee, or Immediate Family Member arises solely from the ownership of securities of a person specified in paragraphs (b)(8)(i) through (b)(8)(viii) of this Item and the director, nominee, or Immediate Family Member receives no extra or special benefit not shared on a pro rata basis by all holders of the class of securities.

10. Transactions include loans, lines of credit, and other indebtedness. For indebtedness, indicate the largest aggregate amount of indebtedness outstanding at any time during the period, the nature of the indebtedness and the transaction in which it was incurred, the amount outstanding as of the latest practicable date, and the rate of interest paid or charged.

11. No information need be given as to any routine, retail transaction. For example, the Fund need not disclose that a director has a credit card, bank or brokerage account, residential mortgage, or insurance policy with a person specified in paragraphs (b)(8)(i) through (b)(8)(viii) of this Item unless the director is accorded special treatment.

(9) Describe briefly any direct or indirect relationship, in which the amount involved exceeds $60,000, of any director or nominee for election as director who is not or would not be an "interested person" of the Fund within the meaning of section 2(a)(19) of the Investment Company Act of 1940 (15 U.S.C. 80a-2(a)(19)), or Immediate Family Member of the director or nominee, that exists, or has existed at any time since the beginning of the last two completed fiscal years of the Fund, or is currently proposed, with any of the persons specified in paragraphs (b)(8)(i) through (b)(8)(viii) of this Item. Relationships include:

(i) Payments for property or services to or from any person specified in paragraphs (b)(8)(i) through (b)(8)(viii) of this Item;

(ii) Provision of legal services to any person specified in paragraphs (b)(8)(i) through (b)(8)(viii) of this Item;

(iii) Provision of investment banking services to any person specified in paragraphs (b)(8)(i) through (b)(8)(viii) of this Item, other than as a participating underwriter in a syndicate; and

(iv) Any consulting or other relationship that is substantially similar in nature and scope to the relationships listed in paragraphs (b)(9)(i) through (b)(9)(iii) of this Item.

Instructions to paragraph (b)(9).

1. Include the name of each director, nominee, or Immediate Family Member whose relationship is described and the nature of the circumstances by reason of which the relationship is required to be described.

2. State the nature of the relationship and the amount of business conducted between the director, nominee, or Immediate Family Member and the person specified in paragraphs (b)(8)(i) through (b)(8)(viii) of this Item as a result of the relationship since the beginning of the last two completed fiscal years of the Fund or proposed to be done during the Fund's current fiscal year.

3. In computing the amount involved in a relationship, include all periodic payments in the case of any agreement providing for periodic payments.

4. If the proxy statement relates to multiple portfolios of a series Fund with different fiscal years, then, in determining the date that is the beginning of the last two completed fiscal years of the Fund, use the earliest date of any series covered by the proxy statement.

5. Disclose indirect, as well as direct, relationships. A person who has a position or relationship with, or interest in, a company that has a relationship with one of the persons listed in paragraphs (b)(8)(i) through (b)(8)(viii) of this Item may have an indirect relationship by reason of the position, relationship, or interest.

6. In determining whether the amount involved in a relationship exceeds $60,000, amounts involved in a relationship of the director (or nominee) should be aggregated with those of his Immediate Family Members.

7. In the case of an indirect interest, identify the company with which a person specified in paragraphs (b)(8)(i) through (b)(8)(viii) of this Item has a relationship; the name of the director, nominee, or Immediate Family Member affiliated with the company and the nature of the affiliation; and the amount of business conducted between the company and the person specified in paragraphs (b)(8)(i) through (b)(8)(viii) of this Item since the beginning of the last two completed fiscal years of the Fund or proposed to be done during the Fund's current fiscal year.

8. In calculating payments for property and services for purposes of paragraph (b)(9)(i) of this Item, the following may be excluded:

A. Payments where the transaction involves the rendering of services as a common contract carrier, or public utility, at rates or charges fixed in conformity with law or governmental authority; or

B. Payments that arise solely from the ownership of securities of a person specified in paragraphs (b)(8)(i) through (b)(8)(viii) of this Item and no extra or special benefit not shared on a pro rata basis by all holders of the class of securities is received.

9. No information need be given as to any routine, retail relationship. For example, the Fund need not disclose that a director has a credit card, bank or brokerage account, residential mortgage, or insurance policy with a person specified in paragraphs (b)(8)(i) through (b)(8)(viii) of this Item unless the director is accorded special treatment.

(10) If an Officer of an investment adviser, principal underwriter, or Sponsoring Insurance Company of the Fund, or an Officer of a person directly or indirectly controlling, controlled by, or under common control with an investment adviser, principal underwriter, or Sponsoring Insurance Company of the Fund, serves, or has served since the beginning of the last two completed fiscal years of the Fund, on the board of directors of a company where a director of the Fund or nominee for election as director who is not or would not be an "interested person" of the Fund within the meaning of section 2(a)(19) of the Investment Company Act of 1940 (15 U.S.C. 80a-2(a)(19)), or Immediate Family Member of the director or nominee, is, or was since the beginning of the last two completed fiscal years of the Fund, an Officer, identify:

(i) The company;

(ii) The individual who serves or has served as a director of the company and the period of service as director;

(iii) The investment adviser, principal underwriter, or Sponsoring Insurance Company or person controlling, controlled by, or under common control with the investment adviser, principal underwriter, or Sponsoring Insurance Company where the individual named in paragraph (b)(10)(ii) of this Item holds or held office and the office held; and

(iv) The director of the Fund, nominee for election as director, or Immediate Family Member who is or was an Officer of the company; the office held; and the period of holding the office.

Instruction to paragraph (b)(10). If the proxy statement relates to multiple portfolios of a series Fund with different fiscal years, then, in determining the date that is the beginning of the last two completed fiscal years of the Fund, use the earliest date of any series covered by the proxy statement.

(11) Provide in tabular form, to the extent practicable, the information required by Items 401(f) and (g), 404(a) and (c), and 405 of Regulation S-K (§§ 229.401(f) and (g), 229.404(a) and (c), and 229.405 of this chapter).

Instruction to paragraph (b)(11). Information provided under paragraph (b)(8) of this Item 22 is deemed to satisfy the requirements of Items 404(a) and (c) of Regulation S-K for information about directors, nominees for election as directors, and Immediate Family Members of directors and nominees, and need not be provided under this paragraph (b)(11).

(12) Describe briefly any material pending legal proceedings, other than ordinary routine litigation incidental to the Fund's business, to which any director or nominee for director or affiliated person of such director or nominee is a party adverse to the Fund or any of its affiliated persons or has a material interest adverse to the Fund or any of its affiliated persons. Include the name of the court where the case is pending, the date instituted, the principal parties, a description of the factual basis alleged to underlie the proceeding, and the relief sought.

(13) For all directors, and for each of the three highest-paid Officers that have aggregate compensation from the Fund for the most recently completed fiscal year in excess of $60,000 ("Compensated Persons"):

(i) Furnish the information required by the following table for the last fiscal year:

Compensation Table

(1)	(2)	(3)	(4)	(5)
Name of Person, Position	Aggregate Compensation From Fund	Pension or Retirement Benefits Accrued as Part of Fund Expenses	Estimated Annual Benefits Upon Retirement	Total Compensation From Fund and Fund Complex Paid to Directors

Instructions to paragraph (b)(13)(i).

1. For column (1), indicate, if necessary, the capacity in which the remuneration is received. For Compensated Persons that are directors of the Fund, compensation is amounts received for service as a director.

2. If the Fund has not completed its first full year since its organization, furnish the information for the current fiscal year, estimating future payments that would be made pursuant to an existing agreement or understanding. Disclose in a footnote to the Compensation Table the period for which the information is furnished.

3. Include in column (2) amounts deferred at the election of the Compensated Person, whether pursuant to a plan established under Section 401(k) of the Internal Revenue Code (26 U.S.C. 401(k)) or otherwise, for the fiscal year in which earned. Disclose in a footnote to the Compensation Table the total amount of deferred compensation (including interest) payable to or accrued for any Compensated Person.

4. Include in columns (3) and (4) all pension or retirement benefits proposed to be paid under any existing plan in the event of retirement at normal retirement date, directly or indirectly, by the Fund or any of its Subsidiaries, or by other companies in the Fund Complex. Omit column (4) where retirement benefits are not determinable.

5. For any defined benefit or actuarial plan under which benefits are determined primarily by final compensation (or average final compensation) and years of service, provide the information required in column (4) in a separate table showing estimated annual benefits payable upon retirement (including amounts attributable to any defined benefit supplementary or excess pension award plans) in specified compensation and years of service classifications. Also provide the estimated credited years of service for each Compensated Person.

6. Include in column (5) only aggregate compensation paid to a director for service on the board and other boards of investment companies in a Fund Complex specifying the number of such other investment companies.

(ii) Describe briefly the material provisions of any pension, retirement, or other plan or any arrangement other than fee arrangements disclosed in paragraph (b)(13)(i) of this Item pursuant to which Compensated Persons are or may be compensated for any services provided, including amounts paid, if any, to the Compensated Person under any such arrangements during the most recently completed fiscal year. Specifically include the criteria used to determine amounts payable under any plan, the length of service or vesting period required by the plan, the retirement age or other event that gives rise to payments under the plan, and whether the payment of benefits is secured or funded by the Fund.

(iii) With respect to each Compensated Person, business development companies must include the information required by Items 402(b)(2)(iv) and 402(c) of Regulation S-K (§§ 229.402(b)(2)(iv) and 229.402(c) of this chapter).

(14) State whether or not the Fund has a separately designated audit committee established in accordance with section 3(a)(58)(A) of the Act (15 U.S.C. 78c(a)(58)(A)). If the entire board of directors is acting as the Fund's audit committee as specified in section 3(a)(58)(B) of the Act (15 U.S.C. 78c(a)(58)(B)), so state. If applicable, provide the disclosure required by § 240.10A-3(d) regarding an exemption from the listing standards for audit committees. Identify the other standing committees of the Fund's board of directors, and provide the following information about each committee, including any separately designated audit committee:

(i) A concise statement of the functions of the committee;

(ii) The members of the committee;

(iii) The number of committee meetings held during the last fiscal year; and

(iv) If the committee is a nominating or similar committee, state whether the committee will consider nominees recommended by security holders and, if so, describe the procedures to be followed by security holders in submitting recommendations.

(c) *Approval of Investment Advisory Contract.* If action is to be taken with respect to an investment advisory contract, include the following information in the proxy statement.

Instruction. Furnish information with respect to a prospective investment adviser to the extent applicable (including the name and address of the prospective investment adviser).

(1) With respect to the existing investment advisory contract:

(i) State the date of the contract and the date on which it was last submitted to a vote of security holders of the Fund, including the purpose of such submission;

(ii) Briefly describe the terms of the contract, including the rate of compensation of the investment adviser;

(iii) State the aggregate amount of the investment adviser's fee and the amount and purpose of any other material payments by the Fund to the investment adviser, or any affiliated person of the investment adviser, during the last fiscal year of the Fund;

(iv) If any person is acting as an investment adviser of the Fund other than pursuant to a written contract that has been approved by the security holders of the company, identify the person and describe the nature of the services and arrangements;

(v) Describe any action taken with respect to the investment advisory contract since the beginning of the Fund's last fiscal year by the board of directors of the Fund (unless described in response to paragraph (c)(1)(vi)) of this Item 22); and

(vi) If an investment advisory contract was terminated or not renewed for any reason, state the date of such termination or non-renewal, identify the parties involved, and describe the circumstances of such termination or non-renewal.

(2) State the name, address and principal occupation of the principal executive officer and each director or general partner of the investment adviser.

Instruction. If the investment adviser is a partnership with more than ten general partners, name:

(i) the general partners with the five largest economic interests in the partnership, and, if different, those general partners comprising the management or executive committee of the partnership or exercising similar authority;

(ii) the general partners with significant management responsibilities relating to the fund.

(3) State the names and addresses of all Parents of the investment adviser and show the basis of control of the investment adviser and each Parent by its immediate Parent.

Instructions.

1. If any person named is a corporation, include the percentage of its voting securities owned by its immediate Parent.

2. If any person named is a partnership, name the general partners having the three largest partnership interests (computed by whatever method is appropriate in the particular case).

(4) If the investment adviser is a corporation and if, to the knowledge of the persons making the solicitation or the persons on whose behalf the solicitation is made, any person not named in answer to paragraph (c)(3) of this Item 22 owns, of record or beneficially, ten percent or more of the outstanding voting securities of the investment adviser, indicate that fact and state the name and address of each such person.

(5) Name each officer or director of the Fund who is an officer, employee, director, general partner or shareholder of the investment adviser. As to any officer or director who is not a director or general partner of the investment adviser and who owns securities or has any other material direct or indirect interest in the investment adviser or any other person controlling, controlled by or under common control with the investment adviser, describe the nature of such interest.

(6) Describe briefly and state the approximate amount of, where practicable, any material interest, direct or indirect, of any director of the Fund in any material transactions since the beginning of the most recently completed fiscal year, or in any material proposed transactions, to which the investment adviser of the Fund, any Parent or Subsidiary of the investment adviser (other than another Fund), or any Subsidiary of the Parent of such entities was or is to be a party.

Instructions.

1. Include the name of each person whose interest in any transaction is described and the nature of the relationship by reason of which such interest is required to be described. Where it is not practicable to state the approximate amount of the interest, indicate the approximate amount involved in the transaction.

2. As to any transaction involving the purchase or sale of assets by or to the investment adviser, state the cost of the assets to the purchaser and the cost thereof to the seller if acquired by the seller within two years prior to the transaction.

3. If the interest of any person arises from the position of the person as a partner in a partnership, the proportionate interest of such person in transactions to which the partnership is a party need not be set forth, but state the amount involved in the transaction with the partnership.

4. No information need be given in response to this paragraph (c)(6) of Item 22 with respect to any transaction that is not related to the business or operations of the Fund and to which neither the Fund nor any of its Parents or Subsidiaries is a party.

(7) Disclose any financial condition of the investment adviser that is reasonably likely to impair the financial ability of the adviser to fulfil its commitment to the fund under the proposed investment advisory contract.

(8) Describe the nature of the action to be taken on the investment advisory contract and the reasons therefor, the terms of the contract to be acted upon, and, if the action is an amendment to, or a replacement of, an investment advisory contract, the material differences between the current and proposed contract.

(9) If a change in the investment advisory fee is sought, state:

(i) The aggregate amount of the investment adviser's fee during the last year;

(ii) The amount that the adviser would have received had the proposed fee been in effect; and

(iii) The difference between the aggregate amounts stated in response to paragraphs (i) and (ii) this item (c)(9) as a percentage of the amount stated in response to paragraph (i) of this item (c)(9).

(10) If the investment adviser acts as such with respect to any other Fund having a similar investment objective, identify and state the size of such other Fund and the rate of the investment adviser's compensation. Also indicate for any Fund identified whether the investment adviser has waived, reduced, or otherwise agreed to reduce its compensation under any applicable contract.

Instruction. Furnish the information in response to this paragraph (c)(10) of Item 22 in tabular form.

(11) Discuss in reasonable detail the material factors and the conclusions with respect thereto which form the basis for the recommendation of the board of directors that the shareholders approve an investment advisory contract. If applicable, include a discussion of any benefits derived or to be derived by the investment adviser from the relationship with the Fund such as soft dollar arrangements by which brokers provide research to the Fund or its investment adviser in return for allocating fund brokerage.

Instruction. Conclusory statements or a list of factors will not be considered sufficient disclosure. The discussion should relate the factors to the specific circumstances of the fund and the investment advisory contract for which approval is sought.

(12) Describe any arrangement or understanding made in connection with the proposed investment advisory contract with respect to the composition of the board of directors of the Fund or the investment adviser or with respect to the selection or appointment of any person to any office with either such company.

(13) For the most recently completed fiscal year, state:

(i) The aggregate amount of commissions paid to any Affiliated Broker; and

(ii) The percentage of the Fund's aggregate brokerage commissions paid to any such Affiliated Broker.

Instruction. Identify each Affiliated Broker and the relationships that cause the broker to be an Affiliated Broker.

(14) Disclose the amount of any fees paid by the Fund to the investment adviser, its affiliated persons or any affiliated person of such person during the most recent fiscal year for services provided to the Fund (other than under the investment advisory contract or for brokerage commissions). State whether these services will continue to be provided after the investment advisory contract is approved.

(d) *Approval of Distribution Plan.* If action is to be taken with respect to a Distribution Plan, include the following information in the proxy statement.

Instruction. Furnish information on a prospective basis to the extent applicable.

(1) Describe the nature of the action to be taken on the Distribution Plan and the reason therefor, the terms of the Distribution Plan to be acted upon, and, if the action is an amendment to, or a replacement of, a Distribution Plan, the material differences between the current and proposed Distribution Plan.

(2) If the Fund has a Distribution Plan in effect:

(i) Provide the date that the Distribution Plan was adopted and the date of the last amendment, if any;

(ii) Disclose the persons to whom payments may be made under the Distribution Plan, the rate of the distribution fee and the purposes for which such fee may be used;

(iii) Disclose the amount of distribution fees paid by the Fund pursuant to the plan during its most recent fiscal year, both in the aggregate and as a percentage of the Fund's average net assets during the period;

(iv) Disclose the name of, and the amount of any payments made under the Distribution Plan by the Fund during its most recent fiscal year to, any person who is an affiliated person of the Fund, its investment adviser, principal underwriter, or Administrator, an affiliated person of such person, or a person that during the most recent fiscal year received 10% or more of the aggregate amount paid under the Distribution Plan by the Fund;

(v) Describe any action taken with respect to the Distribution Plan since the beginning of the Fund's most recent fiscal year by the board of directors of the Fund; and

(vi) If a Distribution Plan was or is to be terminated or not renewed for any reason, state the date or prospective date of such termination or non-renewal, identify the parties involved, and describe the circumstances of such termination or non-renewal.

(3) Describe briefly and state the approximate amount of, where practicable, any material interest, direct or indirect, of any director or nominee for election as a director of the Fund in any material transactions since the beginning of the most recently completed fiscal year, or in any material proposed transactions, to which any person identified in response to Item 22(d)(2)(iv) was or is to be a party.

Instructions.

1. Include the name of each person whose interest in any transaction is described and the nature of the relationship by reason of which such interest is required to be described. Where it is not practicable to state the

approximate amount of the interest, indicate the approximate amount involved in the transaction.

2. As to any transaction involving the purchase or sale of assets, state the cost of the assets to the purchaser and the cost thereof to the seller if acquired by the seller within two years prior to the transaction.

3. If the interest of any person arises from the position of the person as a partner in a partnership, the proportionate interest of such person in transactions to which the partnership is a party need not be set forth but state the amount involved in the transaction with the partnership.

4. No information need be given in response to this paragraph (d)(3) of Item 22 with respect to any transaction that is not related to the business or operations of the Fund and to which neither the Fund nor any of its Parents or Subsidiaries is a party.

(4) Discuss in reasonable detail the material factors and the conclusions with respect thereto which form the basis for the conclusion of the board of directors that there is a reasonable likelihood that the proposed Distribution Plan (or amendment thereto) will benefit the Fund and its shareholders.

Instruction. Conclusory statements or a list of factors will not be considered sufficient disclosure.

Item 23. Delivery of documents to security holders sharing an address.

If one annual report or proxy statement is being delivered to two or more security holders who share an address in accordance with §240.14a-3(e)(1), furnish the following information:

(a) State that only one annual report or proxy statement, as applicable, is being delivered to multiple security holders sharing an address unless the registrant has received contrary instructions from one or more of the security holders;

(b) Undertake to deliver promptly upon written or oral request a separate copy of the annual report or proxy statement, as applicable, to a security holder at a shared address to which a single copy of the documents was delivered and provide instructions as to how a security holder can notify the registrant that the security holder wishes to receive a separate copy of an annual report or proxy statement, as applicable;

(c) Provide the phone number and mailing address to which a security holder can direct a notification to the registrant that the security holder wishes to receive a separate annual report or proxy statement, as applicable, in the future; and

(d) Provide instructions how security holders sharing an address can request delivery of a single copy of annual reports or proxy statements if they are receiving multiple copies of annual reports or proxy statements.

Rule 15c6-1

Settlement Cycle.

(a) Except as provided in paragraphs (b), (c) and (d) of this section, a broker or dealer shall not effect or enter into a contract for the purchase or sale of a security (other than an exempted security, government security, municipal security, commercial paper, bankers' acceptances, or commercial bills) that provides for payment of funds and delivery of securities later than the third business day after the date of the contract unless otherwise expressly agreed to by the parties at the time of the transaction.

(b) Paragraphs (a) and (c) of this section shall not apply to contracts:

(1) For the purchase or sale of limited partnership interests that are not listed on an exchange or for which quotations are not disseminated through an automated quotation system of a registered securities association;

(2) For the purchase or sale of securities that the Commission may from time to time, taking into account then existing market practices, exempt by order from the requirements of paragraph (a) of this section, either unconditionally or on specified terms and conditions, if the Commission determines that such exemption is consistent with the public interest and the protection of investors.

(c) Paragraph (a) of this section shall not apply to contracts for the sale for cash of securities that are priced after 4:30 p.m. Eastern time on the date such securities are priced and that are sold by an issuer to an underwriter pursuant to a firm commitment underwritten offering registered under the Securities Act of 1933 or sold to an initial purchaser by a broker-dealer participating in such offering provided that a broker or dealer shall not effect or enter into a contract for the purchase or sale of such securities that provides for payment of funds and delivery of securities later than the fourth business day after the date of the contract unless otherwise expressly agreed to by the parties at the time of the transaction.

(d) For the purposes of paragraphs (a) and (c) of this section, the parties to a contract shall be deemed to have expressly agreed to an alternate date for payment of funds and delivery of securities at the time of the transaction for a contract for the sale for cash of securities pursuant to a firm commitment offering if the managing underwriter and the issuer have agreed to such date for all securities sold pursuant to such offering and the parties to the contract have not expressly agreed to another date for payment of funds and delivery of securities at the time of the transaction.

Rules 16a-1—16a8: Reports of Directors, Officers and Principal Shareholders

Rule 16a-1. Definition of Terms.

Terms defined in this rule shall apply solely to Section 16 of the Act and the rules thereunder. These terms shall not be limited to Section 16(a) of the Act but also shall apply to all other subsections under Section 16 of the Act.

(a) The term "beneficial owner" shall have the following applications:

(1) Solely for purposes of determining whether a person is a beneficial owner of more than 10 percent of any class of equity securities registered pursuant to Section 12 of the Act, the term "beneficial owner" shall mean any person who is deemed a beneficial owner pursuant to Section 13(d) of the Act and the rules thereunder; provided, however, that the following institutions or persons shall not be deemed the beneficial owner of securities of such class held for the benefit of third parties or in customer or fiduciary accounts in the ordinary course of business (or in the case of an employee benefit plan specified in subparagraph (vi) below, of securities of such class allocated to plan participants where participants have voting power) as long as such shares are acquired by such institutions or persons without the purpose or effect of changing or influencing control of the issuer or engaging in any arrangement subject to Rule 13d-3(b):

(i) A broker or dealer registered under Section 15 of the Exchange Act;

(ii) A bank as defined in Section 3(a)(6) of the Exchange Act;

(iii) An insurance company as defined in Section 3(a)(19) of the Exchange Act;

(iv) An investment company registered under Section 8 of the Investment Company Act;

(v) Any person registered as an investment adviser under Section 203 of the Investment Advisers Act or under the laws of any state;

(vi) An employee benefit plan as defined in Section 3(3) of the Employee Retirement Income Security Act of 1974, as amended, ("ERISA") that is subject to the provisions of ERISA, or any such plan that is not subject to ERISA that is maintained primarily for the benefit of the employees of a state or local government or instrumentality, or an endowment fund;

(vii) A parent holding company or control person, *provided* the aggregate amount held directly by the parent or control person, and directly and indirectly by theirsubsidiaries or affiliates that are not persons specified in paragraphs (a)(1)(i) through (ix), does not exceed one percent of the securities of the subject class;

(viii) A savings association as defined in Section 3(b) of the Federal Deposit Insurance Act;

(ix) A church plan that is excluded from the definition of an investment company under Section 3(c)(14) of the Investment Company Act; and

(x) A group, provided that all the members are persons specified in Rule16a-1(a)(1)(i) through (ix).

(xi) A group, provided that all the members are persons specified in Rule 16a-1(a)(i) through (vii).

Note to Paragraph (a). Pursuant to this section, a person deemed a beneficial owner of more than 10 percent of any class of equity securities registered under Section 12 of the Act would file a Form 3, but the securities holdings disclosed on Form 3, and changes in beneficial ownership reported on subsequent Form 4 or 5 would be determined by the definition of "beneficial owner" in paragraph (a)(2) of this section.

(2) Other than for purposes of determining whether a person is a beneficial owner of more than 10 percent of any class of equity securities registered under Section 12 of the Act, the term "beneficial owner" shall mean any person who, directly or indirectly, through any contract, arrangement, understanding, relationship or otherwise, has or shares a direct or indirect pecuniary interest in the equity securities, subject to the following:

(i) The term "pecuniary interest" in any class of equity securities shall mean the opportunity, directly or indirectly, to profit or share in any profit derived from a transaction in the subject securities.

(ii) The term "indirect pecuniary interest" in any class of equity securities shall include, but not be limited to:

(A) Securities held by members of a person's immediate family sharing the same household; *provided, however,* that the presumption of such beneficial ownership may be rebutted. See also Rules 16a-1(a)(4);

(B) A general partner's proportionate interest in the portfolio securities held by a general or limited partnership. The general partner's proportionate interest, as evidenced by the partnership agreement in effect at the time of the transaction and the partnership's most recent financial statements, shall be the greater of:

(1) The general partner's share of the partnership's profits, including profits attributed to any limited partnership interests held by the general partner and any other interests in profits that arise from the purchase and sale of the partnership's portfolio securities; or

(2) The general partner's share of the partnership capital account, including the share attributable to any limited partnership interest held by the general partner;

(C) A performance-related fee, other than an asset-based fee, received by any broker, dealer, bank, insurance company, investment company, investment adviser, investment manager, trustee or person or entity performing a similar function; *provided, however,* that no pecuniary interest shall be present where:

(1) The performance-related fee, regardless of when payable, is calculated based upon net capital gains and/or net capital appreciation generated from the portfolio or from the fiduciary's overall performance over a period of one year or more; and

(2) Equity securities of the issuer do not account for more than 10 percent of the market value of the portfolio. A right to a non-performance-related fee alone shall not represent a pecuniary interest in the securities;

(D) A person's right to dividends that is separated or separable from the underlying securities. Otherwise, a right to dividends alone shall not represent a pecuniary interest in the securities;

(E) A person's interest in securities held by a trust, as specified in Rule 16a-8(b); and

(F) A person's right to acquire equity securities through the exercise or conversion of any derivative security, whether or not presently exercisable.

(iii) A shareholder shall not be deemed to have a pecuniary interest in the portfolio securities held by a corporation or similar entity in which the person owns securities if the shareholder is not a controlling shareholder of the entity and does not have or share investment control over the entity's portfolio.

(3) Where more than one person subject to Section 16 of the Act is deemed to be a beneficial owner of the same equity securities, all such persons must report as beneficial owners of the securities either separately or jointly, as provided in Rule 16a-3(j). In such cases, the amount of short-swing profit recoverable shall not be increased above the amount recoverable if there were only one beneficial owner.

(4) Any person filing a statement pursuant to Section 16(a) of the Act may state that the filing shall not be deemed an admission that such person is, for purposes of Section 16 of the Act or otherwise, the beneficial owner of any equity securities covered by the statement.

(5) The following interests are deemed not to confer beneficial ownership for purposes of Section 16 of the Act:

(i) Interests in portfolio securities held by any holding company registered under the Public Utility Holding Company Act of 1935;

(ii) Interests in portfolio securities held by any investment company registered under the Investment Company Act of 1940; and

(iii) Interests in securities comprising part of a broad-based, publicly traded market basket or index of stocks, approved for trading by the appropriate federal governmental authority.

(b) The term "call equivalent position" shall mean a derivative security position that increases in value as the value of the underlying equity increases, including, but not limited to, a long convertible security, a long call option, and a short put option position.

(c) The term "derivative securities" shall mean any option, warrant, convertible security, stock appreciation right, or similar right with an exercise or conversion privilege at a price related to an equity security, or similar securities with a value derived from the value of an equity security, but shall not include:

(1) Rights of a pledgee of securities to sell the pledged securities;

(2) Rights of all holders of a class of securities of an issuer to receive securities pro rata, or obligations to dispose of securities, as a result of a merger, exchange offer, or consolidation involving the issuer of the securities;

(3) Rights or obligations to surrender a security, or have a security withheld, upon the receipt or exercise of a derivative security or the receipt or vesting of equity securities, in order to satisfy the exercise price or the tax withholding consequences of receipt, exercise or vesting;

(4) Interests in broad-based index options, broad-based index futures, and broadbased publicly traded market baskets of stocks approved for trading by the appropriate federal governmental authority;

(5) Interests or rights to participate in employee benefit plans of the issuer;

(6) Rights with an exercise or conversion privilege at a price that is not fixed; or

(7) Options granted to an underwriter in a registered public offering for the purpose of satisfying over-allotments in such offering.

(d) The term "equity security of such issuer" shall mean any equity security or derivative security relating to an issuer, whether or not issued by that issuer.

(e) The term "immediate family" shall mean any child, stepchild, grandchild, parent, stepparent, grandparent, spouse, sibling, mother-in-law, father-in-law, son-in-law, daughter-in-law, brother-in-law, or sister-in-law, and shall include adoptive relationships.

(f) The term "officer" shall mean an issuer's president, principal financial officer, principal accounting officer (or, if there is no such accounting officer, the controller), any vice-president of the issuer in charge of a principal business unit, division or function (such as sales, administration or finance), any other officer who performs a policy-making function, or any other person who performs similar policy-making functions for the issuer. Officers of the issuer's parent(s) or subsidiaries shall be deemed officers of the issuer if they perform such policy-making functions for the issuer. In addition, when the issuer is a limited partnership, officers or employees of the general partner(s) who perform policy-making functions for the limited partnership are deemed officers of the limited partnership. When the issuer is a trust, officers or employees of the trustee(s) who perform policy-making functions for the trust are deemed officers of the trust.

Note. "Policy-making function" is not intended to include policy-making functions that are not significant. If pursuant to Item 401(b) of Regulation S-K the issuer identifies a person as an "executive officer," it is presumed that the Board of Directors has made that judgment and that the persons so identified are the officers for purposes of Section 16 of the Act, as are such other persons enumerated in this paragraph (f), but not in Item 401(b).

(g) The term "portfolio securities" shall mean all securities owned by an entity, other than securities issued by the entity.

(h) The term "put equivalent position" shall mean a derivative security position that increases in value as the value of the underlying equity decreases, including, but not limited to, a long put option and a short call option position.

Rule 16a-2. Persons and Transactions Subject to Section 16.

Any person who is the beneficial owner, directly or indirectly, of more than ten percent of any class of equity securities ("ten percent beneficial owner") registered pursuant to Section 12 of the Exchange Act, any director or officer of the issuer of such securities, and any person specified in Section 17(a) of the Public Utility Holding Company Act of 1935 or Section 30(h) of the Investment Company Act of 1940, including any person specified in Exchange Act Rule 16a-8, shall be subject to the provisions of Section 16 of the Exchange Act. The rules under Section 16 of the Act apply to any class of equity securities of an issuer whether or not registered under Section 12 of the Act. The rules under Section 16 of the Act also apply to non-equity securities as provided by the Public Utility Holding Company Act of 1935 and the Investment Company Act of 1940. With respect to transactions by persons subject to Section 16 of the Act:

(a) A transaction(s) carried out by a director or officer in the six months prior to the director or officer becoming subject to Section 16 of the Act shall be subject to Section 16 of the Act and reported on the first required Form 4 only if the transaction(s) occurred within six months of the transaction giving rise to the Form 4 filing obligation and the director or officer became subject to Section 16 of the Act solely as a result of the issuer registering a class of equity securities pursuant to Section 12 of the Act.

(b) A transaction(s) following the cessation of director or officer status shall be subject to Section 16 of the Act only if:

(1) Executed within a period of less than six months of an opposite transaction subject to Section 16(b) of the Act that occurred while that person was a director or officer; and

(2) Not otherwise exempted from Section 16(b) of the Act pursuant to the provisions of this chapter.

Note to Paragraph (b). For purposes of this paragraph, an acquisition and a disposition each shall be an opposite transaction with respect to the other.

(c) The transaction that results in a person becoming a 10 percent beneficial owner is not subject to Section 16 of the Act unless the person otherwise is subject to Section 16 of the Act. A 10 percent beneficial owner not otherwise subject to Section 16 of the Act must report only those transactions conducted while the beneficial owner of more than 10 percent of a class of equity securities of the issuer registered pursuant to Section 12 of the Act.

(d)(1) Transactions by a person or entity shall be exempt from the provisions of Section 16 of the Act for the 12 months following appointment and qualification, to the extent such person or entity is acting as:

(i) Executor or administrator of the estate of a decedent;

(ii) Guardian or member of a committee for an incompetent;

(iii) Receiver, trustee in bankruptcy, assignee for the benefit of creditors, conservator, liquidating agent, or other similar person duly authorized by law to administer the estate or assets of another person; or

(iv) Fiduciary in a similar capacity.

(2) Transactions by such person or entity acting in a capacity specified in paragraph (d)(1) of this section after the period specified in that

paragraph shall be subject to Section 16 of the Act only where the estate, trust or other entity is a beneficial owner of more than 10 percent of any class of equity security registered pursuant to Section 12 of the Act.

Rule 16a-3. Reporting Transactions and Holdings.

(a) Initial statements of beneficial ownership of equity securities required by Section 16(a) of the Act shall be filed on Form 3. Statements of changes in beneficial ownership required by that section shall be filed on Form 4. Annual statements shall be filed on Form 5. At the election of the reporting person, any transaction required to be reported on Form 5 may be reported on an earlier filed Form 4. All such statements shall be prepared and filed in accordance with the requirements of the applicable form.

(b) A person filing statements pursuant to Section 16(a) of the Act with respect to any class of equity securities registered pursuant to Section 12 of the Act need not file an additional statement of Form 3:

(1) When an additional class of equity securities of the same issuer becomes registered pursuant to Section 12 of the Act; or

(2) When such person assumes a different or an additional relationship to the same issuer (for example, when an officer becomes a director).

(c) Any issuer that has equity securities listed on more than one national securities exchange may designate one exchange as the only exchange with which reports pursuant to Section 16(a) of the Act need be filed. Such designation shall be made in writing and shall be filed with the Commission and with each national securities exchange on which any equity security of the issuer is listed at the time of such election. The reporting person's obligation to file reports with each national securities exchange on which any equity security of the issuer is listed shall be satisfied by filing with the exchange so designated.

(d) Any person required to file a statement with respect to securities of a single issuer under both Section 16(a) of the Exchange Act and either Section 17(a) of the Public Utility Holding Company Act of 1935 or Section 30(h) of the Investment Company Act of 1940 may file a single statement containing the required information, which will be deemed to be filed under both Acts.

(e) Any person required to file a statement under Section 16(a) of the Act shall, not later than the time the statement is transmitted for filing with the Commission, send or deliver a duplicate to the person designated by the issuer to receive such statements, or, in the absence of such a designation, to the issuer's corporate secretary or person performing equivalent functions.

(f)(1) A Form 5 shall be filed by every person who at any time during the issuer's fiscal year was subject to Section 16 of the Act with respect to such issuer, except as provided in paragraph (2) below. The form shall be filed within 45 days after the issuer's fiscal year end, and shall disclose the following holdings and transactions not reported previously on Form 3, 4 or 5:

(i) All transactions during the most recent fiscal year that were either exempt from Section 16(b) of the Act, except:

(A) Exercises and conversions of derivative securities exempt under either Exchange Act Rule 16b-3 or 16b-6(b), and any transaction exempt under Exchange Act Rule 16b-3(d), 16b-3(e), or 16b-3(f) (these are required to be reported on Form 4);

(B) Transactions exempt from Section 16(b) of the Act pursuant to Rule 16-b3(c) which shall be exempt from Section 16(a) of the Act; and

(C) Transactions exempt from Section 16(a) of the Act pursuant to another rule;

(ii) Transactions that constituted small acquisitions pursuant to Rule 16a-6(a);

(iii) All holdings and transactions that should have been reported during the most recent fiscal year, but were not; and

(iv) With respect to the first Form 5 requirement for a reporting person, all holdings and transactions that should have been reported in each of the issuer's last two fiscal years but were not, based on the reporting person's reasonable belief in good faith in the completeness and accuracy of the information.

(2) Notwithstanding the above, no Form 5 shall be required where all transactions otherwise required to be reported on the Form 5 have been reported before the due date of the Form 5.

Note. Persons no longer subject to Section 16 of the Act, but who were subject to the section at any time during the issuer's fiscal year, must file a Form 5 unless paragraph (f)(2) is satisfied. *See also* Rule 16a-2(b) regarding the reporting obligations of persons ceasing to be officers or directors.

(g)(1) A Form 4 must be filed to report: all transactions not exempt from Section 16(b) of the Exchange Act; all transactions exempt from Section 16(b) of the Exchange Act pursuant to Exchange Act Rule 16b-3(d), 16b-3(e), or 16-b-3(f); and all exercises and conversions of derivative securities, regardless of whether exempt from Section 16(b) of the Exchange Act. Form 4 must be filed before the end of the second business day following the day on which the subject transaction has been executed.

(2) Solely for purposes of Section 16(a)(2)(C) of the Exchange Act and paragraph (g)(1) of this Rule 16a-3, the date on which the executing broker, dealer or plan administrator notifies the reporting person of the execution of the transaction is deemed the date of execution for a transaction where the following conditions are satisfied:

(i) The transaction is pursuant to a contract, instruction or written plan for the purchase or sale of equity securities of the issuer (as defined in Exchange Act Rule 16a-1(d) that satisfies the affirmative defense conditions of Exchange Act Rule 10b5-1(c) of this chapter; and

(ii) The reporting person does not select the date of execution.

(3) Solely for purposes of Section 16(a)(2)(C) of the Exchange Act and paragraph (g)(1) of this Rule 16a-3, the date on which the plan administrator notifies the reporting person that the transaction has been executed is deemed the date of execution for a discretionary transaction (as defined in Exchange Act Rule 16b-3(b)(1) for which the reporting person does not select the date of execution.

(4) In the case of the transactions described in paragraphs (g)(2) and (g)(3) of this Rule 16a-3, if the notification date is later than the third business day following the trade date of the transaction, the date of execution is deemed to be the third business day following the trade date of the transaction.

(5) At the option of the reporting person, transactions that are reportable on Form 5 may be reported on Form 4, so long as the Form 4 is filed no later than the due date of the Form 5 on which the transaction is otherwise required to be reported.

(h) The date of filing with the Commission shall be the date of receipt by the Commission.

(i) *Signatures.* Where Section 16 of the Act, or the rules or forms thereunder, require a document filed with or furnished to the Commission to be signed, such document shall be manually signed, or signed using either typed signatures or duplicated or facsimile versions of manual signatures. Where typed, duplicated or facsimile signatures are used, each signatory to the filing shall manually sign a signature page or other document authenticating, acknowledging or otherwise adopting his or her signature that appears in the filing. Such document shall be executed before or at the time the filing is made and shall be retained by the filer for a period of five years. Upon request, the filer shall furnish to the Commission or its staff a copy of any or all documents retained pursuant to this section.

(j) Where more than one person subject to Section 16 of the Act is deemed to be a beneficial owner of the same equity securities, all such persons must report as beneficial owners of the securities, either separately or jointly. Where persons in a group are deemed to be beneficial owners of equity securities pursuant to Rule 16a-1(a)(1) due to the aggregation of holdings, a single Form 3, 4 or 5 may be filed on behalf of all persons in the group. Joint and group filings must include all required information for each beneficial owner, and such filings must be signed by each beneficial owner, or on behalf of such owner by an authorized person.

(k) Any issuer that maintains a corporate website shall post on that website by the end of the business day after filing any Form 3, 4 or 5 filed under section 16(a) of the Act as to the equity securities of that issuer. Each such form shall remain accessible on such issuer's website for at least a 12-month period. In the case of an issuer that is an investment company and that does not maintain its own website, if any of the issuer's investment adviser, sponsor, depositor, trustee, administrator, principal underwriter, or any affiliated person of the investment company maintains awebsite that includes the name of the issuer, the issuer shall comply with the posting requirements by posting the forms on one such website.

Rule 16a-4. Derivative Securities.

(a) For purposes of Section 16 of the Act, both derivative securities and the underlying securities to which they relate shall be deemed to be the same class of equity securities, *except that* the acquisition or disposition of any derivative security shall be separately reported.

(b) The exercise or conversion of a call equivalent position shall be reported on Form 4 and treated for reporting purposes as:

(1) A purchase of the underlying security; and

(2) A closing of the derivative security position.

(c) The exercise or conversion of a put equivalent position shall be reported on Form 4 and treated for reporting purposes as:

(1) A sale of the underlying security; and

(2) A closing of the derivative security position.

(d) The disposition or closing of a long derivative security position, as a result of cancellation or expiration, shall be exempt from Section 16(a) of the Act if exempt from Section 16(b) of the Act pursuant to Rule 16b-6(d).

Note to Rule 16a-4. A purchase or sale resulting from an exercise or conversion of a derivative security may be exempt from Section 16(b) of the Act pursuant to Rule 16b-3 or Rule 16b-6(b).

Rule 16a-5. Odd-Lot Dealers.

Transactions by an odd-lot dealer: (a) in odd-lots as reasonably necessary to carry on odd-lot transactions, or (b) in round lots to offset odd-lot transactions previously or simultaneously executed or reasonably anticipated in the usual course of business, shall be exempt from the provisions of Section 16(a) of the Act with respect to participation by such odd-lot dealer in such transaction.

Rule 16a-6. Small Acquisitions.

(a) Any acquisition of an equity security or the right to acquire such securities, other than an acquisition from the issuer (including an employee benefit plan sponsored by the issuer), not exceeding $10,000 in market value shall be reported on Form 5, subject to the following conditions:

(1) Such acquisition, when aggregated with other acquisitions of securities of the same class (including securities underlying derivative securities, but excluding acquisitions exempted by rule from Section 16(b) or previously reported on Form 4 or Form 5) within the prior six months, does not exceed a total of $10,000 in market value; and

(2) The person making the acquisition does not within six months thereafter make any disposition, other than by a transaction exempt from Section 16(b) of the Act.

(b) If an acquisition no longer qualifies for the reporting deferral in paragraph (a) of this Rule 16a-6, all such acquisitions that have not yet been reported must be reported on Form 4 before the end of the second business day following the day on which the conditions of paragraph (a) of this Rule 16a-6 are no longer met.

Rule 16a-7. Transactions Effected in Connection With a Distribution.

(a) Any purchase and sale, or sale and purchase, of a security that is made in connection with the distribution of a substantial block of securities shall be exempt from the provisions of Section 16(a) of the Act, to the extent specified in this rule, subject to the following conditions:

(1) The person effecting the transaction is engaged in the business of distributing securities and is participating in good faith, in the ordinary course of such business, in the distribution of such block of securities; and

(2) The security involved in the transaction is:

(i) Part of such block of securities and is acquired by the person effecting the transaction, with a view to distribution thereof, from the issuer or other person on whose behalf such securities are being distributed or from a person who is participating in good faith in the distribution of such block of securities; or

(ii) A security purchased in good faith by or for the account of the person effecting the transaction for the purpose of stabilizing the market price of securities of the class being distributed or to cover an over-allotment or other short position created in connection with such distribution.

(b) Each person participating in the transaction must qualify on an individual basis for an exemption pursuant to this section.

Rule 16a-8. Trusts.

(a) *Persons Subject to Section 16.*

(1) *Trusts.* A trust shall be subject to Section 16 of the Act with respect to securities of the issuer if the trust is a beneficial owner, pursuant to Exchange Act Rule 16a-1(a)(1), of more than ten percent of any class of equity securities of the issuer registered pursuant to Section 12 of the Act ("ten percent beneficial owner").

(2) *Trustees, Beneficiaries, and Settlors.* In determining whether a trustee, beneficiary, or settlor is a 10 percent beneficial owner with respect to the issuer:

(i) Such persons shall be deemed the beneficial owner of the issuer's securities held by the trust, to the extent specified by Rule 16a-1(a)(1); and

(ii) Settlors shall be deemed the beneficial owner of the issuer's securities held by the trust where they have the power to revoke the trust without the consent of another person.

(b) *Trust Holdings and Transactions.* Holdings and transactions in the issuer's securities held by a trust shall be reported by the trustee on behalf of the trust, if the trust is subject to Section 16 of the Act, except as provided below. Holdings and transactions in the issuer's securities held by a trust (whether or not subject to Section 16 of the Act) may be reportable by other parties as follows:

(1) *Trusts.* The trust need not report holdings and transactions in the issuer's securities held by the trust in an employee benefit plan subject to the Employee Retirement Income Security Act over which no trustee exercises investment control.

(2) *Trustees.* If, as provided by Rule 16a-1(a)(2), a trustee subject to Section 16 of the Act has a pecuniary interest in any holding or transac-

tion in the issuer's securities held by the trust, such holding or transaction shall be attributed to the trustee and shall be reported by the trustee in the trustee's individual capacity, as well as on behalf of the trust. With respect to performance fees and holdings of the trustee's immediate family, trustees shall be deemed to have a pecuniary interest in the trust holdings and transactions in the following circumstances:

(i) A performance fee is received that does not meet the proviso of Rule 16a-1(a)(2)(ii)(C); or

(ii) At least one beneficiary of the trust is a member of the trustee's immediate family. The pecuniary interest of the immediate family member(s) shall be attributed to and reported by the trustee.

(3) *Beneficiaries.* A beneficiary subject to Section 16 of the Act shall have or share reporting obligations with respect to transactions in the issuer's securities held by the trust, if the beneficiary is a beneficial owner of the securities pursuant to Rule 16a-1(a)(2), as follows:

(i) If a beneficiary shares investment control with the trustee with respect to a trust transaction, the transaction shall be attributed to and reported by both the beneficiary and the trust;

(ii) If a beneficiary has investment control with respect to a trust transaction without consultation with the trustee, the transaction shall be attributed to and reported by the beneficiary only; and

(iii) In making a determination as to whether a beneficiary is the beneficial owner of the securities pursuant to Rule 16a-1(a)(2), beneficiaries shall be deemed to have a pecuniary interest in the issuer's securities held by the trust to the extent of their pro rata interest in the trust where the trustee does not exercise exclusive investment control.

Note to Paragraph (b)(3). Transactions and holdings attributed to a trust beneficiary may be reported by the trustee on behalf of the beneficiary, provided that the report is signed by the beneficiary or other authorized person. Where the transactions and holdings are attributed both to the trustee and trust beneficiary, a joint report may be filed in accordance with Rule 16a-3(j).

(4) *Settlors.* If a settlor subject to Section 16 of the Act reserves the right to revoke the trust without the consent of another person, the trust holdings and transactions shall be attributed to and reported by the settlor instead of the trust; *provided, however,* that if the settlor does not exercise or share investment control over the issuer's securities held by the trust, the trust holdings and transactions shall be attributed to and reported by the trust instead of the settlor.

(c) *Remainder Interests.* Remainder interests in a trust are deemed not to confer beneficial ownership for purposes of Section 16 of the Act, *provided* that the persons with the remainder interests have no power, directly or indirectly, to exercise or share investment control over the trust.

(d) A trust, trustee, beneficiary or settlor becoming subject to Section 16(a) of the Act pursuant to this rule also shall be subject to Sections 16(b) and 16(c) of the Act.

Rule 16b-3. Transactions Between an Issuer and Its Officers or Directors.

(a) *General.* A transaction between the issuer (including an employee benefit plan sponsored by the issuer) and an officer or director of the issuer that involves issuer equity securities shall be exempt from Section 16(b) of the Act if the transaction satisfies the applicable conditions set forth in this section.

(b) *Definitions.*

(1) A "Discretionary Transaction" shall mean a transaction pursuant to an employee benefit plan that:

(i) Is at the volition of a plan participant;

(ii) Is not made in connection with the participant's death, disability, retirement or termination of employment;

(iii) Is not required to be made available to a plan participant pursuant to a provision of the Internal Revenue Code; and

(iv) Results in either an intra-plan transfer involving an issuer equity securities fund, or a cash distribution funded by a volitional disposition of an issuer equity security.

(2) An "Excess Benefit Plan" shall mean an employee benefit plan that is operated in conjunction with a Qualified Plan, and provides only the benefits or contributions that would be provided under a Qualified Plan but for any benefit or contribution limitations set forth in the Internal Revenue Code of 1986, or any successor provisions thereof.

(3)(i) A *"Non-Employee Director"* shall mean a director who:

(A) Is not currently an officer (as defined in Rule 16a-1(f)) of the issuer or a parent or subsidiary of the issuer, or otherwise currently employed by the issuer or a parent or subsidiary of the issuer;

(B) Does not receive compensation, either directly or indirectly, from the issuer or a parent or subsidiary of the issuer, for services rendered as a consultant or in any capacity other than as a director, except for an amount that does not exceed the dollar amount for which disclosure would be required pursuant to Rule 404(a) of this chapter;

(C) Does not possess an interest in any other transaction for which disclosure would be required pursuant to Rule 404(a) of this chapter; and

(D) Is not engaged in a business relationship for which disclosure would be required pursuant to Rule 404(b) of this chapter.

(ii) Notwithstanding paragraph (b)(3)(i) of this section, a *"Non-Employee Director"* of a closed-end investment company shall mean a director who is not an "interested person" of the issuer, as that term is defined in Section 2(a)(19) of the Investment Company Act of 1940.

(4) A *"Qualified Plan"* shall mean an employee benefit plan that satisfies the coverage and participation requirements of Sections 410 and 401(a)(26) of the Internal Revenue Code of 1986, or any successor provisions thereof.

(5) A *"Stock Purchase Plan"* shall mean an employee benefit plan that satisfies the coverage and participation requirements of Sections 423(b)(3) and 423(b)(5), or Section 410, of the Internal Revenue Code of 1986, or any successor provisions thereof.

(c) *Tax-Conditioned Plans.* Any transaction (other than a Discretionary Transaction) pursuant to a Qualified Plan, an Excess Benefit Plan, or a Stock Purchase Plan shall be exempt without condition.

(d) *Grants, Awards and Other Acquisitions From the Issuer.* Any transaction involving a grant, award or other acquisition from the issuer (other than a Discretionary Transaction) shall be exempt if:

(1) The transaction is approved by the board of directors of the issuer, or a committee of the board of directors that is composed solely of two or more Non-Employee Directors;

(2) The transaction is approved or ratified, in compliance with Section 14 of the Act, by either: the affirmative votes of the holders of a majority of the securities of the issuer present, or represented, and entitled to vote at a meeting duly held in accordance with the applicable laws of the state or other jurisdiction in which the issuer is incorporated; or the written consent of the holders of a majority of the securities of the issuer entitled to vote; *provided* that such ratification occurs no later than the date of the next annual meeting of shareholders; or

(3) The issuer equity securities so acquired are held by the officer or director for a period of six months following the date of such acquisition, *provided* that this condition shall be satisfied with respect to a derivative security if at least six months elapse from the date of acquisition of the derivative security to the date of disposition of the derivative security (other than upon exercise or conversion) or its underlying equity security.

(e) *Dispositions to the Issuer.* Any transaction involving the disposition to the issuer of issuer equity securities (other than a Discretionary Transaction) shall be exempt,

(3)(i) A *"Non-Employee Director"* shall mean a director who:

(A) Is not currently an officer (as defined in Rule 16a-1(f)) of the issuer or a parent or subsidiary of the issuer, or otherwise currently employed by the issuer or a parent or subsidiary of the issuer;

(B) Does not receive compensation, either directly or indirectly, from the issuer or a parent or subsidiary of the issuer, for services rendered as a consultant or in any capacity other than as a director, except for an amount that does not exceed the dollar amount for which disclosure would be required pursuant to Rule 404(a) of this chapter;

(C) Does not possess an interest in any other transaction for which disclosure would be required pursuant to Rule 404(a) of this chapter; and

(D) Is not engaged in a business relationship for which disclosure would be required pursuant to Rule 404(b) of this chapter.

(ii) Notwithstanding paragraph (b)(3)(i) of this section, a *"Non-Employee Director"* of a closed-end investment company shall mean a director who is not an "interested person" of the issuer, as that term is defined in Section 2(a)(19) of the Investment Company Act of 1940.

(4) A *"Qualified Plan"* shall mean an employee benefit plan that satisfies the coverage and participation requirements of Sections 410 and 401(a)(26) of the Internal Revenue Code of 1986, or any successor provisions thereof.

(5) A *"Stock Purchase Plan"* shall mean an employee benefit plan that satisfies the coverage and participation requirements of Sections 423(b)(3) and 423(b)(5), or Section 410, of the Internal Revenue Code of 1986, or any successor provisions thereof.

(c) *Tax-Conditioned Plans.* Any transaction (other than a Discretionary Transaction) pursuant to a Qualified Plan, an Excess Benefit Plan, or a Stock Purchase Plan shall be exempt without condition.

(d) *Grants, Awards and Other Acquisitions From the Issuer.* Any transaction involving a grant, award or other acquisition from the issuer (other than a Discretionary Transaction) shall be exempt if:

(1) The transaction is approved by the board of directors of the issuer, or a committee of the board of directors that is composed solely of two or more Non-Employee Directors;

(2) The transaction is approved or ratified, in compliance with Section 14 of the Act, by either: the affirmative votes of the holders of a majority of the securities of the issuer present, or represented, and entitled to vote at a meeting duly held in accordance with the applicable laws of the state or other jurisdiction in which the issuer is incorporated; or the written consent of the holders of a majority of the securities of the issuer entitled to vote; *provided* that such ratification occurs no later than the date of the next annual meeting of shareholders; or

(3) The issuer equity securities so acquired are held by the officer or director for a period of six months following the date of such acquisition, *provided* that this condition shall be satisfied with respect to a derivative

security if at least six months elapse from the date of acquisition of the derivative security to the date of disposition of the derivative security (other than upon exercise or conversion) or its underlying equity security.

(e) *Dispositions to the Issuer.* Any transaction involving the disposition to the issuer of issuer equity securities (other than a Discretionary Transaction) shall be exempt, *provided* that the terms of such disposition are approved in advance in the manner prescribed by either paragraph (d)(1) or paragraph (d)(2) of this section.

(f) *Discretionary Transactions.* A Discretionary Transaction shall be exempt only if effected pursuant to an election made at least six months following the date of the most recent election, with respect to any plan of the issuer, that effected a Discretionary Transaction that was:

(1) An acquisition, if the transaction to be exempted would be a disposition; or

(2) A disposition, if the transaction to be exempted would be an acquisition.

Notes to Rule 16b-3.

Note (1). The exercise or conversion of a derivative security that does not satisfy the conditions of this section is eligible for exemption from Section 16(b) of the Act to the extent that the conditions of Rule 16b-6(b) are satisfied.

Note (2). Section 16(a) reporting requirements applicable to transactions exempt pursuant to this section are set forth in Rule 16a-3(f) and (g) and Rule 16a-4.

Note (3). The approval conditions of paragraph (d)(1), (d)(2) and (e) of this section require the approval of each specific transaction, and are not satisfied by approval of a plan in its entirety except for the approval of a plan pursuant to which the terms and conditions of each transaction are fixed in advance, such as a formula plan. Where the terms of a subsequent transaction (such as the exercise price of an option, or the provision of an exercise or tax withholding right) are provided for in a transaction as initially approved pursuant to paragraphs (d)(1), (d)(2) or (e), such subsequent transaction shall not require further specific approval.

Regulation FD

Rule 100. General Rule Regarding Selective Disclosure.

(a) Whenever an issuer, or any person acting on its behalf, discloses any material nonpublic information regarding that issuer or its securities to any person described in paragraph (b)(1) of this Rule 100, the issuer shall make public disclosure of that information as provided in Regulation F-D Rule 101(e):

(1) Simultaneously, in the case of an intentional disclosure; and

(2) Promptly, in the case of a non-intentional disclosure.

(b)(1) Except as provided in paragraph (b)(2) of this Rule 100, paragraph (a) of this Rule 100 shall apply to a disclosure made to any person outside the issuer:

(i) Who is a broker or dealer, or a person associated with a broker or dealer, as those terms are defined in Section 3(a) of the Securities Exchange Act of 1934;

(ii) Who is:

(A) An investment adviser, as that term is defined in Section 202(a)(11) of the Investment Advisers Act of 1940;

(B) An institutional investment manager, as that term is defined in Section 13(f)(5) of the Securities Exchange Act of 1934, that filed a report on Form 13F with the Commission for the most recent quarter ended prior to the date of the disclosure; or

(C) A person associated with either of the foregoing.

For purposes of this paragraph, a "person associated with an investment adviser or institutional investment manager" has the meaning set forth in Section 202(a)(17) of the Investment Advisers Act of 1940, assuming for these purposes that an institutional investment manager is an investment adviser;

(iii) Who is an investment company, as defined in Section 3 of the Investment Company Act of 1940, or who would be an investment company but for Section 3(c)(1) or Section 3(c)(7) thereof, or an affiliated person of either of the foregoing. For purposes of this paragraph, "affiliated person" means only those persons described in Section 2(a)(3)(C), (D), (E), and (F) of the Investment Company Act of 1940, assuming for these purposes that a person who would be an investment company but for Section 3(c)(1) or Section 3(c)(7) of the Investment Company Act of 1940 is an investment company; or

(iv) Who is a holder of the issuer's securities, under circumstances in which it is reasonably foreseeable that the person will purchase or sell the issuer's securities on the basis of the information.

(2) Paragraph (a) of this Rule 100 shall not apply to a disclosure made:

(i) To a person who owes a duty of trust or confidence to the issuer (such as an attorney, investment banker, or accountant);

(ii) To a person who expressly agrees to maintain the disclosed information in confidence;

(iii) To an entity whose primary business is the issuance of credit ratings, provided the information is disclosed solely for the purpose of developing a credit rating and the entity's ratings are publicly available; or

(iv) In connection with a securities offering registered under the Securities Act, other than an offering of the type described in any of Securities Act Rule 415(a)(1)(i)-(vi).

Rule 101. Definitions.

This Rule 101 defines certain terms as used in Regulation F-D.

(a) *Intentional.* A selective disclosure of material nonpublic information is "intentional" when the person making the disclosure either knows, or is reckless in not knowing, that the information he or she is communicating is both material and nonpublic.

(b) *Issuer.* An "issuer" subject to this regulation is one that has a class of securities registered under Section 12 of the Securities Exchange Act of 1934, or is required to file reports under Section 15(d) of the Securities Exchange Act of 1934, including any closed-end investment company (as defined in Section 5(a)(2) of the Investment Company Act of 1940, but not including

(i) Any other investment company or

(ii) Any foreign government or foreign private issuer, as those terms are defined in Rule 405 under the Securities Act.

(c) *Person Acting on Behalf of an Issuer.* "Person acting on behalf of an issuer" means any senior official of the issuer (or, in the case of a closed-end investment company, a senior official of the issuer's investment adviser), or any other officer, employee, or agent of an issuer who regularly communicates with any person described in Regulation F-D Rule 100(b)(1)(i), (ii), or (iii), or with holders of the issuer's securities. An officer, director, employee, or agent of an issuer who discloses material nonpublic information in breach of a duty of trust or confidence to the issuer shall not be considered to be acting on behalf of the issuer.

(d) *Promptly.* "Promptly" means as soon as reasonably practicable (but in no event after the later of 24 hours or the commencement of the next day's trading on the New York Stock Exchange) after a senior official of the issuer (or, in the case of a closed end investment company, a senior official of the issuer's investment adviser) learns that there has been a non-intentional disclosure by the issuer or person acting on behalf of the issuer of information that the senior official knows, or is reckless in not knowing, is both material and nonpublic.

(e) *Public Disclosure.*

(1) Except as provided in paragraph (e)(2) of this Rule 101, an issuer shall make the "public disclosure" of information required by Regulation F-D Rule 100(a) by furnishing to or filing with the Commission a Form 8-K disclosing that information.

(2) An issuer shall be exempt from the requirement to furnish or file a Form 8-K if it instead disseminates the information through another method (or combination of methods) of disclosure that is reasonably designed to provide broad, non-exclusionary distribution of the information to the public.

(f) *Senior Official.* "Senior official" means any director, executive officer (as defined in Exchange Act Rule 3b-7), investor relations or public relations officer, or other person with similar functions.

(g) *Securities Offering.* For purposes of Regulation F-D Rule 100(b)(2)(iv):

(1) *Underwritten Offerings.* A securities offering that is underwritten commences when the issuer reaches an understanding with the broker-dealer that is to act as managing underwriter and continues until the later of the end of the period during which a dealer must deliver a prospectus or the sale of the securities (unless the offering is sooner terminated);

(2) *Non-Underwritten Offerings.* A securities offering that is not underwritten:

(a) If covered by Securities Act Rule 415(a)(1)(x), commences when the issuer makes its first bona fide offer in a takedown of securities and continues until the later of the end of the period during which each dealer must deliver a prospectus or the sale of the securities in that takedown (unless the takedown is sooner terminated);

(b) If a business combination as defined in Securities Act Rule 165(f)(1), commences when the first public announcement of the transaction is made and continues until the completion of the vote or the expiration of the tender offer, as applicable (unless the transaction is sooner terminated);

(c) If an offering other than those specified in paragraphs (a) and (b), commences when the issuer files a registration statement and continues until the later of the end of the period during which each dealer must deliver a prospectus or the sale of the securities (unless the offering is sooner terminated).

Rule 102. No Effect on Antifraud Liability.

No failure to make a public disclosure required solely by Regulation F-D Rule 100 shall be deemed to be a violation of Rule 10b-5 under the Securities Exchange Act.

Rule 103. No Effect on Exchange Act Reporting Status.

A failure to make a public disclosure required solely by Regulation F-D Rule 100 shall not affect whether:

(a) For purposes of Forms S-2, S-3 and S-8 under the Securities Act, an issuer is deemed to have filed all the material required to be filed pursuant to Section 13 or 15(d) of the Securities Exchange Act or, where applicable, has made those filings in a timely manner; or

(b) There is adequate current public information about the issuer for purposes of Rule 144(c) under the Securities Act.

Items Under Regulation S-K

Item 201

(a) *Market information.*

(1) (i) Identify the principal United States market or markets in which each class of the registrant's common equity is being traded. Where there is no established public trading market for a class of common equity, furnish a statement to that effect. For purposes of this Item the existence of limited or sporadic quotations should not of itself be deemed to constitute an "established public trading market." In the case of foreign registrants, also identify the principal established foreign public trading market, if any, for each class of the registrant's common equity.

(ii) If the principal United States market for such common equity is an exchange, state the high and low sales prices for the equity for each full quarterly period within the two most recent fiscal years and any subsequent interim period for which financial statements are included, or are required to be included by Article 3 of Regulation S-X [17 CFR 210], as reported in the consolidated transaction reporting system or, if not so reported, as reported on the principal exchange market for such equity.

(iii) If the principal United States market for such common equity is not an exchange, state the range of high and low bid information for the equity for each full quarterly period within the two most recent fiscal years and any subsequent interim period for which financial statements are included, or are required to be included by Article 3 of Regulation S-X, as regularly quoted in the automated quotation system of a registered securities association, or where the equity is not quoted in such a system, the range of reported high and low bid quotations, indicating the source of such quotations. Indicate, as applicable, that such over-the-counter market quotations reflect interdealer prices, without retail mark-up, mark-down or commission and may not necessarily represent actual transactions. Where there is an absence of an established public trading market, reference to quotations shall be qualified by appropriate explanation.

(iv) Where a foreign registrant has identified a principal established foreign trading market for its common equity pursuant to paragraph (a)(1) of this Item, also provide market price information comparable, to the extent practicable, to that required for the principal United States market, including the source of such information. Such prices shall be stated in the currency in which they are quoted. The registrant may translate such prices into United States currency at the currency exchange rate in effect on the date the price disclosed was reported on the foreign exchange. If the primary United States market for the registrant's common equity trades using American Depositary Receipts, the United States prices disclosed shall be on that basis.

(v) If the information called for by this Item is being presented in a registration statement filed pursuant to the Securities Act or a proxy or information statement filed pursuant to the Exchange Act, the document also shall include price information as of the latest practicable date, and, in the case of securities to be issued in connection with an acquisition, business combination or other reorganization, as of the date immediately prior to the public announcement of such transaction.

(2) If the information called for by this paragraph (a) is being presented in a registration statement on Form S-1 [§239.11 of this chapter] or Form S-18 [§239.28 of this chapter] under the Securities Act or on Form 10 [§249.210 of this chapter] under the Exchange Act relating to a class of common equity for which at the time of filing there is no established United States public trading market, indicate the amount(s) of common equity (i) that is subject to outstanding options or warrants to purchase, or securities convertible into, common equity of the registrant; (ii) that could be sold pursuant to Rule 144 under the Securities Act [§230.144 of this chapter] or that the registrant has agreed to register under the Securities Act for sale by security holders; or (iii) that is being, or has been publicly proposed to be, publicly offered by the registrant (unless such common equity is being offered pursuant to an employee benefit plan or dividend reinvestment plan), the offering of which could have a material effect on the market price of the registrant's common equity.

(b) *Holders.*

(1) Set forth the approximate number of holders of each class of common equity of the registrant as of the latest practicable date.

(2) If the information called for by this paragraph (b) is being presented in a registration statement filed pursuant to the Securities Act or a proxy statement or information statement filed pursuant to the Exchange Act that relates to an acquisition, business combination or other reorganization, indicate the effect of such transaction on the amount and percentage of present holdings of the registrant's common equity owned beneficially by (i) any person (including any group as that term is used in section 13(d)(3) of the Exchange Act) who is known to the registrant to be the beneficial owner of more than five percent of any class of the registrant's common equity and (ii) each director and nominee and (iii) all directors and officers as a group, and the registrant's present commitments to such persons with respect to the issuance of shares of any class of its common equity.

(c) *Dividends.*

(1) State the frequency and amount of any cash dividends declared on each class of its common equity by the registrant for the two most recent fiscal years and any subsequent interim period for which financial statements are required to be presented by §210.3 of Regulation S-X. Where

there are restrictions (including, where appropriate, restrictions on the ability of registrant's subsidiaries to transfer funds to the registrant in the form of cash dividends, loans or advances) that currently materially limit the registrant's ability to pay such dividends or that the registrant reasonably believes are likely to limit materially the future payment of dividends on the common equity so state and either (i) describe briefly (where appropriate quantify) such restrictions, or (ii) cross reference to the specific discussion of such restrictions in the Management's Discussion and Analysis of financial condition and operating results prescribed by Item 303 of Regulation S-K (§229.303) and the description of such restrictions required by Regulation S-X in the registrant's financial statements.

(2) Where registrants have a record of paying no cash dividends although earnings indicate an ability to do so, they are encouraged to consider the question of their intention to pay cash dividends in the foreseeable future and, if no such intention exists, to make a statement of that fact in the filing. Registrants which have a history of paying cash dividends also are encouraged to indicate whether they currently expect that comparable cash dividends will continue to be paid in the future and, if not, the nature of the change in the amount or rate of cash dividend payments.

Instructions to Item 201.

1. Registrants, the common equity of which is listed for trading on more than one securities exchange registered under the Exchange Act, are required to indicate each such exchange pursuant to paragraph (a)(1)(i) of this Item; such registrants, however, need only report one set of price quotations pursuant to paragraph (a)(1)(ii) of this Item; where available, these shall be the prices as reported in the consolidated transaction reporting system and, where the prices are not so reported, the prices on the most significant (in terms of volume) securities exchange for such shares.

2. Market prices and dividends reported pursuant to this Item shall be adjusted to give retroactive effect to material changes resulting from stock dividends, stock splits and reverse stock splits.

3. The computation of the approximate number of holders of registrant's common equity may be based upon the number of record holders or also may include individual participants in security position listings. See Rule 17Ad-8 under the Exchange Act. The method of computation that is chosen shall be indicated.

4. If the registrant is a foreign issuer, describe briefly:

A. Any governmental laws, decrees or regulations in the country in which the registrant is organized that restrict the export or import of capital, including, but not limited to, foreign exchange controls, or that affect the remittance of dividends or other payments to nonresident holders of the registrant's common equity; and

B. All taxes, including withholding provisions, to which United States common equity holders are subject under existing laws and regulations of the foreign country in which the registrant is organized. Include a brief description of pertinent provisions of any reciprocal tax treaty between such foreign country and the United States regarding withholding. If there is no such treaty, so state.

5. If the registrant is a foreign private issuer whose common equity of the class being registered is wholly or partially in bearer form, the response to this Item shall so indicate together with as much information as the registrant is able to provide with respect to security holdings in the United States. If the securities being registered trade in the United States in the form of American Depositary Receipts or similar certificates, the response to this Item shall so indicate together with the name of the depositary issuing such receipts and the number of shares or other units of the underlying security representing the trading units in such receipts.

Item 402

(a) *General*.

(1) *Treatment of Specific Types of Issuers*.

(i) *Small Business Issuers*. A registrant that qualifies as "small business issuer," as defined by Item 10(a)(1) of Regulation S-B [17 CFR 228.10(a)(1)], will be deemed to comply with this item if it provides the information required by paragraph (b) (Summary Compensation Table), paragraphs (c)(1) and (c)(2)(i)-(v) (Option/SAR Grants Table), paragraph (d) (Aggregated Option/SAR Exercise and Fiscal Year-End Option/SAR Value Table), paragraph (e) (Long-Term Incentive Plan Awards Table), paragraph (g) (Compensation of Directors), paragraph (h) (Employment Contracts, Termination of Employment and Change in Control Arrangements) and paragraph (i)(1) and (2) (Report on Repricing of Options/SARs) of this item.

(ii) *Foreign Private Issuers*. A foreign private issuer will be deemed to comply with this item if it provides the information required by Items 11 and 12 of Form 20-F [17 CFR 249.220f], with more detailed information provided if otherwise made publicly available.

(2) *All Compensation Covered*. This item requires clear, concise and understandable disclosure of all plan and non-plan compensation awarded to, earned by, or paid to the named executive officers designated under paragraph (a)(3) of this item, and directors covered by paragraph (g) of this item by any person for all services rendered in all capacities to the registrant and its subsidiaries, unless otherwise specified in this item.

Except as provided by paragraph (a)(5) of this item, all such compensation shall be reported pursuant to this item, even if also called for by another requirement, including transactions between the registrant and a third party where the primary purpose of the transaction is to furnish compensation to any such named executive officer or director. No item reported as compensation for one fiscal year need be reported as compensation for a subsequent fiscal year.

(3) *Persons Covered.* Disclosure shall be provided pursuant to this item for each of the following (the "named executive officers"):

(i) All individuals serving as the registrant's chief executive officer or acting in a similar capacity during the last completed fiscal year ("CEO"), regardless of compensation level;

(ii) The registrant's four most highly compensated executive officers other than the CEO who were serving as executive officers at the end of the last completed fiscal year; and

(iii) up to two additional individuals for whom disclosure would have been provided pursuant to paragraph (a)(3)(ii) of this item but for the fact that the individual was not serving as an executive officer of the registrant at the end of the last completed fiscal year.

Instructions to Item 402(a)(3).

1. *Determination of Most Highly Compensated Executive Officers.* The determination as to which executive officers are most highly compensated shall be made by reference to total annual salary and bonus for the last completed fiscal year (as required to be disclosed pursuant to paragraph (b)(2)(iii)(A) and (B) of this item), but including the dollar value of salary or bonus amounts forgone pursuant to Instruction 3 to paragraph (b)(2)(iii)(A) and (B) of this item, *provided, however,* that no disclosure need be provided for any executive officer, other than the CEO, whose total annual salary and bonus, as so determined, does not exceed $100,000.

2. *Inclusion of Executive Officer of Subsidiary.* It may be appropriate in certain circumstances for a registrant to include an executive officer of a subsidiary in the disclosure required by this item. *See* Rule 3b-7 under the Exchange Act [17 CFR 240.3b-7].

3. *Exclusion of Executive Officer due to Unusual or Overseas Compensation.* It may be appropriate in limited circumstances for a registrant not to include in the disclosure required by this item an individual, other than its CEO, who is one of the registrant's most highly compensated executive officers. Among the factors that should be considered in determining not to name an individual are:

(a) the distribution or accrual of an unusually large amount of cash compensation (such as a bonus or commission) that is not part of a recurring arrangement and is unlikely to continue; and (b) the payment of amounts of cash compensation relating to overseas assignments that may be attributed predominantly to such assignments.

(4) *Information for Full Fiscal Year*. If the CEO served in that capacity during any part of a fiscal year with respect to which information is required, information should be provided as to all of his or her compensation for the full fiscal year. If a named executive officer (other than the CEO) served as an executive officer of the registrant (whether or not in the same position) during any part of a fiscal year with respect to which information is required, information shall be provided as to all compensation of that individual for the full fiscal year.

(5) *Transactions With Third Parties Reported under Item 404*. This item includes transactions between the registrant and a third party where the primary purpose of the transaction is to furnish compensation to a named executive officer. No information need be given in response to any paragraph of this item, other than paragraph (j), as to any such third-party transaction if the transaction has been reported in response to Item 404 of Regulation S-K (§ 229.404).

(6) *Omission of Table or Column*. A table or column may be omitted, if there has been no compensation awarded to, earned by or paid to any of the named executives required to be reported in that table or column in any fiscal year covered by that table.

(7) *Definitions*. For purposes of this item:

(i) The term *stock appreciation rights* ("SARs") refers to SARs payable in cash or stock, including SARs payable in cash or stock at the election of the registrant or a named executive officer.

(ii) The term *plan* includes, but is not limited to, the following: any plan, contract, authorization or arrangement, whether or not set forth in any formal documents, pursuant to which the following may be received: cash, stock, restricted stock or restricted stock units, phantom stock, stock options, SARs, stock options in tandem with SARs, warrants, convertible securities, performance units and performance shares, and similar instruments. A plan may be applicable to one person. Registrants may omit information regarding group life, health, hospitalization, medical reimbursement or relocation plans that do not discriminate in scope, terms or operation, in favor of executive officers or directors of the registrant and that are available generally to all salaried employees.

(iii) The term *long-term incentive plan* means any plan providing compensation intended to serve as incentive for performance to occur over a period longer than one fiscal year, whether such performance is measured by reference to financial performance of the registrant or an affiliate, the registrant's stock price, or any other measure, but excluding restricted stock, stock option and SAR plans.

(8) *Location of Specified Information.* The information required by paragraphs (i), (k) and (l) of this item need not be provided in any filings other than a registrant proxy or information statement relating to an annual meeting of security holders at which directors are to be elected (or special meeting or written consents in lieu of such meeting). Such information will not be deemed to be incorporated by reference into any filing under the Securities Act or the Exchange Act, except to the extent that the registrant specifically incorporates it by reference.

(9) *Liability for Specified Information.* The information required by paragraphs (k) and (l) of this item shall not be deemed to be "soliciting material" or to be "filed" with the Commission or subject to Regulations 14A or 14C [17 CFR 240.14a-1 *et seq.* or 240.14c-1 *et seq.*], other than as provided in this item, or to the liabilities of Section 18 of the Exchange Act [15 U.S.C. 78r], except to the extent that the registrant specifically requests that such information be treated as soliciting material or specifically incorporates it by reference into a filing under the Securities Act or the Exchange Act.

(b) *Summary Compensation Table.*

(1) *General.* The information specified in paragraph (b)(2) of this item, concerning the compensation of the named executive officers for each of the registrant's last three completed fiscal years, shall be provided in a Summary Compensation Table, in the tabular format specified below.

SUMMARY COMPENSATION TABLE

(a)	(b)	(c)	(d)	(e)	(f)	(g)	(h)	(i)
		Annual Compensation			Long Term Compensation			
						Awards	Payouts	
Name and Principal Position	Year	Salary ($)	Bonus ($)	Other Annual Compensation ($)	Restricted Stock Award(s) ($)	Securities Underlying Options/ SARs (#)	LTIP Payouts ($)	All Other Compensation ($)
CEO	— — —							
A	— — —							
B	— — —							
C	— — —							
D	— — —							

(2) The Table shall include:

(i) The name and principal position of the executive officer (column (a));

(ii) Fiscal year covered (column (b));

(iii) Annual compensation (columns (c), (d) and (e)), including:

(A) The dollar value of base salary (cash and non-cash) earned by the named executive officer during the fiscal year covered (column (c));

(B) The dollar value of bonus (cash and non-cash) earned by the named executive officer during the fiscal year covered (column (d)); and

Instructions to Item 402(b)(2)(iii)(A) and (B).

1. Amounts deferred at the election of a named executive officer, whether pursuant to a plan established under Section 401(k) of the Internal Revenue Code [26 U.S.C. 401(k)], or otherwise, shall be included in the salary column (column (c)) or bonus column (column (d)), as appropriate, for the fiscal year in which earned. If the amount of salary or bonus earned in a given fiscal year is not calculable through the latest practicable date, that fact must be disclosed in a footnote and such amount must be disclosed in the subsequent fiscal year in the appropriate column for the fiscal year in which earned.

2. For stock or any other form of non-cash compensation, disclose the fair market value at the time the compensation is awarded, earned or paid.

3. Registrants need not include in the salary column (column (c)) or bonus column (column (d)) any amount of salary or bonus forgone at the election of a named executive officer pursuant to a registrant program under which stock, stock-based or other forms of non-cash compensation may be received by a named executive in lieu of a portion of annual compensation earned in a covered fiscal year. However, the receipt of any such form of non-cash compensation in lieu of salary or bonus earned for a covered fiscal year must be disclosed in the appropriate column of the Table corresponding to that fiscal year (i.e., restricted stock awards (column (f)); options or SARs (column (g)); all other compensation (column (i)), or, if made pursuant to a long-term incentive plan and therefore not reportable at grant in the Summary Compensation Table, a footnote must be added to the salary or bonus column so disclosing and referring to the Long-Term Incentive Plan Table (required by paragraph (e) of this item) where the award is reported.

(C) The dollar value of other annual compensation not properly categorized as salary or bonus, as follows (column (e)):

(*1*) Perquisites and other personal benefits, securities or property, unless the aggregate amount of such compensation is the lesser of either $50,000 or 10% of the total of annual salary and bonus reported for the named executive officer in columns (c) and (d);

(*2*) Above-market or preferential earnings on restricted stock, options, SARs or deferred compensation paid during the fiscal year or payable during that period but deferred at the election of the named executive officer;

(3) Earnings on long-term incentive plan compensation paid during the fiscal year or payable during that period but deferred at the election of the named executive officer;

(4) Amounts reimbursed during the fiscal year for the payment of taxes; and

(5) The dollar value of the difference between the price paid by a named executive officer for any security of the registrant or its subsidiaries purchased from the registrant or its subsidiaries (through deferral of salary or bonus, or otherwise), and the fair market value of such security at the date of purchase, unless that discount is available generally, either to all security holders or to all salaried employees of the registrant.

Instructions to Item 402(b)(2)(iii)(C).

1. Each perquisite or other personal benefit exceeding 25% of the total perquisites and other personal benefits reported for a named executive officer must be identified by type and amount in a footnote or accompanying narrative discussion to column (e).

2. Perquisites and other personal benefits shall be valued on the basis of the aggregate incremental cost to the registrant and its subsidiaries.

3. Interest on deferred or long-term compensation is above-market only if the rate of interest exceeds 120% of the applicable federal long-term rate, with compounding (as prescribed under Section 1274(d) of the Internal Revenue Code, [26 U.S.C. 1274(d)]) at the rate that corresponds most closely to the rate under the registrant's plan at the time the interest rate or formula is set. In the event of a discretionary reset of the interest rate, the requisite calculation must be made on the basis of the interest rate at the time of such reset, rather than when originally established. Only the above-market portion of the interest must be included. If the applicable interest rates vary depending upon conditions such as a minimum period of continued service, the reported amount should be calculated assuming satisfaction of all conditions to receiving interest at the highest rate.

4. Dividends (and dividend equivalents) on restricted stock, options, SARs or deferred compensation denominated in stock ("deferred stock") are preferential only if earned at a rate higher than dividends on the registrant's common stock. Only the preferential portion of the dividends or equivalents must be included.

(iv) Long-term compensation (columns (f), (g) and (h)), including:

(A) The dollar value (net of any consideration paid by the named executive officer) of any award of restricted stock, including share units (calculated by multiplying the closing market price of the registrant's unrestricted stock on the date of grant by the number of shares awarded) (column (f));

(B) The sum of the number of securities underlying stock options granted, with or without tandem SARs, and the number of freestanding SARs (column (g)); and (C) The dollar value of all payouts pursuant to long-term incentive plans ("LTIPs") as defined in paragraph (a)(7)(iii) of this item (column (h)).

Instructions to Item 402(b)(2)(iv).

1. Awards of restricted stock that are subject to performance-based conditions on vesting, in addition to lapse of time and/or continued service with the registrant or a subsidiary, may be reported as LTIP awards pursuant to paragraph (e) of this item instead of in column (f). If this approach is selected, once the restricted stock vests, it must be reported as an LTIP payout in column (h).

2. The registrant shall, in a footnote to the Summary Compensation Table (appended to column (f), if included), disclose:

a. The number and value of the aggregate restricted stock holdings at the end of the last completed fiscal year. The value shall be calculated in the manner specified in paragraph (b)(2)(iv)(A) of this item using the value of the registrant's shares at the end of the last completed fiscal year.

b. For any restricted stock award reported in the Summary Compensation Table that will vest, in whole or in part, in under three years from the date of grant, the total number of shares awarded and the vesting schedule; and

c. Whether dividends will be paid on the restricted stock reported in column (f).

3. If at any time during the last completed fiscal year, the registrant has adjusted or amended the exercise price of stock options or freestanding SARs previously awarded to a named executive officer, whether through amendment, cancellation or replacement grants, or any other means ("repriced"), the registrant shall include the number of options or freestanding SARs so repriced as Stock Options/SARs granted and required to be reported in column (g).

4. If any specified performance target, goal or condition to payout was waived with respect to any amount included in LTIP payouts reported in column (h), the registrant shall so state in a footnote to column (h).

(v) All other compensation for the covered fiscal year that the registrant could not properly report in any other column of the Summary Compensation Table (column (i)). Any compensation reported in this column for the last completed fiscal year shall be identified and quantified in a footnote. Such compensation shall include, but not be limited to:

(A) The amount paid, payable or accrued to any named executive officer pursuant to a plan or arrangement in connection with:

(1) The resignation, retirement or any other termination of such executive officer's employment with the registrant and its subsidiaries; or

(2) A change in control of the registrant or a change in the executive officer's responsibilities following such a change in control;

(B) The sum of the number of securities underlying stock options granted (including options that subsequently have been transferred), with or without tandem SARs, and the number of freestanding SARs (column (g)); and

(C) The dollar value of amounts earned on long-term incentive plan compensation during the fiscal year, or calculated with respect to that period, except that if such amounts are paid during that period, or payable during that period at the election of the named executive officer, this information shall be reported as Other Annual Compensation in column (e);

(D) Annual registrant contributions or other allocations to vested and unvested defined contribution plans; and

(E) The dollar value of any insurance premiums paid by, or on behalf of, the registrant during the covered fiscal year with respect to term life insurance for the benefit of a named executive officer, and, if there is any arrangement or understanding, whether formal or informal, that such executive officer has or will receive or be allocated an interest in any cash surrender value under the insurance policy, either

(1) The full dollar value of the remainder of the premiums paid by, or on behalf of, the registrant;

or

(2) If the premiums will be refunded to the registrant on termination of the policy, the dollar value of the benefit to the executive officer of the remainder of the premium paid by, or on behalf of, the registrant during the fiscal year. The benefit shall be determined for the period, projected on an actuarial basis, between payment of the premium and the refund.

Instructions to Item 402(b)(2)(v).

1. LTIP awards and amounts received on exercise of options and SARs need not be reported as All Other Compensation in column (i).

2. Information relating to defined benefit and actuarial plans should not be reported pursuant to paragraph (b) of this item, but instead should be reported pursuant to paragraph (f) of this item.

3. Where alternative methods of reporting are available under paragraph (b)(2)(v)(E) of this item, the same method should be used for each of the named executive officers. If the registrant chooses to change methods from one year to the next, that fact, and the reason therefor, should be disclosed in a footnote to column (i).

Instruction to Item 402(b). Information with respect to fiscal years prior to the last completed fiscal year will not be required if the registrant was not a reporting company pursuant to Section 13(a) or 15(d) of the Exchange Act at any time during that year, except that the registrant will be required to provide information for any such year if that information previously was required to be provided in response to a Commission filing requirement.

(c) *Option/SAR Grants Table.*

(1) The information specified in paragraph (c)(2) of this item, concerning individual grants of stock options (whether or not in tandem with SARs) and freestanding SARs (including options and SARs that subsequently have been transferred) made during the last completed fiscal year to each of the named executive officers shall be provided in the tabular format specified below:

Option/SAR Grants in Last Fiscal Year

	Individual Grants				Potential Realizable Value at Assumed Annual Rates of Stock Price Appreciation for Option Term		Alternative to (f) and (g): Grant Date Value
(a)	(b)	(c)	(d)	(e)	(f)	(g)	(h)
Name	Number of Securities Underlying Options/ SARs Granted (#)	Percentage of Total Options/ SARs Granted to Employees in Fiscal Year	Exercise of Base Price ($/Sh)	Expiration Date	5% ($)	10% ($)	Grant Date Present Value $
CEO							
A							
B							
C							
D							

(2) The Table shall include, with respect to each grant:

(i) The name of the executive officer (column (a));

(ii) The number of securities underlying options and SARs granted (column (b));

(iii) The percent the grant represents of total options and SARs granted to employees during the fiscal year (column (c));

(iv) The per-share exercise or base price of the options or SARs granted (column (d)). If such exercise or base price is less than the market price of the underlying security on the date of grant, a separate, adjoining column shall be added showing market price on the date of grant;

(v) The expiration date of the options or SARs (column (e)); and

(vi) Either (A) the potential realizable value of each grant of options or freestanding SARs or (B) the present value of each grant, as follows:

(A) The potential realizable value of each grant of options or freestanding SARs, assuming that the market price of the underlying security appreciates in value from the date of grant to the end of the option or SAR term, at the following annualized rates:

(1) 5% (column (f));

(2) 10% (column (g)); and

(3) If the exercise or base price was below the market price of the underlying security at the date of grant, provide an additional column labeled 0%, to show the value at grant-date market price; or

(B) The present value of the grant at the date of grant, under any option pricing model (alternative column (f)).

Instructions to Item 402(c).

1. If more than one grant of options and/or freestanding SARs was made to a named executive officer during the last completed fiscal year, a separate line should be used to provide disclosure of each such grant. However, multiple grants during a single fiscal year may be aggregated where each grant was made at the same exercise and/or base price and has the same expiration date, and the same performance vesting thresholds, if any. A single grant consisting of options and/or freestanding SARs shall be reported as separate grants with respect to each tranche with a different exercise and/or base price, performance vesting threshold, or expiration date.

2. Options or freestanding SARs granted in connection with an option repricing transaction shall be reported in this table. *See* Instruction 3 to paragraph (b)(2)(iv) of this item.

3. Any material term of the grant, including but not limited to the date of exercisability, the number of SARs, performance units or other instruments granted in tandem with options, a performance-based condition to exercisability, a reload feature, or a tax-reimbursement feature, shall be footnoted.

4. If the exercise or base price is adjustable over the term of any option or freestanding SAR in accordance with any prescribed standard or formula, including but not limited to an index or premium

price provision, describe the following, either by footnote to column (c) or in narrative accompanying the Table: (a) the standard or formula; and (b) any constant assumption made by the registrant regarding any adjustment to the exercise price in calculating the potential option or SAR value.

5. If any provision of a grant (other than an antidilution provision) could cause the exercise price to be lowered, registrants must clearly and fully disclose these provisions and their potential consequences either by a footnote or accompanying textual narrative.

6. In determining the grant-date market or base price of the security underlying options or freestanding SARs, the registrant may use either the closing market price per share of the security, or any other formula prescribed for the security.

7. The potential realizable dollar value of a grant (columns (f) and (g)) shall be the product of: (a) the difference between: (i) the product of the per-share market price at the time of the grant and the sum of 1 plus the adjusted stock price appreciation rate (the assumed rate of appreciation compounded annually over the term of the option or SAR); and (ii) the per-share exercise price of the option or SAR; and (b) the number of securities underlying the grant at fiscal year-end.

8. Registrants may add one or more separate columns using the formula prescribed in Instruction 7 toparagraph (c) of this item, to reflect the following:

a. the registrant's historic rate of appreciation over a period equivalent to the term of such options and/or SARs;

b. 0% appreciation, where the exercise or base price was equal to or greater than the market price of the underlying securities on the date of grant; and

c. N% appreciation, the percentage appreciation by which the exercise or base price exceeded the market price at grant. Where the grant included multiple tranches with exercise or base prices exceeding the market price of the underlying security by varying degrees, include an additional column for each additional tranche.

9. Where the registrant chooses to use the grant-date valuation alternative specified in paragraph (c)(2)(vi)(B) of this item, the valuation shall be footnoted to describe the valuation method used. Where the registrant has used a variation of the Black-Scholes or binomial option pricing model, the description shall identify the use of such pricing model and describe the assumptions used relating to the expected volatility, risk-free rate of return, dividend yield and time of exercise. Any adjustments for non-transferability or risk of forfeiture

also shall be disclosed. In the event another valuation method is used, the registrant is required to describe the methodology as well as any material assumptions.

(d) *Aggregated Option/SAR Exercises and Fiscal Year-End Option/SAR Value Table.*

(1) The information specified in paragraph (d)(2) of this item, concerning each exercise of stock options (or tandem SARs) and freestanding SARs during the last completed fiscal year by each of the named executive officers and the fiscal yearend value of unexercised options and SARs, shall be provided on an aggregated basis in the tabular format specified below:

Aggregated Option/SAR Exercises in Last Fiscal Year and FY-End Option/SAR Values

(a)	(b)	(c)	(d)	(e)
			Number of Securities Underlying Unexercised Options/SARs at FY-End (#)	Value of Unexercised In-the-Money Options/SARs at FY-End ($)
Name	Shares Acquired on Exercise (#)	Value Realized ($)	Exercisable/ Unexercisable	Exercisable/ Unexercisable
CEO				
A				
B				
C				
D				

(2) The table shall include:

(i) The name of the executive officer (column (a));

(ii) The number of shares received upon exercise, or, if no shares were received, the number of securities with respect to which the options or SARs were exercised (column (b));

(iii) The aggregate dollar value realized upon exercise (column (c));

(iv) The total number of securities underlying unexercised options and SARs held at the end of the last completed fiscal year, separately identifying the exercisable and unexercisable options and SARs (column (d)); and (v) The aggregate dollar value of in-the-money, unexercised options and SARs held at the end of the fiscal year, separately identifying the exercisable and unexercisable options and SARs (column (e)).

Instructions to Item 402(d)(2).

1. Options or freestanding SARs are in-the-money if the fair market value of the underlying securities exceeds the exercise or base price of the option or SAR. The dollar values in columns (c) and (e) are calculated by determining the difference between the fair market value of the securities underlying the options or SARs and the exercise or base price of the options or SARs at exercise or fiscal year-end, respectively.

2. In calculating the dollar value realized upon exercise (column (c)), the value of any related payment or other consideration provided (or to be provided) by the registrant to or on behalf of a named executive officer, whether in payment of the exercise price or related taxes, shall not be included. Payments by the registrant in reimbursement of tax obligations incurred by a named executive officer are required to be disclosed in accordance with paragraph (b)(2)(iii)(C)(4) of this item.

(e) *Long-Term Incentive Plan ("LTIP") Awards Table.*

(1) The information specified in paragraph (e)(2) of this item, regarding each award made to a named executive officer in the last completed fiscal year under any LTIP, shall be provided in the tabular format specified below:

Long-Term Incentive Plans — Awards in Last Fiscal Year

			Estimated Future Payouts under Non-Stock Price-Based Plans		
(a)	(b)	(c)	(d)	(e)	(f)
Name	Number of Shares, Units or Other Rights (#)	Performance or Other Period Until Maturation or Payout	Threshold ($ or #)	Target ($ or #)	Maximum ($ or #)
CEO					
A					
B					
C					
D					

(2) The Table shall include:

(i) The name of the executive officer (column (a));

(ii) The number of shares, units or other rights awarded under any LTIP, and, if applicable, the number of shares underlying any such unit or right (column (b));

(iii) The performance or other time period until payout or maturation of the award (column (c)); and

(iv) For plans not based on stock price, the dollar value of the estimated payout, the number of shares to be awarded as the payout or a range of estimated payouts denominated in dollars or number of shares under the award (threshold, target and maximum amount) (columns (d) through (f)).

Instructions to Item 402(e).

1. For purposes of this paragraph, the term "long-term incentive plan" or "LTIP" shall be defined in accordance with paragraph (a)(7)(iii) of this item.

2. Describe in a footnote or in narrative text accompanying this table the material terms of any award, including a general descrip-

tion of the formula or criteria to be applied in determining the amounts payable. Registrants are not required to disclose any factor, criterion or performance-related or other condition to payout or maturation of a particular award that involves confidential commercial or business information, disclosure of which would adversely affect the registrant's competitive position.

3. Separate disclosure shall be provided in the Table for each award made to a named executive officer, accompanied by the information specified in Instruction 2 to this paragraph. If awards are made to a named executive officer during the fiscal year under more than one plan, identify the particular plan under which each such award was made.

4. For column (d), "threshold" refers to the minimum amount payable for a certain level of performance under the plan. For column (e), "target" refers to the amount payable if the specified performance target(s) are reached. For column (f), "maximum" refers to the maximum payout possible under the plan.

5. In column (e), registrants must provide a representative amount based on the previous fiscal year's performance if the target award is not determinable.

6. A tandem grant of two instruments, only one of which is pursuant to a LTIP, need be reported only in the table applicable to the other instrument. For example, an option granted in tandem with a performance share would be reported only as an option grant, with the tandem feature noted.

(f) *Defined Benefit or Actuarial Plan Disclosure.*

(1) *Pension Plan Table.*

(i) For any defined benefit or actuarial plan under which benefits are determined primarily by final compensation (or average final compensation) and years of service, provide a separate Pension Plan Table showing estimated annual benefits payable upon retirement (including amounts attributable to any defined benefit supplementary or excess pension award plans) in specified compensation and years of service classifications in the format specified below:

PENSION PLAN TABLE

Remuneration	15	20	Years of Service 25	30	35
125,000					
150,000					
175,000					
200,000					
225,000					
250,000					
300,000					
400,000					
450,000					
500,000					

(ii) Immediately following the Table, the registrant shall disclose:

(A) The compensation covered by the plan(s), including the relationship of such covered compensation to the annual compensation reported in the Summary Compensation Table required by paragraph (b)(2)(iii) of this item, and state the current compensation covered by the plan for any named executive officer whose covered compensation differs substantially (by more than 10%) from that set forth in the annual compensation columns of the Summary Compensation Table;

(B) The estimated credited years of service for each of the named executive officers; and (C) A statement as to the basis upon which benefits are computed (e.g., straight-life annuity amounts), and whether or not the benefits listed in the Pension Plan Table are subject to any deduction for Social Security or other offset amounts.

(2) *Alternative Pension Plan Disclosure.* For any defined benefit or actuarial plan under which benefits are not determined primarily by final compensation (or average final compensation) and years of service, the registrant shall state in narrative form:

(i) The formula by which benefits are determined; and

(ii) The estimated annual benefits payable upon retirement at normal retirement age for each of the named executive officers.

Instructions to Item 402(f).

1. *Pension Levels.* Compensation set forth in the Pension Plan Table pursuant to paragraph (f)(1)(i) of this item shall allow for reasonable increases in existing compensation levels; alternatively, registrants may present as the highest compensation level in the Pension Plan Table an amount equal to 120% of the amount of covered compensation of the most highly compensated individual named in the Summary Compensation Table required by paragraph (b)(2) of this item.

2. *Normal Retirement Age.* The term "normal retirement age" means normal retirement age as defined in a pension or similar plan or, if not defined therein, the earliest time at which a participant may retire without any benefit reduction due to age.

(g) *Compensation of Directors.*

(1) *Standard Arrangements.* Describe any standard arrangements, stating amounts, pursuant to which directors of the registrant are compensated for any services provided as a director, including any additional amounts payable for committee participation or special assignments.

(2) *Other Arrangements.* Describe any other arrangements pursuant to which any director of the registrant was compensated during the registrant's last completed fiscal year for any service provided as a director, stating the amount paid and the name of the director.

Instruction to Item 402(g)(2). The information required by paragraph (g)(2) of this item shall include any arrangement, including consulting contracts, entered into in consideration of the director's service on the board. The material terms of any such arrangement shall be included.

(h) *Employment Contracts and Termination of Employment and Change-in-Control Arrangements.* Describe the terms and conditions of each of the following contracts or arrangements:

(1) Any employment contract between the registrant and a named executive officer; and

(2) Any compensatory plan or arrangement, including payments to be received from the registrant, with respect to a named executive officer, if such plan or arrangement results or will result from the resignation, retirement or any other termination of such executive officer's employment with the registrant and its subsidiaries or from a change-in-control of the registrant or a change in the named executive officer's responsibilities following a change-in-control and the amount involved, including all periodic payments or installments, exceeds $100,000.

(i) *Report on Repricing of Options/SARs.*

(1) If at any time during the last completed fiscal year, the registrant, while a reporting company pursuant to Section 13(a) or 15(d) of the Exchange Act [15 U.S.C. 78m(a), 78o(d)], has adjusted or amended the exercise price of stock options or SARs previously awarded to any of the named executive officers, whether through amendment, cancellation or replacement grants, or any other means ("repriced"), the registrant shall provide the information specified in paragraphs (i)(2) and (i)(3) of this item.

(2) The compensation committee (or other board committee performing equivalent functions or, in the absence of any such committee, the entire board of directors) shall explain in reasonable detail any such repricing of options and/or SARs held by a named executive officer in the last completed fiscal year, as well as the basis for each such repricing.

(3) (i) The information specified in paragraph (i)(3)(*ii*) of this item, concerning all such repricings of options and SARs held by *any* executive officer during the last ten completed fiscal years, shall be provided in the tabular format specified below:

Ten-Year Option/SAR Repricings

(a)	(b)	(c) Number of Securities Underlying Options/ SAR Repriced or Amended (#)	(d) Market Price of Stock at Time of Repricing or Amendment ($)	(e) Exercise Price at Time of Repricing or Amendment ($)	(f)	(g) Length of Original Option Term Remaining at Date of Repricing or Amendment
Name	Date				New Exercise Price ($)	

(ii) The Table shall include, with respect to each repricing:

(A) The name and position of the executive officer (column (a));

(B) The date of each repricing (column (b));

(C) The number of securities underlying replacement or amended options or SARs (column (c));

(D) The per-share market price of the underlying security at the time of repricing (column (d));

(E) The original exercise price or base price of the cancelled or amended option or SAR (column (e));

(F) The per-share exercise price or base price of the replacement option or SAR (column (f)); and

(G) The amount of time remaining before the replaced or amended option or SAR would have expired (column (g)).

Instructions to Item 402(i).

1. The required report shall be made over the name of each member of the registrant's compensation committee, or other board committee performing equivalent functions or, in the absence of any such committee, the entire board of directors.

2. A replacement grant is any grant of options or SARs reasonably related to any prior or potential option or SAR cancellation, whether by an exchange of existing options or SARs for options or SARs with new terms; the grant of new options or SARs in tandem with previously granted options or SARs that will operate to cancel the previously granted options or SARs upon exercise; repricing of previously granted options or SARs; or otherwise. If a corresponding original grant was canceled in a prior year, information about such grant nevertheless must be disclosed pursuant to this paragraph.

3. If the replacement grant is not made at the current market price, describe the terms of the grant in a footnote or accompanying textual narrative.

4. This paragraph shall not apply to any repricing occurring through the operation of:

a. a plan formula or mechanism that results in the periodic adjustment of the option or SAR exercise or base price;

b. a plan antidilution provision; or

c. a recapitalization or similar transaction equally affecting all holders of the class of securities underlying the options or SARs.

5. Information required by paragraph (i)(3) of this item shall not be provided for any repricings effected before the registrant became a reporting company pursuant to Section 13(a) or 15(d) of the Exchange Act.

(j) *Additional Information with Respect to Compensation Committee Interlocks and Insider Participation in Compensation Decisions.* Under the caption "Compensation Committee Interlocks and Insider Participation,"

(1) The registrant shall identify each person who served as a member of the compensation committee of the registrant's board of directors (or board committee performing equivalent functions) during the last completed fiscal year, indicating each committee member who:

(i) was, during the fiscal year, an officer or employee of the registrant or any of its subsidiaries;

(ii) was formerly an officer of the registrant or any of its subsidiaries; or

(iii) had any relationship requiring disclosure by the registrant under any paragraph of Item 404 of Regulation S-K (§229.404). In this event, the disclosure required by Item 404 shall accompany such identification.

(2) If the registrant has no compensation committee (or other board committee performing equivalent functions), the registrant shall identify each officer and employee of the registrant or any of its subsidiaries, and any former officer of the registrant or any of its subsidiaries, who, during the last completed fiscal year, participated in deliberations of the registrant's board of directors concerning executive officer compensation.

(3) The registrant shall describe any of the following relationships that existed during the last completed fiscal year:

(i) an executive officer of the registrant served as a member of the compensation committee (or other board committee performing equivalent functions or, in the absence of any such committee, the entire board of directors) of another entity, one of whose executive officers served on the compensation committee (or other board committee performing equivalent functions or, in the absence of any such committee, the entire board of directors) of the registrant;

(ii) an executive officer of the registrant served as a director of another entity, one of whose executive officers served on the compensation committee (or other board committee performing equivalent functions or, in the absence of any such committee, the entire board of directors) of the registrant; and

(iii) an executive officer of the registrant served as a member of the compensation committee (or other board committee performing equivalent functions or, in the absence of any such committee, the entire board of directors) of another entity, one of whose executive officers served as a director of the registrant.

(4) Disclosure required under paragraph (j)(3) of this item regarding any compensation committee member or other director of the registrant who also served as an executive officer of another entity shall be accompanied by the disclosure called for by Item 404 (§229.404) with respect to that person.

> *Instruction to Item 402(j).* For purposes of this paragraph, the term "entity" shall not include an entity exempt from tax under Section 501(c)(3) of the Internal Revenue Code [26 U.S.C. 501(c)(3)].

(k) *Board Compensation Committee Report on Executive Compensation.*

(1) Disclosure of the compensation committee's compensation policies applicable to the registrant's executive officers (including the named executive officers), including the specific relationship of corporate performance to executive compensation, is required with respect to compensation reported for the last completed fiscal year.

(2) Discussion is required of the compensation committee's bases for the CEO's compensation reported for the last completed fiscal year, including the factors and criteria upon which the CEO's compensation was based. The committee shall include a specific discussion of the relationship of the registrant's performance to the CEO's compensation for the last completed fiscal year, describing each measure of the registrant's performance, whether qualitative or quantitative, on which the CEO's compensation was based.

(3) The required disclosure shall be made over the name of each member of the registrant's compensation committee (or other board committee performing equivalent functions or, in the absence of any such committee, the entire board of directors). If the board of directors modified or rejected in any material way any action or recommendation by such committee with respect to such decisions in the last completed fiscal year, the disclosure must so indicate and explain the reasons for the board's actions, and be made over the names of all members of the board.

> *Instructions to Item 402(k).*
>
> 1. Boilerplate language should be avoided in describing factors and criteria underlying awards or payments of executive compensation in the statement required.
>
> 2. Registrants are not required to disclose target levels with respect to specific quantitative or qualitative performance-related factors considered by the committee (or board), or any factors or criteria involving confidential commercial or business information, the disclosure of which would have an adverse effect on the registrant.

(*l*) *Performance Graph.*

(1) Provide a line graph comparing the yearly percentage change in the registrant's cumulative total shareholder return on a class of common stock registered under Section 12 of the Exchange Act (as measured by dividing (i) the sum of (A) the cumulative amount of dividends for the measurement period, assuming dividend reinvestment, and (B) the difference between the registrant's share price at the end and the beginning of the measurement period; by (ii) the share price at the beginning of the measurement period) with (i) the cumulative total return of a broad equity market index assuming reinvestment of dividends, that includes companies whose equity securities are traded on the same exchange or NASDAQ market or are of comparable market capitalization; *provided, however,* that if the registrant is a company within the Standard & Poor's 500 Stock Index, the registrant must use that index; and (ii) the cumulative total return, assuming reinvestment of dividends, of:

(A) a published industry or line-of-business index;

(B) peer issuer(s) selected in good faith. If the registrant does not select its peer issuer(s) on an industry or lineof-business basis, the registrant shall disclose the basis for its selection; or

(C) Issuer(s) with similar market capitalization(s), but only if the registrant does not use a published industry or line-of-business index and does not believe it can reasonably identify a peer group. If the registrant uses this alternative, the graph shall be accompanied by a statement of the reasons for this selection.

(2) For purposes of paragraph (*l*)(1) of this item, the term "measurement period" shall be the period beginning at the "measurement point" established by the market close on the last trading day before the beginning of the registrant's fifth preceding fiscal year, through and including the end of the registrant's last completed fiscal year. If the class of securities has been registered under section 12 of the Exchange Act for a shorter period of time, the period covered by the comparison may correspond to that time period.

(3) For purposes of paragraph (*l*)(1)(ii)(A) of this item, the term "published industry or line-of-business index" means any index that is prepared by a party other than the registrant or an affiliate and is accessible to the registrant's security holders; provided, however, that registrants may use an index prepared by the registrant or affiliate if such index is widely recognized and used.

(4) If the registrant selects a different index from an index used for the immediately preceding fiscal year, explain the reason(s) for this change and also compare the registrant's total return with that of both the newly selected index and the index used in the immediately preceding fiscal year.

Instructions to Item 402(l).

1. In preparing the required graphic comparisons, the registrant should:

a. use, to the extent feasible, comparable methods of presentation and assumptions for the total return calculations required by paragraph (*l*)(1) of this item; *provided, however,* that if the registrant constructs its own peer group index under paragraph (*l*)(1)(ii)(B), the same methodology must be used in calculating both the registrant's total return and that on the peer group index; and

b. assume the reinvestment of dividends into additional shares of the same class of equity securities at the frequency with which dividends are paid on such securities during the applicable fiscal year.

2. In constructing the graph:

(a) The closing price at the measurement point must be converted into a fixed investment, stated in dollars, in the registrant's stock (or in the stocks represented by a given index), with cumulative returns for each subsequent fiscal year measured as a change from that investment; and

(b) Each fiscal year should be plotted with points showing the cumulative total return as of that point. The value of the investment as of each point plotted on a given return line is the number of shares held at that point multiplied by the then-prevailing share price.

3. The registrant is required to present information for the registrant's last five fiscal years, and may choose to graph a longer period; but the measurement point, however, shall remain the same.

4. Registrants may include comparisons using performance measures in addition to total return, such as return on average common shareholders' equity, so long as the registrant's compensation committee (or other board committee performing equivalent functions or, in the absence of any such committee, the entire board of directors) describes the link between that measure and the level of executive compensation in the statement required by paragraph (k) of this Item.

5. If the registrant uses a peer issuer(s) comparison or comparison with issuer(s) with similar market capitalizations, the identity of those issuers must be disclosed and the returns of each component issuer of the group must be weighted according to the respective issuer's stock market capitalization at the beginning of each period for which a return is indicated.

Item 405

Every registrant having a class of equity securities registered pursuant to Section 12 of the Exchange Act (15 U.S.C. 78(*l*), every closed-end investment company registered under the Investment Company Act of 1940 (15 U.S.C. § 80a-1 *et seq.*), and every holding company registered pursuant to the Public Utility Holding Company Act of 1935 (15 U.S.C. § 79a *et seq.*) shall:

(a) Based solely upon a review of Forms 3 (§ 249.103) and 4 (§ 249.104) and amendments thereto furnished to the registrant pursuant to § 240.16a-3(e) during its most recent fiscal year and Forms 5 and amendments thereto (§ 249.105) furnished to the registrant with respect to its most recent fiscal year, and any written representation referred to in (b)(2)(i) below:

(1) Under the caption "Section 16(a) Beneficial Ownership Reporting Compliance," identify each person who, at any time during the fiscal year, was a director, officer, beneficial owner of more than ten percent of any class of equity securities of the registrant registered pursuant to section 12 of the Exchange Act with respect to the registrant because of the requirements of section 30 of the Investment Company Act ("reporting person") that failed to file on a timely basis, as disclosed in the above Forms, reports required by section 16(a) of the Exchange Act during the most recent fiscal year or prior fiscal years.

(2) For each such person, set forth the number of late reports, the number of transactions that were not reported on a timely basis, and any known failure to file a required Form. A known failure to file would include, but not be limited to, a failure to file a Form 3, which is required by all reporting persons, and a failure to file a Form 5 in the absence of the written representation referred to in paragraph (b)(2)(i) of this section, unless the registrant otherwise knows that no Form 5 is required.

Note: The disclosure requirement is based on a review of the forms submitted to the registrant during and with respect to its most recent fiscal year, as specified above. Accordingly, a failure to file timely need only be disclosed once. For example, if in the most recently concluded fiscal year a reporting person filed a Form 4 disclosing a transaction that took place in the prior fiscal year, and should have been reported in that year, the registrant should disclose that late filing and transaction pursuant to this Item 405 with respect to the most recently concluded fiscal year, but not in material filed with respect to subsequent years.

(b) With respect to the disclosure required by paragraph (a) of this Item:

(1) A form received by the registrant within three calendar days of the required filing date may be presumed to have been filed with the Commission by the required filing date.

(2) If the registrant (i) receives a written representation from the reporting person that no Form 5 is required; and (ii) maintains the representation for two years, making a copy available to the Commission or its staff upon request, the registrant need not identify such reporting person pursuant to paragraph (a) as having failed to file a Form 5 with respect to that fiscal year.

Regulation T

Sec. 220.1 Authority, purpose, and scope.

(a) Authority and purpose. Regulation T (this part) is issued by the Board of Governors of the Federal Reserve System (the Board) pursuant to the Securities Exchange Act of 1934 (the Act) (15 U.S.C.78a et seq.). Its principal purpose is to regulate extensions of credit by brokers and dealers; it also covers related transactions within the Board's authority under the Act. It imposes, among other obligations, initial margin requirements and payment rules on certain securities transactions.

(b) Scope. (1) This part provides a margin account and four special purpose accounts in which to record all financial relations between a customer and a creditor. Any transaction not specifically permitted in a special purpose account shall be recorded in a margin account.

(2) This part does not preclude any exchange, national securities association, or creditor from imposing additional requirements or taking action for its own protection.

(3) This part does not apply to:

(i) Financial relations between a customer and a creditor to the extent that they comply with a portfolio margining system under rules approved or amended by the SEC;

(ii) Credit extended by a creditor based on a good faith determination that the borrower is an exempted borrower;

(iii) Financial relations between a customer and a broker or dealer registered only under section 15C of the Act; and

(iv) Financial relations between a foreign branch of a creditor and a foreign person involving foreign securities.

Sec. 220.2 Definitions.

The terms used in this part have the meanings given them in section 3(a) of the Act or as defined in this section as follows:

Affiliated corporation means a corporation of which all the common stock is owned directly or indirectly by the firm or general partners and employees of the firm, or by the corporation or holders of the controlling stock and employees of the corporation, and the affiliation has been approved by the creditor's examining authority.

Cash equivalent means securities issued or guaranteed by the United States or its agencies, negotiable bank certificates of deposit, bankers acceptances issued by banking institutions in the United States and payable in the United States, or money market mutual funds.

Covered option transaction means any transaction involving options or warrants in which the customer's risk is limited and all elements of the transaction are subject to contemporaneous exercise if:

(1) The amount at risk is held in the account in cash, cash equivalents, or via an escrow receipt; and

(2) The transaction is eligible for the cash account by the rules of the registered national securities exchange authorized to trade the option or warrant or by the rules of the creditor's examining authority in the case of an unregistered option, provided that all such rules have been approved or amended by the SEC.

Credit balance means the cash amount due the customer in a margin account after debiting amounts transferred to the special memorandum account.

Creditor means any broker or dealer (as defined in sections 3(a)(4) and 3(a)(5) of the Act), any member of a national securities exchange, or any person associated with a broker or dealer (as defined in section 3(a)(18) of the Act), except for business entities controlling or under common control with the creditor.

Current market value of:

(1) A security means:

(i) Throughout the day of the purchase or sale of a security, the security's total cost of purchase or the net proceeds of its sale including any commissions charged; or

(ii) At any other time, the closing sale price of the security on the preceding business day, as shown by any regularly published reporting or quotation service. If there is no closing sale price, the creditor may use any reasonable estimate of the market value of the security as of the close of business on the preceding business day.

(2) Any other collateral means a value determined by any reasonable method.

Customer excludes an exempted borrower and includes:

(1) Any person or persons acting jointly:

(i) To or for whom a creditor extends, arranges, or maintains any credit; or

(ii) Who would be considered a customer of the creditor according to the ordinary usage of the trade;

(2) Any partner in a firm who would be considered a customer of the firm absent the partnership relationship; and

(3) Any joint venture in which a creditor participates and which would be considered a customer of the creditor if the creditor were not a participant.

Debit balance means the cash amount owed to the creditor in a margin account after debiting amounts transferred to the special memorandum account.

Delivery against payment, Payment against delivery, or a C.O.D. transaction refers to an arrangement under which a creditor and a customer agree that the creditor will deliver to, or accept from, the customer, or the customer's agent, a security against full payment of the purchase price.

Equity means the total current market value of security positions held in the margin account plus any credit balance less the debit balance in the margin account.

Escrow agreement means any agreement issued in connection with a call or put option under which a bank or any person designated as a control location under paragraph (c) of SEC Rule 15c3-3 (17 CFR 240.15c3-3(c)), holding the underlying asset or required cash or cash equivalents, is obligated to deliver to the creditor (in the case of a call option) or accept from the creditor (in the case of a put option) the underlying asset or required cash or cash equivalent against payment of the exercise price upon exercise of the call or put.

Examining authority means:

(1) The national securities exchange or national securities association of which a creditor is a member; or

(2) If a member of more than one self-regulatory organization, the organization designated by the SEC as the examining authority for the

creditor.

Exempted borrower means a member of a national securities exchange or a registered broker or dealer, a substantial portion of whose business consists of transactions with persons other than brokers or dealers, and includes a borrower who:

(1) Maintains at least 1000 active accounts on an annual basis for persons other than brokers, dealers, and persons associated with a broker or dealer;

(2) Earns at least $10 million in gross revenues on an annual basis from transactions with persons other than brokers, dealers, and persons associated with a broker or dealer; or

(3) Earns at least 10 percent of its gross revenues on an annual basis

from transactions with persons other than brokers, dealers, and persons associated with a broker or dealer.

Exempted securities mutual fund means any security issued by an investment company registered under section 8 of the Investment Company Act of 1940 (15 U.S.C. 80a-8), provided the company has at least 95 percent of its assets continuously invested in exempted securities (as defined in section 3(a)(12) of the Act).

Foreign margin stock means a foreign security that is an equity security that:

(1) Appears on the Board's periodically published List of Foreign Margin Stocks; or

(2) Is deemed to have a "ready market" under SEC Rule 15c3-1 (17 CFR 240.15c3-1) or a "no-action" position issued thereunder.

Foreign person means a person other than a United States person as defined in section 7(f) of the Act.

Foreign security means a security issued in a jurisdiction other than the United States.

Good faith with respect to:

(1) Margin means the amount of margin which a creditor would require in exercising sound credit judgment;

(2) Making a determination or accepting a statement concerning a borrower means that the creditor is alert to the circumstances surrounding the credit, and if in possession of information that would cause a prudent person not to make the determination or accept the notice or certification without inquiry, investigates and is satisfied that it is correct.

Margin call means a demand by a creditor to a customer for a deposit of additional cash or securities to eliminate or reduce a margin deficiency as required under this part.

Margin deficiency means the amount by which the required margin exceeds the equity in the margin account.

Margin equity security means a margin security that is an equity security (as defined in section 3(a)(11) of the Act).

Margin excess means the amount by which the equity in the margin account exceeds the required margin. When the margin excess is represented by securities, the current value of the securities is subject to the percentages set forth in Sec. 220.12 (the Supplement).

Margin security means:

(1) Any security registered or having unlisted trading privileges on a national securities exchange;

(2) After January 1, 1999, any security listed on the Nasdaq Stock Market;

(3) Any non-equity security;

(4) Any security issued by either an open-end investment company or unit investment trust which is registered under section 8 of the Investment Company Act of 1940 (15 U.S.C. 80a-8);

(5) Any foreign margin stock;

(6) Any debt security convertible into a margin security;

(7) Until January 1, 1999, any OTC margin stock; or

(8) Until January 1, 1999, any OTC security designated as qualified for trading in the national market system under a designation plan approved by the Securities and Exchange Commission (NMS security).

Money market mutual fund means any security issued by an investment company registered under section 8 of the Investment Company Act of 1940 (15 U.S.C. 80a-8) that is considered a money market fund under SEC Rule 2a-7 (17 CFR 270.2a-7).

Non-equity security means a security that is not an equity security (as defined in section 3(a)(11) of the Act).

Nonexempted security means any security other than an exempted security (as defined in section 3(a)(12) of the Act).

OTC margin stock means any equity security traded over the counter that the Board has determined has the degree of national investor interest, the depth and breadth of market, the availability of information respecting the security and its issuer, and the character and permanence of the issuer to warrant being treated like an equity security treaded on a national securities exchange. An OTC stock is not considered to be an OTC margin stock unless it appears on the Board's periodically published list of OTC margin stocks.

Payment period means the number of business days in the standard securities settlement cycle in the United States, as defined in paragraph (a) of SEC Rule 15c6-1 (17 CFR 240.15c6-1(a)), plus two business days.

Purpose credit means credit for the purpose of:

(1) Buying, carrying, or trading in securities; or

(2) Buying or carrying any part of an investment contract security which shall be deemed credit for the purpose of buying or carrying the entire security.

Short call or short put means a call option or a put option that is issued, endorsed, or guaranteed in or for an account.

(1) A short call that is not cash-settled obligates the customer to sell the underlying asset at the exercise price upon receipt of a valid exercise notice or as otherwise required by the option contract.

(2) A short put that is not cash-settled obligates the customer to purchase the underlying asset at the exercise price upon receipt of a valid exercise notice or as otherwise required by the option contract.

(3) A short call or a short put that is cash-settled obligates the customer to pay the holder of an in the money long put or long call who has, or has been deemed to have, exercised the option the cash difference between the exercise price and the current assigned value of the option as established by the option contract.

Underlying asset means:

(1) The security or other asset that will be delivered upon exercise of an option; or

(2) In the case of a cash-settled option, the securities or other assets which comprise the index or other measure from which the option's value is derived.

Sec. 220.3 General provisions.

(a) Records. The creditor shall maintain a record for each account showing the full details of all transactions.

(b) Separation of accounts—(1) In general. The requirements of one account may not be met by considering items in any other account. If withdrawals of cash or securities are permitted under this part, written entries shall be made when cash or securities are used for purposes of meeting requirements in another account.

(2) Exceptions. Notwithstanding paragraph (b)(1) of this section:

(i) For purposes of calculating the required margin for a security in a margin account, assets held in the good faith account pursuant to Sec. 220.6(e)(1)(i) or (ii) may serve in lieu of margin;

(ii) Transfers may be effected between the margin account and the special memorandum account pursuant to Secs. 220.4 and 220.5.

(c) Maintenance of credit. Except as prohibited by this part, any credit initially extended in compliance with this part may be maintained regardless of:

(1) Reductions in the customer's equity resulting from changes in market prices;

(2) Any security in an account ceasing to be margin or exempted; or

(3) Any change in the margin requirements prescribed under this part.

(d) Guarantee of accounts. No guarantee of a customer's account shall be given any effect for purposes of this part.

(e) Receipt of funds or securities. (1) A creditor, acting in good faith, may accept as immediate payment:

(i) Cash or any check, draft, or order payable on presentation; or

(ii) Any security with sight draft attached.

(2) A creditor may treat a security, check or draft as received upon written notification from another creditor that the specified security, check, or draft has been sent.

(3) Upon notification that a check, draft, or order has been dishonored or when securities have not been received within a reasonable time, the creditor shall take the action required by this part when payment or securities are not received on time.

(4) To temporarily finance a customer's receipt of securities pursuant to an employee benefit plan registered on SEC Form S-8 or the withholding taxes for an employee stock award plan, a creditor may accept, in lieu of the securities, a properly executed exercise notice, where applicable, and instructions to the issuer to deliver the stock to the creditor. Prior to acceptance, the creditor must verify that the issuer will deliver the securities promptly and the customer must designate the account into which the securities are to be deposited.

(f) Exchange of securities. (1) To enable a customer to participate in an offer to exchange securities which is made to all holders of an issue of securities, a creditor may submit for exchange any securities held in a margin account, without regard to the other provisions of this part, provided the consideration received is deposited into the account.

(2) If a nonmargin, nonexempted security is acquired in exchange for a margin security, its retention, withdrawal, or sale within 60 days following its acquisition shall be treated as if the security is a margin security.

(g) Arranging for loans by others. A creditor may arrange for the extension or maintenance of credit to or for any customer by any person, provided the creditor does not willfully arrange credit that violates parts 221 or 224 of this chapter.

(h) Innocent mistakes. If any failure to comply with this part results from a mistake made in good faith in executing a transaction or calculating the amount of margin, the creditor shall not be deemed in violation of this part if, promptly after the discovery of the mistake, the creditor takes appropriate corrective action.

(i) Foreign currency. (1) Freely convertible foreign currency may be treated at its U.S. dollar equivalent, provided the currency is marked-to-market daily.

(2) A creditor may extend credit denominated in any freely convertible foreign currency.

(j) Exempted borrowers. (1) A member of a national securities exchange or a registered broker or dealer that has been in existence for less than one year may meet the definition of exempted borrower based on a six-month period.

(2) Once a member of a national securities exchange or registered broker or dealer ceases to qualify as an exempted borrower, it shall notify its lender of this fact before obtaining additional credit. Any new extensions of credit to such a borrower, including rollovers, renewals, and additional draws on existing lines of credit, are subject to the provisions of this part.

Sec. 220.4 Margin account.

(a) Margin transactions. (1) All transactions not specifically authorized for inclusion in another account shall be recorded in the margin account.

(2) A creditor may establish separate margin accounts for the same person to:

(i) Clear transactions for other creditors where the transactions are introduced to the clearing creditor by separate creditors; or

(ii) Clear transactions through other creditors if the transactions are cleared by separate creditors; or

(iii) Provide one or more accounts over which the creditor or a third party investment adviser has investment discretion.

(b) Required margin—(1) Applicability. The required margin for each long or short position in securities is set forth in Sec. 220.12 (the Supplement) and is subject to the following exceptions and special provisions.

(2) Short sale against the box. A short sale "against the box" shall be treated as a long sale for the purpose of computing the equity and the required margin.

(3) When-issued securities. The required margin on a net long or net short commitment in a when-issued security is the margin that would be required if the security were an issued margin security, plus any unrealized loss on the commitment or less any unrealized gain.

(4) Stock used as cover. (i) When a short position held in the account serves in lieu of the required margin for a short put, the amount prescribed by paragraph (b)(1) of this section as the amount to be added to the required margin in respect of short sales shall be increased by any unrealized loss on the position.

(ii) When a security held in the account serves in lieu of the required margin for a short call, the security shall be valued at no greater than the exercise price of the short call.

(5) Accounts of partners. If a partner of the creditor has a margin account with the creditor, the creditor shall disregard the partner's financial relations with the firm (as shown in the partner's capital and ordinary drawing accounts) in calculating the margin or equity of the partner's margin account.

(6) Contribution to joint venture. If a margin account is the account of a joint venture in which the creditor participates, any interest of the creditor in the joint account in excess of the interest which the creditor would have on the basis of its right to share in the profits shall be treated as an extension of credit to the joint account and shall be margined as such.

(7) Transfer of accounts. (i) A margin account that is transferred from one creditor to another may be treated as if it had been maintained by the transferee from the date of its origin, if the transferee accepts, in good faith, a signed statement of the transferor (or, if that is not practicable, of the customer), that any margin call issued under this part has been satisfied.

(ii) A margin account that is transferred from one customer to another as part of a transaction, not undertaken to avoid the requirements of this part, may be treated as if it had been maintained for the transferee from the date of its origin, if the creditor accepts in good faith and keeps with the transferee account a signed statement of the transferor describing the circumstances for the transfer.

(8) Sound credit judgment. In exercising sound credit judgment to determine the margin required in good faith pursuant to Sec. 220.12 (the Supplement), the creditor shall make its determination for a specified security position without regard to the customer's other assets or securities positions held in connection with unrelated transactions.

(c) When additional margin is required—(1) Computing deficiency. All transactions on the same day shall be combined to determine whether additional margin is required by the creditor. For the purpose of computing equity in an account, security positions are established or eliminated and a credit or debit created on the trade date of a security transaction. Additional margin is required on any day when the day's transactions create or increase a margin deficiency in the account and shall be for the amount of the margin deficiency so created or increased.

(2) Satisfaction of deficiency. The additional required margin may be satisfied by a transfer from the special memorandum account or by a deposit of cash, margin securities, exempted securities, or any combination thereof.

(3) Time limits. (i) A margin call shall be satisfied within one payment period after the margin deficiency was created or increased.

(ii) The payment period may be extended for one or more limited periods upon application by the creditor to its examining authority unless the examining authority believes that the creditor is not acting in good faith or that the creditor has not sufficiently determined that exceptional circumstances warrant such action. Applications shall be filed and acted upon prior to the end of the payment period or the expiration of any subsequent extension.

(4) Satisfaction restriction. Any transaction, position, or deposit that is used to satisfy one requirement under this part shall be unavailable to satisfy any other requirement.

(d) Liquidation in lieu of deposit. If any margin call is not met in full within the required time, the creditor shall liquidate securities sufficient to meet the margin call or to eliminate any margin deficiency existing on the day such liquidation is required, whichever is less. If the margin deficiency created or increased is $1000 or less, no action need be taken by the creditor.

(e) Withdrawals of cash or securities. (1) Cash or securities may be withdrawn from an account, except if:

(i) Additional cash or securities are required to be deposited into the account for a transaction on the same or a previous day; or

(ii) The withdrawal, together with other transactions, deposits, and withdrawals on the same day, would create or increase a margin deficiency.

(2) Margin excess may be withdrawn or may be transferred to the special memorandum account (Sec. 220.5) by making a single entry to that account which will represent a debit to the margin account and a credit to the special memorandum account.

(3) If a creditor does not receive a distribution of cash or securities which is payable with respect to any security in a margin account on the day it is payable and withdrawal would not be permitted under this paragraph (e), a withdrawal transaction shall be deemed to have occurred on the day the distribution is payable.

(f) Interest, service charges, etc. (1) Without regard to the other provisions of this section, the creditor, in its usual practice, may debit the following items to a margin account if they are considered in calculating the balance of such account:

(i) Interest charged on credit maintained in the margin account;

(ii) Premiums on securities borrowed in connection with short sales or to effect delivery;

(iii) Dividends, interest, or other distributions due on borrowed securities;

(iv) Communication or shipping charges with respect to transactions in the margin account; and

(v) Any other service charges which the creditor may impose.

(2) A creditor may permit interest, dividends, or other distributions credited to a margin account to be withdrawn from the account if:

(i) The withdrawal does not create or increase a margin deficiency in the account; or

(ii) The current market value of any securities withdrawn does not exceed 10 percent of the current market value of the security with respect to which they were distributed.

Sec. 220.5 Special memorandum account.

(a) A special memorandum account (SMA) may be maintained in conjunction with a margin account. A single entry amount may be used to represent both a credit to the SMA and a debit to the margin account. A transfer between the two accounts may be effected by an increase or reduction in the entry. When computing the equity in a margin account, the single entry amount shall be considered as a debit in the margin account. A payment to the customer or on the customer's behalf or a transfer to any of the customer's other accounts from the SMA reduces the single entry amount.

(b) The SMA may contain the following entries:

(1) Dividend and interest payments;

(2) Cash not required by this part, including cash deposited to meet a maintenance margin call or to meet any requirement of a self-regulatory organization that is not imposed by this part;

(3) Proceeds of a sale of securities or cash no longer required on any expired or liquidated security position that may be withdrawn under Sec. 220.4(e); and

(4) Margin excess transferred from the margin account under Sec. 220.4(e)(2).

Sec. 220.6 Good faith account.

In a good faith account, a creditor may effect or finance customer transactions in accordance with the following provisions:

(a) Securities entitled to good faith margin—(1) Permissible transactions. A creditor may effect and finance transactions involving the buying, carrying, or trading of any security entitled to "good faith" margin as set forth in Sec. 220.12 (the Supplement).

(2) Required margin. The required margin is set forth in Sec. 220.12 (the Supplement).

(3) Satisfaction of margin. Required margin may be satisfied by a transfer from the special memorandum account or by a deposit of cash, securities entitled to "good faith" margin as set forth in Sec. 220.12 (the Supplement), any other asset that is not a security, or any combination thereof. An asset that is not a security shall have a margin value determined by the creditor in good faith.

(b) Arbitrage. A creditor may effect and finance for any customer bona fide arbitrage transactions. For the purpose of this section, the term "bona fide arbitrage" means:

(1) A purchase or sale of a security in one market together with an offsetting sale or purchase of the same security in a different market at as nearly the same time as practicable for the purpose of taking advantage of a difference in prices in the two markets; or

(2) A purchase of a security which is, without restriction other than the payment of money, exchangeable or convertible within 90 calendar days of the purchase into a second security together with an offsetting sale of the second security at or about the same time, for the purpose of taking advantage of a concurrent disparity in the prices of the two securities.

(c) "Prime broker" transactions. A creditor may effect transactions for a customer as part of a "prime broker" arrangement in conformity with SEC guidelines.

(d) Credit to ESOPs. A creditor may extend and maintain credit to employee stock ownership plans without regard to the other provisions of this part.

(e) Nonpurpose credit. (1) A creditor may:

(i) Effect and carry transactions in commodities;

(ii) Effect and carry transactions in foreign exchange;

(iii) Extend and maintain secured or unsecured nonpurpose credit, subject to the requirements of paragraph (e)(2) of this section.

(2) Every extension of credit, except as provided in paragraphs (e)(1)(i) and (e)(1)(ii) of this section, shall be deemed to be purpose credit unless, prior to extending the credit, the creditor accepts in good faith from the customer a written statement that it is not purpose credit. The statement shall conform to the requirements established by the Board.

Sec. 220.7 Broker-dealer credit account.

(a) Requirements. In a broker-dealer credit account, a creditor may effect or finance transactions in accordance with the following provisions.

(b) Purchase or sale of security against full payment. A creditor may purchase any security from or sell any security to another creditor or person regulated by a foreign securities authority under a good faith agreement to promptly deliver the security against full payment of the purchase price.

(c) Joint back office. A creditor may effect or finance transactions of any of its owners if the creditor is a clearing and servicing broker or dealer owned jointly or individually by other creditors.

(d) Capital contribution. A creditor may extend and maintain credit to any partner or stockholder of the creditor for the purpose of making a capital contribution to, or purchasing stock of, the creditor, affiliated corporation or another creditor.

(e) Emergency and subordinated credit. A creditor may extend and maintain, with the approval of the appropriate examining authority:

(1) Credit to meet the emergency needs of any creditor; or

(2) Subordinated credit to another creditor for capital purposes, if the other creditor:

(i) Is an affiliated corporation or would not be considered a customer of the lender apart from the subordinated loan; or

(ii) Will not use the proceeds of the loan to increase the amount of dealing in securities for the account of the creditor, its firm or corporation or an affiliated corporation.

(f) Omnibus credit (1) A creditor may effect and finance transactions for a broker or dealer who is registered with the SEC under section 15 of the Act and who gives the creditor written notice that:

(i) All securities will be for the account of customers of the broker or dealer; and

(ii) Any short sales effected will be short sales made on behalf of the customers of the broker or dealer other than partners.

(2) The written notice required by paragraph (f)(1) of this section shall conform to any SEC rule on the hypothecation of customers' securities by brokers or dealers.

(g) Special purpose credit. A creditor may extend the following types of credit with good faith margin:

(1) Credit to finance the purchase or sale of securities for prompt delivery, if the credit is to be repaid upon completion of the transaction.

(2) Credit to finance securities in transit or surrendered for transfer, if the credit is to be repaid upon completion of the transaction.

(3) Credit to enable a broker or dealer to pay for securities, if the credit is to be repaid on the same day it is extended.

(4) Credit to an exempted borrower.

(5) Credit to a member of a national securities exchange or registered broker or dealer to finance its activities as a market maker or specialist.

(6) Credit to a member of a national securities exchange or registered broker or dealer to finance its activities as an underwriter.

Sec. 220.8 Cash account.

(a) Permissible transactions. In a cash account, a creditor, may:

(1) Buy for or sell to any customer any security or other asset if:

(i) There are sufficient funds in the account; or

(ii) The creditor accepts in good faith the customer's agreement that the customer will promptly make full cash payment for the security or asset before selling it and does not contemplate selling it prior to making such payment;

(2) Buy from or sell for any customer any security or other asset if:

(i) The security is held in the account; or

(ii) The creditor accepts in good faith the customer's statement that the security is owned by the customer or the customer's principal, and that it will be promptly deposited in the account;

(3) Issue, endorse, or guarantee, or sell an option for any customer as part of a covered option transaction; and

(4) Use an escrow agreement in lieu of the cash, cash equivalents or underlying asset position if:

(i) In the case of a short call or a short put, the creditor is advised by the customer that the required securities, assets or cash are held by a person authorized to issue an escrow agreement and the creditor independently verifies that the appropriate escrow agreement will be delivered by the person promptly; or

(ii) In the case of a call issued, endorsed, guaranteed, or sold on the same day the underlying asset is purchased in the account and the underlying asset is to be delivered to a person authorized to issue an escrow agreement, the creditor verifies that the appropriate escrow agreement will be delivered by the person promptly.

(b) Time periods for payment; cancellation or liquidation. (1) Full cash payment. A creditor shall obtain full cash payment for customer purchases:

(i) Within one payment period of the date:

(A) Any nonexempted security was purchased;

(B) Any when-issued security was made available by the issuer for delivery to purchasers;

(C) Any "when distributed" security was distributed under a published plan;

(D) A security owned by the customer has matured or has been redeemed and a new refunding security of the same issuer has been purchased by the customer, provided:

(1) The customer purchased the new security no more than 35 calendar days prior to the date of maturity or redemption of the old security;

(2) The customer is entitled to the proceeds of the redemption; and

(3) The delayed payment does not exceed 103 percent of the proceeds of the old security.

(ii) In the case of the purchase of a foreign security, within one payment period of the trade date or within one day after the date on which settlement is required to occur by the rules of the foreign securities market, provided this period does not exceed the maximum time permitted by this part for delivery against payment transactions.

(2) Delivery against payment. If a creditor purchases for or sells to a customer a security in a delivery against payment transaction, the creditor shall have up to 35 calendar days to obtain payment if delivery of the security is delayed due to the mechanics of the transaction and is not related to the customer's willingness or ability to pay.

(3) Shipment of securities, extension. If any shipment of securities is incidental to consummation of a transaction, a creditor may extend the

payment period by the number of days required for shipment, but not by more than one additional payment period.

(4) Cancellation; liquidation; minimum amount. A creditor shall promptly cancel or otherwise liquidate a transaction or any part of a transaction for which the customer has not made full cash payment within the required time. A creditor may, at its option, disregard any sum due from the customer not exceeding $1000.

(c) 90 day freeze. (1) If a nonexempted security in the account is sold or delivered to another broker or dealer without having been previously paid for in full by the customer, the privilege of delaying payment beyond the trade date shall be withdrawn for 90 calendar days following the date of sale of the security. Cancellation of the transaction other than to correct an error shall constitute a sale.

(2) The 90 day freeze shall not apply if:

(i) Within the period specified in paragraph (b)(1) of this section, full payment is received or any check or draft in payment has cleared and the proceeds from the sale are not withdrawn prior to such payment or check clearance; or

(ii) The purchased security was delivered to another broker or dealer for deposit in a cash account which holds sufficient funds to pay for the security. The creditor may rely on a written statement accepted in good faith from the other broker or dealer that sufficient funds are held in the other cash account.

(d) Extension of time periods; transfers. (1) Unless the creditor's examining authority believes that the creditor is not acting in good faith or that the creditor has not sufficiently determined that exceptional circumstances warrant such action, it may upon application by the creditor:

(i) Extend any period specified in paragraph (b) of this section;

(ii) Authorize transfer to another account of any transaction involving the purchase of a margin or exempted security; or

(iii) Grant a waiver from the 90 day freeze.

(2) Applications shall be filed and acted upon prior to the end of the payment period, or in the case of the purchase of a foreign security within the period specified in paragraph (b)(1)(ii) of this section, or the expiration of any subsequent extension.

Sec. 220.9 Clearance of securities, options, and futures.

(a) Credit for clearance of securities. The provisions of this part shall not apply to the extension or maintenance of any credit that is not for more than one day if it is incidental to the clearance of transactions in securities directly between members of a national securities exchange or association or through any clearing agency registered with the SEC.

(b) Deposit of securities with a clearing agency. The provisions of

this part shall not apply to the deposit of securities with an option or futures clearing agency for the purpose of meeting the deposit requirements of the agency if:

(1) The clearing agency:

(i) Issues, guarantees performance on, or clears transactions in, any security (including options on any security, certificate of deposit, securities index or foreign currency); or

(ii) Guarantees performance of contracts for the purchase or sale of a commodity for future delivery or options on such contracts;

(2) The clearing agency is registered with the Securities and Exchange Commission or is the clearing agency for a contract market regulated by the Commodity Futures Trading Commission; and

(3) The deposit consists of any margin security and complies with the rules of the clearing agency that have been approved by the Securities and Exchange Commission or the Commodity Futures Trading Commission.

Sec. 220.10 Borrowing and lending securities.

(a) Without regard to the other provisions of this part, a creditor may borrow or lend securities for the purpose of making delivery of the securities in the case of short sales, failure to receive securities required to be delivered, or other similar situations. If a creditor reasonably anticipates a short sale or fail transaction, such borrowing may be made up to one standard settlement cycle in advance of trade date.

(b) A creditor may lend foreign securities to a foreign person (or borrow such securities for the purpose of relending them to a foreign person) for any purpose lawful in the country in which they are to be used.

(c) A creditor that is an exempted borrower may lend securities without regard to the other provisions of this part and a creditor may borrow securities from an exempted borrower without regard to the other provisions of this part.

Sec. 220.11 Requirements for the list of marginable OTC stocks and the list of foreign margin stocks.

(a) Requirements for inclusion on the list of marginable OTC stocks. Except as provided in paragraph (f) of this section, OTC margin stock shall meet the following requirements:

(1) Four or more dealers stand willing to, and do in fact, make a market in such stock and regularly submit bona fide bids and offers to an automated quotations system for their own accounts;

(2) The minimum average bid price of such stock, as determined by the Board, is at least $5 per share;

(3) The stock is registered under section 12 of the Act, is issued by an insurance company subject to section 12(g)(2)(G) of the Act, is issued by a closed-end investment management company subject to registration pursuant to section 8 of the Investment Company Act of 1940 (15 U.S.C. 80a-8), is an American Depository Receipt (ADR) of a foreign issuer whose securities are registered under section 12 of the Act, or is a stock of an issuer required to file reports under section 15(d) of the Act;

(4) Daily quotations for both bid and asked prices for the stock are continously available to the general public;

(5) The stock has been publicly traded for at least six months;

(6) The issuer has at least $4 million of capital, surplus, and undivided profits;

(7) There are 400,000 or more shares of such stock outstanding in addition to shares held beneficially by officers, directors or beneficial owners of more than 10 percent of the stock;

(8) There are 1,200 or more holders of record, as defined in SEC Rule 12g5-1 (17 CFR 240.12g5-1), of the stock who are not officers, directors or beneficial owners of 10 percent or more of the stock, or the average daily trading volume of such stock as determined by the Board, is at least 500 shares; and

(9) The issuer or a predecessor in interest has been in existence for at least three years.

(b) Requirements for continued inclusion on the list of marginable OTC stocks. Except as provided in paragraph (f) of this section, OTC margin stock shall meet the following requirements:

(1) Three or more dealers stand willing to, and do in fact, make a market in such stock and regularly submit bona fide bids and offers to an automated quotations system for their own accounts;

(2) The minimum average bid price of such stocks, as determined by the Board, is at least $2 per share;

(3) The stock is registered as specified in paragraph (a)(3) of this section;

(4) Daily quotations for both bid and asked prices for the stock are continuously available to the general public; ;

(5) The issuer has at least $1 million of capital, surplus, and undivided profits;

(6) There are 300,000 or more shares of such stock outstanding in addition to shares held beneficially by officers, directors, or beneficial owners of more than 10 percent of the stock; and

(7) There continue to be 800 or more holders of record, as defined in SEC Rule 12g5-1 (17 CFR 240.12g5-1), of the stock who are not officers, directors, or beneficial owners of 10 percent or more of the stock, or the average daily trading volume of such stock, as determined by the Board, is at least 300 shares.

(c) Requirements for inclusion on the list of foreign margin stocks. Except as provided in paragraph (f) of this section, a foreign security shall meet the following requirements before being placed on the List of Foreign Margin Stocks:

(1) The security is an equity security that is listed for trading on or through the facilities of a foreign securities exchange or a recognized foreign securities market and has been trading on such exchange or market for at least six months;

(2) Daily quotations for both bid and asked or last sale prices for the security provided by the foreign securities exchange or foreign securities market on which the security is traded are continuously available to creditors in the United States pursuant to an electronic quotation system;

(3) The aggregate market value of shares, the ownership of which is unrestricted, is not less than $1 billion;

(4) The average weekly trading volume of such security during the preceding six months is either at least 200,000 shares or $1 million;

and

(5) The issuer or a predecessor in interest has been in existence for at least five years.

(d) Requirements for continued inclusion on the list of foreign margin stocks. Except as provided in paragraph (f) of this section, a foreign security shall meet the following requirements to remain on the List of Foreign Margin Stocks:

(1) The security continues to meet the requirements specified in paragraphs (c) (1) and (2) of this section;

(2) The aggregate market value of shares, the ownership of which is unrestricted, is not less than $500 million; and

(3) The average weekly trading volume of such security during the preceding six months is either at least 100,000 shares or $500,000.

(e) Removal from the list. The Board shall periodically remove from the lists any stock that:

(1) Ceases to exist or of which the issuer ceases to exist; or

(2) No longer substantially meets the provisions of paragraphs (b) or (d) of this section or the definition of OTC margin stock.

(f) Discretionary authority of Board. Without regard to other paragraphs of this section, the Board may add to, or omit or remove from the list of marginable OTC stocks and the list of foreign margin stocks an equity security, if in the judgment of the Board, such action is necessary or appropriate in the public interest.

(g) Unlawful representations. It shall be unlawful for any creditor to make, or cause to be made, any representation to the effect that the inclusion of a security on the list of marginable OTC stocks or the list of foreign margin stocks is evidence that the Board or the SEC has in any way passed upon the merits of, or given approval to, such security or any transactions therein. Any statement in an advertisement or other similar communication containing a reference to the Board in connection with the lists or stocks on those lists shall be an unlawful representation.

Sec. 220.12 Supplement: margin requirements.

The required margin for each security position held in a margin account shall be as follows:

(a) Margin equity security, except for an exempted security, money market mutual fund or exempted securities mutual fund, warrant on a securities index or foreign currency or a long position in an option: 50 percent of the current market value of the security or the percentage set by the regulatory authority where the trade occurs, whichever is greater.

(b) Exempted security, non-equity security, money market mutual fund or exempted securities mutual fund: The margin required by the creditor in good faith or the percentage set by the regulatory authority where the trade occurs, whichever is greater.

(c) Short sale of a nonexempted security, except for a non-equity security:

(1) 150 percent of the current market value of the security; or

(2) 100 percent of the current market value if a security exchangeable or convertible within 90 calendar days without restriction other than the payment of money into the security sold short is held in the account, provided that any long call to be used as margin in connection with a short sale of the underlying security is an American-style option issued by a registered clearing corporation and listed or traded on a registered na-

tional securities exchange with an exercise price that does not exceed the price at which the underlying security was sold short.

(d) Short sale of an exempted security or non-equity security: 100 percent of the current market value of the security plus the margin required by the creditor in good faith.

(e) Nonmargin, nonexempted equity security: 100 percent of the current market value.

(f) Put or call on a security, certificate of deposit, securities index or foreign currency or a warrant on a securities index or foreign currency:

(1) In the case of puts and calls issued by a registered clearing corporation and listed or traded on a registered national securities exchange or a registered securities association and registered warrants on a securities index or foreign currency, the amount, or other position specified by the rules of the registered national securities exchange or the registered securities association authorized to trade the option or warrant, provided that all such rules have been approved or amended by the SEC; or

(2) In the case of all other puts and calls, the amount, or other position, specified by the maintenance rules of the creditor's examining authority.

Regulation U

Sec. 221.1 Authority, purpose, and scope.

(a) Authority. Regulation U (this part) is issued by the Board of Governors of the Federal Reserve System (the Board) pursuant to the Securities Exchange Act of 1934 (the Act) (15 U.S.C. 78a et seq.).

(b) Purpose and scope. (1) This part imposes credit restrictions upon persons other than brokers or dealers (hereinafter lenders) that extend credit for the purpose of buying or carrying margin stock if the credit is secured directly or indirectly by margin stock. Lenders include "banks" (as defined in Sec. 221.2) and other persons who are required to register with the Board under Sec. 221.3(b). Lenders may not extend more than the maximum loan value of the collateral securing such credit, as set by the Board in Sec. 221.7 (the Supplement).

(2) This part does not apply to clearing agencies regulated by the Securities and Exchange Commission or the Commodity Futures Trading Commission that accept deposits of margin stock in connection with:

(i) The issuance of, or guarantee of, or the clearance of transactions in, any security (including options on any security, certificate of deposit, securities index or foreign currency); or

(ii) The guarantee of contracts for the purchase or sale of a commodity for future delivery or options on such contracts.

(3) This part does not apply to credit extended to an exempted borrower.

(c) Availability of forms. The forms referenced in this part are available from the Federal Reserve Banks.

Sec. 221.2 Definitions.

The terms used in this part have the meanings given them in section 3(a) of the Act or as defined in this section as follows:

Affiliate means:

(1) For banks:

(i) Any bank holding company of which a bank is a subsidiary within

the meaning of the Bank Holding Company Act of 1956, as amended (12 U.S.C. 1841(d));

(ii) Any other subsidiary of such bank holding company; and

(iii) Any other corporation, business trust, association, or other similar organization that is an affiliate as defined in section 2(b) of the Banking Act of 1933 (12 U.S.C. 221a(c));

(2) For nonbank lenders, affiliate means any person who, directly or indirectly, through one or more intermediaries, controls, or is controlled by, or is under common control with the lender.

Bank. (1) *Bank.* Has the meaning given to it in section 3(a)(6) of the Act (15 U.S.C. 78c(a)(6)) and includes:

(i) Any subsidiary of a bank;

(ii) Any corporation organized under section 25(a) of the Federal Reserve Act (12 U.S.C. 611); and

(iii) Any agency or branch of a foreign bank located within the United States.

(2) *Bank* does not include:

(i) Any savings and loan association;

(ii) Any credit union;

(iii) Any lending institution that is an instrumentality or agency of the United States; or

(iv) Any member of a national securities exchange.

Carrying credit is credit that enables a customer to maintain, reduce, or retire indebtedness originally incurred to purchase a security that is currently a margin stock.

Current market value of:

(1) A security means:

(i) If quotations are available, the closing sale price of the security on the preceding business day, as appearing on any regularly published reporting or quotation service; or

(ii) If there is no closing sale price, the lender may use any reasonable estimate of the market value of the security as of the close of business on the preceding business day; or

(iii) If the credit is used to finance the purchase of the security, the total cost of purchase, which may include any commissions charged.

(2) Any other collateral means a value determined by any reasonable method.

Customer excludes an exempted borrower and includes any person or persons acting jointly, to or for whom a lender extends or maintains credit.

Examining authority means:

(1) The national securities exchange or national securities association of which a broker or dealer is a member; or

(2) If a member of more than one self-regulatory organization, the organization designated by the Securities and Exchange Commission as the examining authority for the broker or dealer.

Exempted borrower means a member of a national securities exchange or a registered broker or dealer, a substantial portion of whose business consists of transactions with persons other than brokers or dealers, and includes a borrower who:

(1) Maintains at least 1000 active accounts on an annual basis for persons other than brokers, dealers, and persons associated with a broker or dealer;

(2) Earns at least $10 million in gross revenues on an annual basis from transactions with persons other than brokers, dealers, and persons associated with a broker or dealer; or

(3) Earns at least 10 percent of its gross revenues on an annual basis from transactions with persons other than brokers, dealers, and persons associated with a broker-dealer.

Good faith with respect to:

(1) The loan value of collateral means that amount (not exceeding 100 per cent of the current market value of the collateral) which a lender, exercising sound credit judgment, would lend, without regard to the customer's other assets held as collateral in connection with unrelated transactions.

(2) Making a determination or accepting a statement concerning a borrower means that the lender or its duly authorized representative is alert to the circumstances surrounding the credit, and if in possession of information that would cause a prudent person not to make the determination or accept the notice or certification without inquiry, investigates and is satisfied that it is correct;

In the ordinary course of business means occurring or reasonably expected to occur in carrying out or furthering any business purpose, or in the case of an individual, in the course of any activity for profit or the management or preservation of property.

Indirectly secured. (1) Includes any arrangement with the customer under which:

(i) The customer's right or ability to sell, pledge, or otherwise dispose of margin stock owned by the customer is in any way restricted while the credit remains outstanding; or

(ii) The exercise of such right is or may be cause for accelerating the maturity of the credit.

(2) Does not include such an arrangement if:

(i) After applying the proceeds of the credit, not more than 25 percent of the value (as determined by any reasonable method) of the assets subject to the arrangement is represented by margin stock;

(ii) It is a lending arrangement that permits accelerating the maturity of the credit as a result of a default or renegotiation of another credit to the customer by another lender that is not an affiliate of the lender;

(iii) The lender holds the margin stock only in the capacity of custodian, depositary, or trustee, or under similar circumstances, and, in good faith, has not relied upon the margin stock as collateral; or

(iv) The lender, in good faith, has not relied upon the margin stock as collateral in extending or maintaining the particular credit.

Lender means:

(1) Any bank; or

(2) Any person subject to the registration requirements of this part.

Margin stock means:

(1) Any equity security registered or having unlisted trading privileges on a national securities exchange;

(2) Any OTC security designated as qualified for trading in the National Market System under a designation plan approved by the Securities and Exchange Commission (NMS security);

(3) Any debt security convertible into a margin stock or carrying a warrant or right to subscribe to or purchase a margin stock;

(4) Any warrant or right to subscribe to or purchase a margin stock; or

(5) Any security issued by an investment company registered under section 8 of the Investment Company Act of 1940 (15 U.S.C. 80a-8), other than:

(i) A company licensed under the Small Business Investment Company Act of 1958, as amended (15 U.S.C. 661); or

(ii) A company which has at least 95 percent of its assets continuously invested in exempted securities (as defined in 15 U.S.C. 78c(a)(12)); or

(iii) A company which issues face-amount certificates as defined in 15 U.S.C. 80a-2(a)(15), but only with respect of such securities; or

(iv) A company which is considered a money market fund under SEC Rule 2a-7 (17 CFR 270.2a-7).

Maximum loan value is the percentage of current market value assigned by the Board under Sec. 221.7 (the Supplement) to specified types of collateral. The maximum loan value of margin stock is stated as a percentage of its current market value. Puts, calls and combinations thereof that do not qualify as margin stock have no loan value. All other collateral has good faith loan value.

Nonbank lender means any person subject to the registration requirements of this part.

Purpose credit is any credit for the purpose, whether immediate, incidental, or ultimate, of buying or carrying margin stock.

Sec. 221.3 General requirements.

(a) Extending, maintaining, and arranging credit—(1) Extending credit. No lender, except a plan-lender, as defined in Sec. 221.4(a), shall extend any purpose credit, secured directly or indirectly by margin stock, in an amount that exceeds the maximum loan value of the collateral securing the credit.

(2) Maintaining credit. A lender may continue to maintain any credit initially extended in compliance with this part, regardless of:

(i) Reduction in the customer's equity resulting from change in market prices;

(ii) Change in the maximum loan value prescribed by this part; or

(iii) Change in the status of the security (from nonmargin to margin) securing an existing purpose credit.

(3) Arranging credit. No lender may arrange for the extension or maintenance of any purpose credit, except upon the same terms and conditions under which the lender itself may extend or maintain purpose credit under this part.

(b) Registration of nonbank lenders; termination of registration; annual report—

(1) Registration. Every person other than a person subject to part 220 of this chapter or a bank who, in the ordinary course of business, extends or maintains credit secured, directly or indirectly, by any margin stock shall register on Federal Reserve Form FR G-1 (OMB control number 7100-0011) within 30 days after the end of any calendar quarter during which:

(i) The amount of credit extended equals $200,000 or more; or

(ii) The amount of credit outstanding at any time during that calendar quarter equals $500,000 or more.

(2) Deregistration. A registered nonbank lender may apply to terminate its registration, by filing Federal Reserve Form FR G-2 (OMB control number 7100-0011), if the lender has not, during the preceding six calendar months, had more than $200,000 of such credit outstanding. Registration shall be deemed terminated when the application is approved by the Board.

(3) Annual report. Every registered nonbank lender shall, within 30 days following June 30 of every year, file Form FR G-4 (OMB control number 7100-0011).

(4) Where to register and file applications and reports. Registration statements, applications to terminate registration, and annual reports shall be filed with the Federal Reserve Bank of the district in which the principal office of the lender is located.

(c) Purpose statement—(1) General rule—(i) Banks. Except for credit extended under paragraph (c)(2) of this section, whenever a bank extends credit secured directly or indirectly by any margin stock, in an amount exceeding $100,000, the bank shall require its customer to execute Form FR U-1 (OMB No. 7100-0115), which shall be signed and accepted by a duly authorized officer of the bank acting in good faith.

(ii) Nonbank lenders. Except for credit extended under paragraph (c)(2) of this section or Sec. 221.4, whenever a nonbank lender extends credit secured directly or indirectly by any margin stock, the nonbank lender shall require its customer to execute Form FR G-3 (OMB control number 7100-0018), which shall be signed and accepted by a duly authorized representative of the nonbank lender acting in good faith.

(2) Purpose statement for revolving-credit or multiple-draw agreements or financing of securities purchases on a payment-against-delivery basis—(i) Banks. If a bank extends credit, secured directly or indirectly by any margin stock, in an amount exceeding $100,000, under a revolving-credit or other multiple-draw agreement, Form FR U-1 must be executed at the time the credit arrangement is originally established and must be amended as described in paragraph (c)(2)(iv) of this section for each disbursement if all of the collateral for the agreement is not pledged at the time the agreement is originally established.

(ii) Nonbank lenders. If a nonbank lender extends credit, secured directly or indirectly by any margin stock, under a revolving-credit or other multiple-draw agreement, Form FR G-3 must be executed at the time the credit arrangement is originally established and must be amended as described in paragraph (c)(2)(iv) of this section for each disbursement if all of the collateral for the agreement is not pledged at the time the agreement is originally established.

(iii) Collateral. If a purpose statement executed at the time the credit arrangement is initially made indicates that the purpose is to purchase or carry margin stock, the credit will be deemed in compliance with this part if:

(A) The maximum loan value of the collateral at least equals the aggregate amount of funds actually disbursed; or

(B) At the end of any day on which credit is extended under the agreement, the lender calls for additional collateral sufficient to bring the credit into compliance with Sec. 221.7 (the Supplement).

(iv) Amendment of purpose statement. For any purpose credit disbursed under the agreement, the lender shall obtain and attach to the executed Form FR U-1 or FR G-3 a current list of collateral which adequately supports all credit extended under the agreement.

(d) Single credit rule. (1) All purpose credit extended to a customer shall be treated as a single credit, and all the collateral securing such credit shall be considered in determining whether or not the credit complies with this part, except that syndicated loans need not be aggregated with other unrelated purpose credit extended by the same lender.

(2) A lender that has extended purpose credit secured by margin stock may not subsequently extend unsecured purpose credit to the same customer unless the combined credit does not exceed the maximum loan value of the collateral securing the prior credit.

(3) If a lender extended unsecured purpose credit to a customer prior to the extension of purpose credit secured by margin stock, the credits shall be combined and treated as a single credit solely for the purposes of the withdrawal and substitution provision of paragraph (f) of this section.

(4) If a lender extends purpose credit secured by any margin stock and non-purpose credit to the same customer, the lender shall treat the credits as two separate loans and may not rely upon the required collateral securing the purpose credit for the nonpurpose credit.

(e) Exempted borrowers. (1) An exempted borrower that has been in existence for less than one year may meet the definition of exempted borrower based on a six-month period.

(2) Once a member of a national securities exchange or registered broker or dealer ceases to qualify as an exempted borrower, it shall notify its lenders of this fact. Any new extensions of credit to such a borrower, including rollovers, renewals, and additional draws on existing lines of credit, are subject to the provisions of this part.

(f) Withdrawals and substitutions. (1) A lender may permit any withdrawal or substitution of cash or collateral by the customer if the withdrawal or substitution would not:

(i) Cause the credit to exceed the maximum loan value of the collateral; or

(ii) Increase the amount by which the credit exceeds the maximum loan value of the collateral.

(2) For purposes of this section, the maximum loan value of the collateral on the day of the withdrawal or substitution shall be used.

(g) Exchange offers. To enable a customer to participate in a reorganization, recapitalization or exchange offer that is made to holders of an issue of margin stock, a lender may permit substitution of the securities received. A nonmargin, nonexempted security acquired in exchange for a margin stock shall be treated as if it is margin stock for a period of 60 days following the exchange.

(h) Renewals and extensions of maturity. A renewal or extension of maturity of a credit need not be considered a new extension of credit if the amount of the credit is increased only by the addition of interest, service charges, or taxes with respect to the credit.

(i) Transfers of credit. (1) A transfer of a credit between customers or between lenders shall not be considered a new extension of credit if:

(i) The original credit was extended by a lender in compliance with this part or by a lender subject to part 207 of this chapter in effect prior to April 1, 1998, (See part 207 appearing in the 12 CFR parts 200 to 219 edition revised as of January 1, 1997), in a manner that would have complied with this part;

(ii) The transfer is not made to evade this part;

(iii) The amount of credit is not increased; and

(iv) The collateral for the credit is not changed.

(2) Any transfer between customers at the same lender shall be accompanied by a statement by the transferor customer describing the circumstances giving rise to the transfer and shall be accepted and signed by a representative of the lender acting in good faith. The lender shall keep such statement with its records of the transferee account.

(3) When a transfer is made between lenders, the transferee shall obtain a copy of the Form FR U-1 or Form FR G-3 originally filed with the transferor and retain the copy with its records of the transferee account. If no form was originally filed with the transferor, the transferee may accept in good faith a statement from the transferor describing the purpose of the loan and the collateral securing it.

(j) Action for lender's protection. Nothing in this part shall require a bank to waive or forego any lien or prevent a bank from taking any action it deems necessary in good faith for its protection.

(k) Mistakes in good faith. A mistake in good faith in connection with the extension or maintenance of credit shall not be a violation of this part.

Sec. 221.4 Employee stock option, purchase, and ownership plans.

(a) Plan-lender; eligible plan. (1) Plan-lender means any corporation, (including a wholly-owned subsidiary, or a lender that is a thrift organization whose membership is limited to employees and former employees of the corporation, its subsidiaries or affiliates) that extends or maintains credit to finance the acquisition of margin stock of the corporation, its subsidiaries or affiliates under an eligible plan.

(2) Eligible plan. An eligible plan means any employee stock option, purchase, or ownership plan adopted by a corporation and approved by its stockholders that provides for the purchase of margin stock of the corporation, its subsidiaries, or affiliates.

(b) Credit to exercise rights under or finance an eligible plan. (1) If a plan-lender extends or maintains credit under an eligible plan, any margin stock that directly or indirectly secured that credit shall have good faith loan value.

(2) Credit extended under this section shall be treated separately from credit extended under any other section of this part except Sec. 221.3(b)(1) and (b)(3).

(c) Credit to ESOPs. A nonbank lender may extend and maintain purpose credit without regard to the provisions of this part, except for Sec. 221.3(b)(1) and (b)(3), if such credit is extended to an employee stock ownership plan (ESOP) qualified under section 401 of the Internal Revenue Code, as amended (26 U.S.C. 401).

Sec. 221.5 Special purpose loans to brokers and dealers.

(a) Special purpose loans. A lender may extend and maintain purpose credit to brokers and dealers without regard to the limitations set forth in Secs. 221.3 and 221.7, if the credit is for any of the specific purposes and meets the conditions set forth in paragraph (c) of this section.

(b) Written notice. Prior to extending credit for more than a day under this section, the lender shall obtain and accept in good faith a written notice or certification from the borrower as to the purposes of the loan. The written notice or certification shall be evidence of continued eligibility for the special credit provisions until the borrower notifies the lender that it is no longer eligible or the lender has information that would cause a reasonable person to question whether the credit is being used for the purpose specified.

(c) Types of special purpose credit. The types of credit that may be extended and maintained on a good faith basis are as follows:

(1) Hypothecation loans. Credit secured by hypothecated customer securities that, according to written notice received from the broker or dealer, may be hypothecated by the broker or dealer under Securities and Exchange Commission (SEC) rules.

(2) Temporary advances in payment-against-delivery transactions. Credit to finance the purchase or sale of securities for prompt delivery, if the credit is to be repaid upon completion of the transaction.

(3) Loans for securities in transit or transfer. Credit to finance securities in transit or surrendered for transfer, if the credit is to be repaid upon completion of the transaction.

(4) Intra-day loans. Credit to enable a broker or dealer to pay for securities, if the credit is to be repaid on the same day it is extended.

(5) Arbitrage loans. Credit to finance proprietary or customer bona fide arbitrage transactions. For the purpose of this section bona fide arbitrage means:

(i) Purchase or sale of a security in one market, together with an offsetting sale or purchase of the same security in a different market at nearly the same time as practicable, for the purpose of taking advantage of a difference in prices in the two markets; or

(ii) Purchase of a security that is, without restriction other than the payment of money, exchangeable or convertible within 90 calendar days of the purchase into a second security, together with an offsetting sale of the second security at or about the same time, for the purpose of taking advantage of a concurrent disparity in the price of the two securities.

(6) Market maker and specialist loans. Credit to a member of a national securities exchange or registered broker or dealer to finance its activities as a market maker or specialist.

(7) Underwriter loans. Credit to a member of a national securities exchange or registered broker or dealer to finance its activities as an underwriter.

(8) Emergency loans. Credit that is essential to meet emergency needs of the broker-dealer business arising from exceptional circumstances.

(9) Capital contribution loans. Capital contribution loans include:

(i) Credit that Board has exempted by order upon a finding that the exemption is necessary or appropriate in the public interest or for the protection of investors, provided the Securities Investor Protection Corporation certifies to the Board that the exemption is appropriate; or

(ii) Credit to a customer for the purpose of making a subordinated loan or capital contribution to a broker or dealer in conformity with the SEC's net capital rules and the rules of the broker's or dealer's examining authority, provided:

(A) The customer reduces the credit by the amount of any reduction in the loan or contribution to the broker or dealer; and

(B) The credit is not used to purchase securities issued by the broker or dealer in a public distribution.

(10) Credit to clearing brokers or dealers. Credit to a member of a national securities exchange or registered broker or dealer whose non-proprietary business is limited to financing and carrying the accounts of registered market makers.

Sec. 221.6 Exempted transactions.

A bank may extend and maintain purpose credit without regard to the provisions of this part if such credit is extended:

(a) To any bank;

(b) To any foreign banking institution;

(c) Outside the United States;

(d) To an employee stock ownership plan (ESOP) qualified under section 401 of the Internal Revenue Code (26 U.S.C. 401);

(e) To any plan lender as defined in Sec. 221.4(a) to finance an eligible plan as defined in Sec. 221.4(b), provided the bank has no recourse to any securities purchased pursuant to the plan;

(f) To any customer, other than a broker or dealer, to temporarily finance the purchase or sale of securities for prompt delivery, if the credit is to be repaid in the ordinary course of business upon completion of the transaction and is not extended to enable the customer to pay for securities purchased in an account subject to part 220 of this chapter;

(g) Against securities in transit, if the credit is not extended to enable the customer to pay for securities purchased in an account subject to part 220 of this chapter; or

(h) To enable a customer to meet emergency expenses not reasonably foreseeable, and if the extension of credit is supported by a statement executed by the customer and accepted and signed by an officer of the bank acting in good faith. For this purpose, emergency expenses include expenses arising from circumstances such as the death or disability of the customer, or some other change in circumstances involving extreme hardship, not reasonably foreseeable at the time the credit was extended. The opportunity to realize monetary gain or to avoid loss is not a "change in circumstances" for this purpose.

Sec. 221.7 Supplement: Maximum loan value of margin stock and other collateral.

(a) Maximum loan value of margin stock. The maximum loan value of any margin stock is fifty per cent of its current market value.

(b) Maximum loan value of nonmargin stock and all other collateral. The maximum loan value of nonmargin stock and all other collateral except puts, calls, or combinations thereof is their good faith loan value.

(c) Maximum loan value of options. Except for options that qualify as margin stock, puts, calls, and combinations thereof have no loan value.

Form 3

INITIAL STATEMENT OF BENEFICIAL OWNERSHIP OF SECURITIES

The Commission is authorized to solicit the information required by this Form pursuant to Sections 16(a) and 23(a) of the Securities Exchange Act of 1934, Sections 17(a) and 20(a) of the Public Utility Holding Company Act of 1935, and Sections 30(h) and 38 of the Investment Company Act of 1940, and the rules and regulations thereunder.

Disclosure of information specified on this form is mandatory, except for disclosure of the I.R.S. identification number of the reporting person if such person is an entity, which is voluntary. If such numbers are furnished, they will assist the Commission in distinguishing reporting persons with similar names and will facilitate the prompt processing of the form. The information will be used for the primary purpose of disclosing the holdings of directors, officers, and beneficial owners of registered companies. Information disclosed will be a matter of public record and available for inspection by members of the public. The Commission can use it in investigations or litigation involving the federal securities laws or other civil, criminal, or regulatory statutes or provisions, as well as for referral to other governmental authorities and self-regulatory organizations. Failure to disclose required information may result in civil or criminal action against persons involved for violations of the federal securities laws and rules.

GENERAL INSTRUCTIONS

1. Who Must File

(a) This Form must be filed by the following persons ("reporting person"):

(i) any director or officer of an issuer with a class of equity securities registered pursuant to Section 12 of the Securities Exchange Act of 1934 ("Exchange Act"); (*Note*: Title is not determinative for purposes of determining "officer" status. *See* Rule 16a-1(f) for the definition of "officer");

(ii) any beneficial owner of greater than 10% of a class of equity securities registered under Section 12 of the Exchange Act, as determined by voting or investment control over the securities pursuant to Rule 16a-1(a)(l) ("ten percent holder");

(iii) any officer or director of a registered holding company pursuant to Section 17 of the Public Utility Holding Company Act of 1935;

(iv) any officer, director, member of an advisory board, investment adviser, affiliated person of an investment adviser or beneficial owner of more than 10% of any class of outstanding securities (other than short-term paper) of a registered closed-end investment company, under Section 30(f) of the Investment Company Act of 1940; and

(v) any trust, trustee, beneficiary or settlor required to report pursuant to Rule 16a-8.

(b) If a reporting person is not an officer, director, or ten percent holder, the person should check "other" in Item 5 (Relationship of Reporting Person to Issuer) and describe the reason for reporting status in the space provided.

(c) If a person described above does not beneficially own any securities required to be reported (*See* Rule 16a-1 and Instruction 5), the person is required to file this Form and state that no securities are beneficially owned.

2. When Form Must be Filed

(a) This Form must be filed within 10 days after the event by which the person becomes a reporting person (*i.e.*, officer, director, ten percent holder or other person). This Form and any amendment is deemed filed with the Commission or the Exchange on the date it is received by the Commission or the Exchange, respectively. *See*, however, Rule 16a-3(h) regarding delivery to a third party business that guarantees delivery of the filing no later than the specified due date.

(b) A reporting person of an issuer that is registering securities for the first time under Section 12 of the Exchange Act must file this Form no later than the effective date of the registration statement.

(c) A separate Form shall be filed to reflect beneficial ownership of securities of each issuer, except that a single statement shall be filed with respect to the securities of a registered public utility holding company and all of its subsidiary companies.

3. Where Form Must be Filed

(a) A reporting person must file this Form in electronic format via the Commission's Electronic Data Gathering Analysis and Retrieval System (EDGAR) in accordance with EDGAR rules set forth in Regulation S-T (17 CFR Part 232), except that a filing person that has obtained a hardship exception under Regulation S-T Rule 202 (17 CFR 232.202) may file the Form in paper. For assistance with technical questions about EDGAR or to request an access code, call the EDGAR Filer Support Office at (202) 942-8900. For assistance with questions about the EDGAR rules, call the Office of EDGAR and Information Analysis at (202) 942-2940.

(b) At the time this Form or any amendment is filed with the Commission, file one copy with each Exchange on which any class of securities of the issuer is registered. If the issuer has designated a single Exchange to receive Section 16 filings, the copy shall be filed with that Exchange only.

(c) Any person required to file this Form or amendment shall, not later than the time the Form or amendment is transmitted for filing with the Commission, send or deliver a copy to the person designated by the issuer to receive the copy or, if no person is so designated, the issuer's corporate secretary (or person performing similar functions) in accordance with Rule 16a-3(e).

NOTE: If filing pursuant to a hardship exception under Regulation S-T Rule 202 (17 CFR 232.202), file three copies of this Form or any amendment, at least one of which is signed, with the Securities and Exchange Commission, 450 5th Street, NW, Washington, DC 20549. (Acknowledgement of receipt by the Commission may be obtained by enclosing a self-addressed stamped postcard identifying the Form or amendment filed.)

4. Class of Securities Reported

(a) (i) Persons reporting pursuant to Section 16(a) of the Exchange Act shall include information as to their beneficial ownership of any class of equity securities of the issuer, even though one or more of such classes may not be registered pursuant to Section 12 of the Act.

(ii) Persons reporting pursuant to Section 17(a) of the Public Utility Holding Company Act of 1935 shall include information as to their beneficial ownership of any class of securities (equity or debt) of the registered holding company and all of its subsidiary companies and specify the name of the parent or subsidiary issuing the securities.

(iii) Persons reporting pursuant to Section 30(f) of the Investment Company Act of 1940 shall include information as to their beneficial ownership of any class of securities (equity or debt) of the registered closed-end investment company (other than "short-term paper" as defined in Section 2(a)(38) of the Investment Company Act).

(b) The title of the security should clearly identify the class, even if the issuer has only one class of securities outstanding; for example, "Common Stock," "Class A Common Stock," "Class B Convertible Preferred Stock," etc.

(c) The amount of securities beneficially owned should state the face amount of debt securities (U.S. Dollars) or the number of equity securities, whichever is appropriate.

5. Holdings Required to be Reported

(a) *General Requirements*. Report holdings of each class of securities of the issuer beneficially owned as of the date of the event requiring the filing of this Form. *See* Instruction 4 as to securities required to be reported.

(b) *Beneficial Ownership Reported (Pecuniary Interest)*.

(i) Although for purposes of determining status as a ten percent holder, a person is deemed to beneficially own securities over which that person has voting or investment control (see Rule 16a-1(a)(1)), for reporting purposes, a person is deemed to be the beneficial owner of securities if that person has or shares the opportunity, directly or indirectly, to profit or share in any profit derived from a transaction in the securities ("pecuniary interest"). See Rule 16a-1(a)(2). See also Rule 16a-8 for the application of the beneficial ownership definition to trust holdings and transactions.

(ii) Both direct and indirect beneficial ownership of securities shall be reported. Securities beneficially owned directly are those held in the reporting person's name or in the name of a bank, broker or nominee for the account of the reporting person. In addition, securities held as joint tenants, tenants in common, tenants by the entirety, or as community property are to be reported as held directly. If a person has a pecuniary interest, by reason of any contract, understanding or relationship (including a family relationship or arrangement) in securities held in the name of another person, that person is an indirect beneficial owner of those securities. *See* Rule 16a-1(a)(2)(ii) for certain indirect beneficial ownerships.

(iii) Report securities beneficially owned directly on a separate line from those beneficially owned indirectly. Report different forms of indirect ownership on separate lines. The nature of indirect ownership shall be stated as specifically as possible; for example, "By Self as Trustee for X," "By Spouse," "By X Trust," "By Y Corporation," etc.

(iv) In stating the amount of securities owned indirectly through a partnership, corporation, trust, or other entity, report the number of securities representing the reporting person's proportionate interest in securities beneficially owned by that entity. Alternatively, at the option of the reporting person, the entire amount of the entity's interest may be reported. *See* Rule 16a-1(a)(2)(ii)(B) and Rule 16a-1(a)(2)(iii).

(v) Where more than one person beneficially owns the same equity securities, such owners may file Form 3 individually or jointly. Joint and group filings may be made by any designated beneficial owner. Holdings of securities owned separately by any joint or group filer are permitted to be included in the joint filing. Indicate only the name and address of the designated filer in Item 1 of Form 3 and attach a list of the names and addresses of each other reporting person. Joint and group filings must include all required information for each beneficial owner, and such filings must be signed by each beneficial owner, or on behalf of such owner by an authorized person. If this Form is being filed in paper pursuant to a hardship exemption and the space provided for signatures is insufficient, attach a signature page. If this Form is being filed in paper, submit any attached listing of names or signatures on another Form 3, copy of Form 3 or separate page of 8 ½ by 11 inch white paper, indicate the number of pages comprising the report (Form plus attachments) at the bottom of each report page (*e.g.*, 1 of 3, 2 of 3, 3 of 3), and include the name of the designated filer and information required by Items 2 and 3 of the Form on the attachment. See Rule 16a-3(i) regarding signatures.

(c) *Non-Derivative and Derivative Securities*.

(i) Report non-derivative securities beneficially owned in Table I and derivative securities (*e.g.*, puts, calls, options, warrants, convertible securities, or other rights or obligations to buy or sell securities) beneficially owned in Table II. Derivative securities beneficially owned that are both equity securities and convertible or exchangeable for other equity securities (*e.g.*, convertible preferred securities) should be reported only on Table II.

(ii) The title of a derivative security and the title of the equity security underlying the derivative security should be shown separately in the appropriate columns in Table II. The "puts" and "calls" reported in Table II include, in addition to separate puts and calls, any combination of the two, such as spreads and straddles. In reporting an option in Table II, state whether it represents a right to buy, a right to sell, an obligation to buy, or an obligation to sell the equity securities subject to the option.

(iii) Describe in the appropriate columns in Table II characteristics of derivative securities, including title, exercise or conversion price, date exercisable, expiration date, and the title and amount of securities underlying the derivative security.

(iv) Securities constituting components of a unit shall be reported separately on the applicable table (*e.g.*, if a unit has a non-derivative security component and a derivative security component, the non-derivative security component shall be reported in Table I and the derivative security component shall be reported in Table II). The relationship between individual securities comprising the unit shall be indicated in the space provided for explanation of responses.

6. Additional Information

(a) If the space provided in the line items on the electronic Form is insufficient, use the space provided for footnotes. If the space provided for footnotes is insufficient, create a footnote that refers to an exhibit to the form that contains the additional information.

(b) If the space provided in the line items on the paper Form or space provided for additional comments is insufficient, attach another Form 3, copy of Form 3 or separate 8 ½ by 11 inch white paper to Form 3, completed as appropriate to include the additional comments. Each attached page must include information required in Items 1, 2 and 3 of the Form. The number of pages comprising the report (Form plus attachments) shall be indicated at the bottom of each report page (*e.g.*, 1 of 3, 2 of 3, 3 of 3).

(c) If one or more exhibits are included, whether due to a lack of space or because the exhibit is, by nature, a separate document (*e.g.*, a power of attorney), provide a sequentially numbered list of the exhibits in the Form. Use the number "24" for any power of attorney and the number "99" for any other exhibit. If there is more than one of either such exhibit, then use numerical subparts. If the exhibit is being filed as a confirming electronic copy under Regulation S-T Rule 202(d) (17 CFR 232.202(d)), then place the designation "CE" (confirming exhibit) next to the name of the exhibit in the exhibit list. If the exhibit is being filed in paper pursuant to a hardship exception under Regulation S-T Rule 202 (17 CFR 232.202), then place the designation "P" (paper) next to the name of the exhibit in the exhibit list.

(d) If additional information is not reported as provided in paragraph (a), (b) or (c) of this instruction, whichever apply, it will be assumed that no additional information was provided.

7. Signature

(a) If the Form is filed for an individual, it shall be signed by that person or specifically on behalf of the individual by a person authorized to sign for the individual. If signed on behalf of the individual by another person, the authority of such person to sign the Form shall be confirmed to the Commission in writing in an attachment to the Form or as soon as practicable in an amendment by the individual for whom the Form is filed, unless such a confirmation still in effect is on file with the Commission. The confirming statement need only indicate that the reporting person authorizes and designates the named person or persons to file the Form on the reporting person's behalf, and state the duration of the authorization.

(b) If the Form is filed for a corporation, partnership, trust, or other entity, the capacity in which the individual signed shall be set forth (*e.g.*, John Smith, Secretary, on behalf of X Corporation).

8. Amendments

(a) If this Form is filed as an amendment in order to add one or more lines of ownership information to Table I or Table II of the Form being amended, provide each line being added, together with one or more footnotes, as necessary, to explain the addition of the line or lines. Do not repeat lines of ownership information that were disclosed in the original Form and are not being amended.

(b) If this Form is filed as an amendment in order to amend one or more lines of ownership information that already were disclosed in Table I or Table II of the Form being amended, provide the complete line or lines being amended, as amended, together with one or more footnotes, as necessary, to explain the amendment of the line or lines. Do not repeat lines of ownership information that were disclosed in the original Form and are not being amended. (c) If this Form is filed as an amendment for any purpose other than or in addition to the purposes described in paragraphs (a) and (b) of this General Instruction 8, provide one or more footnotes, as necessary, to explain the amendment.

FORM 3

OMB APPROVAL
OMB Number: 3235-0104
Expires: January 31, 2005
Estimated average burden
hours per response...... 0.5

UNITED STATES SECURITIES AND EXCHANGE COMMISSION
Washington, D.C. 20549
Form 3

INITIAL STATEMENT OF BENEFICIAL OWNERSHIP OF SECURITIES

Filed pursuant to Section 16(a) of the Securities Exchange Act of 1934, Section 17(a) of the Public Utility
Holding Company Act of 1935 or Section 30(h) of the Investment Company Act of 1940

(Print or Type Responses)

1. Name and Address of Reporting Person*	2. Date of Event Requiring Statement (Month/Day/Year)	3. Issuer Name and Ticker or Trading Symbol
(Last) (First) (Middle)		
(Street)	4. Relationship of Reporting Person(s) to Issuer (Check all applicable) ___ Director ___ 10% Owner ___ Officer (give ___ Other (specify title below) below)	5. If Amendment, Date Original Filed (Month/Day/Year)
(City) (State) (Zip)		6. Individual or Joint/Group Filing (Check Applicable Line) ___ Form filed by One Reporting Person ___ Form filed by More than One Reporting Person

Table I — Non-Derivative Securities Beneficially Owned

1. Title of Security (Instr. 4)	2. Amount of Securities Beneficially Owned (Instr. 4)	3. Ownership Form: Direct (D) or Indirect (I) (Instr. 5)	4. Nature of Indirect Beneficial Ownership (Instr. 5)

Reminder: Report on a separate line for each class of securities beneficially owned directly or indirectly.
* If the form is filed by more than one reporting person, see Instruction 5(b)(v).

**Potential persons who are to respond to the collection of information contained in this form are not
required to respond unless the form displays a currently valid OMB control number.**

(Over)
SEC 1473 (6-03)

FORM 3 (continued)

Table II — Derivative Securities Beneficially Owned (e.g. , puts, calls, warrants, options, convertible securities)

1. Title of Derivative Security (Instr. 4)	2. Date Exercisable and Expiration Date (Month/Day/Year)		3. Title and Amount of Securities Underlying Derivative Security (Instr. 4)		4. Conversion or Exercise Price of Derivative Security	5. Ownership Form of Derivative Security: Direct (D) or Indirect (I) (Instr. 5)	6. Nature of Indirect Beneficial Ownership (Instr. 5)
	Date Exercisable	Expiration Date	Title	Amount or Number of Shares			

Explanation of Responses:

_____ _____
**Signature of Reporting Person   Date

** Intentional misstatements or omissions of facts constitute Federal Criminal Violations. See 18 U.S.C. 1001 and 15 U.S.C. 78ff(a).

Note: File three copies of this Form, one of which must be manually signed. If space is insufficient, *See* Instruction 6 for procedure.

Potential persons who are to respond to the collection of information contained in this form are not required to respond unless the form displays a currently valid OMB Number.

Form 4

STATEMENT OF CHANGES OF BENEFICIAL OWNERSHIP OF SECURITIES

The Commission is authorized to solicit the information required by this Form pursuant to Sections 16(a) and 23(a) of the Securities Exchange Act of 1934, Sections 17(a) and 20(a) of the Public Utility Holding Company Act of 1935, and Sections 30(h) and 38 of the Investment Company Act of 1940, and the rules and regulations thereunder. Disclosure of information specified on this Form is mandatory, except for disclosure of the I.R.S. identification number of the reporting person if such person is an entity, which is voluntary. If such numbers are furnished, they will assist the Commission in distinguishing reporting persons with similar names and will facilitate the prompt processing of the Form. The information will be used for the primary purpose of disclosing the transactions and holdings of directors, officers, and beneficial owners of registered companies. Information disclosed will be a matter of public record and available for inspection by members of the public. The Commission can use it in investigations or litigation involving the federal securities laws or other civil, criminal, or regulatory statutes or provisions, as well as for referral to other governmental authorities and self-regulatory organizations. Failure to disclose required information may result in civil or criminal action against persons involved for violations of the Federal securities laws and rules.

GENERAL INSTRUCTIONS

1. When Form Must Be Filed

(a) This Form must be filed before the end of the second business day following the day on which a transaction resulting in a change in beneficial ownership has been executed (see Rule 16a-1(a)(2) and Instruction 4 regarding the meaning of "beneficial owner," and Rule 16a-3(g) regarding determination of the date of execution for specified transactions). This Form and any amendment is deemed filed with the Commission or the Exchange on the date it is received by the Commission or the Exchange, respectively. *See*, however, Rule 16a-3(h) regarding delivery to a third party business that guarantees delivery of the filing no later than the specified due date.

(b) A reporting person no longer subject to Section 16 of the Securities Exchange Act of 1934 ("Exchange Act") must check the exit box appearing on this Form. However, Form 4 and 5 obligations may continue to be applicable. *See* Rule 16a-3 (f); *see also* Rule 16a-2(b) (transactions after termination of insider status). Form 5 transactions to date may be included on this Form and subsequent Form 5 transactions may be reported on a later Form 4 or Form 5, provided all transactions are reported by the required date.

(c) A separate Form shall be filed to reflect beneficial ownership of securities of each issuer, except that a single statement shall be filed with respect to the securities of a registered public utility holding company and all of its subsidiary companies.

(d) If a reporting person is not an officer, director, or ten percent holder, the person should check "other" in Item 6 (Relationship of Reporting Person to Issuer) and describe the reason for reporting status in the space provided.

2. Where Form Must be Filed

(a) A reporting person must file this Form in electronic format via the Commission's Electronic Data Gathering Analysis and Retrieval System (EDGAR) in accordance with EDGAR rules set forth in Regulation S-T (17 CFR Part 232), except that a filing person that has obtained a hardship exception under Regulation S-T Rule 202 (17 CFR 232.202) may file the Form in paper. For assistance with technical questions about EDGAR or to request an access code, call the EDGAR Filer Support Office at (202) 942-8900. For assistance with questions about the EDGAR rules, call the Office of EDGAR and Information Analysis at (202) 942-2940.

(b) At the time this Form or any amendment is filed with the Commission, file one copy with each Exchange on which any class of securities of the issuer is registered. If the issuer has designated a single Exchange to receive Section 16 filings, the copy shall be filed with that Exchange only.

(c) Any person required to file this Form or amendment shall, not later than the time the Form or amendment is transmitted for filing with the Commission, send or deliver a copy to the person designated by the issuer to receive the copy or, if no person is so designated, the issuer's corporate secretary (or person performing similar functions) in accordance with Rule 16a-3(e).

NOTE: If filing pursuant to a hardship exception under Regulation S-T Rule 202 (17 CFR 232.202), file three copies of this Form or any amendment, at least one of which is signed, with the Securities and Exchange Commission, 450 5th Street, NW, Washington, DC 20549. (Acknowledgement of receipt by the Commission may be obtained by enclosing a self-addressed stamped postcard identifying the Form or amendment filed.)

3. Class of Securities Reported

(a) (i) Persons reporting pursuant to Section 16(a) of the Exchange Act must report each transaction resulting in a change in beneficial ownership of any class of equity securities of the issuer and the beneficial ownership of that class of securities following the reported transaction(s), even though one or more of such classes may not be registered pursuant to Section 12 of the Exchange Act.

(ii) Persons reporting pursuant to Section 17(a) of the Public Utility Holding Company Act of 1935 must report each transaction resulting in a change in beneficial ownership of any class of securities (equity or debt) of the registered holding company and all of its subsidiary companies and the beneficial ownership of that class of securities following the reported transaction(s). Specify the name of the parent or subsidiary issuing thesecurities.

(iii) Persons reporting pursuant to Section 30(h) of the Investment Company Act of 1940 must report each transaction resulting in a change in beneficial ownership of any class of securities (equity or debt) of the registered closedend investment company (other than "short-term paper" as defined in Section 2(a)(38) of the Investment Company Act) and the beneficial ownership of that class of securities following the reported transaction(s).

(b) The title of the security should clearly identify the class, even if the issuer has only one class of securities outstaning; for example, "Common Stock," "Class A Common Stock," "Class B Convertible Preferred Stock," etc.

(c) The amount of securities beneficially owned should state the face amount of debt securities (U.S. Dollars) or the number of equity securities, whichever is appropriate.

4. Transactions and Holdings Required To Be Reported

(a) *General Requirements*

(i) Report, in accordance with Rule 16a-3(g):

(1) all transactions not exempt from §16(b);

(2) all transactions exempt from Section 16(b) pursuant to §240.16b-3(d), §240.16b-3(e), or §240.16b-3(f); and

(3) all exercises and conversions of derivative securities, regardless of whether exempt from Section 16(b) of the Act.

Every transaction must be reported even though acquisitions and dispositions are equal. Report total beneficial ownership following the reported transaction(s) for each class of securities in which a transaction was reported.

Note: The amount of securities beneficially owned following the reported transaction(s) specified in Column 5 of Table I and Column 9 of Table II should reflect those holdings reported or required to be reported by the date of the Form. Transactions and holdings eligible for deferred reporting on Form 5 need not be reflected in the month end total unless the transactions were reported earlier or are included on this Form.

(ii) Each transaction should be reported on a separate line. Transaction codes specified in Item 8 should be used to identify the nature of the transaction resulting in an acquisition or disposition of a security. A deemed execution date must be reported in Column 2A of Table I or Column 3A of Table II only if the execution date for the transaction is calculated pursuant to §240.16a-3(g)(2) or §240.16a-3(g)(3).

Note: Transactions reportable on Form 5 may, at the option of the reporting person, be reported on a Form 4 filed before the due date of the Form 5. (*See* Instruction 8 for the code for voluntarily reported transactions.)

(b) *Beneficial Ownership Reported (Pecuniary Interest)*

(i) Although for purposes of determining status as a ten percent holder, a person is deemed to beneficially own securities over which that person exercises voting or investment control (*see* Rule 16a-1(a)(1)), for reporting transactions and holdings, a person is deemed to be the beneficial owner of securities if that person has the opportunity, directly or indirectly, to profit or share in any profit derived from a transaction in the securities ("pecuniary interest"). *See* Rule 16a-1(a)(2). *See also* Rule 16a-8 for the application of the beneficial ownership definition to trust holdings and transactions.

(ii) Both direct and indirect beneficial ownership of securities shall be reported. Securities beneficially owned directly are those held in the reporting person's name or in the name of a bank, broker or nominee for the account of the reporting person. In addition, securities held as joint tenants, tenants in common, tenants by the entirety, or as community property are to be reported as held directly. If a person has a pecuniary interest, by reason of any contract, understanding or relationship (including a family relationship or arrangement), in securities held in the name of another person, that person is an indirect beneficial owner of the securities. *See* Rule 16a-1(a)(2)(ii) for certain indirect beneficial ownerships.

(iii) Report transactions in securities beneficially owned directly on a separate line from those beneficially owned indirectly. Report different forms of indirect ownership on separate lines. The nature of indirect ownership shall be stated as specifically as possible; for example, "By Self as Trustee for X," "By Spouse," "By X Trust," "By Y Corporation," etc.

(iv) In stating the amount of securities acquired, disposed of, or beneficially owned indirectly through a partnership, corporation, trust, or other entity, report the number of securities representing the reporting person's proportionate interest in transactions conducted by that entity or holdings of that entity. Alternatively, at the option of the reporting person, the entire amount of the entity's interest may be reported. *See* Rule 16a-1(a)(2)(ii)(B) and Rule 16a-1(a)(2)(iii).

(v) Where more than one beneficial owner of the same equity securities must report the same transaction on Form 4, such owners may file Form 4 individually or jointly. Joint and group filings may be made by any designated beneficial owner. Transactions with respect to securities owned separately by any joint or group filer are permitted to be included in the joint filing. Indicate only the name and address of the designated filer in Item 1 of Form 4 and attach a list of the names and addresses of each other reporting person. Joint and group filings must include all required information for each beneficial owner, and such filings must be signed by each beneficial owner, or on behalf of such owner by an authorized person. If this Form is being filed in paper pursuant to a hardship exemption and the space provided for signatures is insufficient, attach a signature page. If this Form is being filed in paper, submit any attached listing of names or signatures on another Form 4, copy of Form 4 or separate page of 8 ½ by 11 inch white paper, indicate the number of pages comprising the report (Form plus attachments) at the bottom of each report page (*e.g.*, 1 of 3, 2 of 3, 3 of 3), and include the name of the designated filer and information required by Items 2 and 3 of the Form on the attachment.

See Rule 16a-3(i) regarding signatures.

(c) *Non-Derivative and Derivative Securities*

(i) Report acquisitions or dispositions and holdings of non-derivative securities in Table I. Report acquisitions or dispositions and holdings of derivative securities (*e.g.*, puts, calls, options, warrants, convertible securities, or other rights or obligations to buy or sell securities) in Table II. Report the exercise or conversion of a derivative security in Table II (as a disposition of the derivative security) and report in Table I the holdings of the underlying security. Report acquisitions or dispositions and holdings of derivative securities that are both equity securities and convertible or exchangeable for other equity securities (*e.g.*, convertible preferred securities) only in Table II.

(ii) The title of a derivative security and the title of the equity security underlying the derivative security should be shown separately in the appropriate columns in Table II. The "puts" and "calls" reported in Table II include, in addition to separate puts and calls, any combination of the two, such as spreads and straddles. In reporting an option in Table II, state whether it represents a right to buy, a right to sell, an obligation to buy, or an obligation to sell the equity securities subject to the option.

(iii) Describe in the appropriate columns in Table II characteristics of derivative securities, including title, exercise or conversion price, date exercisable, expiration date, and the title and amount of securities underlying the derivative security. If the transaction reported is a purchase or a sale of a derivative security, the purchase or sale price of that derivative security shall be reported in column 8. If the transaction is the exercise or conversion of a derivative security, leave column 8 blank and report the exercise or conversion price of the derivative security in column 2.

(iv) Securities constituting components of a unit shall be reported separately on the applicable table (*e.g.*, if a unit has a non-derivative security component and a derivative security component, the non-derivative security component shall be reported in Table I and the derivative security component shall be reported in Table II). The relationship between individual securities comprising the unit shall be indicated in the space provided for explanation of responses. When securities are purchased or sold as a unit, state the purchase or sale price per unit and other required information regarding the unit securities.

5. Price of Securities

(a) Prices of securities shall be reported in U.S. dollars on a per share basis, not an aggregate basis, except that the aggregate price of debt shall be stated. Amounts reported shall exclude brokerage commissions and other costs of execution.

(b) If consideration other than cash was paid for the security, describe the consideration, including the value of the consideration, in the space provided for explanation of responses.

6. Additional Information

(a) If the space provided in the line items on the electronic Form is insufficient, use the space provided for footnotes. If the space provided for footnotes is insufficient, create a footnote that refers to an exhibit to the form that contains the additional information.

(b) If the space provided in the line items on the paper Form or space provided for additional comments is insufficient, attach another Form 4, copy of Form 4 or separate 8 ½ by 11 inch white paper to Form 4, completed as appropriate to include the additional comments. Each attached page must include information required in Items 1, 2 and 3 of the Form. The number of pages comprising the report (Form plus attachments) shall be indicated at the bottom of each report page (*e.g.*, 1 of 3, 2 of 3, 3 of 3).

(c) If one or more exhibits are included, whether due to a lack of space or because the exhibit is, by nature, a separate document (*e.g.*, a power of attorney), provide a sequentially numbered list of the exhibits in the Form. Use the number "24" for any power of attorney and the number

"99" for any other exhibit. If there is more than one of either such exhibit, then use numerical subparts. If the exhibit is being filed as a confirming electronic copy under Regulation S-T Rule 202(d) (17 CFR 232.202(d)), then place the designation "CE" (confirming exhibit) next to the name of the exhibit in the exhibit list. If the exhibit is being filed in paper pursuant to a hardship exception under Regulation S-T Rule 202 (17 CFR 232.202), then place the designation "P" (paper) next to the name of the exhibit in the exhibit list.

(d) If additional information is not reported as provided in paragraph (a), (b) or (c) of this instruction, whichever apply, it will be assumed that no additional information was provided.

7. Signature

(a) If the Form is filed for an individual, it shall be signed by that person or specifically on behalf of the individual by a person authorized to sign for the individual. If signed on behalf of the individual by another person, the authority of such person to sign the Form shall be confirmed to the Commission in writing in an attachment to the Form or as soon as practicable in an amendment by the individual for whom the Form is filed, unless such a confirmation still in effect is on file with the Commission. The confirming statement need only indicate that the reporting person authorizes and designates the named person or persons to file the Form on the reporting person's behalf, and state the duration of the authorization.

(b) If the Form is filed for a corporation, partnership, trust, or other entity, the capacity in which the individual signed shall be set forth (*e.g.*, John Smith, Secretary, on behalf of X Corporation).

(c) If one or more exhibits are included, whether due to a lack of space or because the exhibit is, by nature, a separate document (*e.g.*, a power of attorney), provide a sequentially numbered list of the exhibits in the Form. Use the number "24" for any power of attorney and the number "99" for any other exhibit. If there is more than one of either such exhibit, then use numerical subparts. If the exhibit is being filed as a confirming electronic copy under Regulation S-T Rule 202(d) (17 CFR 232.202(d)), then place the designation "CE" (confirming exhibit) next to the name of the exhibit in the exhibit list. If the exhibit is being filed in paper pursuant to a hardship exception under Regulation S-T Rule 202 (17 CFR 232.202), then place the designation "P" (paper) next to the name of the exhibit in the exhibit list.

(d) If additional information is not reported as provided in paragraph (a), (b) or (c) of this instruction, whichever apply, it will be assumed that no additional information was provided.

8. Transaction Codes

Use the codes listed below to indicate in Table I, Column 3 and Table II, Column 4 the character of the transaction reported. Use the code that most appropriately describes the transaction. If the transaction is not specifically listed, use transaction Code "J" and describe the nature of the transaction in the space for explanation of responses. If a transaction is voluntarily reported earlier than required, place "V" in the appropriate column to so indicate; otherwise, the column should be left blank. If a transaction involves an equity swap or instrument with similar characteristics, use transaction code "K" in addition to the code(s) that most appropriately describes the transaction, *e.g.*, "S/K" or "P/K."

General Transaction Codes

P — Open market or private purchase of non-derivative or derivative security

S — Open market or private sale of non-derivative or derivative security

V — Transaction voluntarily reported earlier than required

Rule 16b-3 Transaction Codes

A — Grant, award or other acquisition pursuant to Rule 16b-3(d)

D — Disposition to the issuer of issuer equity securities pursuant to Rule 16b-3(e)

F — Payment of exercise price or tax liability by delivering or withholding securities incident to the receipt, exercise or vesting of a security issued in accordance with Rule 16b-3

I — Discretionary transaction in accordance with Rule 16b-3(f) resulting in acquisition or disposition of issuer securities

M — Exercise or conversion of derivative security exempted pursuant to Rule 16b-3

Derivative Securities Codes (Except for transactions exempted pursuant to Rule 16b-3)

C — Conversion of derivative security

E — Expiration of short derivative position

H — Expiration (or cancellation) of long derivative position with value received

O — Exercise of out-of-the-money derivative security

X — Exercise of in-the-money or at-the-money derivative security

Other Section 16(b) Exempt Transaction and Small Acquisition Codes (except for Rule 16b-3 codes above)

G — Bona fide gift

L — Small acquisition under Rule 16a-6

W — Acquisition or disposition by will or the laws of descent and distribution

Z — Deposit into or withdrawal from voting trust

Other Transaction Codes

J — Other acquisition or disposition (describe transaction)

K — Transaction in equity swap or instrument with similar characteristics

U — Disposition pursuant to a tender of shares in a change of control transaction

9. Amendments

(a) If this Form is filed as an amendment in order to add one or more lines of transaction information to Table I or Table II of the Form being amended, provide each line being added, together with one or more footnotes, as necessary, to explain the addition of the line or lines. Do not repeat lines of transaction information that were disclosed in the original Form and are not being amended.

(b) If this Form is filed as an amendment in order to amend one or more lines of transaction information that already were disclosed in Table I or Table II of the Form being amended, provide the complete line or lines being amended, as amended, together with one or more footnotes, as necessary, to explain the amendment of the line or lines. Do not repeat lines of transaction information that were disclosed in the original Form and are not being amended.

(c) If this Form is filed as an amendment for any purpose other than or in addition to the purposes described in paragraphs (a) and (b) of this General Instruction 9, provide one or more footnotes, as necessary, to explain the amendment.

FORM 4

☐ Check this box if no longer
subject to Section 16. Form 4 or
Form 5 obligations may continue.
See Instruction 1(b).

(Print or Type Responses)

UNITED STATES SECURITIES AND EXCHANGE COMMISSION
Washington, D.C. 20549

STATEMENT OF CHANGES IN BENEFICIAL OWNERSHIP

Filed pursuant to Section 16(a) of the Securities Exchange Act of 1934, Section 17(a) of the Public Utility
Holding Company Act of 1935 or Section 30(h) of the Investment Company Act of 1940

OMB APPROVAL	
OMB Number:	3235-0287
Expires:	January 31, 2005
Estimated average burden	
hours per response	0.5

1. Name and Address of Reporting Person*	2. Issuer Name **and** Ticker or Trading Symbol	5. Relationship of Reporting Person(s) to Issuer (Check all applicable)
(Last) (First) (Middle)		___ Director ___ 10% Owner
(Street)	3. Date of Earliest Transaction Required to be Reported (Month/Day/Year)	4. If Amendment, Date Original Filed (Month/Day/Year)	___ Officer (give title below) ___ Other (specify below)
(City) (State) (Zip)		6. Individual or Joint/Group Filing (Check Applicable Line) ___ Form filed by One Reporting Person ___ Form filed by More than One Reporting Person

Table I — Non-Derivative Securities Acquired, Disposed of, or Beneficially Owned

1. Title of Security (Instr. 3)	2. Transaction Date (Month/ Day/ Year)	2A. Deemed Execution Date, if any (Month/ Day/Year)	3. Transaction Code (Instr. 8)		4. Securities Acquired (A) or Disposed of (D) (Instr. 3, 4 and 5)			5. Amount of Securities Beneficially Owned Following Reported Transaction (s) (Instr. 3 and 4)	6. Ownership Form: Direct (D) or Indirect (I) (Instr. 4)	7. Nature of Indirect Beneficial Ownership (Instr. 4)
			Code	V	Amount	(A) or (D)	Price			

Reminder: Report on a separate line for each class of securities beneficially owned directly or indirectly.
* If the form is filed by more than one reporting person, see Instruction 4(b)(v).

Potential persons who are to respond to the collection of
information contained in this form are not required to respond
unless the form displays a currently valid OMB control number.

(Over)

SEC 1474 (06-03)

FORM 4 (continued)

Table II — Derivative Securities Acquired, Disposed of, or Beneficially Owned
(*e.g.* puts, calls, warrants, options, convertible securities)

1. Title of Derivative Security (Instr. 3)	2. Conversion or Exercise Price of Derivative Security	3. Transaction Date (Month/ Day/ Year)	3A. Deemed Execution Date, if any (Month/ Day/ Year)	4. Transaction Code (Instr. 8)		5. Number of Derivative Securities Acquired (A) or Disposed of (D) (Instr. 3, 4, and 5)		6. Date Exercisable and Expiration Date (Month/Day/ Year)		7. Title and Amount of Underlying Securities (Instr. 3 and 4)		8. Price of Derivative Security (Instr. 5)	9. Number of derivative Securities Beneficially Owned following Reported Transaction (s)(Instr. 4)	10. Ownership Form of Derivative Security Direct (D) or Indirect (I) (Instr. 4)	11. Nature of Indirect Beneficial Ownership (Instr. 4)
				Code	V	(A)	(D)	Date Exercisable	Expiration Date	Title	Amount or Number of Shares				

Explanation of Responses:

_____   **Signature of Reporting Person   Date

** Intentional misstatements or omissions of facts constitute Federal Criminal Violations. See 18 U.S.C. 1001 and 15 U.S.C. 78ff(a).

Note: File three copies of this Form, one of which must be manually signed. If space is insufficient, see Instruction 6 for procedure.

Potential persons who are to respond to the collection of information contained in this form are not required to respond unless the form displays a currently valid OMB Number.

Page 2

Form 5

ANNUAL STATEMENT OF BENEFICIAL OWNERSHIP OF SECURITIES

The Commission is authorized to solicit the information required by this Form pursuant to Sections 16(a) and 23(a) of the Securities Exchange Act of 1934, Sections 17(a) and 20(a) of the Public Utility Holding Company Act of 1935, and Sections 30(h) and 38 of the Investment Company Act of 1940, and the rules and regulations thereunder. Disclosure of information specified on this Form is mandatory, except for disclosure of the I.R.S. identification number of the reporting person if such person is an entity, which is voluntary. If such numbers are furnished, they will assist the Commission in distinguishing reporting persons with similar names and will facilitate the prompt processing of the Form. The information will be used for the primary purpose of disclosing the transactions and holdings of directors, officers, and beneficial owners of registered companies. Information disclosed will be a matter of public record and available for inspection by members of the public. The Commission can use it in investigations or litigation involving the federal securities laws or other civil, criminal, or regulatory statutes or provisions, as well as for referral to other governmental authorities and self-regulatory organizations. Failure to disclose required information may result in civil or criminal action against persons involved for violations of the Federal securities laws and rules.

GENERAL INSTRUCTIONS

1. When Form Must Be Filed

(a) This Form must be filed on or before the 45th day after the end of the issuer's fiscal year in accordance with Rule 16a-3(f). This Form and any amendment is deemed filed with the Commission or the Exchange on the date it is received by the Commission or Exchange, respectively. *See,* however, Rule 16a-3(h) regarding delivery to a third party business that guarantees delivery of the filing no later than the specified due date.

(b) A reporting person no longer subject to Section 16 of the Securities Exchange Act of 1934 ("Exchange Act") must check the exit box appearing on this Form. Transactions and holdings previously reported are not required to be included on this Form. Form 4 or Form 5 obligations may continue to be applicable. *See* Rule 16a-3(f); *see also* Rule 16a-2(b)(transactions after termination of insider status).

(c) A separate Form shall be filed to reflect beneficial ownership of securities of each issuer, except that a single statement shall be filed with respect to the securities of a registered public utility holding company and all of its subsidiary companies.

(d) If a reporting person is not an officer, director, or ten percent holder, the person should check "other" in Item 6 (Relationship of Reporting Person to Issuer) and describe the reason for reporting status in the space provided.

2. Where Form Must be Filed

(a) A reporting person must file this Form in electronic format via the Commission's Electronic Data Gathering Analysis and Retrieval System (EDGAR) in accordance with EDGAR rules set forth in Regulation S-T (17 CFR Part 232), except that a filing person that has obtained a hardship exception under Regulation S-T Rule 202 (17 CFR 232.202) may file the Form in paper. For assistance with technical questions about EDGAR or to request an access code, call the EDGAR Filer Support Office at (202) 942-8900. For assistance with questions about the EDGAR rules, call the Office of EDGAR and Information Analysis at (202) 942-2940.

(b) At the time this Form or any amendment is filed with the Commission, file one copy with each Exchange on which any class of securities of the issuer is registered. If the issuer has designated a single Exchange to receive Section 16 filings, the copy shall be filed with that Exchange only.

(c) Any person required to file this Form or amendment shall, not later than the time the Form or amendment is transmitted for filing with the Commission, send or deliver a copy to the person designated by the issuer to receive the copy or, if no person is so designated, the issuer's corporate secretary (or person performing similar functions) in accordance with Rule 16a-3(e). NOTE: If filing pursuant to a hardship exception under Regulation S-T Rule 202 (17 CFR 232.202), file three copies of this Form or any amendment, at least one of which is signed, with the Securities and Exchange Commission, 450 5th Street, NW, Washington, DC 20549. (Acknowledgement of receipt by the Commission may be obtained by enclosing a self-addressed stamped postcard identifying the Form or amendment filed.)

3. Class of Securities Reported

(a) (i) Persons reporting pursuant to Section 16(a) of the Exchange Act shall include information as to transactions and holdings required to be reported in any class of equity securities of the issuer and the beneficial ownership at the end of the year of that class of equity securities, even though one or more of such classes may not be registered pursuant to Section 12 of the Exchange Act.

(ii) Persons reporting pursuant to Section 17(a) of the Public Utility Holding Company Act of 1935 shall include transactions and holdings required to be reported in any class of securities (equity or debt) of the registered holding company and any of its subsidiary companies and the beneficial ownership at the end of the issuer's fiscal year of that class of securities. Specify the name of the parent or subsidiary issuing the securities.

(iii) Persons reporting pursuant to Section 30(h) of the Investment Company Act of 1940 shall include transactions and holdings required to be reported in any class of securities (equity or debt) of the registered closed-end investment company (other than "short-term paper as defined in Section 2(a)(38) of the Investment Company Act) and the beneficial ownership at the end of the year of that class of securities.

(b) The title of the security should clearly identify the class, even if the issuer has only one class of securities outstanding; for example, "Common Stock," "Class A Common Stock," "Class B Convertible Preferred Stock," etc.

(c) The amount of securities beneficially owned should state the face amount of debt securities (U.S. Dollars) or the number of equity securities, whichever is appropriate.

4. Transactions and Holdings Required to be Reported

(a) *General Requirements*

(i) Pursuant to Rule 16a-3(f), if not previously reported, the following transactions, and total beneficial ownershipas of the end of the issuer's fiscal year (or an earlier date applicable to a person ceasing to be an insider during the fiscal year) for any class of securities in which a transaction is reported, shall be reported:

(A) any transaction during the issuer's most recent fiscal year that was exempt from Section 16(b) of the Act, except:

(1) any transaction exempt from Section 16(b) pursuant to §240.16b-3(d), §240.16b-3(e), or §240.16b-3(f) (these are required to be reported on Form 4); (2) any exercise or conversion of derivative securities exempt under either §240.16b-3 or §240.16b-6(b) (these are required to be reported on Form 4); (3) any transaction exempt from Section 16(b) of the Act pursuant to §240.16b-3(c), which is exempt from Section 16(a) of the Act; and (4) any transaction exempt from Section 16 of the Act pursuant to another Section 16(a) rule;

(B) any small acquisition or series of acquisitions in a six month period during the issuer's fiscal year not exceeding $10,000 in market value (see Rule 16a-6);

(C) any transactions or holdings that should have been reported during the issuer's fiscal year on a Form 3 or Form 4, but were not reported. The first Form 5 filing obligation shall include all holdings and transactions that should have been reported in each of the issuer's last two fiscal years but were not. *See* Instruction 8 for the code to identify delinquent Form 3 holdings or Form 4 transactions reported on this Form 5.

Note: A required Form 3 or Form 4 must be filed within the time specified by this Form. Form 3 holdings or Form 4 transactions reported on Form 5 represent delinquent Form 3 and Form 4 filings.

(ii) Each transaction should be reported on a separate line. Transaction codes specified in Item 8 should be used to identify the nature of the transactions resulting in an acquisition or disposition of a security. A deemed execution date must be reported in Column 2A of Table I or Column 3A of Table II only if the execution date for the transaction is calculated pursuant to §240.16a-3(g)(2) or §240.16a-3(g)(3).

(iii) Every transaction shall be reported even though acquisitions and dispositions with respect to a class of securities are equal. Report total beneficial ownership as of the end of the issuer's fiscal year for all classes of securities in which a transaction was reported.

(b) *Beneficial Ownership Reported (Pecuniary Interest)*

(i) Although for purposes of determining status as a ten percent holder, a person is deemed to beneficially own securities over which that person exercises voting or investment control (*see* Rule 16a-1(a)(1)), for reporting transactions and holdings, a person is deemed to be the beneficial owner of securities if that person has or shares the opportunity, directly or indirectly, to profit or share in any profit derived from a transaction in the securities ("pecuniary interest").

See Rule 16a-1(a)(2). *See also* Rule 16a-8 for the application of the beneficial ownership definition to trust holdings and transactions.

(ii) Both direct and indirect beneficial ownership of securities shall be reported. Securities beneficially owned directly are those held in the reporting person's name or in the name of a bank, broker or nominee for the account of the reporting person. In addition, securities held as joint tenants, tenants in common, tenants by the entirety, or as community property are to be reported as held directly. If a person has a pecuniary interest, by reason of any contract, understanding or relationship (including a family relationship or arrangement) in securities held in the name of another person, that person is an indirect beneficial owner of the securities. See Rule 16a-1(a)(2)(ii) for certain indirect beneficial ownerships.

(iii) Report transactions in securities beneficially owned directly on a separate line from those beneficially owned indirectly. Report different forms of indirect ownership on separate lines. The nature of indirect ownership shall be stated as specifically as possible; for example, "By Self as Trustee for X," "By Spouse," "By X Trust," "By Y Corporation," etc.

(iv) In stating the amount of securities acquired, disposed of, or beneficially owned indirectly through a partnership, corporation, trust, or other entity, report the number of securities representing the reporting person's proportionate interest in transactions conducted by that entity or holdings of that entity. Alternatively, at the option of the reporting person, the entire amount of the entity's interest may be reported. *See* Rule 16a-1(a)(2)(ii)(B) and Rule 16a-1(a)(2)(iii).

(v) Where more than one beneficial owner of the same equity securities must report the same transaction or holding on Form 5, such owners may file Form 5 individually or jointly. Joint and group filings may be made by any designated beneficial owner. Transactions and holdings with respect to securities owned separately by any joint or group filer are permitted to be included in the joint filing. Indicate only the name and address of the designated filer in Item 1 of Form 5 and attach a list of the names and addresses of each other reporting person. Joint and group filings must include all required information for each beneficial owner, and such filings must be signed by each beneficial owner, or on behalf of such owner by an authorized person.

If this Form is being filed in paper pursuant to a hardship exemption and the space provided for signatures is insufficient, attach a signature page. If this Form is being filed in paper, submit any attached listing of names or signatures on another Form 5, copy of Form 5 or separate page of 8 ½ by 11 inch white paper, indicate the number of pages comprising the report (Form plus attachments) at the bottom of each report page (*e.g.*, 1 of 3, 2 of 3, 3 of 3), and include the name of the designated filer and information required by Items 2 and 3 of the Form on the attachment.

See Rule 16a-3(i) regarding signatures.

(c) *Non-Derivative and Derivative Securities*

(i) Report acquisitions or dispositions and holdings of non-derivative securities in Table I. Report acquisitions or dispositions and holdings of derivative securities (*e.g.*, puts, calls, options, warrants, convertible securities, or other rights or obligations to buy or sell securities) in Table II. Report the exercise or conversion of a derivative security in Table II (as a disposition of the derivative security) and report in Table I the holdings of the underlying security. Report acquisitions or dispositions and holdings of derivative securities that are both equity securities and convertible or exchangeable for other equity securities (*e.g.*, convertible preferred securities) only in Table II.

(ii) The title of a derivative security and the title of the equity security underlying the derivative security should be shown separately in the appropriate columns in Table II. The "puts" and "calls" reported in Table II include, in addition to separate puts and calls, any combination of the two, such as spreads and straddles. In reporting an option in Table II, state whether it represents a right to buy, a right to sell, an obligation to buy, or an obligation to sell the equity securities subject to the option.

(iii) Describe in the appropriate columns in Table II characteristics of derivative securities, including title, exercise or conversion price, date exercisable, expiration date, and the title and amount of securities underlying the derivative security. If the transaction reported is a purchase or a sale of a derivative security, the purchase or sale price of that derivative security shall be reported in column 8. If the transaction is the exercise or conversion of a derivative security, leave column 8 blank and report the exercise or conversion price of the derivative security in column 2.

(iv) Securities constituting components of a unit shall be reported separately on the applicable table (*e.g.*, if a unit has a non-derivative security component and a derivative security component, the non-derivative security component shall be reported in Table I and the derivative security component shall be reported in Table II). The relationship between individual securities comprising the unit shall be indicated in the space provided for explanation of responses. When securities are purchased or sold as a unit, state the purchase or sale price per unit and other required information regarding the unit securities.

5. Price of Securities

(a) Prices of securities shall be reported in U.S. dollars on a per share basis, not an aggregate basis, except that the aggregate price of debt shall be stated. Amounts reported shall exclude brokerage commissions and other costs of execution.

(b) If consideration other than cash was paid for the security, describe the consideration, including the value of the consideration, in the space provided for explanation of responses.

6. Additional Information

(a) If the space provided in the line items on the electronic Form is insufficient, use the space provided for footnotes. If the space provided for footnotes is insufficient, create a footnote that refers to an exhibit to the form that contains the additional information.

(b) If the space provided in the line items on the paper Form or space provided for additional comments is insufficient, attach another Form 5, copy of Form 5 or separate 8 ½ by 11 inch white paper to Form 5, completed as appropriate to include the additional comments. Each attached page must include information required in Items 1, 2 and 3 of the Form. The number of pages comprising the report (Form plus attachments) shall be indicated at the bottom of each report page (*e.g.*, 1 of 3, 2 of 3, 3 of 3).

(c) If one or more exhibits are included, whether due to a lack of space or because the exhibit is, by nature, a separate document (*e.g.*, a power of attorney), provide a sequentially numbered list of the exhibits in the Form. Use the number "24" for any power of attorney and the number "99" for any other exhibit. If there is more than one of either such exhibit, then use numerical subparts. If the exhibit is being filed as a confirming electronic copy under Regulation S-T Rule 202(d) (17 CFR 232.202(d)), then place the designation "CE" (confirming exhibit) next to the name of the exhibit in the exhibit list. If the exhibit is being filed in paper pursuant to a hardship exception under Regulation S-T Rule 202 (17 CFR 232.202), then place the designation "P" (paper) next to the name of the exhibit in the exhibit list.

(d) If additional information is not reported as provided in paragraph (a), (b) or (c) of this instruction, whichever apply, it will be assumed that no additional information was provided.

7. Signature

(a) If the Form is filed for an individual, it shall be signed by that person or specifically on behalf of the individual by a person authorized to sign for the individual. If signed on behalf of the individual by another person, the authority of such person to sign the Form shall be confirmed to the Commission in writing in an attachment to the Form or as soon as practicable in an amendment by the individual for whom the Form is filed, unless such a confirmation still in effect is on file with the Commission. The confirming statement need only indicate that the reporting person authorizes and designates the named person or persons to file the Form on the reporting person's behalf, and state the duration of the authorization.

(b) If the Form is filed for a corporation, partnership, trust, or other entity, the capacity in which the individual signed shall be set forth (*e.g.*, John Smith, Secretary, on behalf of X Corporation).

8. Transaction Codes

Use the codes listed below to indicate in Table I, Column 3 and Table II, Column 4 the character of the transaction reported. Use the code that most appropriately describes the transaction. If the transaction is not specifically listed, use transaction code "J" and describe the nature of the transaction in the space for explanation of responses. If a transaction involves an equity swap or instrument with similar characteristics, use transaction Code "K" in addition to the code(s) that most appropriately describes the transaction, *e.g.*, "S/K" or "P/K."

General Transaction Codes

P — Open market or private purchase of non-derivative or derivative security

S — Open market or private sale of non-derivative or derivative security

Rule 16b-3 Transaction Codes

A — Grant, award or other acquisition pursuant to Rule 16b-3(d)

D — Disposition to the issuer of issuer equity securities pursuant to Rule 16b-3(e)

F — Payment of exercise price or tax liability by delivering or withholding securities incident to the receipt, exercise or vesting of a security issued in accordance with Rule 16b-3

I — Discretionary transaction in accordance with Rule 16b-3(f) resulting in acquisition or disposition of issuer securities

M — Exercise or conversion of derivative security exempted pursuant to Rule 16b-3

Derivative Securities Codes (Except for transactions exempted pursuant to Rule 16b-3)

C — Conversion of derivative security

E — Expiration of short derivative position

H — Expiration (or cancellation) of long derivative position with value received

O — Exercise of out-of-the-money derivative security

X — Exercise of in-the-money or at-the-money derivative security

Other Section 16(b) Exempt Transaction and Small Acquisition Codes (except for Rule 16b-3 codes above)

G — Bona fide gift

L — Small acquisition under Rule 16a-6

W — Acquisition or disposition by will or the laws of descent and distribution

Z — Deposit into or withdrawal from voting trust

Other Transaction Codes

J — Other acquisition or disposition (describe transaction)

K — Transaction in equity swap or instrument with similar characteristics

U — Disposition pursuant to a tender of shares in a change of control transaction

Form 3, 4 or 5 Holdings or Transactions Not Previously Reported

To indicate that a holding should have been reported previously on Form 3, place a "3" in Table I, column 3 or Table II, column 4, as appropriate. Indicate in the space provided for explanation of responses the event triggering the Form 3 filing obligation. To indicate that a transaction should have been reported previously on Form 4, place a "4" next to the transaction code reported in Table I, column 3 or Table II, column 4 (*e.g.*, an open market purchase of a non-derivative security that should have been reported previously on Form 4 should be designated as "P4"). To indicate that a transaction should have been reported on previous Form 5, place a "5" in Table I, column 3 or Table II, column 4, as appropriate. In addition, the appropriate box on the front page of the Form should be checked.

9. Amendments

(a) If this Form is filed as an amendment in order to add one or more lines of transaction or ownership information to Table I or Table II of the Form being amended, provide each line being added, together with one or more footnotes, as necessary, to explain the addition of the line or lines. Do not repeat lines of transaction or ownership information that were disclosed in the original Form and are not being amended.

(b) If this Form is filed as an amendment in order to amend one or more lines of transaction or ownership information that already were disclosed in Table I or Table II of the Form being amended, provide the complete line or lines being amended, as amended, together with one or more footnotes, as necessary, to explain the amendment of the line or lines. Do not repeat lines of transaction or ownership information that were disclosed in the original Form and are not being amended.

(c) If this Form is filed as an amendment for any purpose other than or in addition to the purposes described in paragraphs (a) and (b) of this General Instruction 9, provide one or more footnotes, as necessary, to explain the amendment.

FORM 5

☐ **Check box if no longer subject to Section 16. Form 4 or Form 5 obligations may continue. See Instruction 10b.**

☐ Form 3 Holdings Reported
☐ Form 4 Transactions Reported

OMB APPROVAL
OMB Number: 3235-0362
Expires: January 31, 2005
Estimated average burden hours per response. 1.0

UNITED STATES SECURITIES AND EXCHANGE COMMISSION
Washington, D.C. 20549

ANNUAL STATEMENT OF CHANGES IN BENEFICIAL OWNERSHIP OF SECURITIES

Filed pursuant to Section 16(a) of the Securities Exchange Act of 1934, Section 17(a) of the Public Utility Holding Company Act of 1935 or Section 30(h) of the Investment Company Act of 1940

1. Name and Address of Reporting Person*	2. Issuer Name and Ticker or Trading Symbol	5. Relationship of Reporting Person(s) to Issuer (Check all applicable)
(Last) (First) (Middle)		___ Director ___ 10% Owner ___ Officer (give title below) ___ Other (specify below)
(Street)	3. Statement for Issuer's Fiscal Year Ended (Month/Day/Year)	
(City) (State) (Zip)	4. If Amendment, Date Original Filed (Month/Day/Year)	6. Individual or Joint/Group Reporting (check applicable line) ___ Form Filed by One Reporting Person ___ Form Filed by More than One Reporting Person

Table I — Non-Derivative Securities Acquired, Disposed of, or Beneficially Owned

1. Title of Security (Instr. 3)	2. Transaction Date (Month/Day/Year)	2A. Deemed Execution Date, if any (Month/Day/Year)	3. Transaction Code (Instr. 8)	4. Securities Acquired (A) or Disposed of (D) (Instr. 3, 4 and 5)		5. Amount of Securities Beneficially Owned at end of Issuer's Fiscal Year (Instr. 3 and 4)	6. Ownership Form: Direct (D) or Indirect (I) (Instr. 4)	7. Nature of Indirect Beneficial Ownership (Instr. 4)
				Amount	(A) or (D)	Price		

Reminder: Report on a separate line for each class of securities beneficially owned directly or indirectly.
* If the form is filed by more than one reporting person, see instruction 4(b)(v).

Potential persons who are to respond to the collection of information contained in this form are not required to respond unless the form displays a currently valid OMB control number.

(Over)

SEC 2270 (7-03)

FORM 5 (continued)

Table II — Derivative Securities Acquired, Disposed of, or Beneficially Owned
(e.g., puts, calls, warrants, options, convertible securities)

1. Title of Derivative Security (Instr. 3)	2. Conversion or Exercise Price of Derivative Security	3. Transaction Date (Month/Day/Year)	3A. Deemed Execution Date, if any (Month/Day/Year)	4. Transaction Code (Instr. 8)		5. Number of Derivative Securities Acquired (A) or Disposed of (D) (Instr. 3, 4, and 5)		6. Date Exercisable and Expiration Date (Month/Day/Year)		7. Title and Amount of Underlying Securities (Instr. 3 and 4)		8. Price of Derivative Security (Instr. 5)	9. Number of Derivative Securities Beneficially Owned at End of Issuer's Fiscal Year (Instr. 4)	10. Ownership Form of Derivative Securities: Direct (D) or Indirect (I) (Instr. 4)	11. Nature of Indirect Beneficial Ownership (Instr. 4)
						(A)	(D)	Date Exercisable	Expiration Date	Title	Amount or Number of Shares				

Explanation of Responses:

_____
** Signature of Reporting Person   Date

** Intentional misstatements or omissions of facts constitute Federal Criminal Violations.
See 18 U.S.C. 1001 and 15 U.S.C. 78ff(a).

Note: File three copies of this Form, one of which must be manually signed.
         If space provided is insufficient, see Instruction 6 for procedure.

Potential persons who are to respond to the collection of information contained in this form are not required to respond unless the form displays a currently valid OMB number.

Page 2

New York Stock Exchange Listed Company Manual

303A.02. Independence Tests

In order to tighten the definition of "independent director" for purposes of these standards:

(a) No director qualifies as "independent" unless the board of directors affirmatively determines that the director has no material relationship with the listed company (either directly or as a partner, shareholder or officer of an organization that has a relationship with the company). Companies must identify which directors are independent and disclose the basis for that determination.

Commentary: It is not possible to anticipate, or explicitly to provide for, all circumstances that might signal potential conflicts of interest, or that might bear on the materiality of a director's relationship to a listed company (references to "company" would include any parent or subsidiary in a consolidated group with the company). Accordingly, it is best that boards making "independence" determinations broadly consider all relevant facts and circumstances. In particular, when assessing the materiality of a director's relationship with the listed company, the board should consider the issue not merely from the standpoint of the director, but also from that of persons or organizations with which the director has an affiliation. Material relationships can include commercial, industrial, banking, consulting, legal, accounting, charitable and familial relationships, among others. However, as the concern is independence from management, the Exchange does not view ownership of even a significant amount of stock, by itself, as a bar to an independence finding.

The identity of the independent directors and the basis for a board determination that a relationship is not material must be disclosed in the listed company's annual proxy statement or, if the company does not file an annual proxy statement, in the company's annual report on Form 10-K filed with the SEC. In this regard, a board may adopt and disclose categorical standards to assist it in making determinations of independence and may make a general disclosure if a director meets these standards. Any determination of independence for a director who does not meet these standards must be specifically explained. A company must disclose any standard it adopts. It may then make the general statement that the

All rights in the reprinted materials from the *Listed Company Manual* are owned exclusively by the New York Stock Exchange, Inc., © 2003-2004 New York Stock Exchange, Inc., All rights reserved. See *www.nyse.com*.

independent directors meet the standards set by the board without detailing particular aspects of the immaterial relationships between individual directors and the company. In the event that a director with a business or other relationship that does not fit within the disclosed standards is determined to be independent, a board must disclose the basis for its determination in the manner described above. This approach provides investors with an adequate means of assessing the quality of a board's independence and its independence determinations while avoiding excessive disclosure of immaterial relationships.

(b) In addition, a director is not independent if:

(i) The director is, or has been within the last three years, an employee of the listed company, or an immediate family member is, or has been within the last three years, an executive officer,[1] of the listed company.

Commentary: Employment as an interim Chairman or CEO or other executive officer shall not disqualify a director from being considered independent following that employment.

(ii) The director has received, or has an immediate family member who has received, during any twelve-month period within the last three years, more than $100,000 in direct compensation from the listed company, other than director and committee fees and pension or other forms of deferred compensation for prior service (provided such compensation is not contingent in any way on continued service).

Commentary: Compensation received by a director for former service as an interim Chairman or CEO or other executive officer need not be considered in determining independence under this test. Compensation received by an immediate family member for service as an employee of the listed company (other than an executive officer) need not be considered in determining independence under this test.

(iii) (A) The director or an immediate family member is a current partner of a firm that is the company's internal or external auditor; (B) the director is a current employee of such a firm; (C) the director has an immediate family member who is a current employee of such a firm and who participates in the firm's audit, assurance or tax compliance (but not tax planning) practice; or (D) the director or an immediate family member was within the last three years (but is no longer) a partner or employee of such a firm and personally worked on the listed company's audit within that time.

(iv) The director or an immediate family member is, or has been within the last three years, employed as an executive officer of another company where any of the listed

company's present executive officers at the same time serves or served on that company's compensation committee.

(v) The director is a current employee, or an immediate family member is a current executive officer, of a company that has made payments to, or received payments from, the listed company for property or services in an amount which, in any of the last three fiscal years, exceeds the greater of $1 million, or 2% of such other company's consolidated gross revenues.

Commentary: In applying the test in Section 303A.02(b)(v), both the payments and the consolidated gross revenues to be measured shall be those reported in the last completed fiscal year. The look-back provision for this test applies solely to the financial relationship between the listed company and the director or immediate family member's current employer; a listed company need not consider former employment of the director or immediate family member.

Contributions to tax exempt organizations shall not be considered "payments" for purposes of Section 303A.02(b)(v), provided however that a listed company shall disclose in its annual proxy statement, or if the listed company does not file an annual proxy statement, in the company's annual report on Form 10-K filed with the SEC, any such contributions made by the listed company to any tax exempt organization in which any independent director serves as an executive officer if, within the preceding three years, contributions in any single fiscal year from the listed company to the organization exceeded the greater of $1 million, or 2% of such tax exempt organization's consolidated gross revenues. Listed company boards are reminded of their obligations to consider the materiality of any such relationship in accordance with Section 303A.02(a) above.

General Commentary to Section 303A.02(b): An "immediate family member" includes a person's spouse, parents, children, siblings, mothers and fathers-in-law, sons and daughters-in-law, brothers and sisters-in-law, and anyone (other than domestic employees) who shares such person's home. When applying the look-back provisions in Section 303A.02(b), listed companies need not consider individuals who are no longer immediate family members as a result of legal separation or divorce, or those who have died or become incapacitated.

In addition, references to the "company" would include any parent or subsidiary in a consolidated group with the company.

[1]For purposes of Section 303A, the term "executive officer" has the same meaning specified for the term "officer" in Rule 16a-1(f) under the Securities Exchange Act of 1934.

Transition Rule. Each of the above standards contains a three-year "look-back" provision. In order to facilitate a smooth transition to the new independence standards, the Exchange will phase in the "look-back" provisions by applying only a one-year look-back for the first year after adoption of these new standards. The three-year look-backs provided for in Section 303A.02(b) will begin to apply only from and after November 4, 2004.

As an example, until November 3, 2004, a listed company need look back only one year when testing compensation under Section 303A.02(b)(ii). Beginning November 4, 2004, however, the listed company would need to look back the full three years provided in Section 303A.02(b)(ii).

303A.08. Shareholder Approval of Equity Compensation Plans

Shareholders must be given the opportunity to vote on all equity-compensation plans and material revisions thereto, with limited exemptions explained below.

Equity-compensation plans can help align shareholder and management interests, and equity-based awards are often very important components of employee compensation. To provide checks and balances on the potential dilution resulting from the process of earmarking shares to be used for equity-based awards, the Exchange requires that all equity-compensation plans, and any material revisions to the terms of such plans, be subject to shareholder approval, with the limited exemptions explained below.

Definition of Equity-Compensation Plan

An "equity-compensation plan" is a plan or other arrangement that provides for the delivery of equity securities (either newly issued or treasury shares) of the listed company to any employee, director or other service provider as compensation for services. Even a compensatory grant of options or other equity securities that is not made under a plan is, nonetheless, an "equity-compensation plan" for these purposes.

However, the following are not "equity-compensation plans" even if the brokerage and other costs of the plan are paid for by the listed company:

- Plans that are made available to shareholders generally, such as a typical dividend reinvestment plan.

- Plans that merely allow employees, directors or other service providers to elect to buy shares on the open market or from the listed company for their current fair market value, regardless of whether:

  – the shares are delivered immediately or on a deferred basis; or

– the payments for the shares are made directly or by giving up compensation that is otherwise due (for example, through payroll deductions).

Material Revisions

A "material revision" of an equity-compensation plan includes (but is not limited to), the following:

* A material increase in the number of shares available under the plan (other than an increase solely to reflect a reorganization, stock split, merger, spinoff or similar transaction).

– If a plan contains a formula for automatic increases in the shares available (sometimes called an "evergreen formula") or for automatic grants pursuant to a formula, each such increase or grant will be considered a revision requiring shareholder approval *unless* the plan has a term of not more than ten years.

This type of plan (regardless of its term) is referred to below as a "formula plan." Examples of automatic grants pursuant to a formula are (1) annual grants to directors of restricted stock having a certain dollar value, and (2) "matching contributions," whereby stock is credited to a participant's account based upon the amount of compensation the participant elects to defer.

– If a plan contains no limit on the number of shares available and is not a formula plan, then each grant under the plan will require separate shareholder approval *regardless* of whether the plan has a term of not more than ten years.

This type of plan is referred to below as a "discretionary plan." A requirement that grants be made out of treasury shares or repurchased shares will not, in itself, be considered a limit or pre-established formula so as to prevent a plan from being considered a discretionary plan.

* An expansion of the types of awards available under the plan.

* A material expansion of the class of employees, directors or other service providers eligible to participate in the plan.

* A material extension of the term of the plan.

* A material change to the method of determining the strike price of options under the plan.

– A change in the method of determining "fair market value" from the closing price on the date of grant to the average of the high and low price on the date of grant is an example of a change that the Exchange would not view as material.

* The deletion or limitation of any provision prohibiting repricing of options. See the next section for details.

Note that an amendment will not be considered a "material revision" if it curtails rather than expands the scope of the plan in question.

Repricings

A plan that does not contain a provision that specifically *permits* repricing of options will be considered for purposes of this listing standard as *prohibiting* repricing. Accordingly any actual repricing of options will be considered a material revision of a plan even if the plan itself is not revised. This consideration will not apply to a repricing through an exchange offer that commenced before the date this listing standard became effective.

"Repricing" means any of the following or any other action that has the same effect:

- Lowering the strike price of an option after it is granted.

- Any other action that is treated as a repricing under generally accepted accounting principles.

- Canceling an option at a time when its strike price exceeds the fair market value of the underlying stock, in exchange for another option, restricted stock, or other equity, unless the cancellation and exchange occurs in connection with a merger, acquisition, spin-off or other similar corporate transaction.

Exemptions

This listing standard does not require shareholder approval of employment inducement awards, certain grants, plans and amendments in the context of mergers and acquisitions, and certain specific types of plans, all as described below. However, these exempt grants, plans and amendments may be made only with the approval of the company's independent compensation committee or the approval of a majority of the company's independent directors. Companies must also notify the Exchange in writing when they use one of these exemptions.

Employment Inducement Awards

An employment inducement award is a grant of options or other equity-based compensation as a material inducement to a person or persons being hired by the listed company or any of its subsidiaries, or being re-hired following a bona fide period of interruption of employment. Inducement awards include grants to new employees in connection with a merger or acquisition. Promptly following a grant of any inducement award in reliance on this exemption, the listed company must disclose in a press release the material terms of the award, including the recipient(s) of the award and the number of shares involved.

Mergers and Acquisitions

Two exemptions apply in the context of corporate acquisitions and mergers.

First, shareholder approval will not be required to convert, replace or adjust outstanding options or other equity-compensation awards to reflect the transaction.

Second, shares available under certain plans acquired in corporate acquisitions and mergers may be used for certain post-transaction grants without further shareholder approval. This exemption applies to situations where a party that is not a listed company following the transaction has shares available for grant under pre-existing plans that were previously approved by shareholders. A plan adopted in contemplation of the merger or acquisition transaction would not be considered "pre-existing" for purposes of this exemption.

Shares available under such a pre-existing plan may be used for post-transaction grants of options and other awards with respect to equity of the entity that is the listed company after the transaction, either under the pre-existing plan or another plan, without further shareholder approval, so long as:

- the number of shares available for grants is appropriately adjusted to reflect the transaction;

- the time during which those shares are available is not extended beyond the period when they would have been available under the pre-existing plan, absent the transaction; and

- the options and other awards are not granted to individuals who were employed, immediately before the transaction, by the post-transaction listed company or entities that were its subsidiaries immediately before the transaction.

Any shares reserved for listing in connection with a transaction pursuant to either of these exemptions would be counted by the Exchange in determining whether the transaction involved the issuance of 20% or more of the company's outstanding common stock and thus required shareholder approval under Listed Company Manual Section 312.03(c).

These merger-related exemptions will not result in any increase in the aggregate potential dilution of the combined enterprise. Further, mergers or acquisitions are not routine occurrences, and are not likely to be abused. Therefore, the Exchange considers both of these exemptions to be consistent with the fundamental policy involved in this standard.

Qualified Plans, Parallel Excess Plans and Section 423 Plans

The following types of plans (and material revisions thereto) are exempt from the shareholder approval requirement:

- plans intended to meet the requirements of Section 401(a) of the Internal Revenue Code (e.g., ESOPs);

- plans intended to meet the requirements of Section 423 of the Internal Revenue Code; and

- "parallel excess plans" as defined below.

Section 401(a) plans and Section 423 plans are already regulated under the Internal Revenue Code and Treasury regulations. Section 423 plans, which are stock purchase plans under which an employee can purchase no more than $25,000 worth of stock per year at a plan-specified discount capped at 15%, are also required by the Internal Revenue Code to receive shareholder approval. While Section 401(a) plans and parallel excess plans are not required to be approved by shareholders, U.S. GAAP requires that the shares issued under these plans be "expensed" (i.e., treated as a compensation expense on the income statement) by the company issuing the shares.

An equity-compensation plan that provides non-U.S. employees with substantially the same benefits as a comparable Section 401(a) plan, Section 423 plan or parallel excess plan that the listed company provides to its U.S. employees, but for features necessary to comply with applicable foreign tax law, are also exempt from shareholder approval under this section.

The term "parallel excess plan" means a plan that is a "pension plan" within the meaning of the Employee Retirement Income Security Act ("ERISA") that is designed to work in parallel with a plan intended to be qualified under Internal Revenue Code Section 401(a) to provide benefits that exceed the limits set forth in Internal Revenue Code Section 402(g) (the section that limits an employee's annual pre-tax contributions to a 401(k) plan), Internal Revenue Code Section 401(a)(17) (the section that limits the amount of an employee's compensation that can be taken into account for plan purposes) and/or Internal Revenue Code Section 415 (the section that limits the contributions and benefits under qualified plans) and/or any successor or similar limitations that may hereafter be enacted. A plan will not be considered a parallel excess plan unless (1) it covers all or substantially all employees of an employer who are participants in the related qualified plan whose annual compensation is in excess of the limit of Code Section 401(a)(17) (or any successor or similar limits that may hereafter be enacted); (2) its terms are substantially the same as the qualified plan that it parallels except for the elimination of the limits described in the preceding sentence and the limitation described in clause (3); and (3) no participant receives employer equity contributions under the plan in excess of 25% of the participant's cash compensation.

Transition Rules

Except as provided below, a plan that was adopted before the date of the Securities and Exchange Commission order approving this listing standard will not be subject to shareholder approval under this listing standard unless and until it is materially revised.

In the case of a discretionary plan (as defined in "Material Revisions" above), whether or not previously approved by shareholders, additional grants may be made after the effective date of this listing standard without further shareholder approval only for a limited transition period, defined below, and then only in a manner consistent with past practice. See also "Material Revisions" above. In applying this rule, if a plan can be separated into a discretionary plan portion and a portion that is not discretionary, the non-discretionary portion of the plan can continue to be used separately, under the appropriate transition rule. For example, if a shareholder-approved plan permits both grants pursuant to a provision that makes available a specific number of shares, and grants pursuant to a provision authorizing the use of treasury shares without regard to the specific share limit, the former provision (but not the latter) may continue to be used after the transition period, under the general rule above.

Similarly, in the case of a formula plan (as defined in "Material Revisions" above) that either (1) has not previously been approved by shareholders or (2) does not have a term of ten years or less, additional grants may be made after the effective date of this listing standard without further shareholder approval only for a limited transition period, defined below.

The limited transition period described in the preceding two paragraphs will end upon the first to occur of:

- the listed company's next annual meeting at which directors are elected that occurs more than 180 days after the effective date of this listing standard;

- the first anniversary of the effective date of this listing standard; and

- the expiration of the plan.

A shareholder-approved formula plan may continue to be used after the end of this transition period if it is amended to provide for a term of ten years or less from the date of its original adoption or, if later, the date of its most recent shareholder approval. Such an amendment may be made before or after the effective date of this listing standard, and would not itself be considered a "material revision" requiring shareholder approval.

In addition, a formula plan may continue to be used, without shareholder approval, if the grants after the effective date of this listing standard are made *only* from the shares available immediately before the effective date, in other words, based on formulaic increases that occurred prior to such effective date.

312.03. Shareholder Approval

Shareholder approval is a prequisite to listing in the following situations:

(a) Shareholder approval is required for equity compensation plans. See Section 303A.08.

(b) Shareholder approval is required prior to the issuance of common stock, or of securities convertible into or exercisable for common stock, to:

(1) a director, officer or substantial security holder of the company (a "Related Party");

(2) a subsidiary, affiliate or other closely-related person of a Related Party; or

(3) any company or entity in which a Related Party has a substantial direct or indirect interest;

if the number of shares of common stock to be issued, or if the number of shares of common stock into which the securities may be convertible or exercisable, exceeds either one percent of the number of shares of common stock or one percent of the voting power outstanding before the issuance.

However, if the Related Party involved in the transaction is classified as such solely because such person is a substantial security holder, and if the issuance relates to a sale of stock for cash at a price at least as great as each of the book and market value of the issuer's common stock, then shareholder approval will not be required unless the number of shares of common stock to be issued, or unless the number of shares of common stock into which the securities may be convertible or exercisable, exceeds either five percent of the number of shares of common stock or five percent of the voting power outstanding before the issuance.

(c) Shareholder approval is required prior to the issuance of common stock, or of securities convertible into or exercisable for common stock, in any transaction or series of related transactions if:

(1) the common stock has, or will have upon issuance, voting power equal to or in excess of 20 percent of the voting power outstanding before the issuance of such stock or of securities convertible into or exercisable for common stock; or

(2) the number of shares of common stock to be issued is, or will be upon issuance, equal to or in excess of 20 percent of the number of shares of common stock outstanding before the issuance of the common stock or of securities convertible into or exercisable for common stock.

However, shareholder approval will not be required for any such issuance involving:

- any public offering for cash;

- any bona fide private financing, if such financing involves a sale of:

- common stock, for cash, at a price at least as great as each of the book and market value of the issuer's common stock; or

- securities convertible into or exercisable for common stock, for cash, if the conversion or exercise price is at least as great as each of the book and market value of the issuer's common stock.

(d) Shareholder approval is required prior to an issuance that will result in a change of control of the issuer.

Part II
Taxation

Internal Revenue Code

Sec. 83. Property transferred in connection with performance of services

(a) General rule.—If, in connection with the performance of services, property is transferred to any person other than the person for whom such services are performed, the excess of—

(1) the fair market value of such property (determined without regard to any restriction other than a restriction which by its terms will never lapse) at the first time the rights of the person having the beneficial interest in such property are transferable or are not subject to a substantial risk of forfeiture, whichever occurs earlier, over

(2) the amount (if any) paid for such property,

shall be included in the gross income of the person who performed such services in the first taxable year in which the rights of the person having the beneficial interest in such property are transferable or are not subject to a substantial risk of forfeiture, whichever is applicable. The preceding sentence shall not apply if such person sells or otherwise disposes of such property in an arm's length transaction before his rights in such property become transferable or not subject to a substantial risk of forfeiture.

(b) Election to include in gross income in year of transfer—

(1) In general.—Any person who performs services in connection with which property is transferred to any person may elect to include in his gross income for the taxable year in which such property is transferred, the excess of—

(A) the fair market value of such property at the time of transfer (determined without regard to any restriction other than a restriction which by its terms will never lapse), over

(B) the amount (if any) paid for such property.

If such election is made, subsection (a) shall not apply with respect to the transfer of such property, and if such property is subsequently forfeited, no deduction shall be allowed in respect of such forfeiture.

(2) Election.—An election under paragraph (1) with respect to any transfer of property shall be made in such manner as the Secretary prescribes and shall be made not later than 30 days after the date of such transfer. Such election may not be revoked except with the consent of the Secretary.

(c) Special rules.—For purposes of this section—

(1) Substantial risk of forfeiture.—The rights of a person in property are subject to a substantial risk of forfeiture if such person's rights to full enjoyment of such property are conditioned upon the future performance of substantial services by any individual.

(2) Transferability of property.—The rights of a person in property are transferable only if the rights in such property of any transferee are not subject to a substantial risk of forfeiture.

(3) Sales which may give rise to suit under section 16(b) of the Securities Exchange Act of 1934.—So long as the sale of property at a profit could subject a person to suit under section 16(b) of the Securities Exchange Act of 1934, such person's rights in such property are—

(A) subject to a substantial risk of forfeiture, and

(B) not transferable.

(d) Certain restrictions which will never lapse.—

(1) Valuation.—In the case of property subject to a restriction which by its terms will never lapse, and which allows the transferee to sell such property only at a price determined under a formula, the price so determined shall be deemed to be the fair market value of the property unless established to the contrary by the Secretary, and the burden of proof shall be on the Secretary with respect to such value.

(2) Cancellation.—If, in the case of property subject to a restriction which by its terms will never lapse, the restriction is canceled, then, unless the taxpayer establishes—

(A) that such cancellation was not compensatory, and

(B) that the person, if any, who would be allowed a deduction if the cancellation were treated as compensatory, will treat the transaction as not compensatory, as evidenced in such manner as the Secretary shall prescribe by regulations,

the excess of the fair market value of the property (computed without regard to the restrictions) at the time of cancellation over the sum of—

(C) the fair market value of such property (computed by taking the restriction into account) immediately before the cancellation, and

(D) the amount, if any, paid for the cancellation, shall be treated as compensation for the taxable year in which such cancellation occurs.

(e) Applicability of section.—This section shall not apply to—

(1) a transaction to which section 421 applies,

(2) a transfer to or from a trust described in section 401(a) or a transfer under an annuity plan which meets the requirements of section 404(a)(2),

(3) the transfer of an option without a readily ascertainable fair market value,

(4) the transfer of property pursuant to the exercise of an option with a readily ascertainable fair market value at the date of grant, or

(5) group-term life insurance to which section 79 applies.

(f) Holding period.—In determining the period for which the taxpayer has held property to which subsection (a) applies, there shall be included only the period beginning at the first time his rights in such property are transferable or are not subject to a substantial risk of forfeiture, whichever occurs earlier.

(g) Certain exchanges.—If property to which subsection (a) applies is exchanged for property subject to restrictions and conditions substantially similar to those to which the property given in such exchange was subject, and if section 354, 355, 356, or 1036 (or so much of section 1031 as relates to section 1036) applied to such exchange, or if such exchange was pursuant to the exercise of a conversion privilege—

(1) such exchange shall be disregarded for purposes of subsection (a), and

(2) the property received shall be treated as property to which subsection (a) applies.

(h) Deduction by employer.—In the case of a transfer of property to which this section applies or a cancellation of a restriction described in subsection (d), there shall be allowed as a deduction under section 162, to the person for whom were performed the services in connection with which such property was transferred, an amount equal to the amount included under subsection (a), (b), or (d)(2) in the gross income of the person who performed such services. Such deduction shall be allowed for the taxable year of such person in which or with which ends the taxable year in which such amount is included in the gross income of the person who performed such services.

Sec. 162(m). Certain excessive employee remuneration

(1) In general.—In the case of any publicly held corporation, no deduction shall be allowed under this chapter for applicable employee remuneration with respect to any covered employee to the extent that the

amount of such remuneration for the taxable year with respect to such employee exceeds $1,000,000.

(2) Publicly held corporation.—For purposes of this subsection, the term "publicly held corporation" means any corporation issuing any class of common equity securities required to be registered under section 12 of the Securities Exchange Act of 1934.

(3) Covered employee.—For purposes of this subsection, the term "covered employee" means any employee of the taxpayer if—

(A) as of the close of the taxable year, such employee is the chief executive officer of the taxpayer or is an individual acting in such a capacity, or

(B) the total compensation of such employee for the taxable year is required to be reported to shareholders under the Securities Exchange Act of 1934 by reason of such employee being among the 4 highest compensated officers for the taxable year (other than the chief executive officer).

(4) Applicable employee remuneration.—For purposes of this subsection—

(A) In general.—Except as otherwise provided in this paragraph, the term "applicable employee remuneration" means, with respect to any covered employee for any taxable year, the aggregate amount allowable as a deduction under this chapter for such taxable year (determined without regard to this subsection) for remuneration for services performed by such employee (whether or not during the taxable year).

(B) Exception for remuneration payable on commission basis.—The term "applicable employee remuneration" shall not include any remuneration payable on a commission basis solely on account of income generated directly by the individual performance of the individual to whom such remuneration is payable.

(C) Other performance-based compensation.—The term "applicable employee remuneration" shall not include any remuneration payable solely on account of the attainment of one or more performance goals, but only if—

(i) the performance goals are determined by a compensation committee of the board of directors of the taxpayer which is comprised solely of 2 or more outside directors,

(ii) the material terms under which the remuneration is to be paid, including the performance goals, are disclosed to shareholders and approved by a majority of the vote in a separate shareholder vote before the payment of such remuneration, and

(iii) before any payment of such remuneration, the compensation committee referred to in clause (i) certifies that the performance goals and any other material terms were in fact satisfied.

(D) Exception for existing binding contracts.—The term "applicable employee remuneration" shall not include any remuneration payable under a written binding contract which was in effect on February 17, 1993, and which was not modified thereafter in any material respect before such remuneration is paid.

(E) Remuneration.—For purposes of this paragraph, the term "remuneration" includes any remuneration (including benefits) in any medium other than cash, but shall not include—

(i) any payment referred to in so much of section 3121(a)(5) as precedes subparagraph (E) thereof, and

(ii) any benefit provided to or on behalf of an employee if at the time such benefit is provided it is reasonable to believe that the employee will be able to exclude such benefit from gross income under this chapter.

For purposes of clause (i), section 3121(a)(5) shall be applied without regard to section 3121(v)(1).

(F) Coordination with disallowed golden parachute payments.—The dollar limitation contained in paragraph (1) shall be reduced (but not below zero) by the amount (if any) which would have been included in the applicable employee remuneration of the covered employee for the taxable year but for being disallowed under section 280G.

Sec. 409A. Inclusion in gross income of deferred compensation under nonqualified deferred compensation plans

(a) Rules relating to constructive receipt—

(1) Plan failures—

(A) Gross income inclusion—

(i) In general— If at any time during a taxable year a nonqualified deferred compensation plan—

(I) fails to meet the requirements of paragraphs (2), (3), and (4), or

(II) is not operated in accordance with such requirements,

all compensation deferred under the plan for the taxable year and all preceding taxable years shall be includible in gross income for the taxable year to the extent not subject to a substantial risk of forfeiture and not previously included in gross income.

(ii) Application only to affected participants— Clause (i) shall only apply with respect to all compensation deferred under the plan for participants with respect to whom the failure relates.

(B) Interest and additional tax payable with respect to previously deferred compensation—

(i) In general— If compensation is required to be included in gross income under subparagraph (A) for a taxable year, the tax imposed by this chapter for the taxable year shall be increased by the sum of——

(I) the amount of interest determined under clause (ii), and

(II) an amount equal to 20 percent of the compensation which is required to be included in gross income.

(ii) Interest— For purposes of clause (i), the interest determined under this clause for any taxable year is the amount of interest at the underpayment rate plus 1 percentage point on the underpayments that would have occurred had the deferred compensation been includible in gross income for the taxable year in which first deferred or, if later, the first taxable year in which such deferred compensation is not subject to a substantial risk of forfeiture.

(2) Distributions—

(A) In general— The requirements of this paragraph are met if the plan provides that compensation deferred under the plan may not be distributed earlier than—

(i) separation from service as determined by the Secretary (except as provided in subparagraph (B)(i)),

(ii) the date the participant becomes disabled (within the meaning of subparagraph (C)),

(iii) death,

(iv) a specified time (or pursuant to a fixed schedule) specified under the plan at the date of the deferral of such compensation,

(v) to the extent provided by the Secretary, a change in the ownership or effective control of the corporation, or in the ownership of a substantial portion of the assets of the corporation, or

(vi) the occurrence of an unforeseeable emergency.

(B) Special rules—

(i) Specified employees— In the case of any specified employee, the requirement of subparagraph (A)(i) is met only if distributions may not be made before the date which is 6 months after the date of separation from service (or, if earlier, the date of death of the employee). For purposes of the preceding sentence, a specified employee is a key employee (as defined in section 416(i) without regard to paragraph (5) thereof) of a corporation any stock in which is publicly traded on an established securities market or otherwise.

(ii) Unforeseeable emergency— For purposes of subparagraph (A)(vi)——

(I) In general— The term unforeseeable emergency' means a severe financial hardship to the participant resulting from an illness or accident of the participant, the participant's spouse, or a dependent (as defined in section 152(a)) of the participant, loss of the participant's property due to casualty, or other similar extraordinary and unforeseeable circumstances arising as a result of events beyond the control of the participant.

(II) Limitation on distributions— The requirement of subparagraph (A)(vi) is met only if, as determined under regulations of the Secretary, the amounts distributed with respect to an emergency do not exceed the amounts necessary to satisfy such emergency plus amounts necessary to pay taxes reasonably anticipated as a result of the distribution, after taking into account the extent to which such hardship is or may be relieved through reimbursement or compensation by insurance or otherwise or by liquidation of the participant's assets (to the extent the liquidation of such assets would not itself cause severe financial hardship).

(C) Disabled— For purposes of subparagraph (A)(ii), a participant shall be considered disabled if the participant—

(i) is unable to engage in any substantial gainful activity by reason of any medically determinable physical or mental impairment which can be expected to result in death or can be expected to last for a continuous period of not less than 12 months, or

(ii) is, by reason of any medically determinable physical or mental impairment which can be expected to result in death or can be expected to last for a continuous period of not less than 12 months, receiving income replacement benefits for a period of not less than 3 months under an accident and health plan covering employees of the participant's employer.

(3) Acceleration of benefits— The requirements of this paragraph are met if the plan does not permit the acceleration of the time or schedule of any payment under the plan, except as provided in regulations by the Secretary.

(4) Elections—

(A) In general— The requirements of this paragraph are met if the requirements of subparagraphs (B) and (C) are met.

(B) Initial deferral decision—

(i) In general— The requirements of this subparagraph are met if the plan provides that compensation for services performed during a taxable year may be deferred at the participant's election only if the election to defer such compensation is made not later than the close of the preceding taxable year or at such other time as provided in regulations.

(ii) First year of eligibility— In the case of the first year in which a participant becomes eligible to participate in the plan, such election may be made with respect to services to be performed subsequent to the election within 30 days after the date the participant becomes eligible to participate in such plan.

(iii) Performance-based compensation— In the case of any performance-based compensation based on services performed over a period of at least 12 months, such election may be made no later than 6 months before the end of the period.

(C) Changes in time and form of distribution— The requirements of this subparagraph are met if, in the case of a plan which permits under a subsequent election a delay in a payment or a change in the form of payment—

(i) the plan requires that such election may not take effect until at least 12 months after the date on which the election is made,

(ii) in the case of an election related to a payment not described in clause (ii), (iii), or (vi) of paragraph (2)(A), the plan requires that the first payment with respect to which such election is made be deferred for a period of not less than 5 years from the date such payment would otherwise have been made, and

(iii) the plan requires that any election related to a payment described in paragraph (2)(A)(iv) may not be made less than 12 months prior to the date of the first scheduled payment under such paragraph.

(b) Rules relating to funding—

(1) Offshore property in a trust— In the case of assets set aside (directly or indirectly) in a trust (or other arrangement determined by the Secretary) for purposes of paying deferred compensation under a nonqualified deferred compensation plan, for purposes of section 83 such assets shall be treated as property transferred in connection with the performance of services whether or not such assets are available to satisfy claims of general creditors—

(A) at the time set aside if such assets (or such trust or other arrangement) are located outside of the United States, or

(B) at the time transferred if such assets (or such trust or other arrangement) are subsequently transferred outside of the United States.

This paragraph shall not apply to assets located in a foreign jurisdiction if substantially all of the services to which the nonqualified deferred compensation relates are performed in such jurisdiction.

(2) Employer's financial health— In the case of compensation deferred under a nonqualified deferred compensation plan, there is a transfer of property within the meaning of section 83 with respect to such compensation as of the earlier of—

(A) the date on which the plan first provides that assets will become restricted to the provision of benefits under the plan in connection with a change in the employer's financial health, or

(B) the date on which assets are so restricted,

whether or not such assets are available to satisfy claims of general creditors.

(3) Income inclusion for offshore trusts and employer's financial health— For each taxable year that assets treated as transferred under this subsection remain set aside in a trust or other arrangement subject to paragraph (1) or (2), any increase in value in, or earnings with respect to, such assets shall be treated as an additional transfer of property under this subsection (to the extent not previously included in income).

(4) Interest on tax liability payable with respect to transferred property—

(A) In general— If amounts are required to be included in gross income by reason of paragraph (1) or (2) for a taxable year, the tax imposed by this chapter for such taxable year shall be increased by the sum of—

(i) the amount of interest determined under subparagraph (B), and

(ii) an amount equal to 20 percent of the amounts required to be included in gross income.

(B) Interest— For purposes of subparagraph (A), the interest determined under this subparagraph for any taxable year is the amount of interest at the underpayment rate plus 1 percentage point on the underpayments that would have occurred had the amounts so required to be included in gross income by paragraph (1) or (2) been includible in gross income for the taxable year in which first deferred or, if later, the first taxable year in which such amounts are not subject to a substantial risk of forfeiture.

(c) No inference on earlier income inclusion or requirement of later inclusion— Nothing in this section shall be construed to prevent the inclusion of amounts in gross income under any other provision of this chapter or any other rule of law earlier than the time provided in this section.

Any amount included in gross income under this section shall not be required to be included in gross income under any other provision of this chapter or any other rule of law later than the time provided in this section.

(d) Other definitions and special rules— For purposes of this section:

(1) Nonqualified deferred compensation plan— The term nonqualified deferred compensation plan' means any plan that provides for the deferral of compensation, other than—

(A) a qualified employer plan, and

(B) any bona fide vacation leave, sick leave, compensatory time, disability pay, or death benefit plan.

(2) Qualified employer plan— The term qualified employer plan' means—

(A) any plan, contract, pension, account, or trust described in subparagraph (A) or (B) of section 219(g)(5) (without regard to subparagraph (A)(iii)),

(B) any eligible deferred compensation plan (within the meaning of section 457(b)), and

(C) any plan described in section 415(m).

(3) Plan includes arrangements, etc— The term plan' includes any agreement or arrangement, including an agreement or arrangement that includes one person.

(4) Substantial risk of forfeiture— The rights of a person to compensation are subject to a substantial risk of forfeiture if such person's rights to such compensation are conditioned upon the future performance of substantial services by any individual.

(5) Treatment of earnings— References to deferred compensation shall be treated as including references to income (whether actual or notional) attributable to such compensation or such income.

(6) Aggregation rules— Except as provided by the Secretary, rules similar to the rules of subsections (b) and (c) of section 414 shall apply.

(e) Regulations— The Secretary shall prescribe such regulations as may be necessary or appropriate to carry out the purposes of this section, including regulations—

(1) providing for the determination of amounts of deferral in the case of a nonqualified deferred compensation plan which is a defined benefit plan,

(2) relating to changes in the ownership and control of a corporation or assets of a corporation for purposes of subsection (a)(2)(A)(v),

(3) exempting arrangements from the application of subsection (b) if such arrangements will not result in an improper deferral of United States tax and will not result in assets being effectively beyond the reach of creditors,

(4) defining financial health for purposes of subsection (b)(2), and

(5) disregarding a substantial risk of forfeiture in cases where necessary to carry out the purposes of this section.

Sec. 421. General rules

(a) Effect of qualifying transfer.—If a share of stock is transferred to an individual in a transfer in respect of which the requirements of section 422(a) or 423(a) are met—

(1) no income shall result at the time of the transfer of such share to the individual upon his exercise of the option with respect to such share;

(2) no deduction under section 162 (relating to trade or business expenses) shall be allowable at any time to the employer corporation, a parent or subsidiary corporation of such corporation, or a corporation issuing or assuming a stock option in a transaction to which section 424(a) applies, with respect to the share so transferred; and

(3) no amount other than the price paid under the option shall be considered as received by any of such corporations for the share so transferred.

(b) Effect of disqualifying disposition.—If the transfer of a share of stock to an individual pursuant to his exercise of an option would otherwise meet the requirements of section 422(a) or 423(a) except that there is a failure to meet any of the holding period requirements of section 422(a)(1) or 423(a)(1), then any increase in the income of such individual or deduction from the income of his employer corporation for the taxable year in which such exercise occurred attributable to such disposition, shall be treated as an increase in income or a deduction from income in the taxable year of such individual or of such employer corporation in which such disposition occurred. No amount shall be required to be deducted and withheld under chapter 24 with respect to any increase in income attributable to a disposition described in the preceding sentence.

(c) Exercise by estate.—

(1) In general.—If an option to which this part applies is exercised after the death of the employee by the estate of the decedent, or by a person who acquired the right to exercise such option by bequest or inheritance or by reason of the death of the decedent, the provisions of subsection (a) shall apply to the same extent as if the option had been exercised by the decedent, except that—

(A) the holding period and employment requirements of sections 422(a) and 423(a) shall not apply, and (B) any transfer by the estate of stock acquired shall be considered a disposition of such stock for purposes of section 423(c).

(2) Deduction for estate tax.—If an amount is required to be included under section 423(c) in gross income of the estate of the deceased employee or of a person described in paragraph (1), there shall be allowed to the estate or such person a deduction with respect to the estate tax attributable to the inclusion in the taxable estate of the deceased employee of the net value for estate tax purposes of the option. For this purpose, the deduction shall be determined under section 691(c) as if the option acquired from the deceased employee were an item of gross income in respect of the decedent under section 691 and as if the amount includible in gross income under section 423(c) were an amount included in gross income under section 691 in respect of such item of gross income.

(3) Basis of shares acquired.—In the case of a share of stock acquired by the exercise of an option to which paragraph (1) applies—

(A) the basis of such share shall include so much of the basis of the option as is attributable to such share; except that the basis of such share shall be reduced by the excess (if any) of (i) the amount which would have been includible in gross income under section 423(c) if the employee had exercised the option on the date of his death and had held the share acquired pursuant to such exercise at the time of his death, over (ii) the amount which is includible in gross income under such section; and

(B) the last sentence of section 423(c) shall apply only to the extent that the amount includible in gross income under such section exceeds so much of the basis of the option as is attributable to such share.

Sec. 422. Incentive stock options

(a) In general.—Section 421(a) shall apply with respect to the transfer of a share of stock to an individual pursuant to his exercise of an incentive stock option if—

(1) no disposition of such share is made by him within 2 years from the date of the granting of the option nor within 1 year after the transfer of such share to him, and

(2) at all times during the period beginning on the date of the granting of the option and ending on the day 3 months before the date of such exercise, such individual was an employee of either the corporation granting such option, a parent or subsidiary corporation of such corporation, or a corporation or a parent or subsidiary corporation of such corporation issuing or assuming a stock option in a transaction to which section 424(a) applies.

(b) Incentive stock option.—For purposes of this part, the term "incentive stock option" means an option granted to an individual for any reason connected with his employment by a corporation, if granted by the employer corporation or its parent or subsidiary corporation, to purchase stock of any of such corporations, but only if—

(1) the option is granted pursuant to a plan which includes the aggregate number of shares which may be issued under options and the employees (or class of employees) eligible to receive options, and which is approved by the stockholders of the granting corporation within 12 months before or after the date such plan is adopted;

(2) such option is granted within 10 years from the date such plan is adopted, or the date such plan is approved by the stockholders, whichever is earlier;

(3) such option by its terms is not exercisable after the expiration of 10 years from the date such option is granted; (4) the option price is not less than the fair market value of the stock at the time such option is granted;

(5) such option by its terms is not transferable by such individual otherwise than by will or the laws of descent and distribution, and is exercisable, during his lifetime, only by him; and

(6) such individual, at the time the option is granted, does not own stock possessing more than 10 percent of the total combined voting power of all classes of stock of the employer corporation or of its parent or subsidiary corporation.

Such term shall not include any option if (as of the time the option is granted) the terms of such option provide that it will not be treated as an incentive stock option.

(c) Special rules.—

(1) Good faith efforts to value of stock.—If a share of stock is transferred pursuant to the exercise by an individual of an option which would fail to qualify as an incentive stock option under subsection (b) because there was a failure in an attempt, made in good faith, to meet the requirement of subsection (b)(4), the requirement of subsection (b)(4) shall be considered to have been met. To the extent provided in regulations by the Secretary, a similar rule shall apply for purposes of subsection (d).

(2) Certain disqualifying dispositions where amount realized is less than value at exercise.—If—

(A) an individual who has acquired a share of stock by the exercise of an incentive stock option makes a disposition of such share within either of the periods described in subsection (a)(1), and

(B) such disposition is a sale or exchange with respect to which a loss (if sustained) would be recognized to such individual, then the amount which is includible in the gross income of such individual, and the amount which is deductible from the income of his employer corporation, as compensation attributable to the exercise of such option shall not exceed the excess (if any) of the amount realized on such sale or exchange over the adjusted basis of such share.

(3) Certain transfers by insolvent individuals.—If an insolvent individual holds a share of stock acquired pursuant to his exercise of an incentive stock option, and if such share is transferred to a trustee, receiver, or other similar fiduciary in any proceeding under title 11 or any other similar insolvency proceeding, neither such transfer, nor any other transfer of such share for the benefit of his creditors in such proceeding, shall constitute a disposition of such share for purposes of subsection (a)(1).

(4) Permissible provisions.—An option which meets the requirements of subsection (b) shall be treated as an incentive stock option even if—

(A) the employee may pay for the stock with stock of the corporation granting the option,

(B) the employee has a right to receive property at the time of exercise of the option, or

(C) the option is subject to any condition not inconsistent with the provisions of subsection (b).

Subparagraph (B) shall apply to a transfer of property (other than cash) only if section 83 applies to the property so transferred.

(5) 10-percent shareholder rule.—Subsection (b)(6) shall not apply if at the time such option is granted the option price is at least 110 percent of the fair market value of the stock subject to the option and such option by its terms is not exercisable after the expiration of 5 years from the date such option is granted.

(6) Special rule when disabled.—For purposes of subsection (a)(2), in the case of an employee who is disabled (within the meaning of section 22(e)(3)), the 3-month period of subsection (a)(2) shall be 1 year.

(7) Fair market value.—For purposes of this section, the fair market value of stock shall be determined without regard to any restriction other than a restriction which, by its terms, will never lapse.

(d) $100,000 per year limitation.—

(1) In general.—To the extent that the aggregate fair market value of stock with respect to which incentive stock options (determined without regard to this subsection) are exercisable for the 1st time by any individual during any calendar year (under all plans of the individual's employer corporation and its parent and subsidiary corporations) exceeds $100,000, such options shall be treated as options which are not incentive stock options.

(2) Ordering rule.—Paragraph (1) shall be applied by taking options into account in the order in which they were granted.

(3) Determination of fair market value.—For purposes of paragraph (1), the fair market value of any stock shall be determined as of the time the option with respect to such stock is granted.

Sec. 423. Employee stock purchase plans

(a) General rule.—Section 421(a) shall apply with respect to the transfer of a share of stock to an individual pursuant to his exercise of an option granted after December 31, 1963, under an employee stock purchase plan (as defined in subsection (b)) if—

(1) no disposition of such share is made by him within 2 years after the date of the granting of the option nor within 1 year after the transfer of such share to him; and

(2) at all times during the period beginning with the date of the granting of the option and ending on the day 3 months before the date of such exercise, he is an employee of the corporation granting such option, a parent or subsidiary corporation of such corporation, or a corporation or a parent or subsidiary corporation of such corporation issuing or assuming a stock option in a transaction to which section 424(a) applies.

(b) Employee stock purchase plan.—For purposes of this part, the term "employee stock purchase plan" means a plan which meets the following requirements:

(1) the plan provides that options are to be granted only to employees of the employer corporation or of its parent or subsidiary corporation to purchase stock in any such corporation;

(2) such plan is approved by the stockholders of the granting corporation within 12 months before or after the date such plan is adopted;

(3) under the terms of the plan, no employee can be granted an option if such employee, immediately after the option is granted, owns stock possessing 5 percent or more of the total combined voting power or value of all classes of stock of the employer corporation or of its parent or subsidiary corporation. For purposes of this paragraph, the rules of section 424(d) shall apply in determining the stock ownership of an individual, and stock which the employee may purchase under outstanding options shall be treated as stock owned by the employee;

(4) under the terms of the plan, options are to be granted to all employees of any corporation whose employees are granted any of such options by reason of their employment by such corporation, except that there may be excluded—

(A) employees who have been employed less than 2 years,

(B) employees whose customary employment is 20 hours or less per week,

(C) employees whose customary employment is for not more than 5 months in any calendar year, and

(D) highly compensated employees (within the meaning of section 414(q));

(5) under the terms of the plan, all employees granted such options shall have the same rights and privileges, except that the amount of stock which may be purchased by any employee under such option may bear a uniform relationship to the total compensation, or the basic or regular rate of compensation, of employees, and the plan may provide that no employee may purchase more than a maximum amount of stock fixed under the plan;

(6) under the terms of the plan, the option price is not less than the lesser of—

(A) an amount equal to 85 percent of the fair market value of the stock at the time such option is granted, or

(B) an amount which under the terms of the option may not be less than 85 percent of the fair market value of the stock at the time such option is exercised;

(7) under the terms of the plan, such option cannot be exercised after the expiration of—

(A) 5 years from the date such option is granted if, under the terms of such plan, the option price is to be not less than 85 percent of the fair market value of such stock at the time of the exercise of the option, or

(B) 27 months from the date such option is granted, if the option price is not determinable in the manner described in subparagraph (A)

(8) under the terms of the plan, no employee may be granted an option which permits his rights to purchase stock under all such plans of his employer corporation and its parent and subsidiary corporations to accrue at a rate which exceeds $25,000 of fair market value of such stock (determined at the time such option is granted) for each calendar year in which such option is outstanding at any time. For purposes of this paragraph—

(A) the right to purchase stock under an option accrues when the option (or any portion thereof) first becomes exercisable during the calendar year;

(B) the right to purchase stock under an option accrues at the rate provided in the option, but in no case may such rate exceed $25,000 of fair market value of such stock (determined at the time such option is granted) for any one calendar year;

and

(C) a right to purchase stock which has accrued under one option granted pursuant to the plan may not be carried over to any other option; and

(9) under the terms of the plan, such option is not transferable by such individual otherwise than by will or the laws of descent and distribution, and is exercisable, during his lifetime, only by him.

For purposes of paragraphs (3) to (9), inclusive, where additional terms are contained in an offering made under a plan, such additional terms shall, with respect to options exercised under such offering, be treated as a part of the terms of such plan.

(c) Special rule where option price is between 85 percent and 100 percent of value of stock.—

If the option price of a share of stock acquired by an individual pursuant to a transfer to which subsection (a) applies was less than 100 percent of the fair market value of such share at the time such option was granted, then, in the event of any disposition of such share by him which meets the holding period requirements of subsection (a), or in the event of his death (whenever occurring) while owning such share, there shall be included as compensation (and not as gain upon the sale or exchange of a capital asset) in his gross income, for the taxable year in which falls the date of such disposition or for the taxable year closing with his death, whichever applies, an amount equal to the lesser of—

(1) the excess of the fair market value of the share at the time of such disposition or death over the amount paid for the share under the option, or

(2) the excess of the fair market value of the share at the time the option was granted over the option price.

If the option price is not fixed or determinable at the time the option is granted, then for purposes of this subsection, the option price shall be determined as if the option were exercised at such time. In the case of the disposition of such share by the individual, the basis of the share in his hands at the time of such disposition shall be increased by an amount equal to the amount so includible in his gross income. No amount shall be required to be deducted and withheld under chapter 24 with respect to any amount treated as compensation under this subsection.

Sec. 424. Definitions and special rules

(a) Corporate reorganizations, liquidations, etc..—For purposes of this part, the term "issuing or assuming a stock option in a transaction to which section 424(a) applies" means a substitution of a new option for the old option, or an assumption of the old option, by an employer corporation, or a parent or subsidiary of such corporation, by reason of a corporate merger, consolidation, acquisition of property or stock, separation, reorganization, or liquidation, if—

(1) the excess of the aggregate fair market value of the shares subject to the option immediately after the substitution or assumption over the aggregate option price of such shares is not more than the excess of the aggregate fair market value of all shares subject to the option immediately before such substitution or assumption over the aggregate option price of such shares, and

(2) the new option or the assumption of the old option does not give the employee additional benefits which he did not have under the old option. For purposes of this subsection, the parent-subsidiary relationship shall be determined at the time of any such transaction under this subsection.

(b) Acquisition of new stock.—For purposes of this part, if stock is received by an individual in a distribution to which section 305, 354, 355, 356, or 1036 (or so much of section 1031 as relates to section 1036) applies, and such distribution was made with respect to stock transferred to him upon his exercise of the option, such stock shall be considered as having been transferred to him on his exercise of such option. A similar rule shall be applied in the case of a series of such distributions.

(c) Disposition.—

(1) In general.—Except as provided in paragraphs (2), (3), and (4), for purposes of this part, the term "disposition" includes a sale, exchange, gift, or a transfer of legal title, but does not include—

(A) a transfer from a decedent to an estate or a transfer by request or inheritance;

(B) an exchange to which section 354, 355, 356, or 1036 (or so much of section 1031 as relates to section 1036) applies; or

(C) a mere pledge or hypothecation.

(2) Joint tenancy.—The acquisition of a share of stock in the name of the employee and another jointly with the right of survivorship or a subsequent transfer of a share of stock into such joint ownership shall not be deemed a disposition, but a termination of such joint tenancy (except to the extent such employee acquires ownership of such stock) shall be treated as a disposition by him occurring at the time such joint tenancy is terminated.

(3) Special rule where incentive stock is acquired through use of other statutory option stock.—

(A) Nonrecognition sections not to apply.—If—

(i) there is a transfer of statutory option stock in connection with the exercise of any incentive stock option, and

(ii) the applicable holding period requirements (under section 422(a)(1) or 423(a)(1)) are not met before such transfer,

then no section referred to in subparagraph (B) of paragraph (1) shall apply to such transfer.

(B) Statutory option stock.—For purpose of subparagraph (A), the term "statutory option stock" means any stock acquired through the exercise of an incentive stock option or an option granted under an employee stock purchase plan.

(4) Transfers between spouses or incident to divorce In the case of any transfer described in subsection (a) of section 1041—

(A) such transfer shall not be treated as a disposition for purposes of this part, and

(B) the same tax treatment under this part with respect to the transferred property shall apply to the transferee as would have applied to the transferor.

(d) Attribution of stock ownership.—For purposes of this part, in applying the percentage limitations of sections 422(b)(6) and 423(b)(3)—

(1) the individual with respect to whom such limitation is being determined shall be considered as owning the stock owned, directly or indirectly, by or for his brothers and sisters (whether by the whole or half blood), spouse, ancestors, and lineal descendants; and

(2) stock owned, directly or indirectly, by or for a corporation, partnership, estate, or trust, shall be considered as being owned proportionately by or for its shareholders, partners, or beneficiaries.

(e) Parent corporation.—For purposes of this part, the term "parent corporation" means any corporation (other than the employer corporation) in an unbroken chain of corporations ending with the employer corporation if, at the time of the granting of the option, each of the corporations other than the employer corporation owns stock possessing 50 percent or more of the total combined voting power of all classes of stock in one of the other corporations in such chain.

(f) Subsidiary corporation.—For purposes of this part, the term "subsidiary corporation" means any corporation (other than the employer corporation) in an unbroken chain of corporations beginning with the employer corporation if, at the time of the granting of the option, each of the corporations other than the last corporation in the unbroken chain owns stock possessing 50 percent or more of the total combined voting power of all classes of stock in one of the other corporations in such chain.

(g) Special rule for applying subsections (e) and (f).—In applying subsections (e) and (f) for purposes of section 422(a)(2) and 423(a)(2), there shall be substituted for the term "employer corporation" wherever it appears in subsection (e) and (f) the term "grantor corporation" or the term "corporation issuing or assuming a stock option in a transaction to which section 424(a) applies" as the case may be.

(h) Modification, extension, or renewal of option.—

(1) In general.—For purposes of this part, if the terms of any option to purchase stock are modified, extended, or renewed, such modification, extension, or renewal shall be considered as the granting of a new option.

(2) Special rule for section 423 options.—In the case of the transfer of stock pursuant to the exercise of an option to which section 423 applies and which has been so modified, extended, or renewed, the fair market value of such stock at the time of the granting of the option shall be considered as whichever of the following is the highest—

(A) the fair market value of such stock on the date of the original granting of the option,

(B) the fair market value of such stock on the date of the making of such modification, extension, or renewal, or

(C) the fair market value of such stock at the time of the making of any intervening modification, extension, or renewal.

(3) Definition of modification.—The term "modification" means any change in the terms of the option which gives the employee additional benefits under the option, but such term shall not include a change in the terms of the option—

(A) attributable to the issuance or assumption of an option under subsection (a);

(B) to permit the option to qualify under section 423(b)(9); or

(C) in the case of an option not immediately exercisable in full, to accelerate the time at which the option may be exercised.

(i) Stockholder approval.—For purposes of this part, if the grant of an option is subject to approval by stockholders, the date of grant of the option shall be determined as if the option had not been subject to such approval.

(j) Cross references.—For provisions requiring the reporting of certain acts with respect to a qualified stock option, an incentive stock option, options granted under employer stock purchase plans, or a restricted stock option, see section 6039.

Sec. 1041. Transfers of property between spouses or incident to divorce

(a) General rule.—No gain or loss shall be recognized on a transfer of property from an individual to (or in trust for the benefit of)—

(1) a spouse, or

(2) a former spouse, but only if the transfer is incident to the divorce.

(b) Transfer treated as gift; transferee has transferor's basis

In the case of any transfer of property described in subsection (a)—

(1) for purposes of this subtitle, the property shall be treated as acquired by the transferee by gift, and

(2) the basis of the transferee in the property shall be the adjusted basis of the transferor.

(c) Incident to divorce.—For purposes of subsection (a)(2), a transfer of property is incident to the divorce if such transfer—

(1) occurs within 1 year after the date on which the marriage ceases, or

(2) is related to the cessation of the marriage.

(d) Special rule where spouse is nonresident alien.—Subsection (a) shall not apply if the spouse (or former spouse) of the individual making the transfer is a nonresident alien.

(e) Transfers in trust where liability exceeds basis.—Subsection (a) shall not apply to the transfer of property in trust to the extent that—

(1) the sum of the amount of the liabilities assumed, plus the amount of the liabilities to which the property is subject, exceeds

(2) the total of the adjusted basis of the property transferred.

Proper adjustment shall be made under subsection (b) in the basis of the transferee in such property to take into account gain recognized by reason of the preceding sentence.

Sec. 3401. Definitions

(a) Wages.—For purposes of this chapter, the term "wages" means all remuneration (other than fees paid to a public official) for services performed by an employee for his employer, including the cash value of all remuneration (including benefits) paid in any medium other than cash; except that such term shall not include remuneration paid—

(1) for active service performed in a month for which such employee is entitled to the benefits of section 112 (relating to certain combat zone

compensation of members of the Armed Forces of the United States) to the extent remuneration for such service is excludable from gross income under such section; or

(2) for agricultural labor (as defined in section 3121(g)) unless the remuneration paid for such labor is wages (as defined in section 3121(a)); or

(3) for domestic service in a private home, local college club, or local chapter of a college fraternity or sorority; or

(4) for service not in the course of the employer's trade or business performed in any calendar quarter by an employee, unless the cash remuneration paid for such service is $50 or more and such service is performed by an individual who is regularly employed by such employer to perform such service. For purposes of this paragraph, an individual shall be deemed to be regularly employed by an employer during a calendar quarter only if—

(A) on each of some 24 days during such quarter such individual performs for such employer for some portion of the day service not in the course of the employer's trade or business; or

(B) such individual was regularly employed (as determined under subparagraph (A)) by such employer in the performance of such service during the preceding calendar quarter; or

(5) for services by a citizen or resident of the United States for a foreign government or an international organization; or (6) for such services, performed by a nonresident alien individual, as may be designated by regulations prescribed by the Secretary; or

((7) Repealed. Pub. L. 89-809, title I, Sec. 103(k), Nov. 13, 1966, 80 Stat. 1554)

(8)(A) for services for an employer (other than the United States or any agency thereof)—

(i) performed by a citizen of the United States if, at the time of the payment of such remuneration, it is reasonable to believe that such remuneration will be excluded from gross income under section 911; or

(ii) performed in a foreign country or in a possession of the United States by such a citizen if, at the time of the payment of such remuneration, the employer is required by the law of any foreign country or possession of the United States to withhold income tax upon such remuneration; or

(B) for services for an employer (other than the United States or any agency thereof) performed by a citizen of the United States within a possession of the United States (other than Puerto Rico), if it is reasonable to believe that at least 80 percent of the remuneration to be paid to the employee by such employer during the calendar year will be for such services; or

(C) for services for an employer (other than the United States or any agency thereof) performed by a citizen of the United States within Puerto Rico, if it is reasonable to believe that during the entire calendar year the employee will be a bona fide resident of Puerto Rico; or

(D) for services for the United States (or any agency thereof) performed by a citizen of the United States within a possession of the United States to the extent the United States (or such agency) withholds taxes on such remuneration pursuant to an agreement with such possession; or

(9) for services performed by a duly ordained, commissioned, or licensed minister of a church in the exercise of his ministry or by a member of a religious order in the exercise of duties required by such order; or (10)(A) for services performed by an individual under the age of 18 in the delivery or distribution of newspapers or shopping news, not including delivery or distribution to any point for subsequent delivery or distribution; or

(B) for services performed by an individual in, and at the time of, the sale of newspapers or magazines to ultimate consumers, under an arrangement under which the newspapers or magazines are to be sold by him at a fixed price, his compensation being based on the retention of the excess of such price over the amount at which the newspapers or magazines are charged to him, whether or not he is guaranteed a minimum amount of compensation for such services, or is entitled to be credited with the unsold newspapers or magazines turned back; or

(11) for services not in the course of the employer's trade or business, to the extent paid in any medium other than cash; or (12) to, or on behalf of, an employee or his beneficiary—

(A) from or to a trust described in section 401(a) which is exempt from tax under section 501(a) at the time of such payment unless such payment is made to an employee of the trust as remuneration for services rendered as such employee and not as a beneficiary of the trust; or

(B) under or to an annuity plan which, at the time of such payment, is a plan described in section 403(a); or

(C) for a payment described in section 402(h)(1) and (2) if, at the time of such payment, it is reasonable to believe that the employee will be entitled to an exclusion under such section for payment; or

(D) under an arrangement to which section 408(p) applies; or

(E) under or to an eligible deferred compensation plan which, at the time of such payment, is a plan described in section 457(b) which is maintained by an eligible employer described in section 457(e)(1)(A), or

(13) pursuant to any provision of law other than section 5(c) or 6(1) of the Peace Corps Act, for service performed as a volunteer or volunteer leader within the meaning of such Act; or

(14) in the form of group-term life insurance on the life of an employee; or

(15) to or on behalf of an employee if (and to the extent that) at the time of the payment of such remuneration it is reasonable to believe that a corresponding deduction is allowable under section 217 (determined without regard to section 274(n)); or

(16)(A) as tips in any medium other than cash;

(B) as cash tips to an employee in any calendar month in the course of his employment by an employer unless the amount of such cash tips is $20 or more;

(17) for service described in section 3121(b)(20);

(18) for any payment made, or benefit furnished, to or for the benefit of an employee if at the time of such payment or such furnishing it is reasonable to believe that the employee will be able to exclude such payment or benefit from income under section 127 or 129;

(19) for any benefit provided to or on behalf of an employee if at the time such benefit is provided it is reasonable to believe that the employee will be able to exclude such benefit from income under section 74(c), 117, or 132;

(20) for any medical care reimbursement made to or for the benefit of an employee under a self-insured medical reimbursement plan (within the meaning of section 105(h)(6)); or

(21) for any payment made to or for the benefit of an employee if at the time of such payment it is reasonable to believe that the employee will be able to exclude such payment from income under section 106(b).

(b) Payroll period.—For purposes of this chapter, the term "payroll period" means a period for which a payment of wages is ordinarily made to the employee by his employer, and the term "miscellaneous payroll period" means a payroll period other than a daily, weekly, biweekly, semimonthly, monthly, quarterly, semiannual or annual payroll period.

(c) Employee.—For purposes of this chapter, the term "employee" includes an officer, employee, or elected official of the United States, a State, or any political subdivision thereof, or the District of Columbia, or any agency or instrumentality of any one or more of the foregoing. The term "employee" also includes an officer of a corporation.

(d) Employer.—For purposes of this chapter, the term "employer" means the person for whom an individual performs or performed any service, of whatever nature, as the employee of such person, except that—

(1) if the person for whom the individual performs or performed the services does not have control of the payment of the wages for such services, the term "employer" (except for purposes of subsection (a)) means the person having control of the payment of such wages, and

(2) in the case of a person paying wages on behalf of a nonresident alien individual, foreign partnership, or foreign corporation, not engaged in trade or business within the United States, the term "employer" (except for purposes of subsection (a)) means such person.

(e) Number of withholding exemptions claimed.—For purposes of this chapter, the term "number of withholding exemptions claimed" means the number of withholding exemptions claimed in a withholding exemption certificate in effect under section 3402(f), or in effect under the corresponding section of prior law, except that if no such certificate is in effect, the number of withholding exemptions claimed shall be considered to be zero.

(f) Tips.—For purposes of subsection (a), the term "wages" includes tips received by an employee in the course of his employment. Such wages shall be deemed to be paid at the time a written statement including such tips is furnished to the employer pursuant to section 6053(a) or (if no statement including such tips is so furnished) at the time received.

((g) Repealed. Pub. L. 101-140, title II, Sec. 203(a)(2), Nov. 8, 1989, 103 Stat. 830)

(h) Crew leader rules to apply.—Rules similar to the rules of section 3121(o) shall apply for purposes of this chapter.

Sec. 3402. Income tax collected at source

(a) Requirement of withholding

(1) In general.—Except as otherwise provided in this section, every employer making payment of wages shall deduct and withhold upon such wages a tax determined in accordance with tables or computational procedures prescribed by the Secretary. Any tables or procedures prescribed under this paragraph shall.—

(A) apply with respect to the amount of wages paid during such periods as the Secretary may prescribe, and (B) be in such form, and provide for such amounts to be deducted and withheld, as the Secretary determines to be most appropriate to carry out the purposes of this chapter and to reflect the provisions of chapter 1 applicable to such periods.

(2) Amount of wages.—For purposes of applying tables or procedures prescribed under paragraph (1), the term "the amount of wages" means the amount by which the wages exceed the number of withholding exemptions claimed multiplied by the amount of one such exemption. The

amount of each withholding exemption shall be equal to the amount of one personal exemption provided in section 151(b), prorated to the payroll period. The maximum number of withholding exemptions permitted shall be calculated in accordance with regulations prescribed by the Secretary under this section, taking into account any reduction in withholding to which an employee is entitled under this section.

(b) Percentage method of withholding.—

(1) If wages are paid with respect to a period which is not a payroll period, the withholding exemption allowable with respect to each payment of such wages shall be the exemption allowed for a miscellaneous payroll period containing a number of days (including Sundays and holidays) equal to the number of days in the period with respect to which such wages are paid.

(2) In any case in which wages are paid by an employer without regard to any payroll period or other period, the withholding exemption allowable with respect to each payment of such wages shall be the exemption allowed for a miscellaneous payroll period containing a number of days equal to the number of days (including Sundays and holidays) which have elapsed since the date of the last payment of such wages by such employer during the calendar year, or the date of commencement of employment with such employer during such year, or January 1 of such year, whichever is the later.

(3) In any case in which the period, or the time described in paragraph (2), in respect of any wages is less than one week, the Secretary, under regulations prescribed by him, may authorize an employer to compute the tax to be deducted and withheld as if the aggregate of the wages paid to the employee during the calendar week were paid for a weekly payroll period.

(4) In determining the amount to be deducted and withheld under this subsection, the wages may, at the election of the employer, be computed to the nearest dollar.

(c) Wage bracket withholding.—

(1) At the election of the employer with respect to any employee, the employer shall deduct and withhold upon the wages paid to such employee a tax (in lieu of the tax required to be deducted and withheld under subsection (a)) determined in accordance with tables prescribed by the Secretary in accordance with paragraph (6).

(2) If wages are paid with respect to a period which is not a payroll period, the amount to be deducted and withheld shall be that applicable in the case of a miscellaneous payroll period containing a number of days (including Sundays and holidays) equal to the number of days in the period with respect to which such wages are paid.

(3) In any case in which wages are paid by an employer without regard to any payroll period or other period, the amount to be deducted and withheld shall be that applicable in the case of a miscellaneous payroll period containing a number of days equal to the number of days (including Sundays and holidays) which have elapsed since the date of the last payment of such wages by such employer during the calendar year, or the date of commencement of employment with such employer during such year, or January 1 of such year, whichever is the later.

(4) In any case in which the period, or the time described in paragraph (3), in respect of any wages is less than one week, the Secretary, under regulations prescribed by him, may authorize an employer to determine the amount to be deducted and withheld under the tables applicable in the case of a weekly payroll period, in which case the aggregate of the wages paid to the employee during the calendar week shall be considered the weekly wages.

(5) If the wages exceed the highest wage bracket, in determining the amount to be deducted and withheld under this subsection, the wages may, at the election of the employer, be computed to the nearest dollar.

(6) In the case of wages paid after December 31, 1969, the amount deducted and withheld under paragraph (1) shall be determined in accordance with tables prescribed by the Secretary. In the tables so prescribed, the amounts set forth as amounts of wages and amounts of income tax to be deducted and withheld shall be computed on the basis of the table for an annual payroll period prescribed pursuant to subsection (a).

(d) Tax paid by recipient.—If the employer, in violation of the provisions of this chapter, fails to deduct and withhold the tax under this chapter, and thereafter the tax against which such tax may be credited is paid, the tax so required to be deducted and withheld shall not be collected from the employer; but this subsection shall in no case relieve the employer from liability for any penalties or additions to the tax otherwise applicable in respect of such failure to deduct and withhold.

(e) Included and excluded wages.—If the remuneration paid by an employer to an employee for services performed during one-half or more of any payroll period of not more than 31 consecutive days constitutes wages, all the remuneration paid by such employer to such employee for such period shall be deemed to be wages; but if the remuneration paid by an employer to an employee for services performed during more than one-half of any such payroll period does not constitute wages, then none of the remuneration paid by such employer to such employee for such period shall be deemed to be wages.

(f) Withholding exemptions.—

(1) In general.—An employee receiving wages shall on any day be entitled to the following withholding exemptions:

(A) an exemption for himself unless he is an individual described in section 151(d)(2);

(B) if the employee is married, any exemption to which his spouse is entitled, or would be entitled if such spouse were an employee receiving wages, under subparagraph (A) or (D), but only if such spouse does not have in effect a withholding exemption certificate claiming such exemption;

(C) an exemption for each individual with respect to whom, on the basis of facts existing at the beginning of such day, there may reasonably be expected to be allowable an exemption under section 151(c) for the taxable year under subtitle A in respect of which amounts deducted and withheld under this chapter in the calendar year in which such day falls are allowed as a credit;

(D) any allowance to which he is entitled under subsection (m), but only if his spouse does not have in effect a withholding exemption certificate claiming such allowance; and

(E) a standard deduction allowance which shall be an amount equal to one exemption (or more than one exemption if so prescribed by the Secretary) unless (i) he is married (as determined under section 7703) and his spouse is an employee receiving wages subject to withholding or (ii) he has withholding exemption certificates in effect with respect to more than one employer. For purposes of this title, any standard deduction allowance under subparagraph (E) shall be treated as if it were denominated a withholding exemption.

(2) Exemption certificates.—

(A) On commencement of employment.—On or before the date of the commencement of employment with an employer, the employee shall furnish the employer with a signed withholding exemption certificate relating to the number of withholding exemptions which he claims, which shall in no event exceed the number to which he is entitled.

(B) Change of status.—If, on any day during the calendar year, the number of withholding exemptions to which the employee is entitled is less than the number of withholding exemptions claimed by the employee on the withholding exemption certificate then in effect with respect to him, the employee shall within 10 days thereafter furnish the employer with a new withholding exemption certificate relating to the number of withholding exemptions which the employee then claims, which shall in no event exceed the number to which he is entitled on such day. If, on any day during the calendar year, the number of withholding exemptions to which the employee is entitled is greater than the number of withholding exemptions claimed, the employee may furnish the employer with a new withholding exemption certificate relating to the number of withholding exemptions which the employee then claims, which shall in no event exceed the number to which he is entitled on such day.

(C) Change of status which affects next calendar year.—If on any day during the calendar year the number of withholding exemptions to which the employee will be, or may reasonably be expected to be, entitled at the beginning of his next taxable year under subtitle A is different from the number to which the employee is entitled on such day, the employee shall, in such cases and at such times as the Secretary may by regulations prescribe, furnish the employer with a withholding exemption certificate relating to the number of withholding exemptions which he claims with respect to such next taxable year, which shall in no event exceed the number to which he will be, or may reasonably be expected to be, so entitled.

(3) When certificate takes effect.—

(A) First certificate furnished.—A withholding exemption certificate furnished the employer in cases in which no previous such certificate is in effect shall take effect as of the beginning of the first payroll period ending, or the first payment of wages made without regard to a payroll period, on or after the date on which such certificate is so furnished.

(B) Furnished to take place of existing certificate.—

(i) In general.—Except as provided in clauses (ii) and (iii), a withholding exemption certificate furnished to the employer in cases in which a previous such certificate is in effect shall take effect as of the beginning of the 1st payroll period ending (or the 1st payment of wages made without regard to a payroll period) on or after the 30th day after the day on which such certificate is so furnished.

(ii) Employer may elect earlier effective date.—At the election of the employer, a certificate described in clause (i) may be made effective beginning with any payment of wages made on or after the day on which the certificate is so furnished and before the 30th day referred to in clause (i).

(iii) Change of status which affects next year.— Any certificate furnished pursuant to paragraph (2)(C) shall not take effect, and may not be made effective, with respect to any payment of wages made in the calendar year in which the certificate is furnished.

(4) Period during which certificate remains in effect.—A withholding exemption certificate which takes effect under this subsection, or which on December 31, 1954, was in effect under the corresponding subsection of prior law, shall continue in effect with respect to the employer until another such certificate takes effect under this subsection.

(5) Form and contents of certificate.—Withholding exemption certificates shall be in such form and contain such information as the Secretary may by regulations prescribe.

(6) Exemption of certain nonresident aliens.—Notwithstanding the provisions of paragraph (1), a nonresident alien individual (other than an

individual described in section 3401(a)(6)(A) or (B)) shall be entitled to only one withholding exemption.

(7) Exemption where certificate with another employer is in effect.— If a withholding exemption certificate is in effect with respect to one employer, an employee shall not be entitled under a certificate in effect with any other employer to any withholding exemption which he has claimed under such first certificate.

(g) Overlapping pay periods, and payment by agent or fiduciary.—If a payment of wages is made to an employee by an employer—

(1) with respect to a payroll period or other period, any part of which is included in a payroll period or other period with respect to which wages are also paid to such employee by such employer, or

(2) without regard to any payroll period or other period, but on or prior to the expiration of a payroll period or other period with respect to which wages are also paid to such employee by such employer, or

(3) with respect to a period beginning in one and ending in another calendar year, or

(4) through an agent, fiduciary, or other person who also has the control, receipt, custody, or disposal of, or pays, the wages payable by another employer to such employee,

the manner of withholding and the amount to be deducted and withheld under this chapter shall be determined in accordance with regulations prescribed by the Secretary under which the withholding exemption allowed to the employee in any calendar year shall approximate the withholding exemption allowable with respect to an annual payroll period.

(h) Alternative methods of computing amount to be withheld.—The Secretary may, under regulations prescribed by him, authorize—

(1) Withholding on basis of average wages.—An employer—

(A) to estimate the wages which will be paid to any employee in any quarter of the calendar year,

(B) to determine the amount to be deducted and withheld upon each payment of wages to such employee during such quarter as if the appropriate average of the wages so estimated constituted the actual wages paid, and

(C) to deduct and withhold upon any payment of wages to such employee during such quarter (and, in the case of tips referred to in subsection (k), within 30 days thereafter) such amount as may be necessary to adjust the amount actually deducted and withheld upon the wages of such employee during such quarter to the amount required to be deducted and withheld during such quarter without regard to this subsection.

(2) Withholding on basis of annualized wages.—An employer to determine the amount of tax to be deducted and withheld upon a payment of wages to an employee for a payroll period by—

(A) multiplying the amount of an employee's wages for a payroll period by the number of such payroll periods in the calendar year,

(B) determining the amount of tax which would be required to be deducted and withheld upon the amount determined under subparagraph (A) if such amount constituted the actual wages for the calendar year and the payroll period of the employee were an annual payroll period, and

(C) dividing the amount of tax determined under subparagraph (B) by the number of payroll periods (described in subparagraph (A)) in the calendar year.

(3) Withholding on basis of cumulative wages.—An employer, in the case of any employee who requests to have the amount of tax to be withheld from his wages computed on the basis of his cumulative wages, to—

(A) add the amount of the wages to be paid to the employee for the payroll period to the total amount of wages paid by the employer to the employee during the calendar year,

(B) divide the aggregate amount of wages computed under subparagraph (A) by the number of payroll periods to which such aggregate amount of wages relates,

(C) compute the total amount of tax that would have been required to be deducted and withheld under subsection (a) if the average amount of wages (as computed under subparagraph (B)) had been paid to the employee for the number of payroll periods to which the aggregate amount of wages (computed under subparagraph (A)) relates,

(D) determine the excess, if any, of the amount of tax computed under subparagraph (C) over the total amount of tax deducted and withheld by the employer from wages paid to the employee during the calendar year, and

(E) deduct and withhold upon the payment of wages (referred to in subparagraph (A)) to the employee an amount equal to the excess (if any) computed under subparagraph (D).

(4) Other methods.—An employer to determine the amount of tax to be deducted and withheld upon the wages paid to an employee by any other method which will require the employer to deduct and withhold upon such wages substantially the same amount as would be required to be deducted and withheld by applying subsection (a) or (c), either with respect to a payroll period or with respect to the entire taxable year.

(i) Changes in withholding.—

(1) In general.—The Secretary may by regulations provide for increases in the amount of withholding otherwise required under this section in cases where the employee requests such changes.

(2) Treatment as tax.—Any increased withholding under paragraph (1) shall for all purposes be considered tax required to be deducted and withheld under this chapter.

(j) Noncash remuneration to retail commission salesman.—In the case of remuneration paid in any medium other than cash for services performed by an individual as a retail salesman for a person, where the service performed by such individual for such person is ordinarily performed for remuneration solely by way of cash commission an employer shall not be required to deduct or withhold any tax under this subchapter with respect to such remuneration, provided that such employer files with the Secretary such information with respect to such remuneration as the Secretary may by regulation prescribe.

(k) Tips.—In the case of tips which constitute wages, subsection (a) shall be applicable only to such tips as are included in a written statement furnished to the employer pursuant to section 6053(a), and only to the extent that the tax can be deducted and withheld by the employer, at or after the time such statement is so furnished and before the close of the calendar year in which such statement is furnished, from such wages of the employee (excluding tips, but including funds turned over by the employee to the employer for the purpose of such deduction and withholding) as are under the control of the employer; and an employer who is furnished by an employee a written statement of tips (received in a calendar month) pursuant to section 6053(a) to which paragraph (16)(B) of section 3401(a) is applicable may deduct and withhold the tax with respect to such tips from any wages of the employee (excluding tips) under his control, even though at the time such statement is furnished the total amount of the tips included in statements furnished to the employer as having been received by the employee in such calendar month in the course of his employment by such employer is less than $20. Such tax shall not at any time be deducted and withheld in an amount which exceeds the aggregate of such wages and funds (including funds turned over under section 3102(c)(2) or section 3202(c)(2)) minus any tax required by section 3102(a) or section 3202(a) to be collected from such wages and funds.

(l) Determination and disclosure of marital status.—

(1) Determination of status by employer.—For purposes of applying the tables in subsections (a) and (c) to a payment of wages, the employer shall treat the employee as a single person unless there is in effect with respect to such payment of wages a withholding exemption certificate furnished to the employer by the employee after the date of the enactment of this subsection indicating that the employee is married.

(2) Disclosure of status by employee.—An employee shall be entitled to furnish the employer with a withholding exemption certificate indicating he is married only if, on the day of such furnishing, he is married (determined with the application of the rules in paragraph (3)). An employee whose marital status changes from married to single shall, at such time as the Secretary may by regulations prescribe, furnish the employer with a new withholding exemption certificate.

(3) Determination of marital status.—For purposes of paragraph (2), an employee shall on any day be considered—

(A) as not married, if (i) he is legally separated from his spouse under a decree of divorce or separate maintenance, or (ii) either he or his spouse is, or on any preceding day within the calendar year was, a nonresident alien; or

(B) as married, if (i) his spouse (other than a spouse referred to in subparagraph (A)) died within the portion of his taxable year which precedes such day, or (ii) his spouse died during one of the two taxable years immediately preceding the current taxable year and, on the basis of facts existing at the beginning of such day, the employee reasonably expects, at the close of his taxable year, to be a surviving spouse (as defined in section 2(a)).

(m) Withholding allowances.—Under regulations prescribed by the Secretary, an employee shall be entitled to additional withholding allowances or additional reductions in withholding under this subsection. In determining the number of additional withholding allowances or the amount of additional reductions in withholding under this subsection, the employee may take into account (to the extent and in the manner provided by such regulations)—

(1) estimated itemized deductions allowable under chapter 1 (other than the deductions referred to in section 151 and other than the deductions required to be taken into account in determining adjusted gross income under section 62(a) (other than paragraph (10) thereof)),

(2) estimated tax credits allowable under chapter 1, and (3) such additional deductions (including the additional standard deduction under section 63(c)(3) for the aged and blind) and other items as may be specified by the Secretary in regulations.

(n) Employees incurring no income tax liability.—Notwithstanding any other provision of this section, an employer shall not be required to deduct and withhold any tax under this chapter upon a payment of wages to an employee if there is in effect with respect to such payment a withholding exemption certificate (in such form and containing such other information as the Secretary may prescribe) furnished to the employer by the employee certifying that the employee—

(1) incurred no liability for income tax imposed under subtitle A for his preceding taxable year, and

(2) anticipates that he will incur no liability for income tax imposed under subtitle A for his current taxable year.

The Secretary shall by regulations provide for the coordination of the provisions of this subsection with the provisions of subsection (f).

(o) Extension of withholding to certain payments other than wages.—

(1) General rule.—For purposes of this chapter (and so much of subtitle F as relates to this chapter)—

(A) any supplemental unemployment compensation benefit paid to an individual,

(B) any payment of an annuity to an individual, if at the time the payment is made a request that such annuity be subject to withholding under this chapter is in effect, and

(C) any payment to an individual of sick pay which does not constitute wages (determined without regard to this subsection), if at the time the payment is made a request that such sick pay be subject to withholding under this chapter is in effect,

shall be treated as if it were a payment of wages by an employer to an employee for a payroll period.

(2) Definitions.—

(A) Supplemental unemployment compensation benefits.—For purposes of paragraph (1), the term "supplemental unemployment compensation benefits" means amounts which are paid to an employee, pursuant to a plan to which the employer is a party, because of an employee's involuntary separation from employment (whether or not such separation is temporary), resulting directly from a reduction in force, the discontinuance of a plant or operation, or other similar conditions, but only to the extent such benefits are includible in the employee's gross income.

(B) Annuity.—For purposes of this subsection, the term "annuity" means any amount paid to an individual as a pension or annuity.

(C) Sick pay.—For purposes of this subsection, the term "sick pay" means any amount which—

(i) is paid to an employee pursuant to a plan to which the employer is a party, and

(ii) constitutes remuneration or a payment in lieu of remuneration for any period during which the employee is temporarily absent from work on account of sickness or personal injuries.

(3) Amount withheld from annuity payments or sick pay.—If a payee makes a request that an annuity or any sick pay be subject to withholding

under this chapter, the amount to be deducted and withheld under this chapter from any payment to which such request applies shall be an amount (not less than a minimum amount determined under regulations prescribed by the Secretary) specified by the payee in such request. The amount deducted and withheld with respect to a payment which is greater or less than a full payment shall bear the same relation to the specified amount as such payment bears to a full payment.

(4) Request for withholding.—A request that an annuity or any sick pay be subject to withholding under this chapter—

(A) shall be made by the payee in writing to the person making the payments and shall contain the social security number of the payee,

(B) shall specify the amount to be deducted and withheld from each full payment, and (C) shall take effect—

(i) in the case of sick pay, with respect to payments made more than 7 days after the date on which such request is furnished to the payor, or

(ii) in the case of an annuity, at such time (after the date on which such request is furnished to the payor) as the Secretary shall by regulations prescribe.

Such a request may be changed or terminated by furnishing to the person making the payments a written statement of change or termination which shall take effect in the same manner as provided in subparagraph (C). At the election of the payor, any such request (or statement of change or revocation) may take effect earlier than as provided in subparagraph (C).

(5) Special rule for sick pay paid pursuant to certain collective-bargaining agreements In the case of any sick pay paid pursuant to a collective-bargaining agreement between employee representatives and one or more employers which contains a provision specifying that this paragraph is to apply to sick pay paid pursuant to such agreement and contains a provision for determining the amount to be deducted and withheld from each payment of such sick pay—

(A) the requirement of paragraph (1)(C) that a request for withholding be in effect shall not apply, and

(B) except as provided in subsection (n), the amounts to be deducted and withheld under this chapter shall be determined in accordance with such agreement.

The preceding sentence shall not apply with respect to sick pay paid pursuant to any agreement to any individual unless the social security number of such individual is furnished to the payor and the payor is furnished with such information as is necessary to determine whether the payment is pursuant to the agreement and to determine the amount to be deducted and withheld.

(6) Coordination with withholding on designated distributions under section 3405.— This subsection shall not apply to any amount which is a designated distribution (within the meaning of section 3405(e)(1)).

(p) Voluntary withholding agreements.—

(1) Certain Federal payments.—

(A) In general.—If, at the time a specified Federal payment is made to any person, a request by such person is in effect that such payment be subject to withholding under this chapter, then for purposes of this chapter and so much of subtitle F as relates to this chapter, such payment shall be treated as if it were a payment of wages by an employer to an employee.

(B) Amount withheld.—The amount to be deducted and withheld under this chapter from any payment to which any request under subparagraph (A) applies shall be an amount equal to the percentage of such payment specified in such request. Such a request shall apply to any payment only if the percentage specified is 7 percent, any percentage applicable to any of the 3 lowest income brackets in the table under section 1(c), or such other percentage as is permitted under regulations prescribed by the Secretary.

(C) Specified Federal payments.—For purposes of this paragraph, the term "specified Federal payment" means—

(i) any payment of a social security benefit (as defined in section 86(d)),

(ii) any payment referred to in the second sentence of section 451(d) which is treated as insurance proceeds,

(iii) any amount which is includible in gross income under section 77(a), and

(iv) any other payment made pursuant to Federal law which is specified by the Secretary for purposes of this paragraph.

(D) Requests for withholding.—Rules similar to the rules that apply to annuities under subsection (o)(4) shall apply to requests under this paragraph and paragraph (2).

(2) Voluntary withholding on unemployment benefits.—If, at the time a payment of unemployment compensation (as defined in section 85(b)) is made to any person, a request by such person is in effect that such payment be subject to withholding under this chapter, then for purposes of this chapter and so much of subtitle F as relates to this chapter, such payment shall be treated as if it were a payment of wages by an employer to an employee. The amount to be deducted and withheld under this chapter from any payment to which any request under this paragraph applies shall be an amount equal to 10 percent of such payment.

(3) Authority for other voluntary withholding.—The Secretary is authorized by regulations to provide for withholding—

(A) from remuneration for services performed by an employee for the employee's employer which (without regard to this paragraph) does not constitute wages, and

(B) from any other type of payment with respect to which the Secretary finds that withholding would be appropriate under the provisions of this chapter, if the employer and employee, or the person making and the person receiving such other type of payment, agree to such withholding. Such agreement shall be in such form and manner as the Secretary may by regulations prescribe. For purposes of this chapter (and so much of subtitle F as relates to this chapter), remuneration or other payments with respect to which such agreement is made shall be treated as if they were wages paid by an employer to an employee to the extent that such remuneration is paid or other payments are made during the period for which the agreement is in effect.

(q) Extension of withholding to certain gambling winnings. _

(1) General rule.—Every person, including the Government of the United States, a State, or a political subdivision thereof, or any instrumentalities of the foregoing, making any payment of winnings which are subject to withholding shall deduct and withhold from such payment a tax in an amount equal to the product of the third lowest rate of tax applicable under section 1(c) and such payment.

(2) Exemption where tax otherwise withheld.—In the case of any payment of winnings which are subject to withholding made to a nonresident alien individual or a foreign corporation, the tax imposed under paragraph (1) shall not apply to any such payment subject to tax under section 1441(a) (relating to withholding on nonresident aliens) or tax under section 1442(a) (relating to withholding on foreign corporations).

(3) Winnings which are subject to withholding.—For purposes of this subsection, the term "winnings which are subject to withholding" means proceeds from a wager determined in accordance with the following:

(A) In general.—Except as provided in subparagraphs (B) and (C), proceeds of more than $5,000 from a wagering transaction, if the amount of such proceeds is at least 300 times as large as the amount wagered.

(B) State-conducted lotteries.—Proceeds of more than $5,000 from a wager placed in a lottery conducted by an agency of a State acting under authority of State law, but only if such wager is placed with the State agency conducting such lottery, or with its authorized employees or agents.

(C) Sweepstakes, wagering pools, certain parimutuel pools, jai alai, and lotteries.—Proceeds of more than $5,000 from—

(i) a wager placed in a sweepstakes, wagering pool, or lottery (other than a wager described in subparagraph (B)), or

(ii) a wagering transaction in a parimutuel pool with respect to horse races, dog races, or jai alai if the amount of such proceeds is at least 300 times as large as the amount wagered.

(4) Rules for determining proceeds from a wager.—For purposes of this subsection—

(A) proceeds from a wager shall be determined by reducing the amount received by the amount of the wager, and

(B) proceeds which are not money shall be taken into account at their fair market value.

(5) Exception for bingo, keno, and slot machines.—The tax imposed under paragraph (1) shall not apply to winnings from a slot machine, keno, and bingo.

(6) Statement by recipient.—Every person who is to receive a payment of winnings which are subject to withholding shall furnish the person making such payment a statement, made under the penalties of perjury, containing the name, address, and taxpayer identification number of the person receiving the payment and of each person entitled to any portion of such payment.

(7) Coordination with other sections.—For purposes of sections 3403 and 3404 and for purposes of so much of subtitle F (except section 7205) as relates to this chapter, payments to any person of winnings which are subject to withholding shall be treated as if they were wages paid by an employer to an employee.

(r) Extension of withholding to certain taxable payments of Indian casino profits.—

(1) In general.—Every person, including an Indian tribe, making a payment to a member of an Indian tribe from the net revenues of any class II or class III gaming activity conducted or licensed by such tribe shall deduct and withhold from such payment a tax in an amount equal to such payment's proportionate share of the annualized tax.

(2) Exception.—The tax imposed by paragraph (1) shall not apply to any payment to the extent that the payment, when annualized, does not exceed an amount equal to the sum of—

(A) the basic standard deduction (as defined in section 63(c)) for an individual to whom section 63(c)(2)(C) applies, and

(B) the exemption amount (as defined in section 151(d)).

(3) Annualized tax.—For purposes of paragraph (1), the term "annualized tax" means, with respect to any payment, the amount of tax which would be imposed by section 1(c) (determined without regard to any rate of tax in excess of the fourth lowest rate of tax applicable under section 1(c)) on an amount of taxable income equal to the excess of—

(A) the annualized amount of such payment, over

(B) the amount determined under paragraph (2).

(4) Classes of gaming activities, etc.—For purposes of this subsection, terms used in paragraph (1) which are defined in section 4 of the Indian Gaming Regulatory Act (25 U.S.C. 2701 et seq.), as in effect on the date of the enactment of this subsection, shall have the respective meanings given such terms by such section.

(5) Annualization.—Payments shall be placed on an annualized basis under regulations prescribed by the Secretary.

(6) Alternate withholding procedures.—At the election of an Indian tribe, the tax imposed by this subsection on any payment made by such tribe shall be determined in accordance with such tables or computational procedures as may be specified in regulations prescribed by the Secretary (in lieu of in accordance with paragraphs (2) and (3)).

(7) Coordination with other sections.—For purposes of this chapter and so much of subtitle F as relates to this chapter, payments to any person which are subject to withholding under this subsection shall be treated as if they were wages paid by an employer to an employee.

(s) Exemption from withholding for any vehicle fringe benefit.—

(1) Employer election not to withhold.—The employer may elect not to deduct and withhold any tax under this chapter with respect to any vehicle fringe benefit provided to any employee if such employee is notified by the employer of such election (at such time and in such manner as the Secretary shall by regulations prescribe). The preceding sentence shall not apply to any vehicle fringe benefit unless the amount of such benefit is included by the employer on a statement timely furnished under section 6051.

(2) Employer must furnish W-2.—Any vehicle fringe benefit shall be treated as wages from which amounts are required to be deducted and withheld under this chapter for purposes of section 6051.

(3) Vehicle fringe benefit.—For purposes of this subsection, the term "vehicle fringe benefit" means any fringe benefit—

(A) which constitutes wages (as defined in section 3401), and

(B) which consists of providing a highway motor vehicle for the use of the employee.

Sec. 4999. Golden parachute payments

(a) Imposition of tax.—There is hereby imposed on any person who receives an excess parachute payment a tax equal to 20 percent of the amount of such payment.

(b) Excess parachute payment defined.—For purposes of this section, the term "excess parachute payment" has the meaning given to such term by section 280G(b).

(c) Administrative provisions.—

(1) Withholding.—In the case of any excess parachute payment which is wages (within the meaning of section 3401) the amount deducted and withheld under section 3402 shall be increased by the amount of the tax imposed by this section on such payment.

(2) Other administrative provisions.—For purposes of subtitle F, any tax imposed by this section shall be treated as a tax imposed by subtitle A.

Sec. 6039. Information required in connection with certain options

(a) Furnishing of information.—Every corporation—

(1) which in any calendar year transfers to any person a share of stock pursuant to such person's exercise of an incentive stock option, or

(2) which in any calendar year records (or has by its agent recorded) a transfer of the legal title of a share of stock acquired by the transferor pursuant to his exercise of an option described in section 423(c) (relating to special rule where option price is between 85 percent and 100 percent of value of stock),

shall (on or before January 31 of the following calendar year) furnish to such person a written statement in such manner and setting forth such information as the Secretary may by regulations prescribe.

(b) Special rules.—For purposes of this section—

(1) Treatment by employer to be determinative.—Any option which the corporation treats as an incentive stock option or an option granted under an employee stock purchase plan shall be deemed to be such an option.

(2) Subsection (a)(2) applies only to first transfer described therein.— A statement is required by reason of a transfer described in subsection (a)(2) of a share only with respect to the first transfer of such share by the person who exercised the option.

(3) Identification of stock.—Any corporation which transfers any share of stock pursuant to the exercise of any option described in subsection (a)(2) shall identify such stock in a manner adequate to carry out the purposes of this section.

(c) Cross references.—

For definition of—

(1) the term "incentive stock option", see section 422(b), and

(2) the term "employee stock purchase plan" see section 423(b).

26 CFR § 1-83.6—Deduction by employer

(a) *Allowance of deduction*—

(1) *General rule.* In the case of a transfer of property in connection with the performance of services, or a compensatory cancellation of a nonlapse restriction described in section 83(d) and § 1.83–5, a deduction is allowable under section 162 or 212 to the person for whom the services were performed. The amount of the deduction is equal to the amount included as compensation in the gross income of the service provider under section 83 (a), (b), or (d)(2), but only to the extent the amount meets the requirements of section 162 or 212 and the regulations thereunder. The deduction is allowed only for the taxable year of that person in which or with which ends the taxable year of the service provider in which the amount is included as compensation. For purposes of this paragraph, any amount excluded from gross income under section 79 or section 101(b) or subchapter N is considered to have been included in gross income.

(2) *Special Rule.* For purposes of paragraph (a)(1) of this section, the service provider is deemed to have included the amount as compensation in gross income if the person for whom the services were performed satisfies in a timely manner all requirements of section 6041 or section 6041A, and the regulations thereunder, with respect to that amount of compensation. For purposes of the preceding sentence, whether a person for whom services were performed satisfies all requirements of section 6041 or section 6041A, and the regulations thereunder, is determined without regard to § 1.6041–3(c) (exception for payments to corporations). In the case of a disqualifying disposition of stock described in section 421(b), an employer that otherwise satisfies all requirements of section 6041 and the regulations thereunder will be considered to have done so timely for purposes of this paragraph (a)(2) if Form W–2 or Form W–2c, as appropriate, is furnished to the employee or former employee, and is filed with the federal government, on or before the date on which the employer files the tax return claiming the deduction relating to the disqualifying disposition.

(3) *Exceptions.* Where property is substantially vested upon transfer, the deduction shall be allowed to such person in accordance with his method of accounting (in conformity with sections 446 and 461). In the case of a transfer to an employee benefit plan described in § 1.162–10(a) or a transfer to an employees' trust or annuity plan described in section 404(a)(5) and the regulations thereunder, section 83(h) and this section do not apply.

(4) *Capital expenditure, etc.* No deduction is allowed under section 83(h) to the extent that the transfer of property constitutes a capital expenditure, an item of deferred expense, or an amount properly includible

in the value of inventory items. In the case of a capital expenditure, for example, the basis of the property to which such capital expenditure relates shall be increased at the same time and to the same extent as any amount includible in the employee's gross income in respect of such transfer. Thus, for example, no deduction is allowed to a corporation in respect of a transfer of its stock to a promoter upon its organization, notwithstanding that such promoter must include the value of such stock in his gross income in accordance with the rules under section 83.

(5) *Effective date.* Paragraphs (a)(1) and (2) of this section apply to deductions for taxable years beginning on or after January 1, 1995. However, taxpayers may also apply paragraphs (a)(1) and (2) of this section when claiming deductions for taxable years beginning before that date if the claims are not barred by the statute of limitations. Paragraphs (a) (3) and (4) of this section are effective as set forth in § 1.83– 8(b).

(b) *Recognition of gain or loss.* Except as provided in section 1032, at the time of a transfer of property in connection with the performance of services the transferor recognizes gain to the extent that the transferor receives an amount that exceeds the transferor's basis in the property. In addition, at the time a deduction is allowed under section 83(h) and paragraph (a) of this section, gain or loss is recognized to the extent of the difference between

(1) the sum of the amount paid plus the amount allowed as a deduction under section 83(h), and

(2) the sum of the taxpayer's basis in the property plus any amount recognized pursuant to the previous sentence.

(c) *Forfeitures.* If, under section 83(h) and paragraph (a) of this section, a deduction, an increase in basis, or a reduction of gross income was allowable (disregarding the reasonableness of the amount of compensation) in respect of a transfer of property and such property is subsequently forfeited, the amount of such deduction, increase in basis or reduction of gross income shall be includible in the gross income of the person to whom it was allowable for the taxable year of forfeiture. The basis of such property in the hands of the person to whom it is forfeited shall include any such amount includible in the gross income of such person, as well as any amount such person pays upon forfeiture.

(d) *Special rules for transfers by shareholders—*

(1) *Transfers.* If a shareholder of a corporation transfers property to an employee of such corporation or to an independent contractor (or to a beneficiary thereof), in consideration of services performed for the corporation, the transaction shall be considered to be a contribution of such property to the capital of such corporation by the shareholder, and immediately thereafter a transfer of such property by the corporation to the employee or independent contractor under paragraphs (a) and (b) of this

section. For purposes of this (1), such a transfer will be considered to be in consideration for services performed for the corporation if either the property transferred is substantially nonvested at the time of transfer or an amount is includible in the gross income of the employee or independent contractor at the time of transfer under § 1.83–1(a)(1) or § 1.83–2(a). In the case of such a transfer, any money or other property paid to the shareholder for such stock shall be considered to be paid to the corporation and transferred immediately thereafter by the corporation to the shareholder as a distribution to which section 302 applies. For special rules that may applyto a corporation's transfer of its own stock to any person in consideration of services performed for another corporation or partnership, see § 1.1032–3. The preceding sentence applies to transfers of stock and amounts paid for such stock occurring on or after May 16, 2000.

(2) *Forfeiture.* If, following a transaction described in paragraph (d)(1) of this section, the transferred property is forfeited to the shareholder, paragraph (c) of this section shall apply both with respect to the shareholder and with respect to the corporation. In addition, the corporation shall in the taxable year of forfeiture be allowed a loss (or realize a gain) to offset any gain (or loss) realized under paragraph (b) of this section. For example, if a shareholder transfers property to an employee of the corporation as compensation, and as a result the shareholder's basis of $200x in such property is allocated to his stock in such corporation and such corporation recognizes a short-term capital gain of $800x, and is allowed a deduction of $1,000x on such transfer, upon a subsequent forfeiture of the property to the shareholder, the shareholder shall take $200x into gross income, and the corporation shall take $1,000x into gross income and be allowed a short-term capital loss of $800x.

(e) *Options.* [Reserved]

(f) *Reporting requirements.* [Reserved]

CFR § 1.162-27—Certain employee remuneration in excess of $1,000,000.

(a) *Scope*. This section provides rules for the application of the $1 million deduction limit under section 162(m) of the Internal Revenue Code. Paragraph (b) of this section provides the general rule limiting deductions under section 162(m). Paragraph (c) of this section provides definitions of generally applicable terms. Paragraph (d) of this section provides an exception from the deduction limit for compensation payable on a commission basis. Paragraph (e) of this section provides an exception for qualified performance-based compensation. Paragraphs (f) and (g) of this section provide special rules for corporations that become publicly held corporations and payments that are subject to section 280G, respectively. Paragraph (h) of this section provides transition rules, including the rules for contracts that are grandfathered and not subject to section 162(m). Paragraph (j) of this section contains the effective date provisions. For rules concerning the deductibility of compensation for services that are not covered by section 162(m) and this section, see section 162(a)(1) and § 1.162–7. This section is not determinative as to whether compensation meets the requirements of section 162(a)(1).

(b) *Limitation on deduction*. Section 162(m) precludes a deduction under chapter 1 of the Internal Revenue Code by any publicly held corporation for compensation paid to any covered employee to the extent that the compensation for the taxable year exceeds $1,000,000.

(c) *Definitions*—

(1) *Publicly held corporation*—

(i) *General rule*. A *publicly held corporation* means any corporation issuing any class of common equity securities required to be registered under section 12 of the Exchange Act. A corporation is not considered publicly held if the registration of its equity securities is voluntary. For purposes of this section, whether a corporation is publicly held is determined based solely on whether, as of the last day of its taxable year, the corporation is subject to the reporting obligations of section 12 of the Exchange Act.

(ii) *Affiliated groups*. A publicly held corporation includes an affiliated group of corporations, as defined in section 1504 (determined without regard to section 1504(b)). For purposes of this section, however, an affiliated group of corporations does not include any subsidiary that is itself a publicly held corporation. Such a publicly held subsidiary, and its subsidiaries (if any), are separately subject to this section. If a covered employee is paid compensation in a taxable year by more than one member of an affiliated group, compensation paid by each member of the affiliated group is aggregated with compensation paid to the covered employee by all other members of the group. Any amount disallowed as a deduction by this section must be prorated among the payor corporations in proportion to the amount of compensation paid to the covered employee by each such corporation in the taxable year.

(2) *Covered employee*—

(i) *General rule.* A *covered employee* means any individual who, on the last day of the taxable year, is—

(A) The chief executive officer of the corporation or is acting in such capacity; or

(B) Among the four highest compensated officers (other than the chief executive officer).

(ii) *Application of rules of the Securities and Exchange Commission.* Whether an individual is the chief executive officer described in paragraph (c)(2)(i)(A) of this section or an officer described in paragraph (c)(2)(i)(B) of this section is determined pursuant to the executive compensation disclosure rules under the Exchange Act.

(3) *Compensation*—

(i) *In general.* For purposes of the deduction limitation described in paragraph (b) of this section, *compensation* means the aggregate amount allowable as a deduction under chapter 1 of the Internal Revenue Code for the taxable year (determined without regard to section 162(m)) for remuneration for services performed by a covered employee, whether or not the services were performed during the taxable year.

(ii) *Exceptions. Compensation* does not include—

(A) Remuneration covered in section 3121(a)(5)(A) through section 3121(a)(5)(D) (concerning remuneration that is not treated as *wages* for purposes of the Federal Insurance Contributions Act); and

(B) Remuneration consisting of any benefit provided to or on behalf of an employee if, at the time the benefit is provided, it is reasonable to believe that the employee will be able to exclude it from gross income. In addition, compensation does not include salary reduction contributions described in section 3121(v)(1).

(4) *Compensation Committee.* The *compensation committee* means the committee of directors (including any subcommittee of directors) of the publicly held corporation that has the authority to establish and administer performance goals described in paragraph (e)(2) of this section, and to certify that performance goals are attained, as described in paragraph (e)(5) of this section. A committee of directors is not treated as failing to have the authority to establish performance goals merely because the goals are ratified by the board of directors of the publicly held corporation or, if

applicable, any other committee of the board of directors. See paragraph (e)(3) of this section for rules concerning the composition of the compensation committee.

(5) *Exchange Act*. The *Exchange Act* means the Securities Exchange Act of 1934.

(6) *Examples*. This paragraph (c) may be illustrated by the following examples:

Example 1. Corporation X is a publicly held corporation with a July 1 to June 30 fiscal year. For Corporation X's taxable year ending on June 30, 1995, Corporation X pays compensation of $2,000,000 to A, an employee. However, A's compensation is not required to be reported to shareholders under the executive compensation disclosure rules of the Exchange Act because A is neither the chief executive officer nor one of the four highest compensated officers employed on the last day of the taxable year. A's compensation is not subject to the deduction limitation of paragraph (b) of this section.

Example 2. C, a covered employee, performs services and receives compensation from Corporations X, Y, and Z, members of an affiliated group of corporations. Corporation X, the parent corporation, is a publicly held corporation. The total compensation paid to C from all affiliated group members is $3,000,000 for the taxable year, of which Corporation X pays $1,500,000; Corporation Y pays $900,000; and Corporation Z pays $600,000. Because the compensation paid by all affiliated group members is aggregated for purposes of section 162(m), $2,000,000 of the aggregate compensation paid is nondeductible. Corporations X, Y, and Z each are treated as paying a ratable portion of the nondeductible compensation. Thus, two thirds of each corporation's payment will be nondeductible. Corporation X has a nondeductible compensation expense of $1,000,000 ($1,500,000×$2,000,000/$3,000,000). Corporation Y has a nondeductible compensation expense of $600,000 ($900,000×$2,000,000/$3,000,000). Corporation Z has a nondeductible compensation expense of $400,000 ($600,000×$2,000,000/ $3,000,000).

Example 3. Corporation W, a calendar year taxpayer, has total assets equal to or exceeding $5 million and a class of equity security held of record by 500 or more persons on December 31, 1994. However, under the Exchange Act, Corporation W is not required to file a registration statement with respect to that security until April 30, 1995. Thus, Corporation W is not a publicly held corporation on December 31, 1994, but is a publicly held corporation on December 31, 1995.

Example 4. The facts are the same as in *Example 3*, except that on December 15, 1996, Corporation W files with the Securities and Exchange Commission to disclose that Corporation W is no longer required to be registered under section 12 of the Exchange Act and to terminate its registration of securities under that provision. Because Corporation W is no longer subject to Exchange Act reporting obligations as of December 31, 1996, Corporation W is not a publicly held corporation for taxable year 1996, even though the registration of Corporation W's securities does not terminate until 90 days after Corporation W files with the Securities and Exchange Commission.

(d) *Exception for compensation paid on a commission basis.* The deduction limit in paragraph (b) of this section shall not apply to any compensation paid on a commission basis. For this purpose, compensation is paid on a commission basis if the facts and circumstances show that it is paid solely on account of income generated directly by the individual performance of the individual to whom the compensation is paid. Compensation does not fail to be attributable directly to the individual merely because support services, such as secretarial or research services, are utilized in generating the income. However, if compensation is paid on account of broader performance standards, such as income produced by a business unit of the corporation, the compensation does not qualify for the exception provided under this paragraph (d).

(e) *Exception for qualified performance-based compensation—*

(1) *In general.* The deduction limit in paragraph (b) of this section does not apply to qualified performance-based compensation. Qualified performancebased compensation is compensation that meets all of the requirements of paragraphs (e)(2) through (e)(5) of this section.

(2) *Performance goal requirement—*

(i) *Preestablished goal.* Qualified performance- based compensation must be paid solely on account of the attainment of one or more preestablished, objective performance goals. A performance goal is considered preestablished if it is established in writing by the compensation committee not later than 90 days after the commencement of the period of service to which the performance goal relates, provided that the outcome is substantially uncertain at the time the compensation committee actually establishes the goal. However, in no event will a performance goal be considered to be preestablished if it is established after 25 percent of the period of service (as scheduled in good faith at the time the goal is established) has elapsed. A performance goal is objective if a third party having knowledge of the relevant facts could determine whether the goal is met. Performance goals can be based on one or more business criteria that apply to the individual, a business unit, or the corporation as a whole. Such business criteria could include, for example, stock price, market share, sales, earnings per share, return on equity, or costs. A performance goal need not, however, be based upon an increase or positive result under a business criterion and could include, for example, maintaining the status quo or limiting economic losses (measured, in each case, by reference to a specific business criterion). A performance goal does not include the mere continued employment of the covered employee. Thus, a vesting provision based solely on continued employment would not constitute a performance goal. See paragraph (e)(2)(vi) of this section for rules on compensation that is based on an increase in the price of stock.

(ii) *Objective compensation formula.* A preestablished performance goal must state, in terms of an objective formula or standard, the method for computing the amount of compensation payable to the employee if the goal is attained. A formula or standard is objective if a third party having knowledge of the relevant performance results could calculate the amount to be paid to the employee. In addition, a formula or standard must specify the individual employees or class of employees to which it applies.

(iii) *Discretion.*

(A) The terms of an objective formula or standard must preclude discretion to increase the amount of compensation payable that would otherwise be due upon attainment of the goal. A performance goal is not discretionary for purposes of this paragraph (e)(2)(iii) merely because the compensation committee reduces or eliminates the compensation or other economic benefit that was due upon attainment of the goal. However, the exercise of negative discretion with respect to one employee is not permitted to result in an increase in the amount payable to another employee. Thus, for example, in the case of a bonus pool, if the amount payable to each employee is stated in terms of a percentage of the pool, the sum of these individual percentages of the pool is not permitted to exceed 100 percent. If the terms of an objective formula or standard fail to preclude discretion to increase the amount of compensation merely because the amount of compensation to be paid upon attainment of the performance goal is based, in whole or in part, on a percentage of salary or base pay and the dollar amount of the salary or base pay is not fixed at the time the performance goal is established, then the objective formula or standard will not be considered discretionary for purposes of this paragraph (e)(2)(iii) if the maximum dollar amount to be paid is fixed at that time.

(B) If compensation is payable upon or after the attainment of a performance goal, and a change is made to accelerate the payment of compensation to an earlier date after the attainment of the goal, the change will be treated as an increase in the amount of compensation, unless the amount of compensation paid is discounted to reasonably reflect the time value of money. If compensation is payable upon or after the attainment of a performance goal, and a change is made to defer the payment of compensation to a later date, any amount paid in excess of the amount that was originally owed to the employee will not be treated as an increase in the amount of compensation if the additional amount is based either on a reasonable rate of interest or on one or more predetermined actual investments (whether or not assets associated with the amount originally owed are actually invested therein) such that the amount payable by the employer at the later date will be based on the actual rate of return of a specific investment (including any decrease as well as any increase in the value of an investment). If compensation is payable in the form of property, a change in the timing of the transfer of that property after the attainment of the goal will not be treated as an increase in the amount of compensation for purposes of this paragraph (e)(2)(iii). Thus, for example, if the terms of a stock grant provide for stock to be transferred after the attainment of a performance goal and the transfer of the stock also is subject to a vesting schedule, a change in the vesting schedule that either accelerates or defers the transfer of stock will not be treated as an increase in the amount of compensation payable under the performance goal.

(C) Compensation attributable to a stock option, stock appreciation right, or other stock-based compensation does not fail to satisfy the requirements of this paragraph (e)(2) to the extent that a change in the grant or award is made to reflect a change in corporate capitalization, such as a stock split or dividend, or a corporate transaction, such as any merger of a corporation into another corporation, any consolidation of two or more corporations into another corporation, any separation of a corporation (including a spinoff or other distribution of stock or property by a corporation), any reorganization of a corporation (whether or not such reorganization comes within the definition of such term in section 368), or any partial or complete liquidation by a corporation.

(iv) *Grant-by-grant determination.* The determination of whether compensation satisfies the requirements of this paragraph (e)(2) generally shall be made on a grant-by-grant basis. Thus, for example, whether compensation attributable to a stock option grant satisfies the requirements of this paragraph (e)(2) generally is determined on the basis of the particular grant made and without regard to the terms of any other option grant, or other grant of compensation, to the same or another employee. As a further example, except as provided in paragraph (e)(2)(vi), whether a grant of restricted stock or other stock-based compensation satisfies the requirements of this paragraph (e)(2) is determined without regard to whether dividends, dividend equivalents, or other similar distributions with respect to stock, on such stockbased compensation are payable prior to the attainment of the performance goal. Dividends, dividend equivalents, or other similar distributions with respect to stock that are treated as separate grants under this paragraph (e)(2)(iv) are not performance-based compensation unless they separately satisfy the requirements of this paragraph (e)(2).

(v) *Compensation contingent upon attainment of performance goal.* Compensation does not satisfy the requirements of this paragraph (e)(2) if the facts and circumstances indicate that the employee would receive all or part of the compensation regardless of whether the performance goal is attained. Thus, if the payment of compensation under a grant or award is only nominally or partially contingent on attaining a performance goal, none of the compensation payable under the grant or award will be considered performancebased. For example, if an employee is entitled to a bonus under either of two arrangements, where payment under a non-performance-based arrangement is contingent upon the failure to attain the performance goals under an otherwise performance-based arrangement, then neither arrangement provides for compensation that satisfies the requirements of this paragraph (e)(2). Compensation does not fail to be qualified performance-based compensation merely because the plan allows the compensation to be payable upon death, disability, or change of ownership or control, although compensation actually paid on account of those events prior to the attainment of the performance goal would not satisfy the requirements of this paragraph (e)(2). As an exception to the general rule set forth in the first sentence of paragraph (e)(2)(iv) of this section, the facts-andcircumstances determination referred to in the first sentence of this paragraph (e)(2)(v) is made taking into account all plans, arrangements, and agreements that provide for compensation to the employee.

(vi) *Application of requirements to stock options and stock appreciation rights—*

(A) *In general.* Compensation attributable to a stock option or a stock appreciation right is deemed to satisfy the requirements of this paragraph (e)(2) if the grant or award is made by the compensation committee; the plan under which the option or right is granted states the maximum number of shares with respect to which options or rights may be granted during a specified period to any employee; and, under the terms of the option or right, the amount of compensation the employee could receive is based solely on an increase in the value of the stock after the date of the grant or award. Conversely, if the amount of compensation the employee will receive under the grant or award is not based solely on an increase in the value of the stock after the date of grant or award (e.g., in the case of restricted stock, or an option that is granted with an exercise price that is less than the fair market value of the stock as of the date of grant), none of the compensation attributable to the grant or award is qualified performance-based compensation because it does not satisfy the requirement of this paragraph (e)(2)(vi)(A). Whether a stock option grant is based solely on an increase in the value of the stock after the date of grant is determined without regard to any dividend equivalent that may be payable, provided that payment of the dividend equivalent is not made contingent on the exercise of the option. The rule that the compensation attributable to a stock option or stock appreciation right must be based solely on an increase in the value of the stock after the date of grant or award does not apply if the grant or award is made on account of, or if the vesting or exercisability of the grant or award is contingent on, the attainment of a performance goal that satisfies the requirements of this paragraph (e)(2).

(B) *Cancellation and repricing.* Compensation attributable to a stock option or stock appreciation right does not satisfy the requirements of this paragraph (e)(2) to the extent that the number of options granted exceeds the maximum number of shares for which options may be granted to the employee as specified in the plan. If an option is canceled, the canceled option continues to be counted against the maximum number of shares for which options may be granted to the employee under the plan. If, after grant, the exercise price of an option is reduced, the transaction is treated as a cancellation of the option and a grant of a new option. In such case, both the option that is deemed to be canceled and the option that is deemed to be granted reduce the maximum number of shares for which options may be granted to the employee under the plan. This paragraph (e)(2)(vi)(B) also applies in the case of a stock appreciation right where, after the award is made, the base amount on which stock appreciation is calculated is reduced to reflect a reduction in the fair market value of stock. (vii)

Examples. This paragraph (e)(2) may be illustrated by the following examples:

Example 1. No later than 90 days after the start of a fiscal year, but while the outcome is substantially uncertain, Corporation S establishes a bonus plan under which A, the chief executive officer, will receive a cash bonus of $500,000, if year-end corporate sales are increased by at least 5 percent. The compensation committee retains the right, if the performance goal is met, to reduce the bonus payment to A if, in its judgment, other subjective factors warrant a reduction. The bonus will meet the requirements of this paragraph (e)(2).

Example 2. The facts are the same as in *Example 1,* except that the bonus is based on a percentage of Corporation S's total sales for the fiscal year. Because Corporation S is virtually certain to have some sales for the fiscal year, the outcome of the performance goal is not substantially uncertain, and therefore the bonus does not meet the requirements of this paragraph (e)(2).

Example 3. The facts are the same as in *Example 1,* except that the bonus is based on a percentage of Corporation S's total profits for the fiscal year. Although some sales are virtually certain for virtually all public companies, it is substantially uncertain whether a company will have profits for a specified future period even if the company has a history of profitability. Therefore, the bonus will meet the requirements of this paragraph (e)(2).

Example 4. B is the general counsel of Corporation R, which is engaged in patent litigation with Corporation S. Representatives of Corporation S have informally indicated to Corporation R a willingness to settle the litigation for $50,000,000. Subsequently, the compensation committee of Corporation R agrees to pay B a bonus if B obtains a formal settlement for at least $50,000,000. The bonus to B does not meet the requirement of this paragraph (e)(2) because the performance goal was not established at a time when the outcome was substantially uncertain.

Example 5. Corporation S, a public utility, adopts a bonus plan for selected salaried employees that will pay a bonus at the end of a 3-year period of $750,000 each if, at the end of the 3 years, the price of S stock has increased by 10 percent. The plan also provides that the 10-percent goal will automatically adjust upward or downward by the percentage change in a published utilities index. Thus, for example, if the published utilities index shows a net increase of 5 percent over a 3-year period, then the salaried employees would receive a bonus only if Corporation S stock has increased by 15 percent. Conversely, if the published utilities index shows a net decrease of 5 percent over a 3-year period, then the salaried employees would receive a bonus if Corporation S stock has increased by 5 percent. Because these automatic adjustments in the performance goal are preestablished, the bonus meets the requirement of this paragraph (e)(2), notwithstanding the potential changes in the performance goal.

Example 6. The facts are the same as in *Example 5,* except that the bonus plan provides that, at the end of the 3-year period, a bonus of $750,000 will be paid to each salaried employee if either the price of Corporation S stock has increased by 10 percent or the earnings per share on Corporation S stock have increased by 5 percent. If both the earnings-per-share goal and the stock-price goal are preestablished, the compensation committee's discretion to choose to pay a bonus under either of the two goals does not cause any bonus paid under the plan to fail to meet the requirement of this paragraph (e)(2) because each goal independently meets the requirements of this paragraph (e)(2). The choice to pay under either of the two goals is tantamount to the discretion to choose not to pay under one of the goals, as provided in paragraph (e)(2)(iii) of this section.

Example 7. Corporation U establishes a bonus plan under which a specified class of employees will participate in a bonus pool if certain preestablished performance goals are attained. The amount of the bonus pool is determined under an objective formula. Under the terms of the bonus plan, the compensation committee retains the discretion to determine the fraction of the bonus pool that each employee may receive. The bonus plan does not satisfy the requirements of this paragraph (e)(2). Although the aggregate amount of the bonus plan is determined under an objective formula, a third party could not determine the amount that any individual could receive under the plan.

Example 8. The facts are the same as in *Example 7,* except that the bonus plan provides that a specified share of the bonus pool is payable to each employee, and the total of these shares does not exceed 100% of the pool. The bonus plan satisfies the requirements of this paragraph (e)(2).

In addition, the bonus plan will satisfy the requirements of this paragraph (e)(2) even if the compensation committee retains the discretion to reduce the compensation payable to any individual employee, provided that a reduction in the amount of one employee's bonus does not result in an increase in the amount of any other employee's bonus.

Example 9. Corporation V establishes a stock option plan for salaried employees. The terms of the stock option plan specify that no salaried employee shall receive options for more than 100,000 shares over any 3-year period. The compensation committee grants options for 50,000 shares to each of several salaried employees. The exercise price of each option is equal to or greater than the fair market value at the time of each grant. Compensation attributable to the exercise of the options satisfies the requirements of this paragraph (e)(2). If, however, the terms of the options provide that the exercise price is less than fair market value at the date of grant, no compensation attributable to the exercise of those options satisfies the requirements of this paragraph (e)(2) unless issuance or exercise of the options was contingent upon the attainment of a preestablished performance goal that satisfies this paragraph (e)(2).

Example 10. The facts are the same as in *Example 9,* except that, within the same 3- year grant period, the fair market value of Corporation V stock is significantly less than the exercise price of the options. The compensation committee reprices those options to that lower current fair market value of Corporation V stock. The repricing of the options for 50,000 shares held by each salaried employee is treated as the grant of new options for an additional 50,000 shares to each employee. Thus, each of the salaried employees is treated as having received grants for 100,000 shares. Consequently, if any additional options are granted to those employees during the 3-year period, compensation attributable to the exercise of those additional options would not satisfy the requirements of this paragraph (e)(2). The results would be the same if the compensation committee canceled the outstanding options and issued new options to the same employees that were exercisable at the fair market value of Corporation V stock on the date of reissue.

Example 11. Corporation W maintains a plan under which each participating employee may receive incentive stock options, nonqualified stock options, stock appreciation rights, or grants of restricted Corporation W stock. The plan specifies that each participating employee may receive options, stock appreciation rights, restricted stock, or any combination of each, for no more than 20,000 shares over the life of the plan. The plan provides that stock options may be granted with an exercise price of less than, equal to, or greater than fair market value on the date of grant. Options granted with an exercise price equal to, or greater than, fair market value on the date of grant do not fail to meet the requirements of this paragraph (e)(2) merely because the compensation committee has the discretion to determine the types of awards (i.e., options, rights, or restricted stock) to be granted to each employee or the discretion to issue options or make other compensation awards under the plan that would not meet the requirements of this paragraph (e)(2). Whether an option granted under the plan satisfies the requirements of this paragraph (e)(2) is determined on the basis of the specific terms of the option and without regard to other options or awards under the plan.

Example 12. Corporation X maintains a plan under which stock appreciation rights may be awarded to key employees. The plan permits the compensation committee to make awards under which the amount of compensation payable to the employee is equal to the increase in the stock price plus a percentage "gross up" intended to offset the tax liability of the employee. In addition, the plan permits the compensation committee to make awards under which the amount of compensation payable to the employee is equal to the increase in the stock price, based on the highest price, which is defined as the highest price paid for Corporation X stock (or offered in a tender offer or other arms-length offer) during the 90 days preceding exercise. Compensation attributable to awards under the plan satisfies the requirements of paragraph (e)(2)(vi) of this section, provided that the terms of the plan specify the maximum number of shares for which awards may be made.

Example 13. Corporation W adopts a plan under which a bonus will be paid to the CEO only if there is a 10% increase in earnings per share during the performance period. The plan provides that earnings per share will be calculated without regard to any change in accounting standards that may be required by the Financial Accounting Standards Board after the goal is established. After the goal is established, such a change in accounting standards occurs. Corporation W's reported earnings, for purposes of determining earnings per share under the plan, are adjusted pursuant to this plan provision to factor out this change in standards. This adjustment will not be considered an exercise of impermissible discretion because it is made pursuant to the plan provision.

Example 14. Corporation X adopts a performance- based incentive pay plan with a four-year performance period. Bonuses under the plan are scheduled to be paid in the first year after the end of the performance period (year 5). However, in the second year of the performance period, the compensation committee determines that any bonuses payable in year 5 will instead, for bona fide business reasons, be paid in year 10. The compensation committee also determines that any compensation that would have been payable in year 5 will be adjusted to reflect the delay in payment. The adjustment will be based on the greater of the future rate of return of a specified mutual fund that invests in blue chip stocks or of a specified venture capital investment over the five-year deferral period. Each of these investments, considered by itself, is a predetermined actual investment because it is based on the future rate of return of an actual investment. However, the adjustment in this case is not based on predetermined actual investments within the meaning of paragraph (e)(2)(iii)(B) of this section because the amount payable by Corporation X in year 10 will be based on the greater of the two investment returns and, thus, will not be based on the actual rate of return on either specific investment.

Example 15. The facts are the same as in *Example 14,* except that the increase will be based on Moody's Average Corporate Bond Yield over the five-year deferral period. Because this index reflects a reasonable rate of interest, the increase in the compensation payable that is based on the index's rate of return is not considered an impermissible increase in the amount of compensation payable under the formula.

Example 16. The facts are the same as in *Example 14,* except that the increase will be based on the rate of return for the Standard & Poor's 500 Index. This index does not measure interest rates and thus does not represent a reasonable rate of interest. In addition, this index does not represent an actual investment. Therefore, any additional compensation payable based on the rate of return of this index will result in an impermissible increase in the amount payable under the formula. If, in contrast, the increase were based on the rate of return of an existing mutual fund that is invested in a manner that seeks to approximate the Standard & Poor's 500 Index, the increase would be based on a predetermined actual investment within the meaning of paragraph (e)(2)(iii)(B) of this section and thus would not result in an impermissible increase in the amount payable under the formula.

(3) *Outside directors—*

(i) *General rule.* The performance goal under which compensation is paid must be established by a compensation committee comprised solely of two or more outside directors. A director is an outside director if the director—

(A) Is not a current employee of the publicly held corporation;

(B) Is not a former employee of the publicly held corporation who receives compensation for prior services (other than benefits under a tax-qualified retirement plan) during the taxable year;

(C) Has not been an officer of the publicly held corporation; and

(D) Does not receive remuneration from the publicly held corporation, either directly or indirectly, in any capacity other than as a director. For this purpose, remuneration includes any payment in exchange for goods or services.

(ii) *Remuneration received.* For purposes of this paragraph (e)(3), remuneration is received, directly or indirectly, by a director in each of the following circumstances:

(A) If remuneration is paid, directly or indirectly, to the director personally or to an entity in which the director has a beneficial ownership interest of greater than 50 percent. For this purpose, remuneration is considered paid when actually paid (and throughout the remainder of that taxable year of the corporation) and, if earlier, throughout the period when a contract or agreement to pay remuneration is outstanding.

(B) If remuneration, other than de minimis remuneration, was paid by the publicly held corporation in its preceding taxable year to an entity in which the director has a beneficial ownership interest of at least 5 percent but not more than 50 percent. For this purpose, remuneration is considered paid when actually paid or, if earlier, when the publicly held corporation becomes liable to pay it.

(C) If remuneration, other than de minimis remuneration, was paid by the publicly held corporation in its preceding taxable year to an entity by which the director is employed or selfemployed other than as a director. For this purpose, remuneration is considered paid when actually paid or, if earlier, when the publicly held corporation becomes liable to pay it.

(iii) *De minimis remuneration*—

(A) *In general.* For purposes of paragraphs (e)(3)(ii)(B) and (C) of this section, remuneration that was paid by the publicly held corporation in its preceding taxable year to an entity is de minimis if payments to the entity did not exceed 5 percent of the gross revenue of the entity for its taxable year ending with or within that preceding taxable year of the publicly held corporation.

(B) *Remuneration for personal services and substantial owners.* Notwithstanding paragraph (e)(3)(iii)(A) of this section, remuneration in excess of $60,000 is not de minimis if the remuneration is paid to an entity described in paragraph (e)(3)(ii)(B) of this section, or is paid for personal services to an entity described in paragraph (e)(3)(ii)(C) of this section.

(iv) *Remuneration for personal services.* For purposes of paragraph (e)(3)(iii)(B) of this section, remuneration from a publicly held corporation is for personal services if—

(A) The remuneration is paid to an entity for personal or professional services, consisting of legal, accounting, investment banking, and management consulting services (and other similar services that may be specified by the Commissioner in revenue rulings, notices, or other guidance published in the Internal Revenue Bulletin), performed for the publicly held corporation, and the remuneration is not for services that are incidental to the purchase of goods or to the purchase of services that are not personal services; and

(B) The director performs significant services (whether or not as an employee) for the corporation, division, or similar organization (within the entity) that actually provides the services described in paragraph (e)(3)(iv)(A) of this section to the publicly held corporation, or more than 50 percent of the entity's gross revenues (for the entity's preceding taxable year) are derived from that corporation, subsidiary, or similar organization.

(v) *Entity defined.* For purposes of this paragraph (e)(3), entity means an organization that is a sole proprietorship, trust, estate, partnership, or corporation. The term also includes an affiliated group of corporations as defined in section 1504 (determined without regard to section 1504(b)) and a group of organizations that would be an affiliated group but for the fact that one or more of the organizations are not incorporated. However, the aggregation rules referred to in the preceding sentence do not apply for purposes of determining whether a director has a beneficial ownership interest of at least 5 percent or greater than 50 percent.

(vi) *Employees and former officers.* Whether a director is an employee or a former officer is determined on the basis of the facts at the time that the individual is serving as a director on the compensation committee. Thus, a director is not precluded from being an outside director solely because the director is a former officer of a corporation that previously was an affiliated corporation of the publicly held corporation. For example, a director of a parent corporation of an affiliated group is not precluded from being an outside director solely because that director is a former officer of an affiliated subsidiary that was spun off or liquidated. However, an outside director would no longer be an outside director if a corporation in which the director was previously an officer became an affiliated corporation of the publicly held corporation.

(vii) *Officer.* Solely for purposes of this paragraph (e)(3), *officer* means an administrative executive who is or was in regular and continued service. The term implies continuity of service and excludes those employed for a special and single transaction. An individual who merely has (or had) the title of officer but not the authority of an officer is not considered an officer. The determination of whether an individual is or was an officer is based on all of the facts and circumstances in the particular case, including without limitation the source of the individual's authority, the term for which the individual is elected or appointed, and the nature and extent of the individual's duties.

(viii) *Members of affiliated groups.* For purposes of this paragraph (e)(3), the outside directors of the publicly held member of an affiliated group are treated as the outside directors of all members of the affiliated group.

(ix) *Examples.* This paragraph (e)(3) may be illustrated by the following examples:

Example 1. Corporations X and Y are members of an affiliated group of corporations as defined in section 1504, until July 1, 1994, when Y is sold to another group. Prior to the sale, A served as an officer of Corporation Y. After July 1, 1994, A is not treated as a former officer of Corporation X by reason of having been an officer of Y.

Example 2. Corporation Z, a calendar-year taxpayer, uses the services of a law firm by which B is employed, but in which B has a less-than-5-percent ownership interest. The law firm reports income on a July 1 to June 30 basis. Corporation Z appoints B to serve on its compensation committee for calendar year 1998 after determining that, in calendar year 1997, it did not become liable to the law firm for remuneration exceeding the lesser of $60,000 or five percent of the law firm's gross revenue (calculated for the year ending June 30, 1997). On October 1, 1998, Corporation Z becomes liable to pay remuneration of $50,000 to the law firm on June 30, 1999. For the year ending June 30, 1998, the law firm's gross revenue was less than $1 million. Thus, in calendar year 1999, B is not an outside director. However, B may satisfy the requirements for an outside director in calendar year 2000, if, in calendar year 1999, Corporation Z does not become liable to the law firm for additional remuneration. This is because the remuneration actually paid on June 30, 1999 was considered paid on October 1, 1998 under paragraph (e)(3)(ii)(C) of this section.

Example 3. Corporation Z, a publicly held corporation, purchases goods from Corporation A. D, an executive and less- than-5-percent owner of Corporation A, sits on the board of directors of Corporation Z and on its compensation committee. For 1997, Corporation Z obtains representations to the effect that D is not eligible for any commission for D's sales to Corporation Z and that, for purposes of determining D's compensation for 1997, Corporation A's sales to Corporation Z are not otherwise treated differently than sales to other customers of Corporation A (including its affiliates, if any) or are irrelevant. In addition, Corporation Z has no reason to believe that these representations are inaccurate or that it is otherwise paying remuneration indirectly to D personally. Thus, in 1997, no remuneration is considered paid by Corporation Z indirectly to D personally under paragraph (e)(3)(ii)(A) of this section.

Example 4.

(i) Corporation W, a publicly held corporation, purchases goods from Corporation T. C, an executive and less- than-5- percent owner of Corporation T, sits on the board of directors of Corporation W and on its compensation committee. Corporation T develops a new product and agrees on January 1, 1998 to pay C a bonus of $500,000 if Corporation W contracts to purchase the product. Even if Corporation W purchases the new product, sales to Corporation W will represent less than 5 percent of Corporation T's gross revenues. In 1999, Corporation W contracts to purchase the new product and, in 2000, C receives the $500,000 bonus from Corporation T. In 1998, 1999, and 2000, Corporation W does not obtain any representations relating to indirect remuneration to C personally (such as the representations described in *Example 3*).

(ii) Thus, in 1998, 1999, and 2000, remuneration is considered paid by Corporation W indirectly to C personally under paragraph (e)(3)(ii)(A) of this section. Accordingly, in 1998, 1999, and 2000, C is not an outside director of Corporation W. The result would have been the same if Corporation W had obtained appropriate representations but nevertheless had reason to believe that it was paying remuneration indirectly to C personally.

Example 5. Corporation R, a publicly held corporation, purchases utility service from Corporation Q, a public utility. The chief executive officer, and less-than-5-percent owner, of Corporation Q is a director of Corporation R. Corporation R pays Corporation Q more than $60,000 per year for the utility service, but less than 5 percent of Corporation Q's gross revenues. Because utility services are not personal services, the fees paid are not subject to the $60,000 de minimis rule for remuneration for personal services within the meaning of paragraph (e)(3)(iii)(B) of this section. Thus, the chief executive officer qualifies as an outside director of Corporation R, unless disqualified on some other basis.

Example 6. Corporation A, a publicly held corporation, purchases management consulting services from Division S of Conglomerate P. The chief financial officer of Division S is a director of Corporation A. Corporation A pays more than $60,000 per year for the management consulting services, but less than 5 percent of Conglomerate P's gross revenues. Because management consulting services are personal services within the meaning of paragraph (e)(3)(iv)(A) of this section, and the chief financial officer performs significant services for Division S, the fees paid are subject to the $60,000 de minimis rule as remuneration for personal services. Thus, the chief financial officer does not qualify as an outside director of Corporation A.

Example 7. The facts are the same as in *Example 6*, except that the chief executive officer, and less-than-5-percent owner, of the parent company of Conglomerate P is a director of Corporation A and does not perform significant services for Division S. If the gross revenues of Division S do not constitute more than 50 percent of the gross revenues of Conglomerate P for P's preceding taxable year, the chief executive officer will qualify as an outside director of Corporation A, unless disqualified on some other basis.

(4) *Shareholder approval requirement*—

(i) *General rule.* The material terms of the performance goal under which the compensation is to be paid must be disclosed to and subsequently approved by the shareholders of the publicly held corporation before the compensation is paid. The requirements of this paragraph (e)(4) are not satisfied if the compensation would be paid regardless of whether the material terms are approved by shareholders. The material terms include the employees eligible to receive compensation; a description of the business criteria on which the performance goal is based; and either the maximum amount of compensation that could be paid to any employee or the formula used to calculate the amount of compensation to be paid to the employee if the performance goal is attained (except that, in the case of a formula based, in whole or in part, on a percentage of salary or base pay, the maximum dollar amount of compensation that could be paid to the employee must be disclosed).

(ii) *Eligible employees.* Disclosure of the employees eligible to receive compensation need not be so specific as to identify the particular individuals by name. A general description of the class of eligible employees by title or class is sufficient, such as the chief executive officer and vice presidents, or all salaried employees, all executive officers, or all key employees.

(iii) *Description of business criteria—*

(A) *In general.* Disclosure of the business criteria on which the performance goal is based need not include the specific targets that must be satisfied under the performance goal. For example, if a bonus plan provides that a bonus will be paid if earnings per share increase by 10 percent, the 10-percent figure is a target that need not be disclosed to shareholders. However, in that case, disclosure must be made that the bonus plan is based on an earnings-per-share business criterion. In the case of a plan under which employees may be granted stock options or stock appreciation rights, no specific description of the business criteria is required if the grants or awards are based on a stock price that is no less than current fair market value.

(B) *Disclosure of confidential information.* The requirements of this paragraph (e)(4) may be satisfied even though information that otherwise would be a material term of a performance goal is not disclosed to shareholders, provided that the compensation committee determines that the information is confidential commercial or business information, the disclosure of which would have an adverse effect on the publicly held corporation. Whether disclosure would adversely affect the corporation is determined on the basis of the facts and circumstances. If the compensation committee makes such a determination, the disclosure to shareholders must state the compensation committee's belief that the information is confidential commercial or business information, the disclosure of which would adversely affect the company. In addition, the ability not to disclose confidential information does not eliminate the requirement that disclosure be made of the maximum amount of compensation that is payable to an individual under a performance goal. Confidential information does not include the identity of an executive or the class of executives to which a performance goal applies or the amount of compensation that is payable if the goal is satisfied.

(iv) *Description of compensation.* Disclosure as to the compensation payable under a performance goal must be specific enough so that shareholders can determine the maximum amount of compensation that could be paid to any employee during a specified period. If the terms of the performance goal do not provide for a maximum dollar amount, the disclosure must include the formula under which the compensation would be calculated. Thus, for example, if compensation attributable to the exercise of stock options is equal to the difference in the exercise price and the current value of the stock, disclosure would be required of the maximum number of shares for which grants may be made to any employee and the exercise price of those options (e.g., fair market value on date of grant). In that case, shareholders could calculate the maximum amount of compensation that would be attributable to the exercise of options on the basis of their assumptions as to the future stock price.

(v) *Disclosure requirements of the Securities and Exchange Commission.* To the extent not otherwise specifically provided in this paragraph (e)(4), whether the material terms of a performance goal are adequately disclosed to shareholders is determined under the same standards as apply under the Exchange Act.

(vi) *Frequency of disclosure.* Once the material terms of a performance goal are disclosed to and approved by shareholders, no additional disclosure or approval is required unless the compensation committee changes the material terms of the performance goal. If, however, the compensation committee has authority to change the targets under a performance goal after shareholder approval of the goal, material terms of the performance goal must be disclosed to and reapproved by shareholders no later than the first shareholder meeting that occurs in the fifth year following the year in which shareholders previously approved the performance goal.

(vii) *Shareholder vote.* For purposes of this paragraph (e)(4), the material terms of a performance goal are approved by shareholders if, in a separate vote, a majority of the votes cast on the issue (including abstentions to the extent abstentions are counted as voting under applicable state law) are cast in favor of approval.

(viii) *Members of affiliated group.* For purposes of this paragraph (e)(4), the shareholders of the publicly held member of the affiliated group are treated as the shareholders of all members of the affiliated group. (ix)

Examples. This paragraph (e)(4) may be illustrated by the following examples:

Example 1. Corporation X adopts a plan that will pay a specified class of its executives an annual cash bonus based on the overall increase in corporate sales during the year. Under the terms of the plan, the cash bonus of each executive equals $100,000 multiplied by the number of percentage points by which sales increase in the current year when compared to the prior year. Corporation X discloses to its shareholders prior to the vote both the class of executives eligible to receive awards and the annual formula of $100,000 multiplied by the percentage increase in sales. This disclosure meets the requirements of this paragraph (e)(4). Because the compensation committee does not have the authority to establish a different target under the plan, Corporation X need not redisclose to its shareholders and obtain their reapproval of the material terms of the plan until those material terms are changed.

Example 2. The facts are the same as in *Example 1* except that Corporation X discloses only that bonuses will be paid on the basis of the annual increase in sales. This disclosure does not meet the requirements of this paragraph (e)(4) because it does not include the formula for calculating the compensation or a maximum amount of compensation to be paid if the performance goal is satisfied.

Example 3. Corporation Y adopts an incentive compensation plan in 1995 that will pay a specified class of its executives a bonus every 3 years based on the following 3 factors: increases in earnings per share, reduction in costs for specified divisions, and increases in sales by specified divisions. The bonus is payable in cash or in Corporation Y stock, at the option of the executive. Under the terms of the plan, prior to the beginning of each 3-year period, the compensation committee determines the specific targets under each of the three factors (i.e., the amount of the increase in earnings per share, the reduction in costs, and the amount of sales) that must be met in order for the executives to receive a bonus. Under the terms of the plan, the compensation committee retains the discretion to determine whether a bonus will be paid under any one of the goals. The terms of the plan also specify that no executive may receive a bonus in excess of $1,500,000 for any 3-year period. To satisfy the requirements of this paragraph (e)(4), Corporation Y obtains shareholder approval of the plan at its 1995 annual shareholder meeting. In the proxy statement issued to shareholders, Corporation Y need not disclose to shareholders the specific targets that are set by the compensation committee. However, Corporation Y must disclose that bonuses are paid on the basis of earnings per share, reductions in costs, and increases in sales of specified divisions. Corporation Y also must disclose the maximum amount of compensation that any executive may receive under the plan is $1,500,000 per 3-year period. Unless changes in the material terms of the plan are made earlier, Corporation Y need not disclose the material terms of the plan to the shareholders and obtain their reapproval until the first shareholders' meeting held in 2000.

Example 4. The same facts as in *Example 3,* except that prior to the beginning of the second 3-year period, the compensation committee determines that different targets will be set under the plan for that period with regard to all three of the performance criteria (i.e., earnings per share, reductions in costs, and increases in sales). In addition, the compensation committee raises the maximum dollar amount that can be paid under the plan for a 3-year period to $2,000,000. The increase in the maximum dollar amount of compensation under the plan is a changed material term. Thus, to satisfy the requirements of this paragraph (e)(4), Corporation Y must disclose to and obtain approval by the shareholders of the plan as amended.

Example 5. In 1998, Corporation Z establishes a plan under which a specified group of executives will receive a cash bonus not to exceed $750,000 each if a new product that has been in development is completed and ready for sale to customers by January 1, 2000. Although the completion of the new product is a material term of the performance goal under this paragraph (e)(4), the compensation committee determines that the disclosure to shareholders of the performance goal would adversely affect Corporation Z because its competitors would be made aware of the existence and timing of its new product. In this case, the requirements of this paragraph (e)(4) are satisfied if all other material terms, including the maximum amount of compensation, are disclosed and the disclosure affirmatively states that the terms of the performance goal are not being disclosed because the compensation committee has determined that those terms include confidential information, the disclosure of which would adversely affect Corporation Z.

(5) *Compensation committee certification.* The compensation committee must certify in writing prior to payment of the compensation that the performance goals and any other material terms were in fact satisfied. For this purpose, approved minutes of the compensation committee meeting in which the certification is made are treated as a written certification. Certification by the compensation committee is not required for compensation that is attributable solely to the increase in the value of the stock of the publicly held corporation.

(f) *Companies that become publicly held, spinoffs, and similar transactions—*

(1) *In general.* In the case of a corporation that was not a publicly held corporation and then becomes a publicly held corporation, the deduction limit of paragraph (b) of this section does not apply to any remuneration paid pursuant to a compensation plan or agreement that existed during the period in which the corporation was not publicly held. However, in the case of such a corporation that becomes publicly held in connection with an initial public offering, this relief applies only to the extent that the prospectus accompanying the initial public offering disclosed information concerning those plans or agreements that satisfied all applicable securities laws then in effect. In accordance with paragraph (c)(1)(ii) of this section, a corporation that is a member of an affiliated group that

includes a publicly held corporation is considered publicly held and, therefore, cannot rely on this paragraph (f)(1).

(2) *Reliance period.* Paragraph (f)(1) of this section may be relied upon until the earliest of—

(i) The expiration of the plan or agreement;

(ii) The material modification of the plan or agreement, within the meaning of paragraph (h)(1)(iii) of this section;

(iii) The issuance of all employer stock and other compensation that has been allocated under the plan; or (iv) The first meeting of shareholders at which directors are to be elected that occurs after the close of the third calendar year following the calendar year in which the initial public offering occurs or, in the case of a privately held corporation that becomes publicly held without an initial public offering, the first calendar year following the calendar year in which the corporation becomes publicly held.

(3) *Stock-based compensation.* Paragraph (f)(1) of this section will apply to any compensation received pursuant to the exercise of a stock option or stock appreciation right, or the substantial vesting of restricted property, granted under a plan or agreement described in paragraph (f)(1) of this section if the grant occurs on or before the earliest of the events specified in paragraph (f)(2) of this section.

(4) *Subsidiaries that become separate publicly held corporations—*

(i) *In general.* If a subsidiary that is a member of the affiliated group described in paragraph (c)(1)(ii) of this section becomes a separate publicly held corporation (whether by spinoff or otherwise), any remuneration paid to covered employees of the new publicly held corporation will satisfy the exception for performancebased compensation described in paragraph (e) of this section if the conditions in either paragraph (f)(4)(ii) or (f)(4)(iii) of this section are satisfied.

(ii) *Prior establishment and approval.* Remuneration satisfies the requirements of this paragraph (f)(4)(ii) if the remuneration satisfies the requirements for performance-based compensation set forth in paragraphs (e)(2), (e)(3), and (e)(4) of this section (by application of paragraphs (e)(3)(viii) and (e)(4)(viii) of this section) before the corporation becomes a separate publicly held corporation, and the certification required by paragraph (e)(5) of this section is made by the compensation committee of the new publicly held corporation (but if the performance goals are attained before the corporation becomes a separate publicly held corporation, the certification may be made by the compensation committee referred to in paragraph (e)(3)(viii) of this section before it becomes a separate publicly held corporation). Thus, this paragraph (f)(4)(ii) requires that the outside directors and shareholders (within the meaning of paragraphs (e)(3)(viii) and (e)(4)(viii) of this section) of the corporation before it becomes a separate publicly held corporation establish and approve, respectively, the performance-based compensation for the covered employees of the new publicly held corporation in accordance with paragraphs (e)(3) and (e)(4) of this section.

(iii) *Transition period.* Remuneration satisfies the requirements of this paragraph (f)(4)(iii) if the remuneration satisfies all of the requirements of paragraphs (e)(2), (e)(3), and (e)(5) of this section. The outside directors (within the meaning of paragraph (e)(3)(viii) of this section) of the corporation before it becomes a separate publicly held corporation, or the outside directors of the new publicly held corporation, may establish and administer the performance goals for the covered employees of the new publicly held corporation for purposes of satisfying the requirements of paragraphs (e)(2) and (e)(3) of this section. The certification required by paragraph (e)(5) of this section must be made by the compensation committee of the new publicly held corporation. However, a taxpayer may rely on this paragraph (f)(4)(iii) to satisfy the requirements of paragraph (e) of this section only for compensation paid, or stock options, stock appreciation rights, or restricted property granted, prior to the first regularly scheduled meeting of the shareholders of the new publicly held corporation that occurs more than 12 months after the date the corporation becomes a separate publicly held corporation. Compensation paid, or stock options, stock appreciation rights, or restricted property granted, on or after the date of that meeting of shareholders must satisfy all requirements of paragraph (e) of this section, including the shareholder approval requirement of paragraph (e)(4) of this section, in order to satisfy the requirements for performancebased compensation.

(5) *Example.* The following example illustrates the application of paragraph (f)(4)(ii) of this section:

Example. Corporation P, which is publicly held, decides to spin off Corporation S, a wholly owned subsidiary of Corporation P. After the spinoff, Corporation S will be a separate publicly held corporation. Before the spinoff, the compensation committee of Corporation P, pursuant to paragraph (e)(3)(viii) of this section, establishes a bonus plan for the executives of Corporation S that provides for bonuses payable after the spinoff and that satisfies the requirements of paragraph (e)(2) of this section. If, pursuant to paragraph (e)(4)(viii) of this section, the shareholders of Corporation P approve the plan prior to the spinoff, that approval will satisfy the requirements of paragraph (e)(4) of this section with respect to compensation paid pursuant to the bonus plan after the spinoff. However, the compensation committee of Corporation S will be required to certify that the goals are satisfied prior to the payment of the bonuses in order for the bonuses to be considered performance-based compensation.

(g) *Coordination with disallowed excess parachute payments.* The $1,000,000 limitation in paragraph (b) of this section is reduced (but not below zero) by the amount (if any) that would have been included in the compensation of the covered employee for the taxable year but for being disallowed by reason of section 280G. For example, assume that during a taxable year a corporation pays $1,500,000 to a covered employee and no portion satisfies the exception in paragraph (d) of this section for commissions or paragraph (e) of this section for qualified performance-based compensation. Of the $1,500,000, $600,000 is an excess parachute payment, as defined in section 280G(b)(1) and is disallowed by reason of that section. Because the excess parachute payment reduces the limitation of paragraph (b) of this section, the corporation can deduct $400,000, and $500,000 of the otherwise deductible amount is nondeductible by reason of section 162(m).

(h) *Transition rules—*

(1) *Compensation payable under a written binding contract which was in effect on February 17, 1993—*

(i) *General rule.* The deduction limit of paragraph (b) of this section does not apply to any compensation payable under a written binding contract that was in effect on February 17, 1993. The preceding sentence does not apply unless, under applicable state law, the corporation is obligated to pay the compensation if the employee performs services. However, the deduction limit of paragraph (b) of this section does apply to a contract that is renewed after February 17, 1993. A written binding contract that is terminable or cancelable by the corporation after February 17, 1993, without the employee's consent is treated as a new contract as of the date that any such termination or cancellation, if made, would be effective. Thus, for example, if the terms of a contract provide that it will be automatically renewed as of a certain date unless either the corporation or the employee gives notice of termination of the contract at least 30 days before that date, the contract is treated as a new contract as of the date that termination would be effective if that notice were given. Similarly, for example, if the terms of a contract provide that the contract will be terminated or canceled as of a certain date unless either the corporation or the employee elects to renew within 30 days of that date, the contract is treated as renewed by the corporation as of that date. Alternatively, if the corporation will remain legally obligated by the terms of a contract beyond a certain date at the sole discretion of the employee, the contract will not be treated as a new contract as of that date if the employee exercises the discretion to keep the corporation bound to the contract. A contract is not treated as terminable or cancelable if it can be terminated or canceled only by terminating the employment relationship of the employee.

(ii) *Compensation payable under a plan or arrangement.* If a compensation plan or arrangement meets the requirements of paragraph (h)(1)(i) of this section, the compensation paid to an employee pursuant to the plan or arrangement will not be subject to the deduction limit of paragraph (b) of this section even though the employee was not eligible to participate in the plan as of February 17, 1993. However, the preceding sentence does not apply unless the employee was employed on February 17, 1993, by the corporation that maintained the plan or arrangement, or the employee had the right to participate in the plan or arrangement under a written binding contract as of that date.

(iii) *Material modifications.*

(A) Paragraph (h)(1)(i) of this section will not apply to any written binding contract that is materially modified. A material modification occurs when the contract is amended to increase the amount of compensation payable to the employee. If a binding written contract is materially modified, it is treated as a new contract entered into as of the date of the material modification. Thus, amounts received by an employee under the contract prior to a material modification are not affected, but amounts received subsequent to the material modification are not treated as paid under a binding, written contract described in paragraph (h)(1)(i) of this section.

(B) A modification of the contract that accelerates the payment of compensation will be treated as a material modification unless the amount of compensation paid is discounted to reasonably reflect the time value of money. If the contract is modified to defer the payment of compensation, any compensation paid in excess of the amount that was originally payable to the employee under the contract will not be treated as a material modification if the additional amount is based on either a reasonable rate of interest or one or more predetermined actual investments (whether or not assets associated with the amount originally owed are actually invested therein) such that the amount payable by the employer at the later date will be based on the actual rate of return of the specific investment (including any decrease as well as any increase in the value of the investment).

(C) The adoption of a supplemental contract or agreement that provides for increased compensation, or the payment of additional compensation, is a material modification of a binding, written contract where the facts and circumstances show that the additional compensation is paid on the basis of substantially the same elements or conditions as the compensation that is otherwise paid under the written binding contract. However, a material modification of a written binding contract does not include a supplemental payment that is equal to or less than a reasonable cost-of-living increase over the payment made in the preceding year under that written binding contract. In addition, a supplemental payment of compensation that satisfies the requirements of qualified performance-based compensation in paragraph (e) of this section will not be treated as a material modification.

(iv) Examples. The following examples illustrate the exception of this paragraph (h)(1):

Example 1. Corporation X executed a 3-year compensation arrangement with C on February 15, 1993, that constitutes a written binding contract under applicable state law. The terms of the arrangement provide for automatic extension after the 3-year term for additional 1-year periods, unless the corporation exercises its option to terminate the arrangement within 30 days of the end of the 3-year term or, thereafter, within 30 days before each anniversary date. Termination of the compensation arrangement does not require the termination of C's employment relationship with Corporation X. Unless terminated, the arrangement is treated as renewed on February 15, 1996, and the deduction limit of paragraph (b) of this section applies to payments under the arrangement after that date.

Example 2. Corporation Y executed a 5-year employment agreement with B on January 1, 1992, providing for a salary of $900,000 per year. Assume that this agreement constitutes a written binding contract under applicable state law. In 1992 and 1993, B receives the salary of $900,000 per year. In 1994, Corporation Y increases B's salary with a payment of $20,000. The $20,000 supplemental payment does not constitute a material modification of the written binding contract because the $20,000 payment is less than or equal to a reasonable cost-of-living increase from 1993. However, the $20,000 supplemental payment is subject to the limitation in paragraph (b) of this section. On January 1, 1995, Corporation Y increases B's salary to $1,200,000. The $280,000 supplemental payment is a material modification of the written binding contract because the additional compensation is paid on the basis of substantially the same elements or conditions as the compensation that is otherwise paid under the written binding contract and it is greater than a reasonable, annual cost-of-living increase. Because the written binding contract is materially modified as of January 1, 1995, all compensation paid to B in 1995 and thereafter is subject to the deduction limitation of section 162(m).

Example 3. Assume the same facts as in *Example 2,* except that instead of an increase in salary, B receives a restricted stock grant subject to B's continued employment for the balance of the contract. The restricted stock grant is not a material modification of the binding written contract because any additional compensation paid to B under the grant is not paid on the basis of substantially the same elements and conditions as B's salary because it is based both on the stock price and B's continued service. However, compensation attributable to the restricted stock grant is subject to the deduction limitation of section 162(m). (2) *Special transition rule for outside directors.* A director who is a disinterested director is treated as satisfying the requirements of an outside director under paragraph (e)(3) of this section until the first meeting of shareholders at which directors are to be elected that occurs on or after January 1, 1996. For purposes of this paragraph (h)(2) and paragraph (h)(3) of this section, a director is a disinterested director if the director is disinterested within the meaning of Rule 16b–3(c)(2)(i), 17 CFR 240.16b–3(c)(2)(i), under the Exchange Act (including the provisions of Rule 16b–3(d)(3), as in effect on April 30, 1991).

(3) *Special transition rule for previously-approved plans*—

(i) *In general.* Any compensation paid under a plan or agreement approved by shareholders before December 20, 1993, is treated as satisfying the requirements of paragraphs (e)(3) and (e)(4) of this section, provided that the directors administering the plan or agreement are disinterested directors and the plan was approved by shareholders in a manner consistent with Rule 16b–3(b), 17 CFR 240.16b–3(b), under the Exchange Act or Rule 16b–3(a), 17 CFR 240.16b–3(a) (as contained in 17 CFR part 240 revised April 1, 1990). In addition, for purposes of satisfying the requirements of paragraph (e)(2)(vi) of this section, a plan or agreement is treated as stating a maximum number of shares with respect to which an option or right may be granted to any employee if the plan or agreement that was approved by the shareholders provided for an aggregate limit, consistent with Rule 16b–3(b), 17 CFR 250.16b–3(b), on the shares of employer stock with respect to which awards may be made under the plan or agreement.

(ii) *Reliance period.* The transition rule provided in this paragraph (h)(3) shall continue and may be relied upon until the earliest of—

(A) The expiration or material modification of the plan or agreement;

(B) The issuance of all employer stock and other compensation that has been allocated under the plan; or

(C) The first meeting of shareholders at which directors are to be elected that occurs after December 31, 1996.

(iii) *Stock-based compensation.* This paragraph (h)(3) will apply to any compensation received pursuant to the exercise of a stock option or stock appreciation right, or the substantial vesting of restricted property, granted under a plan or agreement described in paragraph (h)(3)(i) of this section if the grant occurs on or before the earliest of the events specified in paragraph (h)(3)(ii) of this section.

(iv) *Example.* The following example illustrates the application of this paragraph (h)(3):

Example. Corporation Z adopted a stock option plan in 1991. Pursuant to Rule 16b–3 under the Exchange Act, the stock option plan has been administered by disinterested directors and was approved by Corporation Z shareholders. Under the terms of the plan, shareholder approval is not required again until 2001. In addition, the terms of the stock option plan include an aggregate limit on the number of shares available under the plan. Option grants under the Corporation Z plan are made with an exercise price equal to or greater than the fair market value of Corporation Z stock. Compensation attributable to the exercise of options that are granted under the plan before the earliest of the dates specified in paragraph (h)(3)(ii) of this section will be treated as satisfying the requirements of paragraph (e) of this section for qualified performance-based compensation, regardless of when the options are exercised.

(i) [Reserved]

(j) *Effective date—*

(1) *In general.* Section 162(m) and this section apply to compensation that is otherwise deductible by the corporation in a taxable year beginning on or after January 1, 1994.

(2) *Delayed effective date for certain provisions—*

(i) *Date on which remuneration is considered paid.* Notwithstanding paragraph (j)(1) of this section, the rules in the second sentence of each of paragraphs (e)(3)(ii)(A), (e)(3)(ii)(B), and (e)(3)(ii)(C) of this section for determining the date or dates on which remuneration is considered paid to a director are effective for taxable years beginning on or after January 1, 1995. Prior to those taxable years, taxpayers must follow the rules in paragraphs (e)(3)(ii)(A), (e)(3)(ii)(B), and (e)(3)(ii)(C) of this section or another reasonable, good faith interpretation of section 162(m) with respect to the date or dates on which remuneration is considered paid to a director.

(ii) *Separate treatment of publicly held subsidiaries.* Notwithstanding paragraph (j)(1) of this section, the rule in paragraph (c)(1)(ii) of this section that treats publicly held subsidiaries as separately subject to section 162(m) is effective as of the first regularly scheduled meeting of the shareholders of the publicly held subsidiary that occurs more than 12 months after December 2, 1994. The rule for stock-based compensation set forth in paragraph (f)(3) of this section will apply for this purpose, except that the grant must occur before the shareholder meeting specified in this paragraph (j)(2)(ii). Taxpayers may choose to rely on the rule referred to in the first sentence of this paragraph (j)(2)(ii) for the period prior to the effective date of the rule.

(iii) *Subsidiaries that become separate publicly held corporations.* Notwithstanding paragraph (j)(1) of this section, if a subsidiary of a publicly held corporation becomes a separate publicly held corporation as described in paragraph (f)(4)(i) of this section, then, for the duration of the reliance period described in paragraph (f)(2) of this section, the rules of paragraph (f)(1) of this section are treated as applying (and the rules of paragraph (f)(4) of this section do not apply) to remuneration paid to covered employees of that new publicly held corporation pursuant to a plan or agreement that existed prior to December 2, 1994, provided that the treatment of that remuneration as performance- based is in accordance with a reasonable, good faith interpretation of section 162(m). However, if remuneration is paid to covered employees of that new publicly held corporation pursuant to a plan or agreement that existed prior to December 2, 1994, but that remuneration is not performancebased under a reasonable, good faith interpretation of section 162(m), the rules of paragraph (f)(1) of this section will be treated as applying only until the first regularly scheduled meeting of shareholders that occurs more than 12 months after December 2, 1994. The rules of paragraph (f)(4) of this section will apply as of that first regularly scheduled meeting. The rule for stock- based compensation set forth in paragraph (f)(3) of this section will apply for purposes of this paragraph (j)(2)(iii), except that the grant must occur before the shareholder meeting specified in the preceding sentence if the remuneration is not performance-based under a reasonable, good faith interpretation of section 162(m). Taxpayers may choose to rely on the rules of paragraph (f)(4) of this section for the period prior to the applicable effective date referred to in the first or second sentence of this paragraph (j)(2)(iii).

(iv) *Bonus pools.* Notwithstanding paragraph (j)(1) of this section, the rules in paragraph (e)(2)(iii)(A) that limit the sum of individual percentages of a bonus pool to 100 percent will not apply to remuneration paid before January 1, 2001, based on performance in any performance period that began prior to December 20, 1995.

(v) *Compensation based on a percentage of salary or base pay.* Notwithstanding paragraph (j)(1) of this section, the requirement in paragraph (e)(4)(i) of this section that, in the case of certain formulas based on a percentage of salary or base pay, a corporation disclose to shareholders the maximum dollar amount of compensation that could be paid to the employee, will apply only to plans approved by shareholders after April 30, 1995.

26 CFR § 1.6039-1—Information returns required of corporations with respect to certain stock option transactions occurring on or after January 1, 1964

(a) *Requirement of return under section 6039(a)(1).* Every corporation which transfers stock to any person pursuant to such person's exercise on or after January 1, 1964, of a qualified stock option described in section 422(b), or a restricted stock option described in section 424(b), shall make, for each calendar year in which such a transfer occurs, an information return on Form 3921 with respect to each transfer made during such year. The return shall include the following information:

(1) The name, address and employer identification number of the corporation transferring the stock;

(2) The name, address, and identifying number of the person to whom the share or shares of stock were transferred;

(3) The name and address of the corporation the stock of which is the subject of the option (if other than the corporation transferring the stock);

(4) The date the option was granted;

(5) The date the shares were transferred to the person exercising the option;

(6) The fair market value of the stock at the time the option was exercised;

(7) The number of shares of stock transferred pursuant to the option;

(8) The type of option under which the transferred shares were acquired; and

(9) Such other information as may be required by the return or by the instructions issued with respect thereto.

(b) *Requirement of return under section 6039(a)(2).* (1) Every corporation which records, or has by its agent recorded, a transfer of the title to stock acquired by the transferor pursuant to his exercise on or after January 1, 1964, of:

(i) An option granted under an employee stock purchase plan which meets the requirements of section 423(b), and with respect to which the special rule of section 423(c) applied, or

(ii) A restricted stock option which meets the requirements of section 424(b), and with respect to which the special rule of section 424(c)(1) applies, shall make, for each calendar year in which such a recorded transfer of title to such stock occurs, an information return on Form 3922 with respect to each transfer containing the information required by subparagraph (2) of this paragraph.

(2) The return required by subparagraph (1) of this paragraph shall contain the following information:

(i) The name and address of the corporation whose stock is being transferred;

(ii) The name, address, and identifying number of the transferor;

(iii) The date such stock was transferred to the transferor;

(iv) The number of shares to which title is being transferred; and

(v) The type of option under which the transferred shares were acquired.

(3) If the return required by this paragraph is made by the authorized "transfer agent" of the corporation, it shall be deemed to have been made by the corporation. The term "transfer agent", as used in this paragraph, means any designee authorized to keep the stock ownership records of a corporation and to record a transfer of title of the stock of such corporation on behalf of such corporation.

(4) Where a corporation is required by this paragraph to make an information return for the calendar year, such return will only have to supply information relating to the first recorded transfer of title to the share or shares of stock. Thus, for example, if the owner has record title to a share or shares of stock transferred to a recognized broker or financial institution and the stock is subsequently sold by such broker or institution (on behalf of the owner) the corporation is only required to report information relating to the transfer of record title to the broker or financial institution. Similarly, a return is required when a share of stock is transferred by the optionee to himself and another person (or persons) as joint tenants, tenants by the entireties or tenants in common. However, when stock is originally issued to the optionee and another person (or persons) as joint tenants, or as tenants by the entirety, and a stock certificate was not previously actually issued to the optionee as a sole owner, the return required by this paragraph shall be made (at such time and in such manner as is provided by this section with respect to a transfer by the optionee) in respect of the first transfer of the title to such stock by the optionee.

(5) Every corporation which transfers any share of stock pursuant to the exercise of an option described in this paragraph shall identify such stock in a manner sufficient to enable the accurate reporting of the transfer of record title to such shares. Such identification may be accomplished by assigning to the certificates of stock issued pursuant to the exercise of such options a special serial number, or color.

(c) *Time, place, and manner of filing.*

(1) The returns on Forms 3921 and 3922 required by section 6039(a) (1) and (2) and paragraphs (a) and (b) of this section shall be filed as attachments to a summary report on Form 4067 which must be signed by the person required to file the returns or its duly authorized agent. With respect to returns on Form 3921, the summary report on Form 4067 shall indicate the number of returns filed, the number of shares transferred pursuant to exercise of options, the dates on which the options exercised were offered or granted, the fair market value of shares subject to option on such dates, the method by which such value was determined, the type of options under which the transferred shares were acquired, and such other information as may be required by the form or by the instructions issued with respect thereto. With respect to returns on Form 3922, the summary report on Form 4067 shall indicate the number of returns filed, the number of shares transferred, the type of options under which the transferred shares were acquired and such other information as may be required by the form or by the instructions issued with respect thereto. The summary report on Form 4067 and the attached returns on Forms 3921 and 3922 required for any calendar year shall be filed on or before February 28 of the following year with any of the Internal Revenue Service Centers.

(2) If a return is made by the authorized "transfer agent" of the corporation, as described in paragraph (b)(3) of this section, it shall be filed with the district director for the district where the income tax return of the principal corporation is filed after the close of the calendar year for which the return is required, but on or before February 28th of the following calendar year.

(3) For provisions relating to the extension of time for filing the returns required by this section, see § 1.6081–1.

(4) For provisions relating to the time for performance of an act when the last day prescribed for performance falls on Saturday, Sunday, or a legal holiday, see § 301.7503–1 of this chapter (Regulations on Procedure and Administration).

(d) *Stock to which this section applies.* The rules of this section shall apply to any full share of stock acquired pursuant to the exercise of any qualified or restricted stock option, or any option granted under an employee stock purchase plan, irrespective of whether the transfer of stock pursuant to such excercise qualified for the special tax treatment of section 421 and the regulations thereunder. In addition, the rules of paragraph (b) of this section shall apply to any full shares of stock received in respect of stock which was originally acquired pursuant to the exercise of an option described in the preceding sentence. See section 425(b). For definitions of the terms "exercise" and "transfer" see paragraphs (f) and (g) of § 1.421–7. A return is required under paragraph (b) of this section irrespective of whether the transfer of the title constitutes a disposition of such stock as defined by section 425(c).

26 CFR § 1.6039–2.—Statements to persons with respect to whom information is furnished

(a) *Requirement and form of statement.* Every corporation required to make a return on Form 3921 or 3922 under section 6039(a) and § 1.6039–1 shall furnish to each person whose identifying number is (or should be) shown on such return a written statement containing the information required to be shown on such return. This requirement may be met by furnishing a copy of the appropriate return to such person. A statement shall be considered to be furnished to a person within the meaning of this section if it is mailed to such person at his last known address.

(b) *Time for furnishing statements*—(1) *In general.* Each statement required by this section to be furnished to any person for a calendar year shall be furnished to such person on or before January 31, of the year following the year for which the statement is required.

(2) *Extension of time.* For good cause shown upon written application of the corporation required to furnish statements under this section, the district director may grant an extension of time not exceeding 30 days in which to furnish such statements. The application shall be addressed to the district director with whom the income tax returns of the applicant-corporation are filed and shall contain a full recital of the reasons for requesting the extension to aid the district director in determining the period of the extension, if any, which will be granted. Such a request in the form of a letter to the district director signed by the applicant (or its agent) will suffice as an application. The application shall be filed on or before the date prescribed in subparagraph (1) of this paragraph for furnishing the statements required by this section.

(3) *Last day for furnishing statement.* For provisions relating to the time for performance of an act when the last day prescribed for performance falls on Saturday, Sunday, or a legal holiday, see § 301.7503–1 of this chapter (Regulations on Procedure and Administration).

(c) *Penalty.* For provisions relating to the penalty provided for failure to furnish a statement under this section, see § 301.6678–1 of this chapter (Regulations on Procedure and Administration).

Revenue Ruling 2002-22—Transfers Incident to Divorce

2002-19 I.R.B. 849 (May 13, 2002)

ISSUES

(1) Is a taxpayer who transfers interests in nonstatutory stock options and nonqualified deferred compensation to the taxpayer's former spouse incident to divorce required to include an amount in gross income upon the transfer?

(2) Is the taxpayer or the former spouse required to include an amount in gross income when the former spouse exercises the stock options or when the deferred compensation is paid or made available to the former spouse?

FACTS

Prior to their divorce in 2002, A and B were married individuals residing in State X who used the cash receipts and disbursements method of accounting.

A is employed by Corporation Y. Prior to the divorce, Y issued nonstatutory stock options to A as part of A's compensation. The nonstatutory stock options did not have a readily ascertainable fair market value within the meaning of § 1.83–7(b) of the Income Tax Regulations at the time granted to A, and thus no amount was included in A's gross income with respect to those options at the time of grant.

Y maintains two unfunded, nonqualified deferred compensation plans under which A earns the right to receive postemployment payments from Y. Under one of the deferred compensation plans, participants are entitled to payments based on the balance of individual accounts of the kind described in § 31.3121(v)(2)–1(c)(1)(ii) of the Employment Tax Regulations. By the time of A's divorce from B, A had an account balance of $100x under that plan. Under the second deferred compensation plan maintained by Y, participants are entitled to receive single sum or periodic payments following separation from service based on a formula reflecting their years of service and compensation history with Y. By the time of A's divorce from B, A had accrued the right to receive a single sum payment of $50x under that plan following A's termination of employment with Y. A's contractual rights to the deferred compensation benefits under these plans were not contingent on A's performance of future services for Y.

Under the law of State X, stock options and unfunded deferred compensation rights earned by a spouse during the period of marriage are marital property subject to equitable division between the spouses in the event of divorce. Pursuant to the property settlement incorporated into their judgment of divorce, *A* transferred to *B* (1) one-third of the non-statutory stock options issued to *A* by *Y*, (2) the right to receive deferred compensation payments from *Y* under the account balance plan based on $75x of *A*'s account balance under that plan at the time of the divorce, and (3) the right to receive a single sum payment of $25x from *Y* under the other deferred compensation plan upon *A*'s termination of employment with *Y*.

In 2006, *B* exercises all of the stock options and receives *Y* stock with a fair market value in excess of the exercise price of the options. In 2011, *A* terminates employment with *Y*, and *B* receives a single sum payment of $150x from the account balance plan and a single sum payment of $25x from the other deferred compensation plan.

LAW AND ANALYSIS

Section 1041 and the assignment of income doctrine

Section 1041(a) provides that no gain or loss is recognized on a transfer of property from an individual to or for the benefit of a spouse or, if the transfer is incident to divorce, a former spouse. Section 1041(b) provides that the property transferred is generally treated as acquired by the transferee by gift and that the transferee's basis in the property is the adjusted basis of the transferor.

Section 1041 was enacted in part to reverse the effect of the Supreme Court's decision in *United States v. Davis*, 370 U.S. 65 (1962), which held that the transfer of appreciated property to a spouse (or former spouse) in exchange for the release of marital claims was a taxable event resulting in the recognition of gain or loss to the transferor. *See* H.R. Rep. No. 432, 98th Cong., 2d Sess. 1491 (1984). Section 1041 was intended to "make the tax laws as unintrusive as possible with respect to relations between spouses" and to provide "uniform Federal income tax consequences" for transfers of property between spouses incident to divorce, "notwithstanding that the property may be subject to differing state property laws." *Id.* at 1492. Congress thus intended that § 1041 would eliminate differing federal tax treatment of property transfers and divisions between divorcing taxpayers who reside in community property states and those who reside in noncommunity property states.

The term "property" is not defined in § 1041. However, there is no indication that Congress intended "property" to have a restricted meaning under § 1041. To the contrary, Congress indicated that § 1041 should apply broadly to transfers of many types of property, including those that involve a right to receive ordinary income that has accrued in an economic sense (such as interests in trusts and annuities). *Id.* at 1491. Accordingly, stock options and unfunded deferred compensation rights may constitute property within the meaning of § 1041. *See also Balding v. Commissioner*, 98 T.C. 368 (1992) (marital rights to military pension treated as property under § 1041).

Although § 1041 provides nonrecognition treatment to transfers between spouses and former spouses, whether income derived from the transferred property and paid to the transferee is taxed to the transferor or the transferee depends upon the applicability of the assignment of income doctrine. As first enunciated in *Lucas v. Earl*, 281 U.S. 111 (1930), the assignment of income doctrine provides that income is ordinarily taxed to the person who earns it, and that the incidence of income taxation may not be shifted by anticipatory assignments. However, the courts and the Service have long recognized that the assignment of income doctrine does not apply to every transfer of future income rights. *See, e.g., Rubin v. Commissioner*, 429 F.2d 650 (2d Cir. 1970); *Hempt Bros., Inc. v. United States*, 490 F.2d 1172 (3d Cir. 1974), *cert. denied*, 419 U.S. 826 (1974); Rev. Rul. 80–198 (1980–2 C.B. 113). Moreover, in cases arising before the effective date of § 1041, a number of courts had concluded that transfers of income rights between divorcing spouses were not voluntary assignments within the scope of the assignment of income doctrine. *See Meisner v. United States*, 133 F.3d 654 (8th Cir. 1998); *Kenfield v. United States*, 783 F.2d 966 (10th Cir. 1986); *Schulze v. Commissioner*, T.C.M. 1983–263; *Cofield v. Koehler*, 207 F. Supp. 73 (D. Kan. 1962).

In *Hempt Bros., Inc. v. United States*, the court concluded that the assignment of income doctrine should not apply to the transfer of accounts receivable by a cash basis partnership to a controlled corporation in a transaction described in § 351(a), where there was a valid business purpose for the transfer of the accounts receivable together with the other assets and liabilities of the partnership to effect the incorporation of an ongoing business. The court reasoned that application of the assignment of income doctrine to tax the transferor in such circumstances would frustrate the Congressional intent reflected in the nonrecognition rule of § 351(a). Accordingly, the transferee, not the transferor, was taxed as it received payment of the receivables. In Rev. Rul. 80–198, the Service adopted the court's position in *Hempt Bros.*, but ruled that the assignment of income doctrine would nonetheless apply to transfers to controlled corporations where there was a tax avoidance purpose.

Similarly, applying the assignment of income doctrine in divorce cases to tax the transferor spouse when the transferee spouse ultimately receives income from the property transferred in the divorce would frustrate the purpose of § 1041 with respect to divorcing spouses. That tax treatment would impose substantial burdens on marital property settlements involving such property and thwart the purpose of allowing divorcing spouses to sever their ownership interests in property with as little tax intrusion as possible. Further, there is no indication that Congress intended § 1041 to alter the principle established in the pre-1041 cases such as

Meisner that the application of the assignment of income doctrine generally is inappropriate in the context of divorce.

Specific provisions governing nonstatutory stock options

Section 83(a) provides, in general, that if property is transferred to any person in connection with the performance of services, the excess of the fair market value of the property over the amount, if any, paid for the property is included in the gross income of the person performing the services in the first taxable year in which the rights of the person having the beneficial interest in such property are transferable or are not subject to a substantial risk of forfeiture, whichever is applicable. In the case of nonstatutory stock options that do not have a readily ascertainable fair market value at the date of grant, § 83 does not apply to the grant of the option, but applies to property received upon exercise of the option or to any money or other property received in an arm's length disposition of the option. *See* § 83(e) and § 1.83–7(a).

Although a transfer of nonstatutory stock options in connection with a marital property settlement may, as a factual matter, involve an arm's length exchange for money, property, or other valuable consideration, it would contravene the gift treatment prescribed by § 1041 to include the value of the consideration in the transferor's income under § 83. Accordingly, the transfer of nonstatutory stock options between divorcing spouses is entitled to nonrecognition treatment under § 1041.

When the transferee exercises the stock options, the transferee rather than the transferor realizes gross income to the extent determined by § 83(a). Since § 1041 was intended to eliminate differing federal tax treatment for property transferred or divided between spouses in connection with divorce in community property states and in non-community property states, § 83(a) is properly applied in the same manner in both contexts. Where compensation rights are earned through the performance of services by one spouse in a community property state, the portion of the compensation treated as owned by the nonearning spouse under state law is treated as the gross income of the non-earning spouse for federal income tax purposes. *Poe v. Seaborn*, 282 U.S. 101 (1930). Thus, even though the non-employee spouse in a non-community property state may not have state law ownership rights in nonstatutory stock options at the time of grant, § 1041 requires that the ownership rights acquired by such a spouse in a marital property settlement be given the same federal income tax effect as the ownership rights of a non-employee spouse in a community property state. Accordingly, upon the subsequent exercise of the nonstatutory stock options, the property transferred to the non-employee spouse has the same character and is includible in the gross income of the nonemployee spouse under § 83(a) to the same extent as if the non-employee spouse were the person who actually performed the services.

The same conclusion would apply in a case in which an employee transfers a statutory stock option (such as those governed by § 422 or 423(b)) contrary to its terms to a spouse or former spouse in connection with divorce. The option would be disqualified as a statutory stock option, see §§ 422(b)(5) and 423(b)(9), and treated in the same manner as other nonstatutory stock options. Section 424(c)(4), which provides that a § 1041(a) transfer of stock acquired on the exercise of a statutory stock option is not a disqualifying disposition, does not apply to a transfer of the stock option. *See* H.R. Rep. No. 795, 100th Cong., 2d Sess. 378 (1988) (noting that the purpose of the amendment made to § 424(c) is to "clarif[y] that the transfer of stock acquired pursuant to the exercise of an incentive stock option between spouses or incident to divorce is tax free").

CONCLUSION

Under the present facts, the interests in nonstatutory stock options and nonqualified deferred compensation that A transfers to B are property within the meaning of §1041. Section 1041 confers nonrecognition treatment on any gain that A might otherwise realize when A transfers these interests to B in 2002. Further, the assignment of income doctrine does not apply to these transfers. Therefore, A is not required to include in gross income any income resulting from B's exercise of the stock options in 2006 or the payment of deferred compensation to B in 2011. When B exercises the stock options in 2006, B must include in income an amount determined under § 83(a) as if B were the person who performed the services. In addition, B must include the amount realized from payments of deferred compensation in income in the year such payments are paid or made available to B. The same conclusions would apply if A and B resided in a community property state and all or some of these income rights constituted community property that was divided between A and B as part of their divorce.

This ruling does not apply to transfers of property between spouses other than in connection with divorce. This ruling also does not apply to transfers of nonstatutory stock options, unfunded deferred compensation rights, or other future income rights to the extent such options or rights are unvested at the time of transfer or to the extent that the transferor's rights to such income are subject to substantial contingencies at the time of the transfer. *See Kochansky v. Commissioner*, 92 F.3d 957 (9th Cir. 1996). Transfers of certain types of property incident to divorce, the tax consequences of which are governed by a specific provision of the Code or regulations (for example, § 402, 408, 414, 424, or 453B) are not affected by this ruling.

HOLDINGS

(1) A taxpayer who transfers interests in nonstatutory stock options and nonqualified deferred compensation to the taxpayer's former spouse

incident to divorce is not required to include an amount in gross income upon the transfer.

(2) The former spouse, and not the taxpayer, is required to include an amount in gross income when the former spouse exercises the stock options or when the deferred compensation is paid or made available to the former spouse.

PROSPECTIVE APPLICATION

The Service will apply § 7805(b) and assignment of income principles to treat income as gross income of the transferor and not of the transferee if—

(i) The income is attributable to an interest in nonstatutory stock options, unfunded deferred compensation rights, or other similar intangible property rights;

(ii) The options or rights were transferred from one party to a divorce to the other party to the divorce;

(iii) The transfer was required by a provision of an agreement or court order;

(iv) The provision was contained in the agreement or order before November 9, 2002; and

(v) (a) The agreement or court order specifically provides that the transferor must report gross income attributable to the transferred interest, or

(b) It can be established to the satisfaction of the Service that the transferor has reported the gross income for federal income tax purposes.

EFFECT ON OTHER DOCUMENTS

Rev. Rul. 87–112 (1987–2 C.B. 207) which deals with the treatment of transfers of United States savings bonds between spouses or former spouses, is clarified by eliminating references to assignment of income principles. As so clarified, the ruling is reaffirmed respecting the application of § 454 and the regulations thereunder to the transfer and the determination of the transferee's basis.

FURTHER INFORMATION

For further information or questions regarding § 61 or 1041, contact Edward Schwartz of the Office of Associate Chief Counsel (Income Tax and Accounting) at (202) 622–4960. For further information or questions regarding § 83, 402, 408, 414, 422, 423, 424, or 453B, contact Erinn Madden of the Office of the Associate Chief Counsel (Tax Exempt and Government Entities) at (202) 622–6030. These are not toll-free calls.

Revenue Ruling 80-244—Employee Stock Options; Payment with Stock

1980-2 C.B. 234, 1980-36 I.R.B. 9. (September 8, 1980)

[IRS headnote:] Employee stock options; payment with stock. An explanation is provided of the federal income tax consequences of the acquisition of stock pursuant to the exercise of a nonqualified stock option and payment for the stock with identical shares of the corporation's stock that were previously acquired pursuant to the exercise of a qualified stock option.

ISSUE

What are the federal income tax consequences of the acquisition of stock pursuant to the exercise of a nonqualified stock option, if payment for the stock is made with shares of the same corporation's stock that were previously acquired pursuant to the exercise of a qualified stock option?

FACTS

A corporation, whose outstanding stock consists of a single class of common stock, has a qualified stock option plan described in section 422 of the Internal Revenue Code and a nonqualified stock option plan. An optionee who exercises an option granted under the nonqualified plan may pay for the shares (1) in cash, (2) with previously acquired shares having a fair market value equal to the option price, or (3) with cash and previously acquired shares having a fair market value less than the option price.

On May 1, 1977, an employee of the corporation exercised a qualified stock option and acquired 1,000 shares of stock for 2x dollars. The fair market value of the stock steadily increased, and on July 1, 1979, when the employee exercised a nonqualified option (which was granted after April 21, 1969, and did not have a readily ascertainable fair market value when granted) for 2,000 shares of stock, the 1,000 shares of stock acquired pursuant to the qualified option had a fair market value of 6x dollars. The employee paid for the 2,000 shares of stock received pursuant to the nonqualified option with the 1,000 shares of identical stock acquired in 1977 when the employee exercised the qualified option. The nonqualified option price for the 2,000 shares of stock was 6x dollars; however, the fair market value was 12x dollars. Thus, the employee exchanged 1,000 shares of stock with a basis of 2x dollars and a fair market value of 6x dollars for 2,000 shares of stock with a fair market value of 12x dollars.

LAW

Section 421(a)(1) of the Code provides that if a share of stock is transferred to an individual in a transfer in respect of which the requirements of section 422(a) are met, no income results when the share is transferred to the individual upon the exercise of the option with respect to that share.

Section 422(a) of the Code provides that section 421(a) applies with respect to the transfer of a share of stock to an individual pursuant to the exercise of a qualified stock option if no disposition of the share is made by the employee within the three-year period beginning on the day after the day of the transfer of the share.

Section 1.421-8(b) of the Income Tax Regulations provides that a disposition of a share of stock, acquired by the exercise of a statutory option, before the expiration of the applicable holding period, makes section 421 of the Code inapplicable to the transfer of the share. The income attributable to the transfer is treated by the individual as income received in the taxable year in which the disposition occurs.

Section 1.421-8(b)(2) of the regulations provides that section 421 of the Code is not made inapplicable by a transfer before the expiration of the applicable holding period if the transfer is not a disposition of stock as defined in section 425(c).

Section 425(c) of the Code provides that the term 'disposition' includes a sale, exchange, gift, or a transfer of legal title, but does not include an exchange to which section 1036 applies.

Section 1036(a) of the Code provides that no gain or loss shall be recognized if common stock in a corporation is exchanged solely for common stock in the same corporation, or if preferred stock in a corporation is exchanged solely for preferred stock in the same corporation.

Section 1031(d) of the Code provides that if property is acquired in an exchange described in section 1036(a), the basis shall be the same as that of the property exchanged.

Section 83(a) of the Code provides that, if, in connection with the performance of services, property is transferred to any person other than the person for whom such services are performed, the excess of (1) the fair market value of the property at the first time the rights of the person having the beneficial interest in the property are transferable or are not subject to a substantial risk of forfeiture, whichever occurs earlier, over (2) the amount (if any) paid for the property, is included in the gross income of the person who performed the services.

Section 83(e) of the Code provides that section 83 does not apply to the transfer of an option without a readily ascertainable fair market value. However, under section 1.83-7(a) of the regulations, if such option is exercised, section 83(a) applies to the transfer of property pursuant to the exercise, and the employee realizes compensation upon the transfer at the time and in the amount determined under section 83(a).

HOLDINGS

The exercise of the nonqualified stock option caused the realization of 6x dollars of income under section 83(a) of the Code.

(1) The exchange of 6x dollars in value of common stock (1,000 shares) for 6x dollars in value of common stock (1,000 shares) qualifies for nonrecognition of gain under section 1036 of the Code. Pursuant to section 1031(d), the employee-shareholder's basis in this 1,000 shares of stock received pursuant to the exercise of the nonqualified option is the same as the employee-shareholder's basis in the 1,000 shares of stock exchanged therefor (2x dollars). Therefore, a disposition within the meaning of section 425(c) did not occur because section 1036 applies to the exchange of the 1,000 shares of stock that were acquired in 1977 pursuant to the exercise of the qualified option, and the employee-shareholder did not receive income pursuant to section 1.421-8(b) of the regulations.

(2) The additional 1,000 shares of common stock received by the employee-shareholder are compensation for services under section 83(a) of the Code. Accordingly, the employee-shareholder must include in gross income the fair market value (6x dollars) of the additional 1,000 shares of stock received pursuant to the exercise of the nonqualified stock option. The employee-shareholder's basis in the additional 1,000 shares of stock is the same as the amount included in gross income (6x dollars).

Notice 2002-47—Application of Employment Taxes to Statutory Stock Options

I. Purpose and Overview

This notice provides that until Treasury and the Service issue further guidance, in the case of a statutory stock option, i.e., an incentive stock option (ISO) described in section 422(b) of the Internal Revenue Code (Code) or an option granted under an employee stock purchase plan (ESPP) described in section 423(b), the Service will not assess the Federal Insurance Contributions Act (FICA) tax or Federal Unemployment Tax Act (FUTA) tax, or apply federal income tax withholding obligations, upon either the exercise of the option or the disposition of the stock acquired by an employee pursuant to the exercise of the option. This notice further announces that Treasury and the Service anticipate that any final guidance that would apply employment taxes to statutory stock options will not apply to any exercise of a statutory stock option that occurs before the January 1 of the year that follows the second anniversary of the publication of the final guidance. This notice does not relieve individual taxpayers of the obligation to include compensation in income upon a disposition of stock acquired pursuant to the exercise of a statutory stock option and does not relieve employers of any of their reporting obligations.

II. Background

A. Notice 2001-14

On January 18, 2001, the Internal Revenue Service (Service) issued Notice 2001-14, 2001-6 I.R.B. 516, addressing the application of employment taxes to statutory stock options. Notice 2001-14 provides that, in the case of a statutory stock option exercised before January 1, 2003, the Service will not assess FICA or FUTA taxes upon the exercise of the option, and will not treat the disposition of stock acquired by an employee pursuant to the exercise of the option as subject to federal income tax withholding. The notice further provides that information reporting requirements continue to be applicable. The notice also announced the intention to issue administrative guidance clarifying the application of employment taxes to statutory stock options.

B. Proposed Regulations and Related Guidance

On November 13, 2001, the Service and the Treasury Department issued proposed regulations addressing the application of employment taxes to statutory stock options (66 Fed. Reg. 57023 (Nov. 14, 2001)). The proposed regulations provide that FICA and FUTA taxes apply when an individual exercises a statutory stock option and that federal income tax withholding does not apply when an individual exercises a statutory stock option. As proposed, the regulations would have been effective for exercises of statutory stock options occurring on or after January 1, 2003.

On November 13, 2001, the Service also issued two related notices containing proposed guidance: Notice 2001-72, 2001-49 I.R.B. 548, and Notice 2001-73, 2001-49 I.R.B. 549. In Notice 2001-72, the Service provides proposed rules regarding an employer's federal income tax withholding and reporting obligations upon the disposition of stock acquired by an individual pursuant to the exercise of a statutory stock option. The rules would exempt the employer from any federal income tax withholding in such cases. However, under the proposed rules, an employer generally would still be required to make reasonable efforts to report any income on an employee's or former employee's Form W-2.

In Notice 2001-73, the Service provides proposed rules of administrative convenience intended to lessen the administrative burdens related to the application of FICA and FUTA taxes at the time of exercise of a statutory stock option. The rules would allow employers to deem the wages paid due to the exercise of a statutory stock option as being paid at any subsequent date or dates during the calendar year of the date of exercise. In addition, under the proposed rules, an employer would be allowed to spread the deemed wage payments over a period of dates. Notice 2001-73 also proposes other rules of administrative convenience that are intended to assist employers and employees in meeting their employment tax obligations.

III. Comments Received

The Service requested comments as to the proposed regulations and the proposed rules in the accompanying notices. Comments were submitted on a wide variety of issues raised by the application of employment taxes to statutory stock options, including whether imposition of the FICA and FUTA taxes upon an exercise of a statutory stock option was the correct interpretation of the law, and the extent of the administrative burdens upon employers and employees in administering the payments of the taxes. Recognizing the complexity of the issues raised by the proposed guidance and comments, Treasury and the Service have determined that an extension of the moratorium is needed to provide adequate time to consider those issues.

IV. Interim Guidance

The Service and Treasury will continue to consider all of the comments received on the proposed regulations. However, until that review is completed and further guidance is issued, the Service (1) will not assess FICA or FUTA taxes upon the exercise of a statutory stock option or the disposition of stock acquired by an employee pursuant to the exercise of a statutory stock option, and (2) will not treat the exercise of a statutory stock option, or the disposition of stock acquired by an employee pursuant to the exercise of a statutory stock option, as subject to federal income tax withholding.

This Part IV does not relieve individual taxpayers of the obligation to include any compensation in income upon a disposition of stock acquired pursuant to the exercise of a statutory stock option and does not relieve employers of any of their reporting obligations. Regarding the reporting obligations, §1.6041-2(a)(1) of the Income Tax Regulations requires that, under certain circumstances, a payment made by an employer to an employee be reported on Form W-2 even if the payment is not subject to income tax withholding. Specifically, §1.6041-2(a)(1) generally requires reporting of a payment on the Form W-2 if the total amount of the payment, and any other payment of remuneration (including wages, if any) made to the employee (or former employee) that are required to be reported on Form W-2, aggregate at least $600 in a calendar year. Therefore, a disqualifying disposition of stock acquired pursuant to the exercise of a statutory stock option which results in ordinary income generally will result in a reporting obligation on the Form W-2.

V. Effect on Other Documents

In recognition of the need of employers and statutory stock option plan administrators for adequate time to implement any guidance that may be forthcoming, the Service and Treasury anticipate that any final guidance that would apply employment taxes to statutory stock options will not apply to exercises of statutory stock options that occur before the January 1 of the year that follows the second anniversary of the publication of the final guidance.

VI. Drafting Information

The principal author of this notice is Stephen Tackney of the Office of Division Counsel/Associate Chief Counsel (Tax Exempt and Government Entities). For further information regarding this notice contact Stephen Tackney at (202) 622-6040 (not a toll-free call).

Topical Index

T

About the NCEO and Its Publications

The National Center for Employee Ownership (NCEO) is widely considered to be the leading authority in employee ownership in the U.S. and the world. Established in 1981 as a nonprofit information and membership organization, it now has over 3,000 members, including companies, professionals, unions, government officials, academics, and interested individuals. It is funded entirely through the work it does.

The NCEO's mission is to provide the most objective, reliable information possible about employee ownership at the most affordable price possible. As part of the NCEO's commitment to providing objective information, it does not lobby or provide ongoing consulting services. The NCEO publishes a variety of materials on employee ownership and participation and holds dozens of seminars, Webinars, and conferences on employee ownership annually. The NCEO's work includes extensive contacts with the media, both through articles written for trade and professional publications and through interviews with reporters. It has written or edited five books for outside publishers during the past two decades. Finally, the NCEO maintains an extensive Web site at *www.nceo.org*.

Membership Benefits

NCEO members receive the following benefits:

- The bimonthly newsletter, *Employee Ownership Report,* which covers ESOPs, stock options, and employee participation.

- Access to the members-only area of the NCEO's Web site, which includes online tools such as a searchable database of well over 200 NCEO members who are service providers in this field.

- Substantial discounts on publications and events produced by the NCEO (such as this book).

- The right to telephone the NCEO for answers to general or specific questions regarding employee ownership.

An introductory NCEO membership costs $80 for one year ($90 outside the U.S.) and covers an entire company at all locations, a single office of a firm offering professional services in this field, or an individual with a business interest in employee ownership. Full-time students and faculty members who are not employed in the business sector may join at the academic rate of $35 for one year ($45 outside the U.S.).

To join as an NCEO member and/or to order books, see the order form at the end of this section, visit our Web site at *www.nceo.org,* or telephone us at 510-208-1300.

Selected NCEO Publications

The NCEO offers a variety of publications on all aspects of employee ownership and participation. Following are descriptions of a few of our main publications. We publish new books and revise old ones on a yearly basis. To obtain the most current information on what we have available, visit our extensive Web site at *www.nceo.org* or call us at 510-208-1300.

Stock Options and Related Plans

- This book, *Tax and Securities Sources for Equity Compensation,* is a compilation of statutory and regulatory material relevant to the study of equity compensation.

    $35 for NCEO members, $50 for nonmembers

- *The Stock Options Book* is a straightforward, comprehensive overview covering the legal, accounting, regulatory, and design issues involved in implementing a stock option or stock purchase plan. It is our main book on the subject and possibly the most popular book in the field.

    $25 for NCEO members, $35 for nonmembers

- *Selected Issues in Equity Compensation* (formerly titled *Stock Options: Beyond the Basics* and then *Selected Issues in Stock Options*) is more detailed and specialized than *The Stock Options Book,* with chapters on issues such as repricing, securities issues, and evergreen provisions.

    $25 for NCEO members, $35 for nonmembers

- *Beyond Stock Options* is a complete guide, including annotated model plans, to phantom stock, restricted stock, stock appreciation rights, performance awards, and more. Includes a CD with plan documents.

    $35 for NCEO members, $50 for nonmembers

- *Accounting for Equity Compensation* is a guide to the financial accounting rules that govern equity compensation programs in the United States.

    $35 for NCEO members, $50 for nonmembers

- *Communicating Stock Options* offers practical ideas and information about how to explain stock options to a broad group of employees. It includes the views of experienced practitioners as well as detailed examples of how companies communicate tax consequences, financial information, and other matters to employees.

    $35 for NCEO members, $50 for nonmembers

- *Employee Stock Purchase Plans* covers how ESPPs work, tax and legal issues, administration, accounting, communicating the plan to employees, and research on what companies are doing with their plans. The book includes sample plan documents.

$25 for NCEO members, $35 for nonmembers

- *Equity-Based Compensation for Multinational Corporations* describes how companies can use stock options and other equity-based programs across the world to reward a global work force. It includes a country-by-country summary of tax and legal issues.

  $25 for NCEO members, $35 for nonmembers

- *Equity Compensation in a Post-Expensing World* is a collection of essays on strategies for choosing and structuring equity compensation plans when expensing is required.

  $25 for NCEO members, $35 for nonmembers

- *The Employee's Guide to Stock Options* is a guide for the everyday employee that explains in an easy-to-understand format what stock is and how stock options work.

  $25 for both NCEO members and nonmembers

- *Model Equity Compensation Plans* provides examples of incentive stock option, nonqualified stock option, and stock purchase plans, together with brief explanations of the main documents. A disk is included with copies of the plan documents in formats any word processing program can open.

  $50 for NCEO members, $75 for nonmembers

- *Stock Options, Corporate Performance, and Organizational Change* presents the first serious research to examine the relationship between broadly granted stock options and company performance, and the extent of employee involvement in broad option companies.

  $15 for NCEO members, $25 for nonmembers

- *Incentive Compensation and Employee Ownership* takes a broad look at how companies can use incentives, ranging from stock plans to cash bonuses to gainsharing, to motivate and reward employees. It includes both technical discussions and case studies.

  $25 for NCEO members, $35 for nonmembers

Employee Stock Ownership Plans (ESOPs)

- *The ESOP Reader* is an overview of the issues involved in establishing and operating an ESOP. It covers the basics of ESOP rules, feasibility, valuation, and other matters, and then discusses managing an ESOP company, including brief case studies.

  $25 for NCEO members, $35 for nonmembers

- *Selling to an ESOP* is a detailed guide for owners, managers, and advisors of closely held businesses. It explains how ESOPs work and then offers a comprehensive look at legal structures, valuation, financing (including self-financing), and other matters, especially the tax-deferred section 1042 "rollover" that allows owners to indefinitely defer capital gains taxation on the sale proceeds.

    $25 for NCEO members, $35 for nonmembers

- *Leveraged ESOPs and Employee Buyouts* discusses how ESOPs borrow money to buy out entire companies, purchase shares from a retiring owner, or finance new capital. Beginning with a primer on leveraged ESOPs and their uses, it then discusses contribution limits, valuation, accounting, financing, and more.

    $25 for NCEO members, $35 for nonmembers

- *S Corporation ESOPs* covers the advantages of ESOPs in S corporations and the many issues that arise, from legal considerations to valuation to anti-abuse rules.

    $25 for NCEO members, $35 for nonmembers

- *The ESOP Committee Guide* describes the different types of ESOP committees, the range of goals they can address, alternative structures, member selection criteria, training, committee life cycle concerns, and other issues.

    $25 for NCEO members, $35 for nonmembers

- The *ESOP Communications Sourcebook* provides ideas for and examples of communicating an ESOP to employees and customers. It includes a CD with communications materials, including many documents that readers can customize for their own companies.

    $35 for NCEO members, $50 for nonmembers

- *ESOP Valuation* brings together and updates where needed the best articles on ESOP valuation that we have published in our *Journal of Employee Ownership Law and Finance,* described below.

    $25 for NCEO members, $35 for nonmembers

- The *Model ESOP* contains sample plan language, option papers to tailor the plan to individual needs, a section-by-section plain English explanation, and other materials.

    $50 for NCEO members, $75 for nonmembers

- *ESOPs and Corporate Governance* covers everything from shareholder rights to the impact of Sarbanes-Oxley to choosing a fiduciary.

    $25 for NCEO members, $35 for nonmembers

- The *Employee Ownership Q&A Disk* gives Microsoft Windows users (any version from Windows 95 onward) point-and-click access to 500 questions and answers on all aspects of ESOPs in a fully searchable hypertext format. (Note: this is for the general reader and is not a legal reference.) Distributed on a 1.44 MB 3.5-inch diskette with an instruction sheet.

  $75 for NCEO members, $100 for nonmembers

Employee Involvement and Management

- *Ownership Management* draws upon the experience of the NCEO and of leading employee ownership companies to provide ideas and examples for building a culture of lasting innovation by combining employee ownership with employee involvement programs.

  $25 for NCEO members, $35 for nonmembers

- *Front Line Finance Facilitator's Manual* gives step-by-step instructions for teaching business literacy, emphasizing ESOPs.

  $50 for NCEO members, $75 for nonmembers

- *Front Line Finance Diskette* contains the workbook for participants in electronic form (so a copy can be printed out for everyone) in the *Front Line Finance* course.

  $50 for NCEO members, $75 for nonmembers

Other

- *Section 401(k) Plans and Employee Ownership* focuses on how company stock is used in 401(k) plans, both in stand-alone 401(k) plans and combination 401(k)–ESOP plans ("KSOPs").

  $25 for NCEO members, $35 for nonmembers

- *Wealth and Income Consequences of Employee Ownership* is a research study that found pay and benefits were higher in ESOP companies.

  $10 for NCEO members, $15 for nonmembers

- *Ownership Solutions* is a 36-page booklet that introduces the reader to the various equity plans that exist, from ESOPs to stock options to phantom stock.

  $10 NCEO members, $15 nonmembers

- *A Conceptual Guide to Equity-Based Compensation in Non-U.S. Companies* helps non-U.S. companies think through how to approach employee ownership.

  $25 for NCEO members, $35 for nonmembers

- *Employee Ownership Concepts in Nonprofits and Government* discusses how nonprofits and governmental units, despite their lack of stock, can implement employee ownership concepts and build a more productive and satisfying ownership culture in the workplace.

  $25 for NCEO members, $35 for nonmembers

- *Employee Ownership and Corporate Performance* reviews the research that has been done on the link between company stock plans and various aspects of corporate performance.

  $25 for NCEO members, $35 for nonmembers

- *The Journal of Employee Ownership Law and Finance* is the only professional journal solely devoted to employee ownership. Articles are written by leading experts and cover ESOPs, stock options, and related subjects in depth.

  One-year subscription (four issues):
  $75 for NCEO members, $100 for nonmembers

To join the NCEO as a member or to order any of the publications listed on the preceding pages, use the order form on the following page, use the secure ordering system on our Web site at www.nceo.org, or call us at 510-208-1300. If you join at the same time you order publications, you will receive the members-only publication discounts.

Order Form

To order, fill out this form and mail it with your credit card information or check to the NCEO at 1736 Franklin St., 8th Flr., Oakland, CA 94612; fax it with your credit card information to the NCEO at 510-272-9510; telephone us at 510-208-1300 with your credit card in hand; or order at our Web site, *www.nceo.org.* If you are not already a member, you can join now to receive member discounts on any publications you order.

Name

Organization

Address

City, State, Zip (Country)

Telephone   Fax   E-mail

Method of Payment: ☐ Check (payable to "NCEO")   ☐ Visa   ☐ M/C   ☐ AMEX

Credit Card Number

Signature   Exp. Date

Title	Qty.	Price	Total

Subtotal	$
Sales Tax	$
Shipping	$
Membership	$
TOTAL DUE	$

Tax: California residents add 8.75% sales tax (on publications only, not membership or Journal subscriptions)

Shipping: In the U.S., first publication $5, each add'l $1; elsewhere, we charge exact shipping costs to your credit card, plus a $10 handling surcharge; no shipping charges for membership or Journal subscriptions

Introductory NCEO Membership: $80 for one year ($90 outside the U.S.)